Cyber Muslims

ALSO AVAILABLE FROM BLOOMSBURY

Islam through Objects
Edited by Anna Bigelow

*Piety, Politics, and Everyday Ethics in Southeast
Asian Islam: Beautiful Behavior*
Edited by Robert Rozehnal

Sufis, Salafis and Islamists
Sadek Hamid

Cyber Muslims

Mapping Islamic Digital Media in the Internet Age

ROBERT ROZEHNAL

BLOOMSBURY ACADEMIC
LONDON • NEW YORK • OXFORD • NEW DELHI • SYDNEY

BLOOMSBURY ACADEMIC
Bloomsbury Publishing Plc
50 Bedford Square, London, WC1B 3DP, UK
1385 Broadway, New York, NY 10018, USA
29 Earlsfort Terrace, Dublin 2, Ireland

BLOOMSBURY, BLOOMSBURY ACADEMIC and the Diana logo are trademarks
of Bloomsbury Publishing Plc

First published in Great Britain 2022

Cover design: Tjasa Krivec
Cover image © Imar de Waard / Alamy Stock Photo

ISBN: HB: 978-1-3502-3369-0
PB: 978-1-3502-3370-6
ePDF: 978-1-3502-3372-0
eBook: 978-1-3502-3371-3

Typeset by Deanta Global Publishing Services, Chennai, India
Printed and bound in Great Britain

To find out more about our authors and books visit www.bloomsbury.com
and sign up for our newsletters

CONTENTS

ILLUSTRATIONS

Figures

Tables

CONTRIBUTORS

Ismail Fajrie Alatas is Assistant Professor of Middle Eastern and Islamic Studies at New York University and Associate Editor of the *Journal of the Royal Asiatic Society*. He holds a PhD in anthropology and history from the University of Michigan, Ann Arbor, and an MA in history from the National University of Singapore. He is the author of *What Is Religious Authority?: Cultivating Islamic Communities in Indonesia*. He has published articles in leading disciplinary and Islamic studies journals, including *Comparative Studies in Society and History*, *Journal of the Royal Anthropological Institute*, *Islamic Law and Society*, *Journal of Islamic Studies*, and *Die Welt des Islams*. His research interest revolves around questions of religious authority, mobility, social imaginary, and Sufi practices and institutions in historical and contemporary Southeast Asia and South Arabia.

Gary R. Bunt is Professor of Islamic Studies at the University of Wales Trinity Saint David. His research area focuses on Islam, Muslims, and the internet. His most recent book is *Hashtag Islam: How Cyber-Islamic Environments Are Transforming Religious Authority*. Related publications include *iMuslims: Rewiring the House of Islam*; *Islam in the Digital Age: E-Jihad, Online Fatwas and Cyber Islamic Environments*; and *Virtually Islamic: Computer-Mediated Communication and Cyber-Islamic Environments*. For more information, see virtuallyislamic.com

Nabil Echchaibi is Associate Professor of Media Studies and Associate Director of the Center for Media, Religion and Culture at the University of Colorado Boulder. His research and teaching focus on media, religion, and the politics and poetics of Muslim visibility. His work on Muslim media cultures, Islamic modernity, and decoloniality has appeared in various journals and in many book publications. He is the author of *Voicing Diasporas: Ethnic Radio in Paris and Berlin between Culture and Renewal* and coeditor of *International Blogging: Identity, Politics and Networked Publics*; *Media and Religion: The Global View*; and *The Thirdspaces of Digital Religion*. He is currently writing a book, *Unmosquing Islam: Media and Muslim Fugitivity*. Dr. Echchaibi has also written opinion columns in the popular press, including *The Guardian*, *Forbes Magazine*, *Salon*, *Al Jazeera*, *the Huffington Post*, *Religion Dispatches*, *Open Democracy*, and *Latino Rebels*.

Caleb Elfenbein is Associate Professor of History and Religious Studies at Grinnell College, where he also directs the Center for the Humanities. Focusing especially on Muslim communities, he studies how people in different times and places think about, and debate, human welfare in the context of collective life. His work has appeared in the *Journal of the American Academy of Religion*, *Method and Theory in the Study of Religion*, and *The Muslim World*, among other venues. He is the editor and director of *Mapping Islamophobia*, a website documenting anti-Muslim activity and its effects on the participation of American Muslims in public life, and author of *Fear in Our Hearts: What Islamophobia Tells Us about America*.

James B. Hoesterey is Associate Professor and Winship Distinguished Research Professor in the Study of Religion at Emory University. His research focuses broadly on Islam, media, and politics. After completing his PhD in cultural anthropology from the University of Wisconsin-Madison, Hoesterey was the Shorenstein Postdoctoral Fellow at the Asia Pacific Research Center at Stanford University (2009–10); the Andrew W. Mellon Postdoctoral Fellow in Islamic World Studies at Lake Forest College (2011–12); and the ACLS New Faculty Fellow at the Center for Southeast Asian Studies at the University of Michigan. His first book, *Rebranding Islam: Piety, Prosperity, and a Self-Help Guru*, chronicles the rise and fall of Indonesian celebrity preacher K. H. Abdullah Gymnastiar and was awarded runner-up for the 2016 Clifford Geertz Book Prize in the Anthropology of Religion. With generous funding from Notre Dame's "Contending Modernities" project, the Fulbright Foundation, and the Henry Luce Foundation, Hoesterey is currently working on his second book, *Faith in Diplomacy: Indonesia, Soft Power, and the Making of "Moderate Islam."* In addition to serving as executive board member for the Commission for Visual Anthropology (CVA), Hoesterey has worked on documentary television programs broadcast worldwide on Discovery Channel, National Geographic, and the BBC.

Sahar Khamis is Associate Professor in the Department of Communication at the University of Maryland, College Park. She is an expert on Arab and Muslim media, and the former Head of the Mass Communication Department at Qatar University. Dr. Khamis holds a PhD in mass media and cultural studies from the University of Manchester in England. She is a former Mellon Islamic Studies Initiative Visiting Professor at the University of Chicago. She is the coauthor of *Islam Dot Com: Contemporary Islamic Discourses in Cyberspace* and *Egyptian Revolution 2.0: Political Blogging, Civic Engagement and Citizen Journalism*. She is the coeditor of *Arab Women's Activism and Socio-Political Transformation: Unfinished Gendered Revolutions*. She has authored and coauthored numerous book chapters, journal articles, and conference papers, regionally and internationally, in both English and Arabic. She is the recipient of a number of prestigious academic and professional awards and a member of the editorial boards of several journals in the field of communication, in general, and the field of Arab and Muslim media, in particular. Dr. Khamis is a media commentator and analyst, a public speaker, a radio host, and a former human rights commissioner.

Harold D. Morales is Associate Professor in the Department of Philosophy and Religious Studies and Director of the Center for the Study of Religion and the City at Morgan State University. His research focuses on the intersections between race and religion and between lived and mediated experience. He uses these critical lenses to engage Latinx religions in general and Latino Muslim groups in particular. His 2018 book, *Latino and Muslim in America: Race, Religion, and the Making of a New Minority*, engages the use of new media technologies by marginalized groups. Dr. Morales is now focusing on developing public scholarship initiatives through his research on mural art and social justice issues in the city of Baltimore and through the Center for the Study of Religion and the City, which is generously supported by the Henry Luce Foundation.

Madelina Nuñez is a PhD student in American studies at Purdue University and holds an MA in Latin American and Latino studies from the University of Illinois at Chicago. In addition to her current research on *ḥalāl*, or Islamically permissible, Latino food and foodways, her interests include transnational foodways in the Americas, feminist and decolonial epistemologies, and critical race and ethnic studies.

Sana Patel is a PhD candidate at the University of Ottawa. She holds an MA in religion and public life from Carleton University. Her doctoral dissertation examines the intersections of online and offline religion, specifically how young North American Muslims interact with religious authority figures. Her research interests focus on digital religion, religious diversity, religion and immigration, and nonreligion. Sana is Research Assistant for the "Nonreligion in a Complex Future" project at the University of Ottawa and Graduate Student Member-at-Large for the Canadian Society for the Study of Religion. She previously worked as Research Assistant for the "Canadian Muslims Online" (Université du Québec à Montréal) and "Religion and Diversity" (University of Ottawa) projects.

Rosemary Pennington is Associate Professor of Journalism in Miami University's Department of Media, Journalism and Film. A former broadcast journalist, Pennington teaches courses focused on media and society, multimedia journalism, and religion and the news. Her research interests include media representations of Islam and Muslims, the coverage of religion in the news, the use of new media technologies, and global communication. Pennington is the coeditor of two books: *The Media World of ISIS* (2019), with Michael Krona of Malmo University, and *On Islam: Muslims and the Media* (2018), with Indiana University's Hilary Kahn. Her work has also appeared in the journals *New Media & Society*, *International Communication Gazette*, *Communications: The European Journal of Communication Research*, and the *Journal of Communication Inquiry*.

Kristin M. Peterson is Assistant Professor in the Department of Communication at Boston College, teaching courses related to the intersections of media and religion. She earned her PhD in media studies from the University of Colorado Boulder, where she was also a research fellow for the Center for Media, Religion and Culture. Her research focuses on religious expression in digital media, specifically examining how young people engage with online media sites, images, videos, and creative projects as spaces to develop religious meaning. She is currently working on a book project, *Unruly Souls: The Digital Activism of Muslim and Christian Feminists*. She has published articles and book chapters on Muslim Instagram influencers, the digital mourning after the murder of three Muslim college students in Chapel Hill, North Carolina, *ḥijāb* tutorial videos on YouTube, the *Ms. Marvel* comic series, and the Mipsterz fashion video.

Anna Piela is a visiting scholar at the Department of Religious Studies at Northwestern University in Evanston, Illinois. She holds a PhD in women's studies from the University of York, UK. Her research interests include Muslim gendered religious practices and feminist theologies, in particular those mediated through digital technology. Her second book, *Wearing the Niqab: Muslim Women in the UK and the US,* was published in 2021 by Bloomsbury Academic. She has also published articles in the *Journal of American Academy of Religion*, *The Muslim World*, and *Sociology of Religion*. She is currently a co-investigator on a research project on the religious trajectories of Polish female Muslim converts and serves on the steering committee of the American Academy of Religion's "Islam, Gender and Women" program unit.

Babak Rahimi is Director of the Program for the Study of Religion at the Department of Literature, University of California San Diego. His research interests concern the relationship between culture, religion, and technology. The historical and social contexts that inspire his research range from early-modern Islamicate societies to the Global South. He is the author of *Theater-State and Formation of the Early Modern Public Sphere in Iran: Studies on Safavid Muharram Rituals, 1590-1641 C.E.* Rahimi is also the editor of *Performing Iran: Culture, Performance, Theatre* and *Theatre in the Middle East: Between Performance and Politics*; coeditor (with Peyman Eshaghi) of

Muslim Pilgrimage in the Modern World; coeditor (with Armando Salvatore and Roberto Tottoli) of *The Wiley Blackwell History of Islam*; and coeditor (with David M. Faris) of *Social Media in Iran: Politics and Society after 2009*. His articles have appeared in *Thesis Eleven: Critical Theory and Historical Sociology, International Political Science Review, International Communication Gazette, International Journal of Middle East Studies, The Middle East Journal, The Communication Review,* and *Journal of the International Society for Iranian Studies.*

Hussein Rashid, PhD, is an independent scholar and founder of Islamicate, L3C, a consultancy focusing on religious literacy. He is currently teaching at The New School, and his research focuses on Muslims and American popular culture. He coedited a book with Jessica Baldzani on Kamala Khan/ Ms. Marvel, *Ms. Marvel's America: No Normal.* He is currently coediting *The Bloomsbury Handbook on Muslims and Popular Culture* with Kristian Petersen and another volume with Huma Mohibullah on Islam in North America. He previously coauthored an SSRC report on Religion and Digital Humanities with Chris Cantwell and worked with the Children's Museum of Manhattan as a content expert on their exhibit "America to Zanzibar: Muslim Cultures Near and Far." His other current projects include an independent film, a documentary project on Muslims in the United States, and a museum project on religion and jazz.

Robert Rozehnal is Professor in the Department of Religion Studies and Founding Director of the Center for Global Islamic Studies at Lehigh University. He holds a PhD in Islamic studies from Duke University and an MA in South Asian studies from the University of Wisconsin-Madison. In addition to the history and practice of Sufism in South Asia, his research and teaching interests include ritual studies, postcolonial theory, religious nationalism, globalization, and digital religion. He is the author of numerous articles and three books: *Cyber Sufis: Virtual Expressions of the American Muslim Experience*; *Piety, Politics, and Everyday Ethics in Southeast Asian Islam: Beautiful Behavior*; and *Islamic Sufism Unbound: Politics and Piety in Twenty-First Century Pakistan*. He previously served as the national cochair of the "Islamic Mysticism" program unit at the American Academy of Religion.

Megan Adamson Sijapati is Professor of Religious Studies at Gettysburg College. She holds a PhD in religious studies from the University of California, Santa Barbara, and an MA in religious studies from the University of Colorado at Boulder. In addition to the history and practice of Islam and religions of South Asia, her interests include the body in religion, religion and modernity, contemporary Sufism, digital religion, and religious revival and reform. She is the author of numerous articles and three books: *Muslim Communities* *and Cultures of the Himalaya: Conceptualizing the Global Ummah*; *Religion and Modernity in the Himalaya*; and *Islamic Revival in Nepal: Religion and a New Nation*. She currently serves as the national cochair of the "Body in Religion" program unit at the American Academy of Religion and on the Executive Board of the South Asian Muslim Studies Association.

Andrea Stanton is Associate Professor of Islamic Studies and Chair of the Department of Religious Studies at the University of Denver. She is an affiliate faculty member at D.U.'s Center for Middle East Studies. She obtained her MA and PhD in Middle Eastern history from Columbia University and her BA in history and religion from Williams College. She publishes regularly in the fields of digital religion (with a focus on Islamic studies) and media history (with a focus on the Middle East). She has received grants from the American Academy of Religion, the National Endowment for the Humanities, and the U.S. Institute of Peace.

ACKNOWLEDGMENTS

This volume was completed amid the widespread chaos and unprecedented challenges of the 2020–21 Covid-19 pandemic. In planning this project, I looked to assemble a group of scholars whose work I encountered and learned a lot from when conducting research for my book *Cyber Sufis: Virtual Expressions of the American Muslim Experience* (Oneworld Academic, 2019). In yet another reminder of the utility of digital media, the interactions with the volume's contributors this past year were limited entirely to online communication. I am immensely grateful to my colleagues' dedication, determination, and unwavering faith in this collaborative effort. They all endured my endless email requests and editorial tweaks with good humor and equanimity. Unfortunately, not everyone who was originally involved was ultimately able to participate. Several scholars whose research explores different dimensions of the digital media productions of African American Muslims were forced to withdraw amid trying circumstances. In the end, the limits of time (submission deadlines) and space (word count) also prevented me from including other talented scholars doing important work in this rapidly expanding academic field.

This book spotlights case studies from multiple geographic and cultural locations, moving between a variety of languages (Arabic, Persian, Bahasa Indonesia, and Spanish). The transliteration and diacritics for all Arabic terms have been standardized throughout. The only exceptions to this rule are Standard English renderings for common names, religious institutions, and political organizations (e.g., al-Qaeda, rather than *al-Qāʿidah*), the Prophet Muhammad (rather than Muḥammad), and *Eid al-Adha* (rather than *ʿīd al-ʿaḍḥā*). The original spelling of non-English terms in the quotations from other sources and the bibliographic references has also been maintained.

Given the intrinsic fluidity and dynamism of digital media, the case studies in this book are by nature contextualized, contingent, temporal, and ultimately temporary. After all, as primary sources, websites and social media platforms are living "texts" that constantly expand, contract, transform, and even disappear, leaving no trace behind. In this sense, this entire volume is best viewed as a snapshot—or, to be more precise, a *screenshot*—of the complex, shape-shifting world of cyber Islam at a particular moment in its ongoing, unfolding evolution. Although the digital resources referenced in this book will inevitably change (or evaporate altogether), they were all accurate and up to date as of June 2021.

This is the second volume I have edited during my time as the founding director of Lehigh University's Center for Global Islamic Studies (https://cgis.cas.lehigh.edu/). In 2016, the Center hosted a conference on Islam in Southeast Asia on the Lehigh campus, launching a conversation that ultimately culminated in the publication of *Piety, Politics, and Everyday Ethics in Southeast Asian Islam: Beautiful Behavior* (Bloomsbury Academic, 2019). With that past as precedent, it has been a great pleasure to work with the acquisition editor Lalle Pursglove and the entire Bloomsbury editorial team once again. Their assistance, insights, and expertise are deeply appreciated.

This project benefited from the generous support of the Dean's Office in Lehigh's College of Arts and Sciences, as well as a 2021 Faculty Research Grant from the Office of Research and Graduate Studies. For their friendship, encouragement, and sage advice, I offer sincere thanks to my sublime faculty colleagues in the Department of Religion Studies and the Center for Global Islamic Studies. And as ever, I owe a special debt of gratitude to my wife, Kelly Choi, for the daily gifts of laughter, patience, and perspective.

Introduction

Mapping Islamic Digital Media in the Internet Age

Robert Rozehnal

In the twenty-first century, digital media offer tech-savvy Muslims around the globe alternative pathways for self-imagining and social networking, piety and performance, politics and polemics, communication and community-building. This interdisciplinary volume spotlights the cutting-edge research of sixteen scholars with unique perspectives and novel insights on the flourishing landscape of cyber Islam. Their chapters explore the digital expressions of distinct groups of cyber Muslims, including religious clerics and Sufi masters, feminists and fashionistas, artists and activists, pilgrims and online influencers. The granular case studies chart the variety and vibrancy of Islamic digital media against the backdrop of broader social trends: racism and Islamophobia, gender dynamics, celebrity culture, identity politics, and the shifting modes of religious piety and practice. These stories span a vast cultural and geographic terrain: Indonesia, Iran, the Arab Middle East, and North America. In their analysis and interpretations, the authors employ a panoply of digital multimedia technologies as primary sources. These "virtual texts" include websites, podcasts, blogs, Twitter, Facebook, Instagram, YouTube channels, online magazines and discussion forums, and religious apps.

Throughout the book we spotlight the term "cyberspace" to capture the unique capacity of digital media to engage the realm of the imagination. The "internet" is the vast global communication network, both hardware and software infrastructure, that links smaller computer networks around the globe. The "World Wide Web" defines the system of interlinked, hypertext websites and web pages that are accessed via the internet. Together, they form the machinery and tools of digital media—the superhighway for virtual communication. Popularized by science fiction writer William Gibson in his 1984 genre-busting, cyberpunk novel *Neuromancer*, "cyberspace" designates the more abstract, creative, and generative capacities enabled by digital multimedia technologies.[1] Going beyond the black-and-white limits of printed text, cyberspace offers an enhanced sensorium that facilitates evocative storytelling with its visceral displays of both images and sounds. In the Internet Age, it is through digital narratives that identity, subjectivity, and community are most readily formulated, expressed, and experienced by innovative cyber Muslims.

This book is aimed at students, scholars, and nonexpert readers interested in the interface of digital media with the lived, local contexts of contemporary global Islam. To set the stage for informed reading, this Introduction outlines salient issues in the investigation of cyberspace and digital media—and briefly surveys the scholarship on digital Islam. Turning to the book's chapters, I highlight key patterns, trajectories, and conclusions raised by each of the volume's authors—and explain the thematic frames that bind their diverse investigations into a coherent whole.

Cyberspace and Digital Networks

In 2020–1, the Covid-19 pandemic turned the world upside down. As the virus spread, mask mandates, social distancing, and public lockdowns forced life indoors—and online. Amid the chaos and uncertainty, people by necessity turned to the internet to educate their children, buy groceries, conduct business, meet and socialize, express political opinions, and even practice their religion. At the same time, the global scale of the public health disaster exposed deep, entrenched structural problems—shedding a bright hot light on socioeconomic disparities, the vulnerability of marginalized groups, the precarity of "essential workers," the pervasive inequities of the digital divide, and the trade-offs between personal privacy, corporate power, and government surveillance. Amplifying and exacerbating existing trends, Covid-19 clearly revealed the symbiotic relationship between online and offline worlds—and the tantalizing possibilities (and glaring limitations) of that interdependence.

Digital media are now so integrated into every dimension of contemporary life that it is easy to forget the World Wide Web was invented in 1990 and that the iPhone, Android, and Kindle did not exist before 2007. Today there are nearly one billion websites accessible on the internet. And with more than ten billion gadgets—from desktops, laptops, and cellphones to cars, vacuum cleaners, and refrigerators—now connected to digital networks, the "Internet of Things" is no longer a science fiction fantasy. Each passing year, the avalanche of digital information and the reach of electronic communication networks accelerate. Coupled with the integration of cloud-based computing on ever faster, cheaper, and more accessible mobile devices, the growth curve of online multimedia usage continues to expand exponentially. Amid the torrential pace of technological change, digital media have been quickly domesticated as the "new normal" of our wired lives.

Digital networks have the potential to radically reconfigure the everyday experience of both space and time. With streaming downloads, spontaneous live interactions, and the instantaneous exchange of words, images, and sounds, virtual reality transcends the solid, fixed boundaries of territory and temporality. Via web pages, blogs, dating sites, podcasts, wikis, chat rooms, and myriad social networking platforms, today's cyber surfers encounter new ways to meet, interact, build communities, and reshape ways of thinking, acting, and being in the world. In this dynamic process, electronic multimedia technologies are radically reconfiguring the rules of identity and subjectivity, economic consumption, social interaction, political discourse, and religious life.

Once online, cyber surfers enter a virtual Wild West that, at first glance, appears to be an open and limitless (if often chaotic and anarchic) space. Even for the privileged minority with easy access to a computer or smartphone, a viable internet connection, and the requisite cultural capital, however, utopian visions of the World Wide Web do not last long. The sense of unbridled freedom and endless possibility online is ultimately illusory. As a 2016 report from Freedom House documents, internet freedom around the world has in fact steadily declined in the early decades of the twenty-first century. More than two-thirds of all internet users today—including most of the world's Muslims—live in countries where criticism of the government, military, or ruling dynasties is subject to strict censorship.[2] And for all people everywhere, there simply is no escape from the long reach of the web's gatekeepers (media conglomerates and service providers, governments, militaries, and intelligence agencies) and the five horseman of the neoliberal Digital Economy: Amazon, Apple, Facebook, Microsoft, and Google.

Yet despite the barriers and restrictions to the increasingly corporatized, controlled, and surveilled digital domain, cyberspace still provides ample space for imagination and invention, innovation and agency. As recent history attests, digital media have a proven track record of facilitating novel forms of individual empowerment, cultural expression, social organization, and political mobilization. In multiple locations, cyberspace has amplified the voices of individuals and communities, who speak and act beyond the purview of traditional nodes of authority and power. In recent years, a wide variety of social outsiders, outliers, and marginalized groups have learned to leverage digital media. For these technophiles, the internet has quickly proved to be a great equalizer—offering fertile ground to upend the social status quo like no other form of mass media before it. I argue that cyberspace's unique affordances, along with its underlying messiness, facilitate what Homi Bhabha calls a "contradictory and ambivalent space of enunciation," opening up new avenues for individual agency, social transformation, and the inversion of offline, "real world" power dynamics.[3] The subversive potential of digital media is an outgrowth of its asymmetric power. Armed with the bullhorn of internet access, the "little guys" can punch above their proverbial weight, reaching vast audiences with a speed, focus, and volume they could never otherwise hope to attain.

Cyberspace now constitutes a distinct public sphere—though certainly not in the mode of Jurgen Habermas's vision of an open, democratic "middle space" mediating between individual citizens and government authorities.[4] Unlike the coffeehouses, public squares, street cafes, and print media of previous centuries, discourse on the World Wide Web is deterritorialized and diffuse. Moreover, digital communication is often anonymous and by definition not mediated via direct, face-to-face exchanges. If interpersonal interactions remain exclusively virtual, then cyberspace is ultimately a one-way street, a dead-end echo chamber. But the "nowhere" of cyberspace is in fact populated by real people who are embodied in concrete locations and embedded in local communities—and cyber networks can (and frequently do) circle back to the mundane realm of terrestrial life. In everyday practice, online encounters often lead to new offline relationships. People who meet in chatrooms often later meet for coffee. Virtual conversations frequently inspire individuals to attend community events or political protests in local neighborhoods. And even cybernauts who never meet their social media "friends" in the flesh still discover new ideas, attitudes, and desires online that impact their worldviews and alter their life trajectories. When true symbiosis between the digital and analog worlds occurs, the virtual is made real.

As digital networks continue to spread their tentacles wider and deeper, scholars have scrambled to map the tectonic shifts of the Internet Age. The expanding archive of digital media studies draws on multiple academic disciplines: communications and media studies, sociology, cultural anthropology, and, more recently, religious studies. The field remains "under construction," however. At present, there is no unanimity among scholars on terminology, methodology, or theoretical approach. In the face of overwhelming evidence, what everyone seems to agree on is that the digital revolution is here to stay and that its influence on religious life is trending upward at an accelerating pace. Chapter 1 of my book *Cyber Sufis* surveys the research on the interface between digital media and comparative religions. My analysis spotlights key thinkers, overarching patterns, and competing paradigms in the interdisciplinary study of digital religion. In keeping with the theme of this volume, however, here I narrow the focus to a vital subset of this evolving scholarly field: Islamic digital media.[5]

Mapping Islamic Digital Media

In Europe and North America, mainstream media outlets too often erase the incredible complexity of Islam and the dazzling diversity of Muslims. On cable television, blogs, web pages, social media, and newspapers, daily headlines typically spotlight sensationalist stories, simplistic narratives, and reductive stereotypes. With rare exceptions, this coverage reduces Islam's global cultural kaleidoscope to a one-dimensional caricature, reinforced by the constant recirculation of stock images of Muslims: silent, invisible women in black veils, angry bearded men, shouting political slogans and wielding guns, and smoldering cities in distant desert lands.

These kinds of essentializing tropes pertain to Islamic digital media as well. It is certainly true that in recent decades no Muslims have proved more adept at exploiting the internet than militant *jihādi* groups. For al-Qaeda, the Taliban, Boko Haram, ISIS, and their myriad affiliates and offshoots, sophisticated and highly stylized YouTube videos (including "martyr" testimonials, filmed executions, and live feeds of terrorist attacks), online magazines, websites, and social media campaigns provide an effective and affective conduit for advertising and recruitment. Not surprisingly, political Islam, extremist ideology, and *jihādi* militancy have typically dominated both journalistic and academic coverage of cyber Islam as well.[6] In everyday practice, however, Islamic digital media are vastly more expansive, multidimensional, and complex—mirroring the incredible diversity of the contemporary *ummah* (the global community of Muslims) itself.

As the chapters in this volume demonstrate, cyberspace has quickly opened up new channels for Muslim community-building, social networking, political participation, self-expression, storytelling, and meaning-making. Muslims around the world have joined the global digital revolution, integrating social media into every dimension of their lives with incredible speed and remarkable skill. By embracing the disruptions of electronic multimedia, a new generation of Muslims has learned to leverage digital media to find their voices, question cultural taboos, circumvent traditional gatekeepers of religious authority, and challenge entrenched political powers. Year by year (even day by day), increasing numbers of Muslims operate in the virtual realm—and many of them clearly spend a great deal of time, energy, and resources maintaining active (and often elaborate) websites and social media platforms. These virtual productions display an array of Muslim identities, blending culture, ethnicity, class, gender, sectarianism, nationalism, and political ideology into complex digital mosaics.

When it comes to Muslims and media, the past is prologue. In diverse cultural locations and historical moments, Muslims have effectively leveraged the power of media as a tool to communicate their own distinct visions of religious identity, piety, and practice. Print technology was not established in the Islamic world until the nineteenth century, 400 years after

Gutenberg's invention of moveable type facilitated the dissemination of Martin Luther's German translation of the Bible. Though late to arrive, it quickly spread during the colonial and postcolonial eras as a broad spectrum of Muslim political actors readily adopted print media to broadcast their messages and build their own "imagined communities."[7] These trends have rapidly expanded in the digital era. Regardless of the medium, however, new articulations of Muslim faith, identity, and community are always built on the same bedrock foundations. As miriam cooke and Bruce Lawrence argue:

> The boundaries of digital Islam reflect the scriptural, creedal, and historical boundaries of Islamic thinking. There can be no Islam without limits or guideposts. You cannot have a straight path unless you know what is beyond or outside or against the straight path. Cyberspace, like social space, must be monitored to be effectively Muslim. . . . The horizontal, open-ended nature of the Internet makes the boundaries of digital Islam at once more porous and more subject to change than those of its predecessors. There are still the same guideposts: the scripture (the noble Qur'an), the person (the Last Prophet), and the law (the *shari'a*, or broad path, with the *'ulama*, or religious specialists, as its custodians). Each term—the book, the prophet, the law—has to be defined historically and then redefined in cyberspace in order to reflect the diversity of resources and worldviews within the *umma*.[8]

Given the persistence of tradition, what exactly is "new" about Muslim "new media"? Beyond the obvious affordances of digital technologies (speed, cost, access), cyberspace has upended entrenched social hierarchies and power dynamics. In the twenty-first century, amid a cacophonous (and at time combative) competition over the mantle of Islamic authority and authenticity, Muslim religious leaders and laypeople alike employ electronic multimedia platforms to speak for Islam. Access to canonical religious resources—the Qur'ān, *ḥadīth* (traditions of the Prophet Muhammad), and the sources of Islamic jurisprudence (*fiqh*)—is no longer the exclusive monopoly of religious scholars and the educated elite. Neither are public claims to the right to interpret Islamic tradition. The increasing volume as well as intensity of public debate via digital media has only accelerated the fracturing of traditional modes of communal identity and social cohesion. The participation of new Muslim social actors has also radically reconfigured the dynamics of the public sphere, both locally and globally. As Dale Eickelman and Jon Anderson note,

> This combination of new media and new contributors to religious and political debates fosters an awareness on the part of all actors of the diverse ways in which Islam and Islamic values can be created and feeds into new senses of a public sphere that is discursive, performative and participative, and not confined to formal institutions recognized by state authorities.[9]

In the Internet Age, new media facilitate new messages and empower new messengers.

Though relatively limited in scope and scale, scholarship on Islamic digital media has made important theoretical, methodological, and ethnographic contributions to the broader field of digital religion. As my Bibliography attests, many of the contributors in this volume have been at the forefront of this rapidly expanding subfield. Research on cyber Islam began in the late 1990s with the groundbreaking work of anthropologist Jon W. Anderson. In a series of wide-ranging articles, Anderson charts how a diverse array of Muslims in the Middle East and the global diaspora employ digital media. These Muslim netizens include students (in both traditional Islamic *madrassahs* and modern universities), religious scholars (*'ulamā'*), middle-class technocrats, labor migrants, government gatekeepers, corporate workers, Islamist ideologues, as well as members of established religious institutions.[10] "They range from political activists to Sufi orders, from mobilization to witness," Anderson argues.

> They both recruit and propagandize, bringing their issues into a wider, already public sphere in some cases but in others carving out a new one that encompasses or repackages existing ones, compelling dialogue by leveraging forms of communication that reshape the social field ... Islam on the Internet is first a story of new interpreters, newly emboldened by confidence in and command of the channel.[11]

As Anderson documents, the rise of internet Islam in the West began during the 1980s, led initially by Arab Muslim university students studying in the burgeoning IT fields. These diasporic Muslim techies worked to build nascent online communities and services by creating experimental websites that included scanned copies of the Qur'ān and *ḥadīth* collections "as pious acts of witness for Islam in cyberspace."[12] During the mid-1990s, groups such as Muslim Students Associations on North American college campuses followed their lead, developing more sophisticated web pages and online discussion forums in the absence of local networks of *'ulamā'* and *madrassahs*. Since the late 1990s, a wide range of established Muslim leaders and institutions with varied agendas and interpretations of the faith have joined this fertile digital commons. As Anderson illustrates, these new virtual Muslim voices include conventional religious institutions, publishing houses, government agencies, Islamist and *jihādi* groups, and institutional Sufi orders.

Anderson divides Muslim digital entrepreneurs into three distinct groupings: "creole" pioneers, activists, and "officializing" interpreters.[13] Collectively, these hybrid and polyvalent groups represent competing voices, multiple claims to authority, and contested assertions of legitimacy. They employ divergent intellectual techniques to forge new linkages and social networks while occupying an "intermediate social space that they in part define and help to build."[14] In Anderson's view, digital media facilitate

Muslim agency by providing entirely novel avenues for communication and community. At the same time, this democratization of knowledge and discursive power disrupts and fragments established nodes of religious power and authority. In his words,

> communication on the Internet model is unstructured by existing canons and enforcers of authority; it puts an unaccustomed measure of agency (not to mention of self-authorization) in the hands of a browser, a channel-surfer, a mobile-phone user, a desktop publisher. On the receiving end, the freedom to look implies a corresponding freedom to sample alternative role models, alternative legitimation and models of authority, not just to the state but in competition with religious authorities and also the family.[15]

The most prominent and prolific chronicler of cyber Islam is Gary R. Bunt (author of Chapter 1 in this volume). In the past two decades, Bunt has published dozens of essays, articles, and book reviews on the subject, in addition to four influential monographs: *Hashtag Islam: How Cyber-Islamic Environments Are Transforming Religious Authority* (2018); *iMuslims: Rewiring the House of Islam* (2009); *Islam in the Digital Age: E-Jihad, Online Fatwas and Cyber Islamic Environments* (2003); and *Virtually Islamic: Computer-Mediated Communication and Cyber Islamic Environments* (2002).[16] Bunt's research explores multiple dimensions of the global "digital *ummah*" in a wide array of "cyber Islamic environments"—two of the author's key neologisms.[17] His work traces the complex interconnections, tensions, and messiness of internet Islam, offering important insights into how digital media simultaneously facilitate and reconfigure Muslim discourse and practice. Like Anderson, Bunt emphasizes the contestations over the mantle of Islamic authority in cyberspace—an alternative ecosystem that simultaneously facilitates novel personal interactions and reconfigures normative modes of hierarchy, power, and social interaction. "Rewiring the House of Islam has not been without its difficulties," he argues. "The Internet has reshaped the boundaries of Muslim networks, created new dialogues, and presented new transaction routes within the Islamic knowledge economy."[18]

Bunt's work is distinguished by its descriptive, encyclopedic approach. His publications provide abundant real world/virtual world examples, mapping Muslim voices online through paradigmatic case studies. Bunt's writings survey a plethora of websites, cataloging Muslim community networking, cultural practices, and identity politics across an expansive social, political, and cultural spectrum. His analysis demonstrates how new technologies and new media spaces—podcasting, video blogs, social networking sites—access new Muslim audiences and create alternative markets for Islamic knowledge, all of which bend and stretch the boundaries of normative tradition. Bunt's eclectic case studies investigate a wide range of digital resources and interfaces, including Qur'ān recitations, translations, and interpretations;[19]

ḥadīth and debates over Islamic law;[20] *fatāwā* (juridical opinions) and *fiqh* (jurisprudence);[21] ritual performance;[22] Islamic music;[23] social networking sites;[24] mobile device applications;[25] and the Islamic blogosphere.[26]

Bunt's methodology often focuses on key exemplars, tracking how different Muslim actors employ digital technologies to communicate their own distinct religious interpretations, ideological agendas, political goals, and discrete claims to Islamic authority. In *iMuslims*, for example, he analyzes the digital media footprint of the Qatar-based Shaykh Yusuf al-Qaradawi, Iraq's Ayatollah al-Sistani, and the Egyptian popular preacher, Amr Khaled.[27] In other work, Bunt spotlights the digital media interfaces of Sunni leaders and institutions;[28] Shī'ī religious leaders;[29] Sufis;[30] Muslim governments and political dissidents;[31] and Muslim hackers, hacktivists, and government censors.[32] Most significantly, Bunt has been at the forefront of research on the use of the internet as a critical tool in the propaganda, recruitment, and logistical operations of Muslim militants.[33] His work provides ample documentation of the multiple media forums used by tech-savvy *jihādi* movements, from video clips and blogs to e-magazines. Charting a variety of *e-jihād* cyber networks in multiple political contexts, Bunt highlights the "use of violent and elaborately choreographed online pronouncements and performances."[34]

Building on these foundations, a recent wave of scholarship offers different vistas and alternative perspectives on the variety and vibrancy of cyber Islam. This new generation of scholars continues to expand the analytical frame, asking new questions about method and theory while tracking the virtual lives of Muslims in different social contexts. In *Islam Dot Com: Contemporary Islamic Discourses in Cyberspace*, for example, Mohammed el-Nawawy and Sahar Khamis (author of Chapter 6 in this volume) examine the Arabic and English language discussion forums of three popular Islamic websites: *www.islamonline.net*, *www.amrkhaled.net*, and *www.islamway.com*.[35] Other scholars have followed suit with detailed, multidimensional case studies of particular Muslim web pages.[36] In similar fashion, recent research documents the multimodal usage of digital media by local Muslim communities in diverse cultural settings and political contexts, including the United States,[37] Iran,[38] the Arab world (particularly during the "Arab Spring"),[39] and Southeast Asia.[40] Other notable contributions investigate the use of cyberspace by Muslim women;[41] generational divides in electronic media usage and attitudes;[42] Islamic authority and authenticity in cyberspace;[43] the Qur'ān online;[44] Muslim legal scholars, media preachers, and online celebrities;[45] Islamism and political Islam online;[46] the Muslim blogosphere and discussion groups;[47] Islamic dating and matchmaking sites;[48] Islamic-themed video games;[49] and cyber Sufism.[50] The emergence of focused reports on digital religion, digital studies of Islamophobic networks, and digital journals such as *Cyber Orient: Online Journal of the Virtual Middle East and Islamic World* signals the growing sophistication of this fertile scholarly subfield.[51]

This academic scholarship confirms that digital media are precipitating deep structural changes to the public face of Islam around the globe. It is abundantly clear that emergent media technologies are quickly altering the expectations, attitudes, and practices of both producers and consumers within the Islamic knowledge economy. Though still limited by the boundaries of class, gender, and the digital divide—with young, male, urban, middle-class professionals dominating the discourse—Islamic digital media are nonetheless growing at a remarkable pace. Social dynamics, both large and small, are reconstituted in the process. As Nabil Echchaibi (author of Chapter 15 in this volume) argues,

> the Internet has enabled a new cultural space for Muslims to create new networks of Islamic learning, praxis, and deliberation, causing an important shakeup in top-down approaches to religious authority and introducing new influential actors as the face of a public, visible, and global Islam. Digital media are also reconfiguring the kind of public hailed by this highly performative, engaged, and confident Islam.[52]

With increasing self-reflexivity, creativity, and assertiveness, cyber Muslims are embracing digital multimedia to amplify their individual voices, rewire community networks, and reshape the contours of their own public identities.

Thematic Frames and Chapter Layout

This volume builds on the current scholarship on cyber Islam while pushing the field in new directions. Each of the book's fifteen chapters is a self-contained universe with its own story to tell. Every chapter focuses on a particular cultural and geographical location (or locations) with case studies that examine how specific Muslims—individuals, groups, or organizations—deploy various forms of digital media to access diverse audiences and to project a wide array of messages. At the same time, chapters are grouped together around four distinct thematic frames.

Part I, "Authority and Authenticity," examines how digital media reconfigure the networks of Islamic knowledge. The three chapters in this part each ponder a series of pressing questions: Who exactly is authorized to speak for and interpret Islamic faith online? In what ways does digital media either expand or disassemble entrenched structures of institutional power and the predominance of established gatekeepers of tradition?

In Chapter 1, "The Net *Imam* Effect: Digital Contestation of #Islam and Religious Authority," Gary R. Bunt documents the ongoing shifts in the representation of Islamic authority within the competitive "online marketplace of ideas." His analysis foregrounds how an array of Muslim authority figures, legal experts, and online influencers adroitly leveraged their digital media footprints to expand influence during the Covid-19 pandemic. Bunt's illustrative examples range from TikTok *fatāwā* and digital Qur'ān sites to apps for *hajj* pilgrims and the podcasts, blogs, e-books, YouTube channels, and personal websites of prominent institutional leaders.

Chapter 2, "Hybrid *Imams*: Young Muslims and Religious Authority on Social Media," traces generational changes among Muslim "digital natives," who search for guidance, advice, and inspiration online. Drawing on extensive fieldwork interviews from the annual "Reviving the Islamic Spirit" (RIS) conference in Toronto, Sana Patel describes how young North American Muslims fluidly integrate digital media into their everyday religious lives. Her case studies spotlight the "virtual and hybrid presence" of celebrity Sunni *imams* who maintain highly personalized connections with their legions of followers via social media (Facebook, Twitter, Instagram), punctuated with in-person appearances and interactions.

In Chapter 3, "Mediating Authority: A Sufi *Shaykh* in Multiple Media," Ismail Fajrie Alatas explores how Islamic religious authority "takes shape and is configured through different practices of mediatization" through the story of an influential contemporary Indonesian Sufi master: Shaykh Habib Luthfi Bin Yahya. Alatas's insightful analysis compares the utility and efficacy of print and digital media technologies, contrasting Habib Luthfi's public profile, discourses, and audience engagement in a bimonthly print magazine, *alKisah* (The Parable), with the official website, Facebook page, and Twitter account established and curated by his disciples to help spread his message.

Part II, "Community and Identity," illuminates how cyber Muslims from different social, ethnic, and cultural backgrounds harness cyberspace to initiate conversations, expand networks, and champion their own unique visions of Muslim subjectivity. Each of the four chapters offers granular case studies that show how digital media are deployed to complement, extend, or reformulate "real world" offline Muslim communities.

Chapter 4, "Stream If You Want: *See Something, Say Something* and the Humanizing Potential of Digital Islam," describes how an eclectic crowdfunded podcast creates an open and interactive space for multiple publics to engage a host of compelling (and often controversial) issues—and to humanize the lived experiences of American Muslims. Caleb Elfenbein's interviews with the podcast's Muslim producer and select non-Muslim listeners reveal how the strategic use of digital media can work to upend the burdens of Muslim self-representation and combat the pervasive silence, stereotypes, and misunderstandings that fuel Islamophobia.

In Chapter 5, "Latinx Muslim Digital Landscapes: Locating Networks and Cultural Practices," Madelina Nuñez and Harold D. Morales outline the history of the Latinx Muslim community in the United States, along with the parallel evolution and increasing sophistication of its diverse digital multimedia productions. Spotlighting prominent national organizations and key online influencers, their study clarifies the vital roles that emerging digital technologies (social media outlets, cloud file sharing and streaming platforms, video conference rooms) and, in particular, Latinx Muslim food websites and celebrity bloggers have played in the formation of a distinct cultural and communal identity.

In Chapter 6, "Revisiting Digital Islamic Feminism: Multiple Resistances, Identities, and Online Communities," Sahar Khamis investigates the digital footprints of Muslim feminists, fashionistas, activists, and community organizers across an expansive local and diasporic landscape. Her study explores a wide range of websites, Twitter feeds, and private Facebook groups. These case studies illustrate the creative, innovative strategies of diverse, hybrid groups of tech-savvy Muslim women who skillfully deploy cyberspace to claim agency, amplify their own voices, challenge patriarchy and social marginalization, resist reductive narratives and stereotypes, and build networks of solidarity and support.

Chapter 7, "#MuslimGirlWoke: A Muslim Lifestyle Website Challenges Intersectional Oppression," focuses on the online lifestyle magazine and website *Muslim Girl*, aimed at an audience of Muslim American teenage girls, most of them children of immigrants. Through a nuanced examination of the content of online articles, Kristin M. Peterson shows how *Muslim Girl* engages pressing social issues, critiques the representations of Muslim women in mainstream media and popular culture, promotes a community of shared support, encourages social awareness and engagement, and champions a progressive politics "rooted in Islamic teaching and intersectional feminism."

Part III, "Piety and Performance," considers how Islamic pedagogy, performative practices, and embodied rituals are mirrored in virtual spaces. The four case-study chapters document how digital media open up new spaces for Muslim experience and expression and ask: What is gained (or lost) in the transfer of intimate, personal acts of piety into the public dimensions of cyberspace?

In Chapter 8, "The Digital *Niqābosphere* as a Hypermediated Third Space," Anna Piela explores the "multilayered self-mediation" and "theological bricolage" of an ambitious online influencer who publishes content on YouTube, Facebook, Twitter, Instagram, and review blogs while operating an Etsy business selling Islamic art, jewelry, and clothing. Rivka Sajida constructs and performs a complex amalgam of hybrid, non-normative identities through her multiple digital media platforms. A *niqāb*-wearing Jewish-Muslim, Muslim-Queer, Muslim-Feminist, and Orthodox-Sufi, she advocates for people with disabilities while leading prayers and offering sermons from her own online mosque.

Chapter 9, "Islamic Meditation: Mindfulness Apps for Muslims in the Digital Spiritual Marketplace," charts the emergence of a new genre of Islamic guided meditation apps. With attention to texts, soundscapes, and visual displays, Megan Adamson Sijapati highlights three distinct apps that echo the wellness industry's promises of improved mental health, emotional stability, and stress reduction while grounding meditation practice in the cultural, theological, and epistemological frames of Islamic piety. Designed by and for Muslims, these apps draw on traditional Sufi techniques (and terminology) while erasing any "explicit reference to any institutional or authoritative sources."

In Chapter 10, "From Mecca with Love: Muslim Religious Apps and the Centering of Sacred Geography," Andrea Stanton examines the interface between digital media, sacred space, and the complex ritual nexus of Islamic pilgrimage. Her study tracks the content of hundreds of *hajj and 'umrah* mobile apps in English, Arabic, and Persian available for downloading on various online markets. These digital material objects, she argues, intentionally frame a particular version of the city of Mecca for contemporary, global Muslim pilgrims—and serve to both augment ritual performance and shape "affective pious self-fashioning."

Chapter 11, "Seeing a Global Islam?: *Eid al-Adha* on Instagram," traces the application of digital media to the experience and expression of Muslim piety during *Ramaḍān*. Focusing on hashtags, textual narratives, and visual imagery, Rosemary Pennington analyzes an array of inspirational, contemplative, and celebratory posts circulated to mark the end of the Islamic month of fasting. Viewing these digital messages as evidence of lived religion, she highlights how they both reflect diverse versions of individual piety and envision a global "Muslim social body" that is expansive, inclusive, and interconnected.

Part IV, "Visual and Cultural (Re)presentation," explores the sensual, aesthetic, and affective affordances (and limitations) of Muslim digital multimedia. Moving across a vast cultural terrain and between online and offline worlds, the four chapters in this final thematic section document how various cyber Muslims leverage the unique sensorial capacities of cyberspace to display and re-present Islam to multiple local audiences in heterogeneous public spheres.

Chapter 12, "Defining Islamic Art: Practices and Digital Reconfigurations," examines the assumptions and prejudices that (mis)inform the display of Islamicate art in both offline and online spaces. Hussein Rashid's case studies compare the curation of Islamic material culture, history, and knowledge in prominent public museums (the Metropolitan Museum of Art in New York City, the British Museum in London, and the Children's Museum of Manhattan) with digital websites (Archnet and Artstor). Drawing on multiple theoretical models and his own personal experiences, he calls for more nuanced, inclusive, imaginative, and Muslim-centric approaches.

Chapter 13, "Dousing the Flame: The Political Work of Religious Satire in Contemporary Indonesia," focuses on the strategic use of levity and humor in Indonesian cyberspaces. James B. Hoesterey foregrounds the formation of numerous "Funny Brigades" by diverse groups of young, media-savvy online activists whose carefully crafted posts and memes promote civic pluralism, intra-Muslim harmony, and interreligious tolerance through visual jokes and theological representations. Juxtaposing digital texts and images, his analysis illustrates how "lucid play" on Indonesian social media works to "side-step, if not disarm, the problem of online (and offline) rancor."

Chapter 14, "The Instagram Cleric: History, Technicity, and Shī'ī Iranian Jurists in the Age of Social Media," surveys the evolution and impact of media technologies in Iran—from early Shī'īsm, to the formation of an Islamist state in 1979, to the contemporary digital era. Through a detailed analysis of the visual imagery, political rhetoric, and highly personalized styles displayed on the Instagram accounts of two contemporary jurists, Babak Rahimi explores the multivalent and nuanced ways that Shī'ī religious authority and identity "undergoes dynamic change amid a visual and cultural repertoire of self (re)presentations."

In Chapter 15, "Muslims between Transparency and Opacity," Nabil Echchaibi ponders the limits and costs of Muslim visibility. Amid the politics and aesthetics of the "War on Terror," reductive, essentializing, and dehumanizing discourses and disciplinary systems frame Muslims as Others, outsiders, strangers, and potentially dangerous threats. Spotlighting the creative work of writers, street performers, documentary filmmakers, video bloggers, and digital artists, Echchaibi reveals how Muslims can leverage digital media to resist control, manipulation, and erasure to discover "an ethics of Muslim narration that defies the totalizing frames of transparency."

Conclusion

As a key marker of twenty-first-century global modernity, cyberspace now serves as a vital alternative ecosystem for Muslims for piety and practice, narratives and networking, experience and expression. Since all digital culture is local, however, there is simply no single, seamless pattern to cyber Islam. When it comes to online digital cultures, hybridity and heterogeneity, diversity and difference are the norm, not the exception.

Engaging a bricolage of digital media platforms, the cyber Muslims in this book each display their own distinct versions of Islamic identity. They do so within local and global environments where other Muslims—drawing on the same foundational history, sacred sources, and religious symbols— imagine and enact markedly different models of Islamic normativity, subjectivity, authority, and community. This state of multiplicity is nothing new. From its origins, Islam has never been monolithic or static. Throughout history, Islam has flowed through diverse landscapes like water, adapting to the contours of local geographies and taking on the colors of local cultures. With the past as precedent, the transplantation of Muslim piety and practices across the virtual realm of cyberspace repeats a deeply engrained pattern of constant accommodation, adaptation, and transformation.

While predicting the future of technology is a fool's errand, it is safe to say that the internet is not going away and that digital media will only become increasingly powerful and omnipresent in the years ahead. Current trajectories, common sense, and Moore's Law all suggest that we are at the tipping point of another major technological and social paradigm shift, with momentous changes already underway.[53] Global tech giants, venture capital firms, and corporate media conglomerates continue to pour massive financial investments into quantum computers; big data analytics, metadata mining, and digital advertising; mobile, cloud, and social media applications; and VR (virtual reality), AR (augmented reality), and AI (artificial intelligence) technology. These seismic shifts in the digital media matrix raise a host of vexing (and unresolved) ethical questions surrounding the proper balance between unbridled capitalism, government oversight and regulation, and individual privacy. Exactly where all this energy, effort, and expense leads is impossible to say. But if, as the tech pundits and prognosticators suggest, we are in fact moving inexorably toward an increasingly integrated, interactive, and immersive hyper-reality with Web 3.0., past precedent suggests that cyber Muslims will quickly adapt to the next wave of emergent digital media technologies to keep pace with changing times.

Amid the momentous paradigm shift of the Internet Age, the challenge for scholars is to keep up with the changing attitudes and practices of Muslims, who increasingly deploy cyberspace in divergent ways to diverse ends. In order to account for the heterodox, polycentric expressions of mediated Muslim subjectivities, scholars need new tools. As the chapters in this book illustrate, granular case studies are essential to capture the particularities and multiplicities of Islamic digital media. Building on these examples, future research will also require more granular, 360-degree studies of the reciprocal flows between online digital Islam and the day to day, "on the ground" dynamics of Muslim community life. To that end, scholars will need to better document how digital media help Muslims forge offline relationships, build networks, and transcend geographic and cultural boundaries—and how the "real world," in turn, reinforces or reformulates virtual experiences. Detailed studies that combine online ethnography with offline interviews and interactions with the producers and users of these spaces will help illuminate the gaps and divergences between digital fantasies and lived realities. Most importantly, the field will benefit from new methodological approaches to digital narratives and practices—along with more nuanced theoretical frameworks—to explain precisely how religious life is augmented or altered in cyberspace.

This volume is most certainly not the last word on cyber Muslims. It is instead meant to be an intervention that will, I hope, serve as a catalyst for further scholarly investigations in the years ahead. As digital religion and cyber Islam continue to expand, morph, and evolve, this flourishing field of scholarly inquiry and investigation remains wide open—primed for new voices, new analytical paradigms, and alternative perspectives.

Part I

Authority and Authenticity

CHAPTER 1

The Net *Imam* Effect:

Digital Contestations of #Islam and Religious Authority

Gary R. Bunt

Introduction

This chapter explores the contestation on issues of representation and religious authority in cyber Islamic environments. In an era where authority networks transcend geographical boundaries, and when digital proficiency can be more important than religious status, there has been an evolution in the dynamics of Islamic authority and leadership. Today, digital technology is reshaping how Muslims across vast territories relate to religious authorities in fulfilling spiritual, mystical, and legalistic agendas. Millennials and "digital natives" may respond more to aspects of online authority than "analog" equivalents, impacting everyday concepts of religious knowledge and identity, and also raising concerns regarding radicalization. Online environments often challenge traditional models of authority; "traditional" in this context refers to the purview of *imams*, *mullahs*, and *shaykhs* located in the historically rooted "analog" locations of religious authority such as *madrassahs* or mosques.[1] The term is ambiguous, as it can also refer to those adhering to diverse notions of expertise associated with Islamic sources relating to the Prophet Muhammad, his followers, and/or the descendants of projected authority, scholarship, and interpretation. This does not preclude gatekeepers in these contexts articulating notions of religious authority online, with a blurring between analog and digital authority. One result is the impact of digitally literate religious scholars, authorities, and "influencers," whose impact goes beyond these demarcated boundaries of established spiritual exemplars and legal experts.[2]

This chapter examines how diverse religious perspectives contest for audiences, reflecting on multimedia approaches from a variety of players in the spectrum of Muslim zones of cyberspace. It questions the impact of social media pronouncements and explores how religious institutional organizations and their corresponding digital platforms respond to contemporary concerns in the light of continually shifting religious and media contexts. I also demonstrate how the global Covid-19 crises focused attention on the ways in which Islamic digital interfaces could be utilized within Muslim communities and by religious institutions to negotiate questions of spirituality, interpretation, and ritual propriety within the rapidly changing pandemic context.

Exploring Islamic Cyberspace

Any analysis of cyber Muslims should reflect upon the exponential growth in internet technologies and gradual increases in digital access spurred by a rapid growth in online Islamic discourse in a multiplicity of formats and religious zones, all of which featured in my initial definition of "cyber Islamic environments."[3] This term has evolved in line with technological shifts and their applications in diverse Muslim contexts but has not yet become redundant given its flexibility in encompassing a complex range of digital media forms from content providers who define themselves as "Muslims." Although *jihād*-oriented discourse has proportionally distorted the field for some observers, it actually constitutes a small component in a much more substantial and varied set of online networks, affiliations, and voices associated with the articulation of Muslim identities and knowledge. In observing and monitoring the constant shifts in these cyber Islamic environments, one becomes conscious of the utilization of increasingly innovative and digitally literate applications as digital natives become embedded in platforms and organizations—while also establishing their own novel outlets online. The separation between on- and offline is increasingly anachronistic, with mobile devices coupled with enhanced digital literacy and access making the internet a natural zone for all elements of Muslims' lives. In fact, the complexity of content associated with religion comprises a minor component of a much wider pattern of digital media consumption in Muslim population zones.

The early phases of online Islamic expression prompted reactions from apathy to resistance from some established Muslim religious authorities toward the new media, for multiple reasons: a lack of digital literacy, "technophobia," generational divides, and concerns that the internet would "distract" and "corrupt" people were common views. Resistance to the usage of online media in religious spaces such as mosques, concerns about the presence of the Qur'ān on the internet, and fears that digital media would challenge or subvert traditional norms through digital influences were also frequent fears. Amid the information "vacuum" caused by initial inactivity from these conventional Muslim authorities, there emerged a wave of digital content generated by enthusiasts and opportunists. These users presented a new vision of how a "market share" in cyber Islamic environments would lead to influence in and impact on an exponentially growing online context. New voices and platforms focusing on a digital rather than analog presence contested for influence, encompassing a range of religious perspectives. This trend accelerated when web-focused content expanded into growing social media applications and spaces, zones where technological innovation and application in presenting alternative interpretations of Islamic content left a number of conventional authorities in their wake.[4] In response, those established authorities, experts, and institutions that had ignored or condemned the internet changed course, realizing that their influence across generations (especially among younger people) would wane in the absence of a digital presence. The increasing expectations among Muslims that religious questions could be answered by an authentic authority through an internet search—and that the hierarchy of search linked to algorithms, metadata, and links was more influential than scholarly reputations— meant that a "shopping around" for opinions became more prevalent.[5] In everyday practice, religiously oriented content was increasingly integrated into much wider content consumption patterns. This included, for example, the production of apps for specific Islamic purposes, such as reading the Qur'ān, determining prayer direction, and generating reminders of specific prayer times.[6]

The utilization of a search engine to seek basic knowledge on Islam can expose the surfer to a multitude (or cacophony) of different voices and opinions. While this information overload exposes the reader to a range of options, it can also be challenging and confusing, necessitating detailed research rather than providing an instant answer. Content providers who are able to present themselves as the "go-to" source for information may offer their adherents a shortcut, one that already relates to their existing worldview. Alternatively, this may impact or alter religious perspectives entirely. Occasionally, this reshaping may go against the traditional values of a community network. This has certainly been a contributing factor in the political-religious framing of opinions, which have led to so-called radicalization, with militant groups such as al-Qaeda and "Islamic State" now forming part of the marketplace of ideas open to all web users. Attempts to mediate or provide gatekeeping options that reflect specific cultural and religious outlooks within communities are not always successful, especially in the face of intergenerational disconnects based on differences in ideas about (and approaches to) knowledge, as well as more prosaic factors such as digital literacy limitations. Overall, however, the competitive nature of online content, the need to ensure design is fresh and navigable, and the constant demands for immediacy, identity, and affiliation with networks and causes have meant that opportunities for exposure to alternative worldviews and interpretations have extended exponentially amid the reduced digital divide and corresponding increases in digital literacy. Even when censorship and monitoring impede this exposure, tech-savvy Muslims have found many ways around local internet restrictions.

Digital Contestation of Islamic Influence

In the twenty-first century, mosques, Muslim organizations, religious lifestyle influencers, and diverse Islamic interpretative frameworks contest online for impact on issues of belief, identity, politics, and community through diverse digital media forms. In 2020 this was highlighted with an intensified utilization of technological interfaces aimed to bring together socially distanced communities and networks during the Covid-19 pandemic—manifested in YouTube *Ramaḍān* rituals, TikTok religious advice, and online activist mobilization through social media. Authority is increasingly shaped by its approaches to online questions, the "searchability" and immediacy of responses, and the ease in which it can be navigated and accessed online via diverse media formats. Specific strands of belief draw on these digital spaces to present granular ideas of interpretation, leadership, and religious identities—capturing these formulations through Islamic digital media that increasingly have responded to the "always on" nature of mobile devices, building content that factors in immediacy and responsiveness. Marginalized perspectives outside of the mainstreams of interpretation and practice have also taken advantage of online opportunities to open up new audiences for their interpretations, on issues as varied as sexuality and *jihād* radicalization. Traditional boundaries rooted in historical layers of scholarship, interpretation, and ritualistic practices have broken through globalizing online influences, introducing a range of digitally literate players unencumbered by governments and organizational limitations.[7] This includes individuals presenting Islamic lifestyles and ideas through social media, capturing and influencing young audiences in the process. Contesting notions of "authentic" Islamic messages can be found online, part of long-standing debates that pre-date digital media, often reflected in the emergence of diverse interpretative strands, multiple "schools" of thought, and the political manifestation of religious authority.[8] This can be a cause of conflict, contestation, and even antagonistic "trolling" and abuse between different factions.

   Among increasingly globalized Muslim communities, there is a pervasive evolution in terms of notions of authority and leadership, and this extends into digital technologies which shape how Muslims across vast territories relate to religious authorities in fulfilling their spiritual mystical and legalistic agendas.[9] The contestation for authority through different models appears online and offline (and at points in-between). Pre-technological approaches of authority dissemination continue, even as innovative approaches toward interpreting Islam as a "lifestyle" play out through streaming media with little differentiation between the on- and offline worlds—especially for those digital natives and technologically literate generations for whom devices are embedded throughout their daily activities. The notion of Islam being "always on" takes on a different dimension in online contexts, with devices continually presenting reminders, updates, prayers, and networking affiliations across diverse Muslim networks. The capture and presentation of ritual through digital media acts in some zones serve as a reinforcement of authority, especially when societal norms are challenged by other influences outside of conventional religious reference points. Traditional narratives rooted in time-bound layers of interpretation and scholarship can achieve a continuity through their electronic presence online, even as "innovative" interpretations and ideas filter through to receptive and curious audiences.

Voices of Religious Authority

The projection of religious authority online now serves as a vital focal point for those seeking to position themselves as significant voices within a complex Islamic milieu. Individuals providing opinions on well-designed web interfaces compete with the "major players," acquiring influence and prestige for their religious interpretations which might contradict "traditional" perspectives. This can unsettle the status quo, but also open up spaces to access new audiences. The mediation power of the local *imam* (or otherwise titled "religious authority") may be challenged by an online (and, at times, anonymous) authority projecting an "authentic" interpretative voice. Conversely, the local *imam* may transform into a net *imam* when developing a global voice through online articulation and presentation of their worldview. The creative application of online media is influential in this context, especially in an increasingly competitive marketplace for ideas and influences. Presenting Islamic authority online requires investment of time and resources, especially if an individual or group seeks to develop interactive and responsive digital spaces where affiliations and memberships can be engineered. The online marketplace for ideas can also stretch into micro-areas. As with other sectors of the internet, the "long tail" of micro-demand means that highly specialized perspectives and "products" can be strategically targeted; networks of individuals may communicate a specific set of interpretative values which they cannot easily express in their local, analog context. This might include allegiance to a political-religious perspective which is prohibited in the local context or online observance of religious practices and rituals that are not permitted or encouraged in local mosques.

Some key players now have a digital heritage stretching back to the 1990s, with a continuity of content and an established brand and profile within the authority marketplace. Other Muslim media stars have come and gone: burnt out, censored, or eclipsed in this contested space. Some net *imams* have profiles which are monetized, either literally or figuratively in terms of the number of "likes," clicks, and reposts. At the same time, they compete with other forms of online influencers with Islamic identities and ideas of religious authority that are projected through YouTube lifestyle channels, Instagram brand promotion, and tweets. A subtle underpinning religious ethos filtered through content more aligned with motivational speakers, "edutainment," and personality culture has effectively recalibrated contemporary notions of authority projection. The emergence of both self-proclaimed "scholars" and net *imams* into these zones as a means of asserting influence suggests skill development, which goes well beyond the conventional religious structures of knowledge dissemination.

Advocates of diverse religious perspectives have recognized these factors. The spectrum of authority, from *jihād*-oriented content to Sufi performance, relies on the production of dynamic content attuned to different online consumption patterns, interfaces, and influences in the contested marketplace. Digital material is designed to attract attention immediately, before an individual swipes through to other content; attention spans in digital spaces can waver, especially with the myriad distractions available for consumers, including message alerts and pop-ups which interfere with the consumption of content. Marketing is key. Affiliation and continuity with pre-digital Muslim networks and interests can also be a significant factor, albeit with a reframing of the parameters of knowledge and identity in the digital context. There is a continuity of themes as well. Notions of interpretation, prophethood, and Islamic piety, for example, are often interpreted by what I have defined as "iMuslims" (or digitally connected Muslims) in line with traditional understandings. This includes how significant questions of identity, theology, law, and epistemology are approached. For example, in some Sunni contexts, the application of *ijtihād* (a pragmatic interpretation of Islam in the light of contemporaneous circumstances) may include all of the traditional processes and components of knowledge interpretation and dissemination. The key difference lies in the fact that the circulation of legal opinions is instantaneous through online channels and frequently hyperlinked to other opinions and information sources. As a result, interpretations of Sunni law may become part of a multimedia output—rather than being sent through a laborious process of editing, proofing, publication, and distribution. In Islam's formative historical period, especially in the centuries following the death of Muhammad in 632 CE, religious interpretations were distributed through written forms or oral transmission. Their emphasis and immediate impact are significantly altered within the digital context, however.

Audience expectations are also different in digital contexts. Petitioners may attempt to acquire or search for alternative responses from a range of online scholars, prior to formulating a decision based on the response that most closely fits their own individual outlook or circumstances. The net *imam* effect in this instance is the notion of immediacy: the pressure to provide an opinion before competitors can result in reduced opportunities to reflect on and research the complex nuances within a religious opinion. Search engine algorithms impact online information acquisition, including in Islamic contexts. Some religious perspectives place greater emphasis on the production of a religious opinion (*fatāwā*) than others. Institutions such as the Deobandis, for example, have dedicated *fatwā* departments to answer questions;[10] machine-generated responses to common questions are also evolving in the UAE.[11] Searching online through specific databases—as well as general searches—offers another way to access legal opinions. The extended shelf life of a *fatwā* is itself a further consequence of cyber Islamic environments: the pronouncements of generations of deceased scholars compete with contemporary perspectives through digitized archives, augmented by audiovisual materials. In effect, the advocates of specific legal authorities subtly project their own views through the edited opinions of others.

Into this context emerge new players and perspectives, drawing on alternative approaches to online media which go well beyond websites. These voices gain traction through social media, applying innovative approaches to dissemination. Over time, there have been some major shifts and changes in terms of responses to different platforms. Content has "evolved" to accommodate these transformations, whether through compressing written thoughts into the format of a tweet (initially 140 characters, currently 280 characters) or developing a dynamic digital format to discuss the Qur'ān. Adapting traditional source materials for specific audiences also increased edutainment content for children, such as animated *Sīra* biographical films, whose narratives combined the latest iteration of a communication process with a reliance on traditional Islamic sources.[12] Some of these presentations even linked to opportunities to subscribe to dedicated online channels for further or more extensive content.

The exponential rise of TikTok, in which concise video clips are created and circulated on cellphones, offered a further opportunity to project ideas about Islam, especially toward a youth demographic. Some authorities have expressed concerns that the app might be *ḥarām* (forbidden) because it contained immoral content, showed "gender mixing," dancing, and had addictive qualities.[13] Others, like Zimbabwean preacher Mufti Ismail Menk, acknowledged the complex issues of TikTok's utilization by religious scholars but did not dismiss it.[14] None of these debates, however, prevented TikTok becoming popular with young people, a point that has not been lost on religious authorities and those seeking to present religious values. Although there have been concerns from authorities in Mecca over the use of cellphones in the *Ka'bah* precincts over the years, for example, this has not stopped the phenomena and the incremental increase in clips made in Mecca uploaded online. Following suit, the presentation of "official" content from Mecca is now allowed on TikTok, including clips from *hajj* and *'umrah* filmed close to the *Ka'bah*.[15] The Qur'ān and its recitation also feature extensively on TikTok, a natural format for brief presentations and audiovisual recitations.[16] In 2020, this included the presentation of a *du'ā'* (prayer) on the Coronavirus.[17] In a similar fashion, the rise of TikTok *fatāwā* has facilitated the circulation of religious opinions among broad audiences. Some of these have explored relatively controversial topics, such as a widely shared TikTok on the "Islamic ruling for Or@l $ex" (the use of this spelling designed to avoid inappropriate links to other sites).[18]

Some cyber Islamic environments do not necessarily require a traditionally trained religious scholar to mediate ideas of authority and influence. Performative and ritual practices articulated online emanate from diverse sources, including those who could be identified as "Islamic influencers." The presentation of the Qur'ān online features on numerous translation and recitation sites and apps, offering searchable digital interfaces which open up the Revelation to audiences ranging from the curious to the devoted, from Muslim and other perspectives. Social media have also played a role in projecting different approaches toward the Qur'ān, often attracting substantial online audiences in the process. While many famous reciters can be found online (including via archive recordings), there are also some atypical, niche approaches to the science of recitation, with new trends developing around female reciters and examples of children presenting *suwar*.[19]

The Net *Imam* Effect and Covid-19

The impact of the Covid-19 pandemic in 2020 led to an increasing digitized mediatization of Islam, especially relating to ritualistic practices and expressions of religious authority. This built on existing practices and structures within cyber Islamic environments but amplified and, in some cases, adapted them to suit situations, where lockdown and limited social mixing meant that access to mosques was restricted or prohibited. Multiple Islamic authorities and institutions that had previously been reluctant to place sermons and prayers online on a regular basis, for example, determined that the pandemic circumstances required some pragmatic interpretive approaches toward this unprecedented situation. This included responses to key events in the Islamic calendar such as *Ramaḍān*, which acquired a digital dimension through the facilitation of online *ifṭār* (a pre-pandemic phenomenon that acquired added impetus and poignancy because of the Covid-19 situation), as well as recitations and sermons specific to *Laylat al-Qadr* that would usually have taken place in the mosque context.[20] The responses from Muslim scholars and authorities to this situation required new rules within this crisis mode. I am not suggesting here that these digital outputs and concerns were priorities for everyone, however, given how content competes for attention amid the continued digital divides that inhibit access.

Responses to the pandemic from religious authorities reflected the pressures of their rapidly developing contextual situations. In numerous locales, religious opinions were placed online as a quick response to significant questions associated with the outbreak. In the UK, this included countering rumors that started to emerge on issues which were impacting communities. There had been concerns in London that bodies of Muslim Covid-19 victims in hospitals were being cremated—in violation of Islamic practices for burial. In response, a religious scholar had to go online in order to counter these rumors which, though unsubstantiated, had wide social media circulation, causing disquiet within local communities.[21]

A particularly revealing indicator of the role of social media, religious authority, and the net *imam* effect during Covid-19 was reflected in Mecca, where investments in multimedia rapidly intensified. This included the enhanced development and promotion of apps presenting streaming content broadcasting specific ritual practices associated with *hajj* and *'umrah*, as well as specific responses to the pandemic. This was significant in terms of projecting ideas of religious influence and "appropriate" practice during the Covid-19 outbreak, from social distancing during prayer to the wearing of masks in the precincts of the *Ka'bah*. An implication of these apps was the authorization of the use of digital interfaces for religious purposes during circumstances where normative practices and rituals were in crisis mode. The cliché of the "new normal" played out in empty pilgrimage sites and social-distanced prayer rituals. Particularly striking were images of an empty *mataf* (the precincts surrounding the *Ka'bah*) and of cleaners praying toward the *Ka'bah*. An especially instructive example of these apps came from Haramain Recordings, part of a suite of apps associated with the precincts of Mecca, including for the practice of *hajj* and *'umrah* (available via Android and Apple platforms). This app features recordings and streaming of prayers and sermons, while its Instagram page displays socially distanced adapted activities such as prayer and sermons—alongside photos of religious and other functionaries observing protocols (from *imams* to security personnel).

Since the 2020 *hajj* was exclusively open to limited numbers of pilgrims based in Saudi Arabia, others could only observe activities online through channels such as these. Some of this imagery was taken from cellphones, which had previously been banned or restricted near the *Ka'bah* (an edict that has steadily eroded with the presence of improved Wi-Fi in the *Ka'bah* precincts and digitally connected pilgrimage devices and apps). These images were frequently taken on and reposted by other Islamic digital media platforms, especially with the striking and unusual images of sparsely attended *'umrah* and *hajj* rituals. The Haramain social media feeds, such as Twitter, further intensified attention on these focal points with clips from recitations and livestreaming (some drawn from other online broadcast channels), along with poignant photos from a relatively empty Mecca and Medina. This was a digital projection of religious authenticity from the focal point of Islamic authority.

In a similar fashion, Islamic media outlets in local and international contexts spotlighted the efforts of religious authorities to mitigate the impact of social distancing, along with their advice, as restrictions slowly eased. These sites also reproduced specific recommendations on pilgrimage, especially concerning the prescribed restrictions. The socially distanced 2020 *hajj* was strictly regulated to keep participants safely away from each other, generating in the process some striking and unusual photographs of the resulting practices. This included time lapse photography of the *ṭawāf*, as well as the final circumambulation of the *Ka'bah* at the completion of pilgrimage.[22] At the time of *Ramaḍān*'s conclusion, the image of a solitary woman praying by the *Ka'bah* was widely circulated, described by one social media commentator as "a beautiful metaphor of how many Muslims have spent Ramadan and Eid. Physically alone, but spiritually (and digitally) connected. As a friend said to me, Muslims have rich interior lives."[23]

Other Islamic portals offer entry into diverse online content, from a variety of usage perspectives and levels of interest. Amid the pandemic, this included the incorporation of advice about Covid-19, drawn from a range of sources. The About Islam channel was one of several platforms that offered advice on "Holding Virtual *Jumu'ahs* and *Taraweek* [*sic*] Prayers," reproducing an article from Sheikh Ahmad Kutty, which originally appeared on a Toronto Islamic website.[24] It provided a *fatwā* on how a virtual congregational prayer could be instituted in order to enable the continuity of practice until the reinstatement of "normal" prayers. Kutty argued, "With the situation being unprecedented, it calls for an exceptional ruling or opinion." However, he also noted that this was not a principle for the long term: "In the age of increasing trends of individualism, and movements away from mosques (i.e. being unmosqued), we must never adopt online gatherings as a general rule."[25] While accepting a temporary break due to the Covid-19 situation, Kutty advised that the prospect of a long-term cancellation would break mosque attending habits, thereby endangering the community.

Congregational prayers are a cornerstone of Muslim ritual practice and religious life, with continuity going back to the time of the Prophet Muhammad. Because they require physical meeting points, their enactment in virtual settings necessitated a responsive interpretation of sources according to the needs of the day. Different sectors within diverse Muslim contexts responded online to the Covid-19 crisis with pronouncements indicating shifting attitudes to this issue. The Council of Senior Scholars in Al-Azhar in Egypt, for example, advised the avoidance of congregational prayers entirely due to the pandemic.[26] The Minister of Endowments Muhammad Mukhtar Jumaa responded with partial restrictions in mosque settings, rather than closing congregational prayer, emphasizing that the Ministry had been focusing on preventing the spread of infection through intensified cleaning and sterilization campaigns. Dr. Jumaa also noted that rumors on "suspicious pages and websites" were causing difficulties with regard to these issues. In response, he advised that while it was not compulsory to attend mosque during this situation, ablutions should be performed at home before entering a mosque, and the traditional hand shake greetings should be avoided.[27] As an international center of Sunni Islamic learning, Al-Azhar has broad influence beyond the Egyptian borders, increasingly mediated through its digital output. Mixed messages emerged from other authority channels as well, including debates on the origins of the virus and assertions that it was a "punishment" for China's restrictions on Uighur Muslims.[28] The International Union of Muslim Scholars issued prohibitions on any congregational prayers as part of a detailed *fatwā* on preventing the spread of Covid-19.[29]

As a further manifestation of the net *imam* effect, the Covid-19 crises also became a dominant theme within online *fatāwā* sites. This genre of Islamic digital media is a long-standing phenomenon, which has survived and thrived within different technological iterations of the internet and World Wide Web. Indeed, there are digital sites related to all the complex and competing shades of opinion within the Muslim spectrum. This is part of a much wider phenomenon associated with online religious opinions and "Question and Answer" (Q&A) sites, which have been utilized since the emergence of the earliest Islamic websites. As new iterations of newspaper Q&A sites, these innovative platforms presented scholars in their own rights as authentic authorities. Personal profiles and academic credentials were emphasized. Since *fatāwā* sites have formed part of the contestation for religious authority online, it was not surprising that a number of digital platforms devoted resources to respond to Covid-19. A few salient examples of Covid-related *fatāwā* are illustrative of these phenomena.

IslamQA.info was founded by the Syrian-born Shaykh Muhammad Saalih al-Munajjid (1960–) in Saudi Arabia in 1997, making it one of the long-standing *fatwā* sites in a web format. The content has evolved since *IslamQA*'s inception to include in 2020 material in sixteen languages, integrating diverse social media including WhatsApp. Al-Munajjid has been described as a leading Salafi, who allegedly influenced the ideology of al-Qaeda and ISIS.[30] Al-Munajjid was arrested in 2017 in Saudi Arabia; he remained detained in 2021, having been charged with encouraging people to fight in Syria and supporting the Muslim Brotherhood and the Houthi movement.[31] Even so, *IslamQA* continues to operate. The site describes al-Munajjid as "General Supervisor" and continues to widely circulate his videos and statements despite his incarceration.

During the pandemic, this meant that "endorsed" responses to readers' questions about Covid-19 continued to appear on *IslamQA*. This included inquiries about ritual practices such as *ghusl* (the ritual bathing prior to prayer) and whether a Covid-19 death was the equivalent to martyrdom. Many of the *IslamQA* responses in the archive are "timeless" in that they refer to general issues of faith, practice, ritual, and interpretation which do not connect to specific events. The Covid-19 tranche of questions, however, responds specifically to a set of circumstances surrounding the virus—offering yet another example of the use of *ijtihād* in response to specific issues. In 2020, some readers inquired about whether *ruqyah* (exorcism) might be effective in the pandemic situation. More "practical" questions were also raised as to whether the traditional approach toward the deceased regarding ritual washing and the funeral prayer could be performed in absentia when it is too difficult to be in the presence of the body (with a response citing precedents drawn from the Prophet Muhammad's own practice). *IslamQA* condemned as *bid'ah,* or "innovation," the practice of offering the funeral prayer every night for all Muslims who had died on a specific day.

Given al-Munajjid's status in prison, it was not surprising to see that statements from the Council of Senior Scholars in Saudi Arabia started to appear on *IslamQA*. This included a statement in response to a "question" (solicited or otherwise) asking for a ruling on attending *Jumu'ah* prayers in the pandemic context; the resulting opinion cited *aḥādīth* sources as analogous for prohibiting an infected person to attend the mosque.[32] *IslamQA* also highlighted that quarantine should be observed, if pronounced by a specialist, authoritative medical body.[33] Another Covid-19 specific question related to whether personal protective equipment (PPE) could be worn by someone during prayers. This was deemed permissible "as long as the worshipper is able to place his nose and forehead on the ground when prostrating," again citing *aḥādīth* sources in justification.[34] Additional responses outlined the modification of prayers for the sick.[35]

Other online Islamic perspectives also sought to exert influence and promote their interpretations of religious authority during the pandemic, seeing it as a duty to help their local communities. The UK-based *Islamic Portal* responded to the preponderance of internet-based content—and specifically issues surrounding the transmission of *aḥādīth*—via Zoom, Skype, and similar platforms. Although this contrasts with the traditional methods of face-to-face transmission of knowledge, it was deemed acceptable in light of the pandemic situation.[36] The site's digital discourse illuminated an interesting exploration of the minutiae of details associated with prayer during Covid-19. This included issues associated with socially distanced prayers and mosque prayers requiring physical space between congregants, including the introduction of ticketed systems requiring the registration of personal details.[37] Mask-wearing was also a resonant issue, especially around the question of whether the use of masks contravened a principle in the *hajj*, requiring an extra sacrifice. In this case, the special circumstances of the pandemic were seen as a mitigating factor, altering how and when the state of *iḥrām* (ritual purity and symbolic clothing required for participating in pilgrimage) commenced.[38]

Online approaches to lockdown also adopted other forms of digital media in order to disseminate opinions and attract audiences. The Scottish *Deenspiration* channel offered a "chat show" format in its online Q&A on how to approach *Ramaḍān* (especially fasting) during the Covid-19 outbreak.[39] A further episode featuring Shaykh Ruzwan Mohammed, a Scottish religious scholar and education advisor, discussed aspects of spirituality during the pandemic while also promoting an online course on Islam which was a response to Covid-19.[40] *Deenspiration* is part of a wider set of podcasts, blogs, e-books, and digital resources seeking to communicate ideas to make readers "better Muslims" through "authentic" interpretative processes. Given its multimedia outlets, it was well positioned to adapt and effectively project its ideas within the lockdown situation.

Social media were applied across diverse Muslim contexts internationally in order to present perspectives on the Covid-19 situation. This included images from Istanbul in May 2020, showing socially distanced prayers at Fatih Mosque via aerial photographs. In contrast, the August 2020 repositioning and reopening of Aya Sophia as a mosque (after eighty-six years as a national museum) was seen by online critics as disregarding social distancing conventions.[41] In Egypt, Al-Azhar University drew on Periscope as a means to present video clips and images demonstrating social distancing during *Ramaḍān*, marking the Islamic New Year with recitations of the Qur'ān in an otherwise empty mosque.[42] Al-Azhar also extensively utilized Twitter to present its views on Covid-19 measures, with photos of sermons emphasizing social distancing measures.[43] Social media became a significant channel for Al-Azhar on a broader range of issues as well, including speeches and conference proceedings embedded into numerous activities. In November, for example, the Grand Imam of Al-Azhar was seen discussing terrorism measures—following attacks in France—with the French Minister of Europe and Foreign Affairs, Jean-Yves Le Drian. The clip of the meeting was immediately translated and uploaded online, accompanied by music more in line with a cinematic epic than an information clip.[44]

Instagram also became a significant channel for the amplification of diverse religious perspectives. This included Shīʿī Iranian clerics promoting their activities on *TalabeToday*. Posts displayed various clerics undertaking their everyday activities and jobs while negotiating the difficulties of the Covid-19 situation; others were shown being proactive in hospital wards, conducting prayers with patients and working with medical teams.[45] Some Covid-19 content responses centered on a specific personality. This included the use of brief videos using Snapchat by the American *imam* Suhaib Webb who developed "Snapwas" (a combination of Snapchat and *fatwā*) to present extremely concise religious opinions. Webb's pioneering use of social media extended from the virtual *ifṭār* to *Eid* prayers and *Ramaḍān* sermons.[46]

In a similar fashion, many international Muslim religious organizations drew on online video delivery channels such as Zoom to present their *iftār* celebrations to broad audiences during the pandemic lockdowns.

Conclusion

Digital media have provided an ideal—and at times the only—way to project ideas of religious authority and authenticity during a time of social isolation in diverse social settings. In 2020, the Covid-19 pandemic expanded the application of internet technologies in Islamic contexts. This is the latest iteration of the net *imam* effect, drawing upon existing social media and internet techniques, and extending their application across diverse cyber Islamic environments. Amid the global pandemic, organizations and individuals intensified social media deployment to articulate divergent approaches to religious authority, including *fatāwā*, prayers, and interactive content. Some preexisting barriers to usage diminished in a pragmatic recognition of potential utility in an increasingly connected milieu. This recognition heightened an appreciation of how social media can reinforce religiosity—especially in crisis mode—within a competitive marketplace for influence and audience. Mosques and religious organizations operating in this context developed innovative solutions to atypical issues and situations, illuminating a dynamic of change and transition through digital content.

Presenting religious opinions online was not without potential problems, however, especially for activists, advocates, and authorities using media against governmental authority or established norms—and facing possible sanction or imprisonment as a result. The potential for any digitally proficient individual to set up a channel and pronounce on religious issues—whether or not it was endorsed by religious conventions—has led to censorship and prosecution in some contexts. Clearly, it is important to avoid idealizing any notions of digital media as a universal "liberation" force. In local and global contexts, they encompass complex perspectives, sometimes opening up audiences for potential "radicalization" under the guise of conspiracy theories, *jihād* narratives, and "jihādi" identities. Al-Qaeda, "Islamic State," and their variants project an interpretation of values, propaganda, and responses through public and clandestine networks of digital authority to diverse audiences (from supporters to curious and speculative observers) where, in some zones, ownership of content is itself a prosecutable offense.

In continually shifting media contexts, salient questions emerge on how various Muslim gatekeepers will continue to respond and adapt to this information overload of authority, *fatāwā,* and alternate opinions. In online zones with limited or no "central" authority, there is clearly a complex marketplace of online influences and ideas. The design of sites and the application of algorithms to enhance searchability can be as influential as the reputation of any individual scholar. For academics, the capture and analysis of this continually shifting online context raise vexing methodological and research challenges.

Islamic organizations compete with fluid social media from diverse sources within diverse cyber Islamic environments, responding to the intensified relationship between iMuslims and their devices. Many project competing messages of authenticity, authority, and direct connection to core Islamic principles. Amid this ongoing contestation, funding considerations shape the terms of influence, as apps and other media require increasingly significant investments of time, money, experience, and input. The increased integration of digital threads into the overall discourse about Islam and Muslims in contemporary contexts demonstrates that the net *imam* effect is in a process of continual development, refinement, and innovation in line with technological advancements. Amid these momentous changes, digital media narratives and practices retain a continuity with traditional roots and routes of knowledge—the latest iteration of a message emanating from a seventh-century prophet.

CHAPTER 2

Hybrid *Imams*:

Young Muslims and Religious Authority on Social Media

Sana Patel

Introduction

For many religious communities, central religious authority is an essential part of identity, piety, and practice. Most Catholics look to the Pope for guidance in their everyday lives. Many Tibetan Buddhist communities consider the Dalai Lama to be the embodiment of religious authority. For Muslims, however, the definition of central religious authority is hotly debated—and often a cause of intrareligious conflict. Ismaili Muslims regard the Agha Khan as the one true authority, while the Bohri Muslim community looks up to Mufaddal Saifuddin as the supreme spiritual leader. Many Sufi Muslims are members of formal institutional *ṭarīqah* orders ("spiritual path") led by spiritual leaders who offer guidance. For the majority of Sunni Muslims around the globe, however, the concept of universal, exclusive, and absolute religious authority is not considered valid. Although *imams*—Muslim clerics who lead others in congregational prayer, often as head of mosques—are publicly recognized as authority figures who are well-versed in Islamic jurisprudence (*fiqh*), they do not claim any sort of divine lineage (unlike in other Muslim communities such as Shī'ī Islam). While *imams* operate at both local and international levels, they do not link *fatāwā* (Islamic legal rulings) to a single source of religious authority. Today, in many Sunni communities *imams* operate in both online and offline spaces, providing services such as counseling, giving *khuṭbah*s (public lectures/sermons), and performing *nikah* (Islamic marriage rites), among other roles. In doing so, however, they typically do not claim to act as central religious authorities.

Before the digital media era—and the ubiquitous access to social media applications and networks on phones, laptops, and tablets—Sunni Muslims would often interact with *imams* in person at the local mosque or by telephone. As Muslims rapidly embraced "digital religion" by adopting an online presence on message boards, Question and Answer (Q&A) websites, institutional web pages, and other social media platforms, *imams* have learned to adapt to the virtual world.[1] With the expansive rise and easy accessibility of social media, accelerated by the unprecedented changes of Covid-19, *imams* and established religious institutions have increasingly shifted from offline to online spaces, creating a virtual and hybrid presence.

This chapter examines how young Muslims (aged eighteen to forty) in North America feel about religious authority in both online and offline spaces, and how certain prominent religious authority figures influence religious identity and religious/spiritual practices in their followers' everyday lives. My analysis illustrates how particular groups of young Muslims access religious authority—both virtually and in-person—in ways that shape the construction and experience of their religious identities, understandings, and practices. The data for this study comes from my own dissertation research based on fieldwork conducted between 2018 and 2019.[2] The participants were recruited from the Reviving the Islamic Spirit (RIS) conference: an annual gathering in Toronto that attracts over 20,000 Muslims and non-Muslims from around the world.[3] Pre-Covid-19, RIS took place in-person at the Toronto Metro Convention Centre. Many speakers at this event are considered to be prominent religious authority figures in the Sunni community, including Hamza Yusuf from California, Suleiman Moola from South Africa, Tariq Jamil from Pakistan, among others. I conducted semi-structured qualitative interviews with selected participants regarding their religious identity and authority, their religious and spiritual practices in their everyday lives, their personal experiences as Muslims in Canada and the United States, their encounters with Islamophobia, and their use of the internet for religious purposes.

Narrowing the focus, this chapter spotlights issues relating to religious authority and social media, with a particular emphasis on lived religion. I begin with a brief survey of the scholarship on "digital religion" and Muslim religious authority on the internet before outlining my own theoretical and methodological frameworks. An analysis of the data from qualitative interviews documents how young Muslims perceive religious authority and authenticity in both online and offline spaces by spotlighting their interactions with prominent religious authority figures: Yasir Qadhi, Suhaib Webb, Mufti Menk, and Omar Suleiman. This inquiry aims to address a number of key questions: How do young Muslims practice their religion in their everyday lives? How do they "do" Islam on the internet? Which religious authorities do young Muslims "follow"/"like" on social media? And what specific roles do these authority figures play in the identity formation, worldviews, and practices of Muslim youth?

Surveying the Scholarship

In recent years, a select group of scholars have explored religion online in an effort to document how young people seek religious information and religious authority on the internet. For this chapter, the works of Heidi Campbell, Christopher Helland, and Stewart Hoover are especially relevant.

Campbell's edited volume *Digital Religion: Understanding Religious Practices in New Media Worlds* consists of multiple essays on the topic of "digital religion" in various different cultural contexts.[4] In framing the volume, Campbell explains that the term "digital religion" does not simply refer to religion online but rather engages how digital media spaces and religious practices shape each other. Previously, scholars often employed the term "cyber-religion" to describe new activities online in relation to religious communities and rituals in cyberspace. By contrast, Campbell suggests that "digital religion" offers a more nuanced way to approach the technological and cultural landscapes that have made online and offline spaces integrated and blended. As the data in this chapter confirms, digital media—specifically social media—have facilitated new pathways for a new generation of young Muslims to connect with religious authority online.

Helland's article, "Diaspora on the Electric Frontier: Developing Virtual Connections with Sacred Homelands," illustrates how diasporic religious traditions have leveraged the internet to develop network connections among themselves and with their places of origin.[5] Helland emphasizes the significance of community in religion, documenting how these diaspora groups deploy the internet not only to discuss religion and develop new religious practices but also to fulfill the particular needs of their communities by raising money, organizing volunteer labor, and networking with its members. Many of the participants in my research identified as members of diaspora communities—identities that at least partially influenced their ways of practicing Islam.

Hoover's edited collection *The Media and Religious Authority* examines the notion of religious authority in different traditions and how it is transformed by new media.[6] He argues that in order to understand the dynamic changes between religion and media, scholars should document the shifting forms of religious claims, values, and symbols. Accounting for these factors reveals new contexts of authority formation and the evolving contours of religious authenticity. In the interviews that I conducted, for example, some participants asserted that a clear definition of authority and authenticity is vitally important for Muslims, because it allows them to navigate amid the vast array of religious leaders available in both online and offline spaces.

As a subset of the scholarship on digital religions, there is also a significant amount of research on Muslims in cyberspace, specifically on the complex interplay between Muslim religious authority and the internet. Among others, Gary R. Bunt, Nabil Echchaibi, Kristin M. Petersen, and Robert Rozehnal (all contributors to this edited volume) are considered important scholars in this expanding field. Notably, however, within the study of digital Islam research on how young Muslims—young Canadians and Americans in this case—navigate the world of online *imams* and negotiate religious information online is somewhat lacking. My research aims to address this gap.

Bunt's *Hashtag Islam* covers theoretical approaches for cyber Islamic environments (CIE)—a term that he coined to refer to the incredible variety of Muslim expressions on the internet. His study examines the emergent technologies impacting CIE, and their impact on faith and representation, religious authorities and its influences, and *jihād* online.[7] In relation to the question of religious authority online, Bunt focuses on how certain authorities are authenticated through the application of *ijtihād* (independent reasoning) and examines what the development of the internet means for celebrity religious figures. In addition, he critically analyzes prominent *fatwā* websites like *IslamQA.info* and *eShaykh.com*. In my own interviews, many participants identified *IslamQA* as a website that they surfed in search of answers to their own religious questions.

Discussing how Muslim women engage with urban styles, fashion, and popular culture to challenge stereotypes of their own oppression, Kristin M. Peterson and Nabil Echchaibi analyze the #Mipsterz video in their article, "Mipsterz: Hip, American and Muslim."[8] In this video, young Muslim women challenge pervasive mass media stereotypes—like the standard trope that all Muslim women are oppressed—and illustrate, by contrast, how they exercise their own freewill and agency in their everyday lives. In presenting themselves in a non-normative way, these young women assert that they have their own distinct ways of practicing Islam. In a similar fashion, participants in my study embraced their own unique approach to religious practices and emphasized the importance of seeking religious authority outside of traditional religious institutions.

Rozehnal's method of analyzing Sufism online in *Cyber Sufis: Virtual Expressions of the American Muslim Experience* approaches digital media as "carefully crafted and authorized documents that reveal a great deal about the values and priorities, the networks and narratives, of discrete American Sufi groups."[9] He suggests that many prominent American Sufi communities that are active in offline and online spaces display a hybrid religious identity that is modern, Muslim, and mystic. He demonstrates this by focusing on the Inayati Order and its sophisticated use of digital media as a case study throughout the book. Although my own fieldwork deals with young Muslims who identify more with a traditional Sunni affiliation rather than

Sufi orders, discovering Islam on social media apps also profoundly shapes how they think about and experience religious practices, the competing claims to authority and authenticity, and Islamic discourse online.

Theoretical and Methodological Frameworks

This chapter places a significant emphasis on lived religion because it provides a framework to explore the ways that Islam is practiced in nonofficial and often unrecognized ways, outside the purview of established religious institutions like mosques and *madrassah*s (Islamic schools). Prominent scholars who have taken this approach include Robert A. Orsi,[10] Nancy Ammerman,[11] Meredith McGuire,[12] and Nadia Jeldt oft (who applies the theory to Islam).[13] Scholars of religious studies have often examined how religious institutions influence the piety and formal activities of practitioners such as attending church, praying *ṣalāh* (the formal act of prayer by Muslims five times a day), or volunteering in the community. Measuring religiosity solely by means of church or mosque attendance is problematic, however, because it focuses exclusively on those that are active within established religious institutions and ignores the less visible elements of religious life. Many people consider some of the normal activities that they engage in their everyday lives as religious or spiritual. According to Orsi, lived religion is about mundane practices, vital religious narratives, and anything that falls outside of institutional religion.[14] Ammerman also points out that the "everyday" of lived religion consists of (non) religious practices, rituals performed by people who are nonexperts, and daily practices that are outside the scope of institutional religious events in both public and private spheres.[15] Similarly, McGuire emphasizes that some of the participants in her research considered ordinary things like gardening or healing as vital religious or spiritual activities.[16] Jeldtoft uses the term "reconfigured religious practices" to describe how Muslims in her research customized their own individual routines of daily religious life—ritual activities that were not necessarily connected with an institutional form of Islam.[17]

A focus on lived religion allows us to look at how young Muslims engage with religious authority and to consider the non-normative ways that Islam is lived and understood. Are young Muslims in North America practicing Islam exclusively through religious institutions, or do they experience and express their own particular ways of being Muslim which includes distinct understandings of authenticity and authority? In this study, the lived religion approach brought to the surface a diversity of thinking about Muslim religious authority among my respondents. Their presence on social media—specifically on websites and apps like Facebook, Twitter, and Instagram—illustrated their connectedness with religious authority figures, whose content they "followed," "liked," and "retweeted." Some participants also actively utilized social media and the internet to conduct their own independent searches on religious matters, illuminating how they approach religious institutions and authority online.

For this study, I conducted a total of fifty interviews with young Muslims recruited at the RIS conference in 2018 and 2019. I informally recruited participants in 2018 by socializing with people at the RIS bazaar (marketplace). This large space was dedicated for businesses, nonprofit organizations, and food vendors who sell products and distribute information to curious conference-goers. A separate site was also designated for congregational prayer within this sprawling bazaar. The following year, I was given a formal booth at the bazaar to recruit participants for my research. I set up the booth by displaying recruitment material which consisted of interview invitations and posters. Potential participants approached me directly this time, instead of me having to reach out to them. Figure 2.1 shows how just crowded it can get in some areas of the RIS conference. This photo was taken right after a break had ended as attendees were waiting to enter the lecture halls for the next set of speakers. At this time, people were coming back from eating and praying in the bazaar.

In order to participate in my study, conference attendees had to meet the following criteria: citizens or permanent residents of the United States

FIGURE 2.1 *The crowd at the RIS conference in December 2019. This image displays the entrance area near the lecture halls on the left, with the bazaar straight ahead in the gymnasium area. Photo by the author.*

or Canada, between the ages of eighteen and forty—,[18] self-identified as Muslims, maintain an active presence on social media, and attended the RIS conference in the past.[19] The criteria allowed me to focus on participants who identified as Muslim millennials (born between 1981 and 1996). Most of them identified as Sunni, with only a small subset identifying as Shi'a or members of other Muslim minority communities. Over the course of the two years, fifty people volunteered to participate in semi-structured interviews. These interactions were conducted both in-person and virtually on Skype, Facetime video, or WhatsApp video. The average length of each interview was one hour.

In addition to these interpersonal interviews, my methodology also employed participant observation. RIS takes place over three days during the Christmas holidays, and people from all around the world come to attend and take part in the myriad activities. During these events, I observed many things including how people interacted with each other and, in particular, how some of them engaged with celebrity *imams* in attendance. Prominent speakers and celebrity *imams* like Zaid Shakir and Tariq Jamil were typically followed around by groups of admirers in the bazaar. Individuals would rush over to them to ask them a question or to offer a simple greeting. There was also an instance at the 2019 event, where an attendee jumped onto the stage to greet Tariq Jamil while he was giving his talk. This style of communication and interaction illustrated the dynamics of hierarchy created in the hybrid space of RIS. In my assessment, that hybridity emerges because the conference merges online and offline worlds, allowing participants to meet celebrity *imams* from their social media experience in a "real world," offline event. The following sections encapsulate these findings, with a spotlight on the central issue of religious authority.

Hybrid *Imams*: Online and Offline Religious Authority

Yasir Qadhi

Even though the idea of central religious authority is contested within the Muslim community, RIS effectively acts as a space where multiple religious authorities are brought together from both online and offline worlds. At each annual conference, many of the featured speakers are recognized as prominent religious authority figures for the North American Sunni Muslim community.

In 2018 and 2019, Yasir Qadhi was one of the featured speakers at RIS. Qadhi is an Islamic scholar based in Houston, Texas, and is one of the founders of AlMaghrib Institute, an online Islamic institution where users can take virtual classes with various Islamic teachers on a range of topics.[20] He has a doctorate from Yale University and teaches at Rhodes College in Memphis, Tennessee. In interviews, participants confirmed that they were motivated to attend this conference to learn from key religious authority figures like Qadhi. For example, Participant 26, a twenty-seven-year-old male who had recently immigrated to Canada, stated that he especially enjoyed Qadhi's lecture. In his words:

> I got to meet Shaykh Yasir Qadhi. I walked up to him and I was quite happy and very excited to meet him. . . . I think that was sensational, absolutely sensational, being there, sitting there and listening to him. It was a powerful twenty-to-twenty-five-minute speech that he gave. I've been trying to see, but it is still not up on YouTube. I would say hearing him, not just what he said but also the way he said it, his eloquence, his delivery, both languages. Everything was so powerful, so powerful.[21]

Since Qadhi is based in the United States, Canadians like P26 do not typically have easy access to interact with him in person, making this a special moment for him. Qadhi does have a prominent online presence and regularly posts on Facebook and Twitter; on Facebook one million people like and follow him, and there are more than 549,000 followers on Twitter. Although these social media platforms allow people to have some type of interaction with celebrity *imams*, these impersonal interactions do not compare to meeting them at an event or seeing them live in person. Young Muslims describe a fascination with seeing such religious authority figures face-to-face, equating it with meeting a popular celebrity. Participants talked in similar glowing terms about other well-known social media figures they got to see at RIS who they would otherwise never meet IRL ("in real life"). This included performers like Khaled Siddiq, a British musician and YouTuber, and Brother Ali, an American rapper and activist. Figure 2.2 is a photograph of Brother Ali performing at RIS in 2019—in an area reserved for musical performances, poetry, and small Q&A sessions with some of the invited guests.

In an interview, I asked Participant 20 (a thirty-two-year-old female who has spent the majority of her life in Canada) about how she navigates the internet when researching Islamic matters. She replied by saying, "I will have to learn it [Arabic] myself or get the trusted version [of the Qur'ān's translation] from somebody who's actually truly studied the Qur'ān like Yasir Qadhi or Nouman Ali Khan. I would think that would be the best because they've gone out of their way to study the Qur'ān itself."[22] Her response speaks to the issues of authenticity, the validity of religious information available online, and the legitimacy of these celebrity *imams*. What exactly makes the information that they preach and talk about trustworthy? P26 expressed a confidence in the educational credentials of these religious

FIGURE 2.2 *Brother Ali performing songs from his previous albums at RIS 2019. This performance took place at the bazaar's 360 Stage. Photo by the author.*

authority figures. In most cases, celebrity *imams* like Yasir Qadhi have traditional Sunni educational backgrounds. Although Qadhi has a Western educational background with a PhD from Yale, he also has a master's degree in Islamic theology from his studies in Saudi Arabia at the Islamic University of Medina. These dual qualifications raise his status with young Muslims who acknowledge the importance of both Western and Islamic education. Qadhi is regarded as an Islamic scholar who can relate to Muslims living in the West, hence his popularity with the Muslim millennials in this study.

Although many participants pointed to the educational backgrounds of these Islamic scholars as a measure of legitimacy and trustworthiness, others raised concerns regarding their authenticity. Participant 45, a twenty-eight-year-old female who has spent half of her life in Canada, revealed doubts about Qadhi and his Islamic teachings:

I didn't know most of them [the speakers at RIS], but just recently I heard that Yasir Qadhi is not great. He was actually my favorite speaker. Apparently, the stuff that he says is not based on Qur'ān and *ḥadīth* [collections of the sayings and acts of Prophet Mohammed]. He just says things that are actually not allowed in Islam, which make me very concerned. I'm afraid to listen to the stuff, to his lectures because I don't know if I'm going be learning something that is wrong.[23]

Although Qadhi was previously one of her favorite speakers, the woman now questions his authority based on what she has heard from others. Her comment confirms that young Muslims in this community do not universally agree on the authenticity of particular clerics, even those with traditional backgrounds and formal training in Islamic jurisprudence. Participant 37, a twenty-three-year-old male who was born and raised in the United States, expressed a similar concern with the lack of knowledge and expertise of some of the RIS speakers. In his words, "Some of the speakers . . . I was confused as to why they were speaking on certain matters when they themselves acknowledged that they had no experienced knowledge on that matter, so I was a little bit confused by that I would say."[24] In my view, both these statements spotlight an underlying ambiguity and ambivalence about central religious authority figures in Sunni Islam. Analyzing the thoughts and experiences of participants on issues of religious authority reveals that some young Muslims are simply overwhelmed with the choices of religious authority in online spaces. Although most respondents were impressed with some of the authority figures accessible online, they were careful and deliberate about assessing trustworthiness and authenticity before accepting them as legitimate authority figures.

Suhaib Webb, Mufti Menk, and Omar Suleiman

In interviews, many participants stressed that in addition to looking forward to interacting with famous Islamic scholars at conferences like RIS, they actively "followed" them on social media as well. For example, Participant 9 (a thirty-five-year-old man born in Canada) described himself as a social media follower of Suhaib Webb, one of the most prolific online *imams*. Webb was previously the *imam* at the Islamic Society of Boston. In 2016, he was especially popular among North American Muslim youth, famous for delivering eight-second *fatāwā* on Snapchat and his virtual sermons (*khuṭbah*s) that integrated references to popular media like the TV show, *The Walking Dead*.

Mufti Menk is another religious authority figure with a popular online profile among RIS conference participants. Based in Zimbabwe, Menk has over seven million global followers on Twitter. He is particularly known for his motivational tweets and *khuṭbah*s that incorporate comedy to attract attention from young Muslims. For a twenty-eight-year-old Canadian female, Mufti Menk is as motivational as Jalal ad-Din Rumi (1207–73).

"Mufti Menk was another person who I hadn't listened to, but someone was like you should read his posts," she stated.

> I follow him, his posts on social media because I absolutely love them. That guy is so synced in his words and some of them hit so close to home in my opinion, he's like Rumi. That's a big thing but some of his things are so well-said. It's so well written and I'm like he needs to start a book or calendar because we need one of those every day.[25] This woman's comparison of Menk to the famous thirteenth-century Persian Sufi master, Rumi, is revealing—even though Rumi has frequently been romanticized in the West as a poet who writes about love and spirituality, rather than Islam per se.[26]

Menk's online messaging clearly resonates with young Muslims living in the West. His tweets are typically communicated in comforting and encouraging tones, rather than a preaching rhetorical style. To take one example, on January 31, 2021, Menk tweeted: "There are some who will misunderstand you no matter what you say or do. They're just not meant to be on your journey. Remember, you're fulfilling your purpose, not theirs. So it calls for a different path. Don't worry. The Almighty will send people who should be in your life!" Menk's charisma has a unique appeal among his millions of loyal Twitter followers who are often mesmerized by his messages and admire his soft tone, as opposed to the stern preaching style of other *imams* like Yasir Qadhi. His legions of online fans, both Muslims and non-Muslims, even include celebrities like rappers Nicki Minaj. When Nicki Minaj first followed Menk on Twitter, it created a frenzy among young Muslims and non-Muslims alike who debated what Menk had to offer her. In response to this tweet storm, Menk posted a YouTube video, stating that the Islamic information that he preaches is available to anyone, regardless of background (Figure 2.3).

FIGURE 2.3 *Screenshot of Mufti Menk's YouTube video on Nicki Minaj following him on Twitter. This video, posted in August 2020, elicited more than 1.3 million views (https://www.youtube.com/watch?v=Eczk1Ofk8UE).*

Omar Suleiman is yet another celebrity *imam* who was especially popular among the young Muslims at RIS. Also based in the United States, Suleiman is a founder of Yaqeen Institute for Islamic Research—which mainly operates online—and an adjunct professor of Islamic studies at Southern Methodist University. He too maintains an active and dynamic digital profile, with over two million followers on Facebook. Like Menk, many participants emphasized Suleiman's charismatic personality when giving *khuṭbah*s and public lectures at events like RIS. When asked whether she was looking forward to seeing any specific *imams*, Participant 25 (a twenty-eight-year-old female, who immigrated to Canada from Jordan) responded:

> I guess one person that I was really looking forward to from the talk was Shaykh Omar Suleiman. I really respect his work and his approach taking certain topics and addressing them in a very easy to understand kind of way and in a way that makes you feel uplifted and feeling hopeful that there's something that you can do, whether personally or communally as a community.[27]

In a similar fashion, Participant 10, a twenty-three-year-old female born in Canada, described being moved by Suleiman's speech at the 2018 RIS conference. In her words, "Omar Suleiman's speech was all about forgiveness and how [to] go through life when someone hurts you intentionally or not, and I feel like that really affected me. I even bought the CD. Because I thought it was really good what he said because everybody goes through hardships and everybody experiences someone that hurts them."[28] In these instances, the attraction to Suleiman was about more than his ability to relate to Muslims living in non-Muslim Western countries. Participants highlighted instead the unique environment that Suleiman created when delivering his lectures. They were drawn to his captivating style and clearly resonated with the message that he was trying to get across to the audience. This is one salient example of how Muslim authority figures like Suleiman capture their audience's attention by cultivating a unique personal communication style, both online and offline.

Authenticity and Social Media

Since cyberspace is so vast, unlimited, and malleable, it creates spaces for all kinds of communities and individuals to share information, develop friendships and relationships, and discover pathways to navigate online in relation to religious matters. Many of the participants in this research, however, also described their thoughts and anxieties about the authenticity of information accessible on the internet. A key concern was the sheer volume and varying quality of sources of Islamic information online. Participants found that it was ultimately up to them to filter through the ocean of digital information to find what they personally would consider authentic and to then interpret those materials via *ijtihād*.

Some participants emphasized that they turned to the internet for guidance on specific topics. Participant 9, for example, a thirty-five-year-old male who worked as a chaplain in the Canadian army, said that he only utilizes the internet for matters like Islamic finance since he already has trustable sources for other issues. "Sometimes I go on the internet though, for questions that are very new, and very kind of . . . things like Islamic finance . . . the internet is a pretty good resource," he stated. "But I know how the people are. When people say, 'I know who the authority is who I can rely upon.'"[29] Participant 3, a twenty-one-year-old female who was born and raised in the United States, described her preference for "authentic" websites that she trusts such as *Seeker's Hub*, an Islamic institution based in Toronto: "I think if it is an authentic website, then I would use it. Like I think *Seeker's Hub* has a question-and-answer forum. So, I mean I would go there if the answer was there, I would go there. I would trust it. Just randomly Googling it, I wouldn't trust."[30]

For most RIS participants, however, this search for dependable resources prompted them to look for particular textual sources such as canonical collections of *ḥadīth* like Sahih Bukhari or direct *āyāt* (verses) from the Qur'ān as a signal of authenticity. Several respondents described a desire to learn Arabic themselves in order to translate and interpret these religious sources on their own. Participant 45 emphasized that she specifically searches for online sources that cite the Qur'ān and *sunnah* (practices of Prophet Mohammad): "If it is from Qur'ān and *sunnah*, *ḥadīth* . . . authentic *ḥadīth* then I have to believe that. The other thing is the best thing we can do is learn Arabic to learn the highest possible translation and do your own reading and even in *ḥadīth* and so on."[31] In my view, this can be considered a form of democratizing *ijtihād*—a process of interpretation that was historically done exclusively by Islamic scholars who were trained in traditional Islamic jurisprudence. Increasingly, young Muslims who lack such classical training but do have access to digital materials that aid in reading and understanding Islamic legal concepts are claiming the right and responsibility to interpret tradition on their own. In this sense, Islamic authority is no longer reserved exclusively for trained clerics.

Table 2.1 displays the number of followers for each of the religious authority figures discussed earlier on three of the most popular social media platforms that were identified by the participants: Facebook, Twitter, and Instagram. In interviews, participants described using social media on a regular basis and most of them confirmed that they actively follow celebrity *imams* and Muslim influencers on these specific digital apps. Although select respondents expressed some concern in relation to the scholars' authority and authenticity, these celebrity *imams* have nonetheless managed to build massive online platforms which draw large audiences to their virtual preaching and conversations. This following includes people from all around the world where social media is accessible, including considerable numbers of non-Muslims. The global popularity of these Islamic scholars shows that they have adapted to the social media age, finding creative ways to continue to preach in new ways to new audiences. Given the ubiquity, speed, and reach of social media apps, young Muslims can easily reach out

TABLE 2.1 Followers of Each Islamic Scholar. Tabulated as of March 2021

	Facebook	Twitter	Instagram
Yasir Qadhi[a]	1,104,400	549,500	187,000
Mufti Menk[b]	4,340,900	7,200,00	2,900,00
Suhaib Webb[c]	964,000	122,500	105,000
Omar Suleiman[d]	2,583,800	447,200	816,000

[a]Qadhi's Facebook: https://www.facebook.com/yasir.qadhi/
[b]Menk's Facebook: https://www.facebook.com/muftimenk/
[c]Webb's Facebook: https://www.facebook.com/suhaib.webb/
[d]Suleiman's Facebook: https://www.facebook.com/imamomarsuleiman/

to and access material from these celebrity *imams* rather than turning to local, analog resources. The remarkably large numbers of followers illustrate again how trust and authenticity are built by these celebrity *imams* via a savvy deployment social media platform.

Being a celebrity *imam* is about more than just preaching at a local mosque. Even so, these *imams* display a wide variety of linkages to (or distance from) established religious institutions. It is important to note that in some cases their social media platforms are independently owned and operated. For example, Webb and Menk do not affiliate with any formal religious institutions and post on social media independently. Other celebrity *imams*, by contrast, expressly link their digital media profiles to particular institutions—emphasizing their official relationships with prominent Islamic institutions and established careers within large organizations such as ISNA (Islamic Society of North America) or Qalam Institute. Qadhi was previously associated with AlMaghrib Institute but now affiliates with the Islamic Seminary of America based in Dallas, Texas. Suleiman emphasizes his links to the religious institution that he founded and regularly posts on Yaqeen Institute's social media accounts.

This new dynamic of finding and interacting with religious authority figures on social media resonates with the broader concepts of digital media, religion online, and online religion. Rather than going to the local mosque to ask a religious question to the *imam*, young Muslims increasingly opt to simply go online. There they have access to multiple trained scholars, as well as a wide range of self-styled Islamic "experts" who can answer their inquiries. If users are not satisfied or want to learn more, they can decide to interpret meaning for themselves by studying Islamic materials and practicing independent *ijtihād*. In my view, these online opportunities for lived religion provide young Muslims with alternative methods to take matters into their own hands, bypassing the traditional gatekeepers of institutional religious authority. These alternative pathways of practicing Islam illustrate a new sense of freedom to define the parameters of religious authority and to choose how and where to access it. Many participants in this study identified more than one celebrity *imam* that they looked up to. Factors that contributed to their selection included having easy access to them on social media platforms, their relevance to young Muslims living in the West, and the background of their traditional educational training. For those participants who wanted to practice *ijtihād,* the easy accessibility of religious information online allowed them to do so. Pervasive questions about authenticity, however, prompted most of them to refer back to celebrity *imams* who offered informed and practical advice on all kinds of matters, from general questions about Qur'ān interpretation and ritual practice to specific issues like Islamic finance.

When asked about how they practice Islam in their everyday lives, almost all of the RIS participants mentioned the "five pillars" of mainstream Islam: expressing belief in the oneness of Allah, praying five times a day, giving to charity, fasting during *Ramaḍān*, and performing pilgrimage to Mecca. At the same time, they also identified some additional ritual practices that shape their daily, lived piety. This included reciting a certain amount of *juz'* (one of thirty sections that the Qur'ān is divided into) every day, fasting every Monday and Thursday per *sunnah,* and sitting in a silent space and speaking directly to God as a form of meditation. The concept of lived religion allows us to account for the importance of these kinds of personal religious and spiritual practices that are often done outside of formal religious institutions—and beyond the influence of formal religious authority.

The ways that participants navigated and negotiated the spoken and unspoken rules and regulations of Islamic practices suggest that they frequently interpreted the viability of some everyday practices on their own (*ijtihād*), without the need for religious authority or institutions. For example, Participant 12 (a twenty-eight-year-old female born in the United States) talked about the (in)significance of wearing makeup while doing *wuḍū'* (ablution)—even though there is a general understanding among the majority of *imams* in the Sunni community that makeup invalidates the *wuḍū'* required before praying *ṣalāh*. She explained that she has bigger things to be concerned about than worry about makeup and ablution:

> Some people ask like can you wear mascara with *wuḍū'*. Like to me, that's not a big deal, like I'm sure God is worried about other things than something so trivial . . . like okay good if you really want to know, but I'm not dying to know that answer. I'm focusing on the bigger picture personally. Which is why I like RIS, it was very big picture.[32]

Participant 50 (a twenty-three-year-old female who immigrated to Canada from Pakistan) echoed similar concerns about the regulation of small matters, such as the visibility of a Muslim woman's hair or the proper positions for prayer. In her view, some issues are not as relevant as some religious authorities make them out to be. In her words:

> I don't think God is going to judge me if I misfolded a leg this way while I am praying, Oh no!, a strand of hair came out while I am praying and all of a sudden, my prayer is not completed. I don't like the idea of overregulation and I feel like those things come to light when you're looking for very specific answers. For example, I know *IslamQ&A* is a go-to site for everyone. I will go there but then I will see very aggressive replies sometimes or they will be like no, this is wrong.[33]

Significantly, her critique questions the authority and authenticity of the popular *fatwā* website, *IslamQ&A*—a digital resource that is designed for Muslim users to search for questions that they have, with answers provided by *imams* formally trained in Islamic jurisprudence.

When navigating through the limitless Islamic resources and digital *fatāwā* on the internet, young Muslims in North America not only have to choose between different *imams* for guidance, they also have to define what is "authentically" Islamic. The massive volume of religious information online informs their religious identities and understandings of Islam in unprecedented ways. Amid the multiplicity of websites like *IslamQ&A,* social media interactions with celebrity *imams,* and the constant stream of materials found on Twitter, Facebook, and Instagram, young Muslims seek to create their own ways of practicing Islam and formulate religious identity. While it is true that having unlimited access to religious resources on the internet is beneficial for many young Muslims, the unprecedented volume of information also presents doubts and tensions. The participants in my study displayed a hesitation to default to one or more resources in relation to Islamic questions. They always questioned the legitimacy of sources of information that they found online. Although they did frequently identify certain websites that they found trustable—like *IslamQ&A* and *Seeker's Hub*—they typically filtered through these websites to research certain topics or to look out for specific references to *āyāt* and *sunnah*. Similarly, they also questioned the authenticity of the celebrity *imams* that they themselves "followed" or "liked" on social media. This illustrates the key point that within the North American Sunni community there is no central religious authority—a reality that, in turn, has encouraged young Muslims in North America to practice *ijtihād* to help them navigate through the immense online landscape.

Conclusion

In the twenty-first century, religious authority online is readily available, offering multiple perspectives on a wide range of matters public and private, spiritual and mundane. In response to this new dynamic, tech-savvy celebrity *imams* have quickly adapted to the social media age by amplifying their online profiles, curating accounts on trendy social media platforms, and encouraging their followers to interact with them on these apps. Young Muslims who have a difficult time with religious authority figures at the local level increasingly discover what they are searching for online via social media and *fatwā* websites. In keeping with the concept of lived religion, it is clear that Muslim millennials have a diverse approach to religious authority and authenticity. While some participants at the RIS conference still look up to certain religious authority figures, they also described a pattern of turning to online searches for religious matters. In discussing the accessibility of Islamic authority figures online, RIS participants consistently highlighted issues of authenticity and the significance of the hybridity of celebrity *imams*. My research found that the accessibility and personal styles of celebrity *imams* in *both* online and offline spaces are crucially important factors for young Muslims in North America. Even when conducting independent *ijtihād* using online resources, Muslim millennials tend to defer back to the expertise of *imams* when their uncertainties or doubts remain unresolved.

Although many young Muslims in North America turn to the internet to search for what they are lacking in offline spaces, they still find that issues of religious authority and authenticity are not so easily resolved. The participants in this study struggled for new answers to old questions: What does religious authority look like and how can its authenticity be determined? Celebrity *imams* like Yasir Qadhi, Suhaib Webb, Mufti Menk, and Omar Suleiman offer these young Muslims novel opportunities to relate to figures of religious authority in online spaces where they can "follow," "like," and "retweet." The annual RIS conference plays an important role in uniting young Muslims with celebrity *imams* in an offline forum, where they interact face-to-face in a hybrid setting. With new trends continuing to emerge online—and with an endless array of social media apps like TikTok constantly adapting in response to these changes—celebrity *imams* will have to continuously transform how they engage and interact with their followers if they hope to stay relevant in the years ahead.

CHAPTER 3

Mediating Authority:
A Sufi *Shaykh* in Multiple Media

Ismail Fajrie Alatas

Introduction

Recent anthropological works on religion and media have called attention to how religious actors utilize the media as part of religious practice.[1] Instead of positing the development of new media as inevitably detrimental to religion or assimilating religious practice and sociality into their logic and modes of existence, these works suggest the ways in which religious actors use and reshape different media forms as part of changing religious practice.[2] Mediatization of religious texts in novel technological contexts, for example, has produced new aesthetic experiences that could not be accomplished by earlier media, as well as alternative modalities that have helped to solidify religious identity across a vast distance.[3] Instead of treating media simply as channels of communication and dissemination, these anthropological perspectives push us to think about mediation or mediatization as involving qualitative transformations of that which is being mediated. It is precisely for this reason that the use of novel media technologies for religious purposes has generated new possibilities that engender not only excitement but also anxiety.[4] Building on these insights, this chapter observes how the changing practice of mediatization shapes and reconfigures Muslim religious authority and the parameters of Islamic authenticity. My analysis examines the engagement of a contemporary Indonesian Sufi master, Habib Luthfi Bin Yahya (b. 1947), with different media forms to explore how religious authority takes shape and is configured through different practices of mediatization.

Authority, as Hannah Arendt explains, is a hierarchical relationship that is defined in contradistinction to coercion by force and persuasion through arguments. The term "authority," Arendt explains, comes from the Latin *auctoritas*, which is derived from the verb *augere*, meaning "to augment." What is being augmented is a foundation built by others in the past and deemed to be sacred. Those endowed with authority are people recognized to have a connection to that foundational past, the capacity to transform and augment that past into examples for the present, and the ability to effect obedience without resorting to coercion.[5] Authority, Arendt adds, "rests neither on common reason nor on the power of the one who commands" but on the recognition of the hierarchy deemed by all parties involved to be right and legitimate.[6] What is analytically useful about this definition is its construal of authority as taking shape in and through two kinds of contingent relationships: a relationship with a particular discursive tradition and history, and a corresponding relationship with contemporaneous others who come to recognize, accept, or contest that frame. Positing authority as a contingent relationship allows us to think more concretely about its formation, maintenance, and modification. This, in turn, opens up the possibility for thinking about authority as an assemblage, involving not only the actors deemed to be authoritative and those who recognize that authority but also other actors and semiotic forms that mediate, stabilize, and shape that relationship.

The case of Habib Luthfi allows us to further complicate Arendt's theorization of authority by foregrounding the questions of mediation that have not received adequate treatment in her essay but have nevertheless played central roles in the formation, reconfiguration, and diversification of religious authority. Media forms, including digital media, serve as infrastructure that facilitates social practice and relations while shaping sensory experience.[7] They generate the possibility of thought, recognition, and experience, thereby creating the material preconditions for recognizing authority. While media forms enable transmission, they also work to "transform, translate, distort, and modify the meaning or elements they are supposed to carry."[8] Focusing on Habib Luthfi's engagement with different media technologies thus accentuates how divergent media platforms and practices qualitatively shape and transform the hierarchical relationship that shapes the contours of religious authority.

The chapter begins by introducing Habib Luthfi and his role as a Sufi master and a mobile preacher active in rural Javanese communities. Over the years, many of Habib Luthfi's audience have joined his Sufi order and taken initiation as formal disciples. My analysis spotlights the infrastructures used by Habib Luthfi to maintain his relationship with his disciples. In 2003, a newly established bimonthly Islamic print magazine, *alKisah* (The Parable), introduced a Q&A rubric dedicated to Sufism and requested Habib Luthfi to become its expert host. Having his own print media outlet allowed Habib Luthfi to become known as an authority of Sufism outside of his traditional

Sufi circle. With the increasing popularity of social media, however, the market for the Islamic magazine dwindled, and *alKisah* closed down. In 2010, several of Habib Luthfi's disciples established the official website, Facebook page, and Twitter account of their Sufi master with the aim to spread his ideas. By presenting a short history of Habib Luthfi's engagement with different media forms, this chapter observes the contrastive relationship of authority that is formed in and through both print and digital media technologies.

The Sufi Master

Habib Luthfi Bin Yahya of Pekalongan (Central Java) is one of the most influential Muslim scholars of contemporary Indonesia. Born into an Indonesian-Ḥaḍramī family that claims descent from the Prophet Muhammad, Habib Luthfi studied under numerous scholars of Islamic law, theology, and Sufism in Java before being appointed by one of his teachers to succeed him as a master of the Naqshbandiyya-Khālidiyya and Shādhilīyya Sufi orders. As a Sufi spiritual leader, he worked for years to maintain and expand the Sufi congregation that he inherited from his teacher. His success in doing so gradually propelled him into national prominence. In 2000, he was elected by a council of senior Sufi masters as the head of the Association of Sufi Orders in Indonesia (Jam'iyyah Ahlith Thariqah al-Mu'tabarah an-Nahdliyah, JATMAN), one of the autonomous bodies under the traditionalist Nahdlatul Ulama, Indonesia's largest Islamic organization, claiming more than fifty million members. Considered by many of his followers as a living saint, Habib Luthfi has prominently nested himself in various social networks including political, military, scholarly, and business circles.

Over several decades, Habib Luthfi has indefatigably preached in many and varied localities, interacting with highly diverse audiences. Such encounters have introduced Habib Luthfi to a wide range of people, many of whom have decided to become disciples by pledging allegiance (*bay'a*) to him. Being a disciple of a Sufi master establishes a substantively different kind of hierarchical relationship than that between Muslim preachers and their audience. Sufi discipleship involves the continuous effort of maintaining a direct and intimate connection to the master, notwithstanding the geographic distance that separates them. Modeled on the paradigmatic relationship between the Prophet Muhammad and his companions, Sufis posit discipleship as the privileged site of religious learning and spiritual growth.[9]

Like most Sufi masters in Java, Habib Luthfi's relationship with his disciples mainly hinges on the maintenance of direct interpersonal relations. Disciples who are deeply committed to learning from Habib Luthfi spend time living with him. This ranges from those who spend a month in a year (like the holy month of *Ramaḍān*) to others who live continuously in his presence for years. The majority, however, only come once a month to Pekalongan to attend a mass gathering held at Habib Luthfi's congregational center. For the disciples, attending these monthly gatherings is understood to fulfill the minimum requirement of *suḥba*, or companionship with their master. While non-initiates attend to simply learn something about their religion by listening to Habib Luthfi, for his disciples the substance of the sermon itself is secondary to the impact and import of being in the presence of their master and establishing bodily contact with him.

Beyond attending the monthly gathering, disciples are also required to maintain their connection to the master through the recitation of the daily litany. Entitled "Litany of the Shādhilī-ʿAlawī Sufi Order" (*Awrād al-ṭarīqah al-shādhiliya al-ʿalawiyya*), this series of prayers were compiled and systematized by Habib Luthfi and entextualized in the form of a privately printed prayer manual sold during the monthly gathering. Disciples are obligated to buy the manual and recite the litany on a daily basis. The manual does not contain substantive teachings of Sufism, apart from outlining the basic practical rules that ought to be observed by initiated disciples. While the text helps to maintain the durability of the relationship of authority between the disciples and their master when they are physically estranged from him, it does not substitute for the imperative to spend time with Habib Luthfi. The substantive teachings of Sufism are instead handed down gradually during the monthly gathering, when Habib Luthfi delivers a thirty- to forty-minute sermon. In effect, for disciples who live with Habib Luthfi, such teachings are transmitted in a piecemeal manner through everyday interactions with the master. The basic logic at work in this process is that of the control of knowledge. The master transmits knowledge differently to different disciples based on what he deems appropriate for each individual. Disciples are expected to act as empty receptacles, whose main duty is to observe and listen attentively to the master. Posing a question to the master is generally seen to be inappropriate, except in exceptional circumstances.

Another means for maintaining a direct connection to the master is the practice of *rābiṭa* (bonding). This term refers to a technique of visualization in which the image of the master is preserved in the disciples' hearts. Such a practice has historically been aided by various technologies that serve to evoke the visual imagination, including hagiographical texts, paintings, sketches of shrines and relics, or photographs of modern-day saints and Sufi masters.[10] Many disciples, for example, have told me how they recite the daily litany while gazing directly at Habib Luthfi's photo. Others confessed that at times they converse with a hung portrait of their master, particularly when they want to complain about something. An elderly man even cautioned me that if a disciple has portraits of the Sufi master in his bedroom, they should be covered when engaging in sexual intercourse.

The pledge of allegiance, the congregational center, the prayer manual, and the practice of companionship and bonding are all conceptual and practical apparatuses that make up a Sufi order. Together, they work to constitute, formalize, and maintain discipleship as a durable hierarchical relationship that is iconic of, and indexically connected to, a foundational past—namely, the Prophetic past—constituted through the master's chain of Sufi initiation (*silsila*). These apparatuses allow the master to transmit and augment Prophetic teachings, eliciting obedience without resorting to coercion.

The Expert Host

The hierarchical relationship I have sketched thus far stands in marked contrast to the dynamics configured through the "Spiritual Consultation" (*konsultasi spiritual*) rubric that Habib Luthfi maintains in the popular Islamic magazine, *alKisah*. Founded in 2003, *alKisah* began as an Islamic bimonthly catering to the emerging Muslim market that has expanded significantly since the 1990s, a period often described as the era of Islamic revival in Indonesia.[11] This period witnessed the Islamization of state and society, ushering in a more liberated atmosphere in which Indonesians began to feel more comfortable with public expressions of Islam. Several state-directed initiatives facilitated Islamic manifestations in the public sphere, such as the establishment of Islamic banking systems and Muslim intellectual organizations, the application of Islamic family law, permission for women to wear the veil in public schools, the publication of Islamic magazines, and the broadcasting of Islamic programs on television.[12] These developments resulted in vivid public manifestations of Islamic piety.

One such trend was Sufism's increasing prominence among urban-based, middle-class Muslims in search of authentic Islamic teachings. The Sufism popularized among urbanized Muslims, however, was quite different from more traditional rural-based variants. Rather than equating Sufism exclusively with Sufi orders, it emphasized instead a set of thoughts and practices aimed at internalizing ethical principles within the self, without mandating a formal pledge of allegiance to a Sufi master within an established institutional order.[13] During this time, Indonesian bookshops were flooded by translations of classical Sufi texts while Sufi-oriented Islamic programs were aired on television. This new trend drove the media entrepreneurs Harun and Nuniek Musawa, known for their teenage pop magazine *Aneka Yess!*, to establish a new magazine called *alKisah* in 2003 in the hope of tapping into this emerging market. The magazine focused on profiles of Muslim saints and scholars, reports on the agendas of Islamic study groups (*majelis taklim*) and saintly commemorations (*haul*) in

FIGURE 3.1 *Three editions of* alKisah *magazine, purchased by the author in Jakarta. Photo by the author.*

Indonesia, discussions of different prayers and litanies, along with several Q&A rubrics on legal, theological, and spiritual issues such as dream interpretation (Figure 3.1).

In its heyday, the bimonthly magazine's circulation ranged from 60,000 to 90,000 per edition. Its active readership consisted mostly of young people (between fifteen and forty years old) with a high school or university education, living mainly in the urban centers of Java. This suggests that *alKisah*'s readership was quite different from the traditional congregation of a Sufi master like Habib Luthfi, namely rural and provincial town-based Muslims, many with *pesantren* (traditional Islamic boarding school) backgrounds. Instead, *alKisah*'s reading public was comprised largely of young, secular-educated, urban-based Muslims actively studying or working in formal sectors who, despite their interest in Sufism, did not have adequate time to maintain an active relationship with a living Sufi master.

Among the scholars frequently covered by *alKisah* was Habib Luthfi. In 2004 alone, the magazine featured two extended reports on the Sufi master, entitled "Habib Luthfi bin Yahya: Shading the heart of the *umma* through prayers" and "A figure with thirty million followers."[14] Both articles are introductory in that they acquaint the readers with Habib Luthfi's biography, life trajectory, activism, daily activity, and family life. Another extended report explored Habib Luthfi's position as the chairman of JATMAN, along with a discussion of the association's history and function.[15] These reports incorporate hagiographic elements, including discussions of several saintly marvels (*karāma*) performed by Habib Luthfi based on the testimonies of his followers and disciples. Habib Luthfi was frequently featured on the magazine's cover as well. In at least two issues, *alKisah* included a detachable pin-up photo of Habib Luthfi that readers could frame and hang on their walls (Figure 3.2). I have personally seen these *alKisah* photos adorning the houses of Habib Luthfi's disciples.

FIGURE 3.2 *A pin-up photograph of Habib Luthfi from the* alKisah *magazine, purchased by the author in Jakarta. Photo by the author.*

In early 2004, *alKisah*'s editorial board asked Habib Luthfi to serve as the expert host for the magazine's "Spiritual Q&A" rubric. Previously, the column was managed by *alKisah*'s in-house team of researchers. The sense that one gets from reading these articles is that the team largely refrained from giving conclusive answers to the questions posed by the readers. In an issue from September 2003, for example, Basundari from Jakarta asks about whispers that she began to hear after habitually reciting a particular litany. The answer to this question mainly deals with the possibility that such whispers come from either angels or *jinns* (intelligent spirits or supernatural creatures in Arabian and Islamic mythology). The team advises Basundari to only follow the instructions given through the whispers insofar as they do not oppose Islamic law. Although the team admits to their lack of specific knowledge regarding the litany, they conclude that "seen from the actual text, the prayer itself is good as it petitions God for beneficial things."[16] It is this lack of expertise that led the magazine's founders to approach Habib Luthfi, who responded affirmatively to their request. Every fortnight, a journalist from *alKisah* visited Habib Luthfi to read him the questions that had been submitted. Habib Luthfi then dictated his answer, and the journalist prepared them for publication. Harun Musawa told me in one of our conversations that *alKisah*'s readers responded positively to the rubric's new expert host. Their excitement was evident from the significant increase in the number of questions pouring into *alKisah*.

As the new host of the "Spiritual Q&A" column, Habib Luthfi is presented not as a master of a particular Sufi order but as an expert of spiritual knowledge. Such a presentation configures a different relationship from that formed between a Sufi master and his disciples. For one, knowledge production is contingent on questions from readers, many of whom do not have personal ties to Habib Luthfi. Several questioners, in fact, admit to first learning about Habib Luthfi from *alKisah*'s coverage of the Sufi master. Equally important is the way in which this relationship involves new actors who sustain and shape its contours, including the journalist who transcribed Habib Luthfi's answers and the editors who modified the transcripts. Significantly, Habib Luthfi's position as a host of this rubric is a salaried position. He is professionally expected to answer every question posed to him by the readers. In that capacity, Habib Luthfi has to address myriads of questions—from topics relating to the legality of *tumpeng* (a cone-shaped rice dish traditionally featured in Javanese thanksgiving rituals) to the side effects of particular litanies, the meaning of different Sufi concepts, and the duties involved in discipleship. In every instance, his answers to readers' inquiries are decisive. They are not based on textual research but rather on sedimented knowledge that weaves textual references with orally transmitted sayings of Sufi masters and Habib Luthfi's own experience as a seasoned Sufi master. In time, the magazine column became so popular that *alKisah* decided to work with a publishing house to select and compile Habib Luthfi's answers into a book entitled *Spiritual Advice: The Sufi Path according to Habib Luthfi bin Yahya* (*Nasihat Spiritual: Mengenal Tarekat ala Habib Luthfi bin Yahya*). Advertised in every issue of *alKisah*, more than 80,000 copies of the book have been sold.

Despite the anxiety of many Sufi-oriented scholars over the dissemination of Islamic esoteric knowledge through the medium of a popular magazine, I argue that it would be a mistake to characterize Habib Luthfi's role as an expert host as a radical break from his role as a traditional Sufi master. To begin with, not everyone who comes to visit Habib Luthfi on a regular basis in his house in Pekalongan is a Sufi disciple. Many guests come to see Habib Luthfi simply to consult on various issues, including spiritual matters. In fact, the magazine's popularity also helps to reinforce the institution of Sufi discipleship. The following three examples are illustrative of this point.

In an edition from April 2007, Yendra Muchraman of East Jakarta poses a question regarding a particular prayer to alleviate financial hardship that Habib Luthfi prescribed in an earlier issue of the magazine to another questioner, Agus. Muchraman asks Habib Luthfi whether the permission (*ijāza*) for reciting that prayer was only issued to Agus or whether Habib Luthfi has granted permission to every reader of *alKisah*. Muchraman explains that he is experiencing the same difficulty faced by Agus. In his response, Habib Luthfi explains that all of the prescriptions that he has issued in *alKisah* are unrestricted, meaning that he has given anyone the permission to recite the prayer. Nevertheless, he also cautions that it is better for Muchraman to come and see him directly precisely because every problem is particular in nature, even if they are similar on the surface. The best remedy to a problem, Habib Luthfi advises, can only be given after a proper diagnosis.[17] Here we see how the magazine column reinforces the importance of direct interpersonal relations.

Another salient example pertains to several questions posed by readers interested in joining a Sufi order. Habib Luthfi addresses such questions by applauding their resolution to join a Sufi community and recommends the names of Sufi masters who reside not far from where they live, rather than inviting them to become his own disciples. In this case, while Habib Luthfi is playing the role of an expert host, he nevertheless reaffirms the importance of Sufi orders and formal discipleship as a mode of spiritual self-cultivation.[18] A final example has to do with several questions posed by readers who identify themselves as Habib Luthfi's disciples. These questions are interesting in that they demonstrate how the magazine acts as a medium that allows disciples to indirectly pose questions to their master. For Habib Luthfi's disciples, posing a direct question to the master is generally discouraged since, in keeping with a famous Sufi adage, disciples ought to behave like "corpses in the hands of morticians." Indeed, when I lived with Habib Luthfi for two years, I personally witnessed how most disciples were reluctant to pose questions directly to their master, either because they did not see it as proper or because they were too shy to do so. In this sense, the magazine provides an alternative platform where Habib Luthfi's disciples can pose questions to their spiritual guide, thereby reproducing discipleship with a new twist. In effect, the magazine serves as a supplementary pedagogical apparatus that augments the infrastructure of a Sufi order.

The Virtual Master

The advent and exponential growth of digital media posed an unprecedented challenge to print media in Indonesia. In the early decades of the twenty-first century, several leading newspapers and magazines were forced to bid farewell to their readers as others were left gasping for breath. Though some print publications successfully transitioned to digital formats, that was not the case for *alKisah*. Beginning in 2014, the Islamic magazine had to face the reality that their market had significantly dwindled—with similar content now readily available from various digital media platforms. Indonesian

Muslim scholars with substantial followings and various other Islamic movements and organizations increasingly manage their own websites, Facebook pages, and Twitter accounts. Amid these expansive changes, *alKisah* went out of business in January 2015.

Far from being mere channels of communication and information dissemination, social media engender negotiations over traditional forms of Islamic authority and authenticity, which have become more intensely contested amid the increasingly plural, often competing, social and intellectual formations of post-authoritarian Indonesia.[19] The expansion of modern Islamic movements often tied to transnational Islamic networks hostile to Sufism, competing claims of religious authenticity made by different Muslim leaders and communities, and secular intellectual formations facilitated by modern media, schools, and universities have all opened up complex and conflictual terrains which are reproduced in and through social media. Traditional Sufi orders and the hierarchical relationship linking Sufi masters and their disciples have persistently become objects of criticism in online debates, with some even going as far as questioning whether they are authentically Islamic. At the same time, social media have also afforded Habib Luthfi's followers with new ways of responding to such challenges.

In 2009, a disciple of Habib Luthfi, Ahmad Tsauri (b. 1985), decided to create the official website of his master to disseminate his teachings. Tsauri came to this idea while cataloging and archiving Habib Luthfi's written works, many of which were scattered in loose leaf and notebooks. To facilitate this work, he began enlisting the support of other young disciples and subsequently launched the website. This was followed by a Facebook fan page and a Twitter account. Today, Habib Luthfi's website is accessed by 100–300,000 visitors each month, mostly from Indonesia. His official Facebook fan page and Twitter account have more than 2.4 million and more than 200,000 followers, respectively. The materials for these online platforms consist of excerpts from Habib Luthfi's sermons, informal conversations, and written works. Habib Luthfi himself has not been personally involved in this project, although he granted Tsauri full permission to manage his internet presence. Tsauri and his team did not receive any financial support from Habib Luthfi or his family. In order to keep the website afloat, they founded a small graphic design company catering to local businesses.

Tsauri believed that the internet affords new opportunities for the dissemination of the Sufi master's thoughts among the wider Indonesian public, including those skeptical of Sufism and Sufi orders. To do so, he presented Habib Luthfi not as a Sufi master but as an Islamic public intellectual concerned with the common good of the nation, or in Tsauri's own words, "the well-being of the nation" (*kemaslahatan bangsa*). Tsauri was particularly concerned with the rapid circulation of anecdotes that recount Habib Luthfi's saintly marvels (*karāma*) among the Sufi master's followers. In his view, these proliferating stories obscured Habib Luthfi's intellectual contributions. During our conversations, Tsauri often bemoaned the dearth of sources that point to the intellectual contributions of eminent Sufi scholars of the past. Except for a few who actually took the time to commit their ideas to paper, most of these renowned scholars are only known posthumously as miracle-working saints. Tsauri was determined to use social media not only to disseminate Habib Luthfi's ideas to the broader public but also to construct a different persona of the master, one that conformed to the rationality of the modern public. To do so, Tsauri consciously minimized—and, at times, excluded—Habib Luthfi's discourse on Sufi metaphysics, focusing instead on the Sufi master's civic and nationalist ideas which are presented as *opini persuasif* (persuasive opinion) designed to elicit responses and engender discussions.

Tsauri's digital project, however, alarmed other disciples, particularly because Habib Luthfi himself—despite his authorization—was not directly involved in managing the website and social media accounts. Central to their concern is the issue of authorial absence that results when the discourses of the Sufi master are disseminated in decentered forms.[20] Informed by this culturally specific logocentrism, some disciples went as far as characterizing the internet, and the kind of sociality it engenders, as a source of *fitna* (i.e., temptation, trial, sedition, slander). *Fitna*, as Stefania Pandolfo suggests, can be understood as a concept denoting "semiotic disorder." Like cancer, *fitna* is a "trope of growth out of control," like the "straying of language," or when discourse takes on a life of its own and starts creating a world independent of its author.[21] In this view, the circulatory possibility afforded by social media, together with the absence of recitational control, can lead to the fracturing of discourse from authorial intent, thereby aggravating the risk of *fitna*. Using a Qur'ānic phrase, one senior disciple explained to me that the internet and social media "*yuḥarrifūna al-kalima 'an mawāḍi'ihi*" ("take words out of their contexts"), thereby exacerbating the risk for distortion and displacement of meaning.

Tsauri was certainly current in his prediction that Habib Luthfi's social media presence would generate interest from the broader public. Even non-Muslim Indonesians are now following the Sufi master's social media. What he did not anticipate, however, was the ensuing increase of internet usage among Habib Luthfi's disciples, facilitated by the availability of affordable China-made smartphones and the decreasing price of internet data plans due to increasing competition among local phone service providers. These disciples use the internet to gaze at their master's latest photos, read his newest posts, and maintain their spiritual connections to Habib Luthfi. The term that kept coming up during my conversations with them was "bonding" (*rabiṭa*), which, as previously explained, refers to a technique of visualizing the image of the master in the disciples' heart. Bonding maintains the affective bond between the disciples and their master beyond shared, bodily presence. Since the practice of *rabiṭa* has historically been aided by different technologies that serve to evoke visual imaginations, there is nothing fundamentally new in using novel media platforms for the purpose of bonding—except that social media now allow the disciples to "interact" with their master in a virtual space shared with and accessible to other netizens of varying backgrounds.

Consequently, most interactions that take place in Habib Luthfi's Facebook page tend to reproduce the forms of hierarchically organized sociality within a Sufi congregation. Habib Luthfi's followers respond to new postings with deference rather than engaging with the actual message. They treat what Tsauri described as "persuasive opinions" as the authoritative dictates of a Sufi master and react by uttering Islamic formulae like "God is Great" (*Allāhu akbar*), "Praise be to God" (*alhamdulillāh*), "Glory be to God" (*subhanaAllāh*), or by offering prayers for Habib Luthfi. Some respond by asking Habib Luthfi about the meaning of a dream they experienced, requesting supplication or names for their newborn children, or seeking advice and spiritual guidance. Others request permission to recite litanies, ask to be recognized as disciples, or apologize to Habib Luthfi for not being able to attend the monthly gathering. From speaking to some of the disciples, however, I got the sense that they were not expecting any response—and the absence of a reply certainly does not deter most of them from continuing to pose such comments, questions, and requests. When used to facilitate Sufi bonding, the content of the message itself becomes less important than the actual forms of connectivity (and visuality) that these media allow.

As the administrator, Tsauri himself does not respond to any of the comments. Unlike other Muslim scholars who use social media to directly interact with their followers and critics, Tsauri only employs social media to simply relay Habib Luthfi's ideas that are already articulated offline. When one senior disciple who started to follow Habib Luthfi on Twitter was followed back, he sent an irritated private message to Tsauri requesting to be unfollowed, stating as his reason the impropriety of a master following his disciple. In this case, the act of following a Twitter account is perceived through the prism of Sufi etiquette (*adab*).

One repercussion of the reproduction of Sufi sociality in social media is the rising tendency to police critical comments, not by the administrator (who welcomes such engagements) but by other followers who are also Habib Luthfi's initiated disciples. Netizens voicing critical comments toward Habib Luthfi are often bullied by disciples, who use expressions like "Who do you think you are talking to?"; "Please be more polite!"; "Watch it, you are talking to a saint"; "God's wrath upon those who criticize His friends"; and so on. Some devotees respond to critical comments by telling the critics to go and visit Habib Luhtfi and clarify the matter directly with him. Others fault the administrator for liberally posting Habib Luthfi's statements which, in their view, generate misunderstandings. It is important to note that while policing, bullying, or censorious expressions toward others in the actual physical presence of the master would be deemed inappropriate, these responses are considered acceptable vis-à-vis his "virtual presence." This suggests that social media facilitate but also reconfigure Sufi sociality.

In 2015, Facebook launched a livestreaming video feature. Taking advantage of this innovation, Tsauri and his team added live coverage of Habib Luthfi's monthly gathering to the Sufi master's Facebook fan page. Viewers of the coverage ranged from 40,000 to 70,000 people each month. This new feature has allowed people—including disciples—who wanted to attend the gathering but were unable to do so to virtually experience Habib Luthfi's sermon and perform *dhikr* (rhythmic repetition of God's name and other devotional formulas) with him from remote locations. Similarly, the feature has also enabled people who are not familiar with Habib Luthfi, or those who have not attended the in-person gatherings, to get acquainted with the Sufi rituals and the master's sermons by accessing the widely shared videos. At the same time, this new development has also generated anxiety among senior disciples I talked to who were worried that video livestreaming would provide excuses for people to not attend the monthly gathering. One senior disciple assured me that merely tuning in to the live coverage could never substitute for bodily co-presence. "The spiritual elixir transmitted through companionship (*suḥba*) cannot be relayed through social media," he explained. Another disciple told me that Habib Luthfi's sermons delivered during the monthly gatherings are aimed at people who are already oriented toward Sufism. In her view, livestreaming the sermons on Facebook makes them available to those who are critical of Sufism— and who would only listen to scrutinize them. In her assessment, making the monthly sermons publicly available on Facebook exposes Habib Luthfi Luthfi to unwarranted criticism from those who question Sufism's Islamic authenticity or do not share its epistemic assumptions.

These concerns notwithstanding, new possibilities have certainly been opened up by the livestreaming of Habib Luthfi's monthly gathering. For one, those who watch the live coverage can see the Sufi master clearly, a luxury that is often difficult to enjoy when they attend the mass gathering in person. This is particularly the case for women who are confined to a separate section and cannot sit near Habib Luthfi during the live ritual. Given these circumstances, I have seen attendees of the monthly gathering tune in to the live coverage to witness what their naked eyes cannot see. It is important to remember, however, that one cannot watch live coverage with a cheap internet data plan. This suggests that only viewers with the financial means to access decent Wi-Fi connections or to purchase more expensive internet data plans can enjoy the livestreaming Facebook feature.

Similar to the prominent platform in *alKisah* magazine, Habib Luthfi's Facebook fan page and Twitter account are managed by administrative gatekeepers who curate and relay information based on the Sufi master's sermons, talks, and even informal conversations. While the *alKisah*-mediated relationship between Habib Luthfi and his public was dialogical, the social dynamics formed in and through social media are unidirectional. Social media outlets are not dialogical, since Habib Luthfi does not respond to questions and queries from his followers. Instead, we see here a return to the logic and mechanics of the earlier hierarchical relationship, whereby disciples are expected to listen attentively to the master and not ask questions—even though the relationship is more complex when mediated by social media as it involves double curation. That is, administrators filter knowledge and information that have been initially curated by the Sufi master himself. As a result, it is not surprising that many senior disciples were concerned with the curatorial power of the administrative gatekeepers, most of whom are younger and technologically savvy disciples.

Tensions between senior disciples and these social media curators came to a boiling point in early 2017. It so happened that in a conversation between Habib Luthfi and his guests, the Sufi master remarked that in a democracy all citizens should enjoy the same right and responsibility to serve their country, regardless of their religious affiliation. When this remark was subsequently relayed on Habib Luthfi's Twitter feed, it was construed by critics as suggesting the permissibility of having a non-Muslim political leader in Indonesia. The tweet quickly went viral and sparked controversies on Twitter and Facebook. Many users expressed their disappointment in Habib Luthfi's statement, while others praised the Sufi master for his pluralist stance. Modernist Muslims and Salafis in particular intensified their criticism of Habib Luthfi. One Muslim activist went as far as writing, "a *murshid* (Sufi master) who believes that a non-Muslim can become the leader of a Muslim nation, is not a *murshid*, but a *mufsid* (one who spreads corruption)." Such critiques, in turn, enraged Habib Luthfi's followers who responded with anger, provoking a series of further tweet wars. The controversial tweet even circulated beyond social media, prompting the displeasure of several senior traditionalist scholars. The principals of Java's leading traditional Islamic boarding schools like Sidogiri, Ploso, Lirboyo, and Langitan, all of whom respect Habib Luthfi and recognize him as their peer, requested clarification by sending emissaries to Pekalongan to discern what legal precedent Habib Luthfi based his opinion upon.

In the wake of these events, several senior disciples of Habib Luthfi—who are traditionally trained scholars in their own right—came to the conclusion that Tsauri and his team were to blame for these controversies. In their view, the official website and social media have downplayed Habib Luthfi's role as a Sufi master by focusing on contentious civic ideas that may spark misunderstandings and public critique. They also accused Tsauri of projecting a nonrepresentative portrait of their master. These senior disciples brought the matter directly to Habib Luthfi and suggested the need to institute control over the materials disseminated through the master's website and social media. Thereafter, an editorial board was formed consisting of four senior disciples, with the role of Tsauri and his team reduced to mere technicalities. Subsequently, any post or tweet from Habib

Luthfi's official accounts requires prior approval from the board. Since then, Habib Luthfi's website, Facebook, and Twitter accounts no longer disseminate Habib Luthfi's civic ideas. Instead, they now function solely as media platforms for transmitting the less contentious spiritual messages of the Sufi master to his own congregation.

Conclusion

In this chapter, I have documented the direct and indirect engagement of a Sufi master with multiple media. Rather than treating media simply as channels of communication and dissemination distinct from the actors involved, I have demonstrated how engagement with a variety of media forms engenders different dynamics of presence and relationship that link the Sufi master to his own community and a broader public. Distinct forms of mediatization reconfigure Habib Luthfi's authority in contrasting ways, generating both new possibilities of networking and connection, as well as new forms of discordance and anxiety.

In my view, the case of Habib Luthfi's media engagement reinforces the need to desist from treating religious authority as an essentialized and immutable formation that is incompatible with the consumerist conventions that shape contemporary mass media. Nor should scholars fall into the ideological trap of assuming that the development of new media technologies heralds emancipation, rational debates, and the weakening of traditional religious authority.[22] As a sociological reality, religious authority takes shape through a "materializing process" that "must be concretized through material mediation."[23] This means that materiality and material mediation should not be seen as distinct from, but rather as the condition for, religious authority. As a result, media should not be analytically separated from authority, as the presentation and materialization of authority itself presuppose a mediatic structure. In short: different media forms do not simply or necessarily absorb and transform religious authority in accordance with their own modes of functioning. Instead, new media technologies and novel forms of mediation may themselves be integrated and transfigured in different ways by religious practices.

As illustrated in this chapter, the Sufi logics of interaction are reproduced and reconfigured, even if inadvertently, in and through different media interfaces that may transfigure them into new virtual sacred spaces.[24] This, in turn, points to how Sufi institutional frameworks continue to shape— without necessarily determining—technologically mediated interpretations and interactions. Different actors, even those who belong to the same Sufi order, understand mediation and mediatization in contrasting ways. They often question the relationship between physical and virtual presence, and debate whether companionship (*suḥba*) can or should be effectively conveyed and experienced through social media. The fact that such questions are periodically raised by various media users reveals the workings of different semiotic (or media) ideologies, that is, "assumptions about what signs [media] are, what function signs [media] do or do not serve, and what consequences they might or might not produce."[25] Beyond provoking excitement or concern, different media allow for creative engagement by diverse actors in ways that transcend their own commodified logics of production. Amid these complex dynamics, media create, expand, and reconfigure social relationships that complicate the formation and reproduction of religious authority while facilitating old and new debates over what is authentically Islamic.

Acknowledgment

I would like to thank Harun and Nuniek Musawa for providing me with a complete set of the *alKisah* magazine, and Martin Slama, Carla Jones, Patrick Eisenlohr, Bart Barendregt, Fatimah Husein, Julian Millie, and James Hoesterey for their comments on earlier iterations of this chapter. I also benefited from the helpful feedback I received from two workshops (2016 and 2018) organized by Martin Slama at the Institute for Social Anthropology, Austrian Academy of Sciences, Vienna. A previous iteration of some parts of this article appeared in a 2017 American Ethnologist Online forum, "Piety, Celebrity, and Sociality: A Forum on Islam and Social Media in Southeast Asia," edited by Martin Slama and Carla Jones. Finally, I am grateful to Rob Rozehnal for his meticulous reading and editing of this chapter.

Part II

Community
and Identity

CHAPTER 4

Stream If You Want:

See Something, Say Something and the Humanizing Potential of Digital Islam

Caleb Elfenbein

Introduction

From the beginning of 2010 through the close of 2020 there were nearly 2,000 media reports documenting various instances of Muslim communities in the United States reaching out in some way to non-Muslim communities.[1] These accounts describe a range of activities undertaken by Muslims unaffiliated with national advocacy organizations, including participating in interfaith gatherings, both their own and others; hosting open mosque events; coordinating "Ask a Muslim" and "Meet a Muslim" programming; and organizing fair-style events offering a variety of activities meant to introduce non-Muslims to their Muslim neighbors. According to many participants, these efforts are meant to humanize Muslims, to show that they are just like everyone else. Many of the participants who feature in news reports, Muslim and non-Muslim alike, express joy at the prospects of making connections with others in their local communities. Yet it is difficult to imagine that Muslims and non-Muslims are speaking from the same position.

As one frequent Muslim participant in "humanizing" programming, Dr. Mohammad Qamar of Sioux Falls, South Dakota, told an audience in 2017, amid an historic rise in anti-Muslim sentiment and activity, "outreach is not just important. It is a necessity."[2] Non-Muslim participants sometimes express a similar sentiment, explaining that developing intercultural understanding is a necessity in today's world or some variation on that theme. When set in the context of anti-Muslim sentiment and hostility, however, "necessity" can take on a different significance. The point here is not to criticize non-Muslims who take time out of their own lives to attend—and sometimes to plan and co-host—such humanizing events. They are deciding to use their time in the service of building community and making connections with people different from themselves. That is laudable. The key here is that they are *choosing* to engage in acts of *voluntary* participation, a vital element of public life in democratic societies.

During the decade in question, there is a direct correlation between a rise in anti-Muslim activity across the country and the extent of "humanizing" work by American Muslims. There is necessity, and then there is *necessity*. The stakes are different, with real implications for the individuals and communities doing the work.

Some "back of the napkin" math can help us grasp the scope of humanizing work from 2010 to 2020. We know that there were at least 2,000 instances of outreach events during this period; in fact, this is a conservative estimate because it includes only those events that received local media coverage. As anyone with experience planning events knows, even an hour-long event requires many hours of labor. If each humanizing event requires five hours of work, which is a very reasonable if not conservative estimate, this comes to 10,000 hours over ten years, multiplied by all those individuals who contributed to each instance of outreach.

American Muslims have not spent this much time humanizing themselves because of anything they have done to warrant questions or doubts about their commitment to local communities across the country. Rather, such work has been a necessity because of non-Muslim fears and suspicions that rarely reflect people's actual experiences with Muslims and Muslim communities. Through these "in real life" (IRL) events, Muslims are effectively ministering to other people's fears, stereotypes, and misconceptions, often having to overcome fears of their own relating to anti-Muslim sentiment and activity in the process. The burden to make other people feel safe, to remind others of one's own humanity, and to share what it means to have a particular identity—in this case, being Muslim—is born by only some communities in the United States. The burden is in some ways part of the cost of admission for being part of a broader American public, in terms of a capacity both to be safe in public and to be seen by others as American. These two facets are of course deeply connected.

It makes perfect sense that Muslims in the contemporary United States, as individuals and communities, have identified relational, local outreach work as a key strategy in countering anti-Muslim sentiment. Americans who report knowing someone who is Muslim are more likely to have positive views of Muslims in general. Yet only about 55 percent of non-Muslim Americans report knowing someone who is Muslim.[3] It would seem to follow therefore that more outreach, more meetings, more in-person humanizing work is the best way to change perceptions of Muslims. In his remarks to Rotarians in Sioux Falls, Dr. Qamar joked that Muslims had finally been making some progress, finally surpassing zombies in esteem. Funny not funny.

There are a number of reasons, however, that we ought to pause in assessing what on its face seems like a logical progression: non-Muslims who know Muslims have warmer feelings toward Muslims, therefore more Muslims should reach out to more non-Muslims. One reason is a simple question of numbers. There are about 3.45 million Muslims living in the United States, just over 1 percent of the general population. No matter how much humanizing work Muslims in local communities do, it will be hard to meaningfully increase the number of people who report knowing someone who is Muslim without creating an ever-growing burden on the time, effort, and emotional energy outreach requires.

A second and related reason to pause in assessing the "ergo" of humanizing outreach work is that Muslims have lives to lead. Muslims are parents. Muslims are caregivers. Muslims have jobs. Muslims have lots of things they could be doing other than ministering to other people's fears. Some Muslims want to engage in outreach work. Some Muslims garner immense satisfaction from interfaith work. There is a good chance they are already engaging in such activities. Even so, given what we all experience of the many competing demands in our human lives, expecting even more Muslims to turn over nights and weekends to various kinds of humanizing work is in itself *de*humanizing.

A third reason to pause in imagining that more outreach work will lead to more people having ever-warmer feelings about Muslims—a popular metric of assessing sentiment about a particular group of people—reflects the nature of much of the work itself. As programming meant for "outsiders," humanizing work may often offer a curated, and perhaps sanitized, portrait. This is not a criticism of the enormous efforts Muslims have undertaken over the past decades. But it is worth asking how many people, especially those already in a vulnerable position, would share their own struggles, their own doubts, their own searching questions, in a room full of strangers? (Would you?) Yet, these struggles, doubts, and questions are the very things that make us most human.

These three reasons for pause led me to investigate other ways that Muslims are actively countering Islamophobia in the United States. More specifically, they led me to seek out other ways that Muslims are countering Islamophobia that might address the limits of numbers, the realities of human lives, and the pitfalls of programming that is "not just important, but a necessity"—in short, alternative strategies that address the burdens and limits of IRL efforts to minister to others' fears. This search led me to an instance of digital Islam, a podcast called *See Something, Say Something*. Through a close analysis of the podcast episodes, interviews with the host, and interviews with non-Muslim listeners, I have learned that certain forms of cultural production by Muslims—and meant primarily for Muslims—can offer a less burdensome, more sustainable complement to other kinds of efforts meant to counter anti-Muslim sentiment.

A resonant example of such cultural production, the *See Something, Say Something* podcast engages the complexities of Muslim experiences in (North) America in a way that is also accessible, and perhaps relatable, to a broad non-Muslim audience. There are other examples of digital Islam that find this balance, which is admittedly a tall order. Much like *See Something, Say Something*, Taz Ahmed and Zahra Noorbakhsh's podcast, *#GoodMuslimBadMuslim,* provides an excellent model for future work.[4] Both are examples of what I call a "stream if you want" approach to humanization. As I explain in this chapter, a "stream if you want" approach prioritizes community-building for Muslims through exploring aspects of their identities and experiences while also offering non-Muslim audiences the chance to "listen in" on conversations to which they would not otherwise have access.

Before moving to a detailed analysis of *See Something, Say Something*, I situate the humanizing work of Muslims across the United States in a theoretical framework of publics and counterpublics which attends to the operations of power inherent in the conditions of public life. Within this framework, I highlight the role of audience when people are speaking to diverse groups, drawing on insights from Black writers to consider how power affects to whom and for whom people speak.

Publics, Counterpublics, and the Humanizing Work of American Muslims

In December of 2015, Mona Haydar and her husband stood outside a public library in Cambridge, Massachusetts, between signs that read "Talk to a Muslim" and "Ask a Muslim." They also offered free coffee and donuts from a venerable New England institution, Dunkin' Donuts. Explaining her motivations to *The Boston Globe*, Mona Haydar said, "We just wanted to talk to people and we didn't see any harm in doing that. We are just normal people. There is definitely fear [in America], and I want to talk about it, because it's actually misplaced and misguided—I am really nice!"[5] That same month, Abu Muhammad al-Maghribee, an *imam* at the Islamic Center of Palm Beach in Florida, described his community's decision to hold an open house to *The Palm Beach Post*: "You don't have to be afraid of who we are. We shop in the same mall and have coffee in the same Starbucks. We go to the same Whole Foods. We don't come from another planet."[6]

In a 2018 interview with the *East Bay Times*, Munir Safi, who coordinates outreach efforts for a number of mosques in Hayward, California, articulated his motivations in similar terms: "I think it's just a matter of normalizing ourselves in the community and saying that we're really just average folk and pretty boring, actually. That's the message I'm trying to put across—it really is—and it's sad that we have to do this, to say that we are boring, average folk."[7]

As these responses illustrate, a central goal for Muslim public outreach is to show non-Muslims just how normal Muslims really are. We all eat the same donuts, enjoy the same coffee, and share the same public spaces. Given that Muslims and non-Muslims share basic elements of our lives in common, non-Muslims need not be afraid. As Mohammad Qamar explained in 2017, and Munir Safi echoed a year later, such efforts are necessary because the conditions of public life for Muslims in the United States are marked by pervasive suspicion and the threat of anti-Muslim sentiment and activity. In these conditions, ministering to other people's fears functions as a prerequisite to participating in public life—being part of the American public—beyond shared pleasures of donuts, coffee, and shopping. Prerequisites for participating in public life, which do not exist in the same way for members of majority communities, can impede authentic engagement.

The fact of prerequisites for authentic engagement in public life brings to mind the important work of Nancy Fraser. Back in 1990, Fraser pointed out that the idea of "the public," a collective group of citizens participating in the life of democratic countries on equal terms, was much more an ideal than a reality.[8] In everyday practice as well as law, from the very first moments of modern democracies, many people were not welcome in "the public" because they did not fit dominant norms of race, gender, class, sexuality. As a result, she argued, subordinated social groups begin to form "counterpublics" in which they are (more) free to participate in collective life. Modern democratic societies, then, consist of multiple publics. Writing almost a decade later, Michael Warner built on Fraser's foundational insights to suggest that in some instances members of counterpublics seek to become part of dominant publics, while in other cases they prefer to remain apart.[9]

Taken together, Fraser and Warner provide a framework to help us make sense of contemporary Muslim public outreach efforts—and why it is important to consider other, especially digital, means of countering Islamophobia. Importantly, when Fraser and Warner talk about participating in public life (or, perhaps more accurately, the life of publics), they are not referring to formal elements of citizenship, such as voting. Instead, they refer to the things that make it possible for groups of people to explore and debate topics that are important to them. Fraser includes "journals, bookstores, publishing companies, film and video distribution networks, lecture series, research centers, academic programs, conferences, conventions, festivals, and local meeting places" as examples of what enables and constitutes public life. Thirty-odd years later, we of course need to add digital public life to this list. With this important addition, Fraser's list remains just as relevant today as it was to life in the early 1990s. It captures two essential dimensions of public life: the means through which we express ideas and the spaces in which we discuss and debate them.

Through their public outreach, Mohammad, Mona, Abu Muhammad, and Munir are trying to show non-Muslims that it really is safe to welcome Muslims into "the public." Mona wants people to learn that she is really nice. Abu Muhammad lets readers know that he likes Starbucks, Whole Foods, and the mall. Munir emphasizes that he is normal—boring, actually. This is not to say that the three of them, and the thousands of other American Muslims engaging in similar work, do not also want to maintain distinct spaces for discussion of ideas particular to being an American Muslim. But they see that the possibility of participating in non-Muslim publics, dominant publics, requires humanizing work. It is not just important, it is a necessity.

A significant amount of humanizing work undertaken by Muslims in the United States unfolds in the kinds of venues and spaces Fraser identifies as being crucial to public life. All of this outreach unfolds with dominant, non-Muslim, largely white publics in mind—a fact that shapes how Muslims engaging in humanizing work direct their minds, talents, and time. Other people's fears, in effect, determine to what publics tens of thousands of Muslims across the country contribute. To paraphrase Toni Morrison, the anti-Muslim sentiment that creates the necessity of humanizing work by Muslims functions as a distraction from whatever else they might otherwise be doing as individuals with rich lives and multifaceted desires.[10] Dominant publics loom large. It is entirely possible that some or many Muslims who engage in humanizing work do so because they truly seek to become part of dominant publics.[11] For those who do not have that goal, however, it is vital to ask what avenues exist to contribute to Muslim counterpublics in a way that is less distracting from more closely held goals *and* address the reality that what members of dominant publics think about Muslims have concrete implications for Muslim lives.

The Distraction of a Non-Muslim Audience

In 2018, as Muslim communities were working harder than ever to humanize themselves in response to anti-Muslim sentiment in the United

States, Mychal Denzel Smith shared his experience as a Black writer with readers of *Harper's Magazine*. In his words, "As a writer, I have spent more time asking white people to see me as human than I have thinking about the world I want to live in."[12] Smith's sentiment echoes Morrison's from back in 1975: racism, of which anti-Muslim sentiment is a species, distracts people from what would otherwise be their work. Being a writer is one way in which a person might contribute to public discussions about the worlds in which they (we) want to live. Fraser's list of the means and spaces of participation points to a much wider variety of possibilities, however. Given what we know of the intended audiences of humanizing work, we can productively extend Smith's insight to the full diversity of activities in which Muslim communities speak to dominant publics.[13] This is not to say that Muslim communities should not engage in outreach to non-Muslim publics. Rather, it is to simply acknowledge that it comes at a cost. The payoff is not always clear. Again, Smith's words are instructive: "Writing to white people about the black experience is meant to engender their sympathy. Yet it never comes. . . . Appeals to the white conscience have not worked, and there are no signs they ever will. It is a strategy whose burial may be long overdue."

To be clear, I am not equating the experience of Muslims in the United States with the experience of Black Americans, though the two are linked in important ways. Nearly 20 percent of Muslims in the contemporary United States are Black,[14] and the history of Islam in the United States always has been inextricably linked with Black experience.[15] Yet beyond these direct interconnections, the persistence of white racism against Black and brown communities in general suggests that we can extend Smith's insight beyond the experiences of Black Muslims.

The distraction of racism and the limits of white sympathy raise important questions about public engagement, whose chief purpose is to humanize Muslims to dominant publics. Is ministering to the fears of dominant publics an effective and sustainable approach to addressing anti-Muslim sentiment? In the end, is it an effective use of time, energy, and resources?

It is clear that for many Muslim communities humanizing work is necessary because of real and immediate fears about safety and security. I do not want to discount that reality. Still, I am left with a question about long-term efficacy, as Smith suggests.

Toward the end of his article, Smith shares an excerpt from a conversation between James Baldwin and Audre Lorde, published in *Essence* magazine in 1984. In that exchange, Lorde challenges what she sees as a masculinist understanding of freedom in Baldwin's work and, more generally, in Black American communities. Smith marvels at the exchange and quotes from a passage in Baldwin's final book to demonstrate that his conversation with Lorde had a subsequent effect on Baldwin's understanding of gender and liberation.

Smith concludes his article by saying, "Provided the space to challenge one another without the distraction of a white audience, Baldwin and Lorde were better able to engage in debate around the social life of black people and blackness." Published in *Essence*, this interaction between Baldwin and Lorde was meant for a Black public—or perhaps more accurately, a Black counterpublic. Its primary purpose was to push members of Black communities to think more deeply about gender and liberation. Does this mean that it might not also be a resource for members of other publics to learn about Black life in the United States? In short: Can dominant publics learn from things that are not meant primarily for them?

According to Kiese Laymon, one of the most celebrated contemporary Black writers in the United States, we all—Black, brown, white—regularly benefit from reading, watching, and listening to material not expressly meant for us. There is of course an essential difference to keep in mind. Long ago, speaking to white audiences, James Baldwin pointed out that Black Americans know white America because they have no choice but to know white America. In a similar fashion, Laymon asserts that even though he writes primarily with Black audiences in mind, he always has to consider white audiences because of the demography of the publishing industry and consuming publics. Still, he noted, "As a political project, Black and brown writers have to think a lot about what it means to decenter the people and the power we have been taught to center." "It is liberatory," he argued, "to focus on an audience that's different from the audience we were taught to write for our entire lives."[16]

As with Mychal Denzel Smith, Laymon's insights into race, audience, and writing are applicable to virtually any activity that is meant for a public, which I define as a group of people who share a common engagement with an idea, an activity, or a creative expression or program of some kind. The question for Laymon is whom one is *primarily* considering when creating or planning something meant for a public or publics. "We know there are all these registers," he says, some of which will be accessible to certain publics and others that will not. Accounting for white audiences (or publics) by including accessible registers is not the same as engaging in public work expressly aimed at white audiences. Dominant publics need not be a distraction from the work that members of Black and brown publics want to accomplish. Likewise, dominant publics need not be a distraction for members of Muslim counterpublics who are working toward a world in which they want to live.

We now turn to a case study of digital Islam that exemplifies the political vision of cultural production Smith and Laymon articulate: *See Something, Say Something*. This podcast is primarily and very intentionally for Muslims, yet it also draws non-Muslim listeners who find it accessible and very meaningful. It acknowledges dominant publics without prioritizing them and humanizes Muslims without placing a burden on them to meet the needs of white audiences.

Let's Talk about Some Big Life Questions

See Something, Say Something started as a weekly Buzzfeed News production in 2016. In late 2018, Buzzfeed discontinued its podcast division, ending the show's two-year run. I must admit that I was disappointed, having become a regular non-Muslim listener. The show offered honest, in-depth looks at Muslim experiences across a great many topics, ranging of devotional practices and holidays to sexuality and mental health. Its guests reflected the great diversity of Muslim communities in the United States and North America.

In March of 2019, Ahmed Ali Akbar, who hosted the podcast during its run at Buzzfeed, released an episode titled "Processing Christchurch" about the white supremacist-fueled attacks on a Christchurch, New Zealand, mosque that left fifty-one dead and forty injured. The episode features Ahmed's father, Waheed, and the conversation between them was beautiful and heartbreaking. The two tenderly discussed the loss of life in a faraway land and, understandably, wondered what it means for Muslim communities elsewhere, including the United States. Although the podcast seemed to be designed primarily to help Muslims to process what had happened, I was grateful for it in that moment. It helped me consider what happened in Christchurch by creating a window into their experience of a tragedy to which their identity as Muslims connected them. Soon after, Ahmed rebooted the show as a crowdfunded podcast.[17]

Ahmed Ali Akbar grew up in Saginaw, Michigan, home to a small Muslim community heavily steeped in Black Muslim histories and experiences. In the first of a series of personal interviews, Ahmed explained to me that his family believed deeply in their responsibility to change perceptions of Muslims.[18] As a teenager, he said, he "took being Muslim on [his] shoulders," feeling a lot of pressure to do the same kind of outreach work as Mohammad Qamar, Mona Haydar, and Munir Safi—and thousands of other Muslims across the United States. When we spoke, Ahmed told stories of his parents encouraging him to give presentations in schools and churches about Islam and being Muslim. He also recounted experiences countering the anti-Muslim sentiment that he regularly encountered in online gaming forums.

In his late teens, just as he was developing doubts about the efficacy of outreach work of the kind in which he was engaged, he was beginning to seek out ways of engaging other Muslims online. He described much of what he found online as emphasizing "orthodox sensibilities," which did not fit with his own personal experience of being Muslim. He did, however, discover ways of connecting with others who, like him, had questions about "common understandings of being Muslim."

Eventually, starting in 2013 while he was in graduate school, he experimented with creating digital community using forms of social media. These early efforts included a Tumblr page called "Rad Brown Dads," a digital space where Ahmed meant to foster "self-love and retrospection via the struggles, beauty and power of parents of color," along with a Twitter handle of the same name.

The *See Something, Say Something* podcast, which began in October 2016 after he was already an established Buzzfeed reporter covering Muslim lives in the United States, reflects Ahmed's own life experiences: growing up in a diverse, close-knit Muslim community in a majority white, non-Muslim city; engaging in humanizing outreach work for non-Muslim audiences; and developing community through, and audiences for, his digital work. The original pitch for the show, which Ahmed shared with me, is instructive.

From its start, he explained, the show had three core goals. First, to provide a platform for Muslim voices that is representative of different experiences. Second, to use storytelling to complicate the idea of what it means to be a Muslim in America beyond how they are typically represented, both by media and by Muslims themselves. And third, to develop a broad audience base by plugging into national conversations about race, religion, and immigration, both within and outside of Muslim communities in the United States and North America. Significantly, as Ahmed himself pitched to producers, "Ideally, the show does not fit into a niche of speaking exclusively to Muslims, nor exclusively explaining to non-Muslims. I want us to cover all sorts of experiences in an intersectional way. Talking class, gender, sexuality, race, religion, and more."[19]

Like Mychal Denzel Smith, Ahmed saw *See Something, Say Something* as a space in which Muslims—himself, his guests, listeners—could explore the world in which they live and imagine the world in which they want to live. Like Kiese Laymon, Ahmed envisioned *See Something, Say Something*, which he often shortens to "*See Something*" on the show, as also having multiple registers, as being available and meaningful to diverse audiences, or publics, for different reasons.

In the series preview, Ahmed explains, "This is a show where we talk about our experiences, and not for Muslims—or on behalf of all Muslims— like we are so often asked to do." He continues, "And as a Muslim myself, I want to talk about the burden of representation that Muslims feel right now."[20] The point of the show is very much *not* to represent Muslims, but rather to "think about big life questions," human questions, as Muslims.

The list of episode topics would be familiar to anyone living today, especially in the United States, whatever their identity. Ahmed and his guests— writers, poets, scholars, musicians, organizers, journalists, politicians, among many others—discuss a huge range of issues: relationships, pop culture, race, parents, food, music, holidays, television, podcasts, self-care, mental health, addiction, the supernatural, religion, gender, sexuality, and #metoo. They talk about how these and other topics unfold in Muslim lives, their lives, often situating their own experiences in the broader context of being Muslim in America.

Unsurprisingly, anti-Muslim sentiment figures into many of these discussions. Even with long histories of anti-Muslim sentiment in the United States, the podcast's first full year unfolded amid a backdrop of staggering levels of anti-Muslim hostility and activity, ranging from everyday harassment and violence to several attempts by the federal government to enact Muslim bans. These realities color most episodes and even play a central place in some of them. Despite this backdrop, the podcast continued, and continues, to explore big life questions and the full range of joys, complexities, and sorrows of human life.

Through its presentation of the reality of diverse Muslim experiences, *See Something, Say Something* is able to engage life questions in a way that avoids moralizing. An excellent example of its approach in this regard is a two-part series on intoxicants. In the first episode, Najam Haider, a professor of religion at Barnard College, visits for an episode called "Lost in the Sauce." Haider discusses alcohol consumption from legal and historical perspectives, intoxication in Sufi devotional practices, coffee culture, and debates about trace amounts of alcohol in desserts. In the second episode, author and activist Arnesa Buljusmic-Kustura discusses drinking culture in Bosnian Muslim communities, trauma and alcoholism, gender and drinking, and social pressure related to drinking.

With these two episodes, *See Something, Say Something* takes on the idea that "Muslims don't drink," a generalization that operates both within Muslim communities to police boundaries of "Muslimness" and outside of Muslim communities to further stereotypes about all Muslims being especially, and often dangerously, "religious." In other words, the episodes operate within different registers simultaneously. They contribute thoughtfully to debates within Muslim communities (and families) *and*, without sacrificing any nuance necessary to make the material meaningful to Muslim listeners, offer a way for non-Muslims to think beyond flattened media representations of Muslims.

Importantly, many of the topics in these particular episodes are relevant to contemporary human experience in general. Social pressures around drinking, especially as they relate to gender expectations, are a part of many young peoples' lives in the United States, with effects that extend well into adulthood. Trauma and alcoholism, or addiction more generally, affect lives of all kinds. These are big life questions, and the podcast's episodes offer learning opportunities to Muslims and non-Muslims alike, even if in different ways. In this sense, "Lost in the Sauce" illustrates an approach to humanizing Muslims—and thus countering anti-Muslim sentiment— that does not place a burden on Muslims in the process. It is an approach that allows a Muslim host and Muslim guests to delve into sensitive topics without centering non-Muslim publics, maintaining in some ways a counterpublic that is purposefully aloof from the needs or demands of dominant publics. At the same time, it is this very approach, especially in a digital medium like podcasting that is given to intimate interviews and conversations, that appeals to listeners in search of content that feels "authentic."

It's Like I'm Eavesdropping

During one interview, Ahmed shared that according to his best estimates about a third of *See Something, Say Something* listeners are non-Muslim. So, what is it that draws these listeners to a podcast that is not primarily meant for them? With his support, I engaged Ahmed's significant social media following, circulating a short survey to learn more about Muslim and non-Muslim listeners alike. Almost all of the responses I received were from non-Muslim listeners. I chose three respondents for follow-up interviews. What I learned from them underscores the promise of digital Islam to engage non-Muslim audiences, performing "humanizing" work without the burden of catering to them specifically.

Each of the three non-Muslim listeners I selected identify as female, reflecting the overall trend of survey respondents. Each is also a member of dominant publics in the United States. All are white, two identify as Christian, and one as not particularly religious. All three are originally from the midwest and describe themselves as liberal politically. While their political leanings may give pause about the efficacy of digital Islam as a tool to reach beyond those who already might be inclined to seek out opportunities to learn about people different from themselves, it is essential to point out that anti-Muslim sentiment is not particular to any political or demographic group.[21] Questions about the "Americanness" of Muslims cut across political and ideological commitments.

Moreover, as with racism in general, anti-Muslim sentiment extends beyond explicitly Islamophobic attitudes—the reach of common misconceptions about Muslims affects everyone, including sometimes Muslims themselves. As I learned in my interviews with Ahmed and *See Something, Say Something* listeners, the humanizing potential of digital expressions of Islam includes helping people of all backgrounds, identities, and political persuasions learn how to be more inclusive of Muslim neighbors and fellow community members.

One person I interviewed, Alice, grew up with a number of Muslims in Michigan. She said that she was struck with how big a gap there was between her own experiences and what she began hearing about Muslims in the wake of September 11. In my interview with her, Alice noted, "I did not think Muslim people were scary or violent or any of those things because they were just my friends and neighbors."[22] Still, because Muslims were simply friends and neighbors when she was growing up in the years preceding September 11, she had never bothered to learn all that much about how their lives—or considered how their experiences—might have been different from her own. *See Something, Say Something*, therefore, offers Alice an opportunity to continue to learn without burdening those in her life.

In her questionnaire response, Alice stated, "As a white, non-Muslim woman, it [*See Something, Say Something*] gives me a chance to 'eavesdrop' on Muslim conversations and then when I talk about issues with my Muslim friends I am working from a more educated space."[23] I followed up with Alice on this point during our interview. "Right after Trump's election and the Muslim travel ban," she said, "living in an area where I do have some Muslim friends and work in an area with a Muslim population, I was sort of feeling at a loss trying to be the well-intentioned white lady, but to do that in a way that is not more about me than about the people most affected." The podcast, in her view, helped her be a better friend and ally: "Hearing conversations between Muslims, where I'm not there as a factor, made me feel less dumb when checking in and spending time with Muslim friends and people I work with." Hearing these conversations, she said, gave her some insights into how Muslims might be feeling and what they might have on their minds. "The fact that it's not for me," she noted, "is what makes it useful."

Alice singled out some *See Something, Say Something* episodes that were especially meaningful for her given the particulars of her own life. She noted that when she was growing up, she was not very aware of Black Muslims, but "Now that I'm in Detroit, that's a bigger presence in public life and the history of the city." Invoking an episode with an *imam* from Michigan, Abdurrahim Rashada, who had begun his life as a Muslim in the Nation of Islam and eventually settled in a Sunni community, Alice said, "Hearing that history directly from someone who was involved enriched my knowledge a lot. I definitely run into a lot of people in Detroit who were part of the Nation, or who grew up in the nation, and have gone in different directions since then."

Alice also mentioned episodes centering on the Muslim ban enacted early in 2017. Alice explained that she works at a time bank, which organizes bartering arrangements between community members, and the neighborhood the time bank serves has a significant Yemeni community. The podcast episodes on the Muslim ban helped educate Alice and her friends and colleagues in a way that made them more sensitive to how the policy might be affecting others in their lives, especially those with family in Yemen. These comments demonstrate how *See Something, Say Something*, as a digital resource that is not for her but is available to her, has made Alice a better friend, neighbor, and service provider. For others, the benefits of listening to the podcast may be a bit more attenuated—though no less significant—given how the show helps them navigate whiteness in America—in themselves and across their social circles.

Like Alice, another listener, Megan, noted that one of the great values of the podcast is that it provides a public space in which Muslims do not need to think of non-Muslim listeners. As such, it creates a positive space for Muslims that simultaneously benefits, and challenges, other listeners. Guests on the show, she said, "aren't apologizing for who they are, and I don't think they need to. That matters. I try to encourage people to listen—that may not be their comfort zone. I like to get people out of their comfort zone."[24] It is important to note that Megan works in Presbyterian ministry.

Given her background, Megan finds the podcast an especially valuable resource for people who might be hesitant about learning about Muslims or Islam. In her words, "I get to say, 'This is a really great podcast,' and I know if people listen to it, they're not going to . . . it's not scary. If you are scared of the world that you don't know, listen. Just listen in and understand that you don't need to be afraid of what you don't know." Although Megan did not use the word "eavesdrop," there is some resonance between Alice's description and the way that Megan views the value of *See Something, Say Something* for non-Muslim, and presumably white, audiences.

For another listener, Maureen, *See Something, Say Something* has been part of a larger effort to burst the white bubble in which she was raised. She began seeking out resources after experiencing what she described as a "white privilege wakeup moment." Not knowing where to go from there, she outlined the process that followed: "The first thing I can do is start getting different inputs. Media was the easiest way."[25] Maureen found that she was most engaged by media produced by, and largely for, people of color. That was, she noted, one of the reasons she likes the podcast: "It feels like sitting in and observing what's really happening in real Muslim lives— not someone trying to tell me about it."

Unlike Alice, Maureen does not live in an area with Muslim communities. Still, the diversity of the Muslim community that the podcast shares with listeners helps her remember that people who have similar backgrounds, or who share some parts of their identities, may very well have very different views and experiences of the world. In this way, *See Something, Say Something*, a show not meant for her but available to her, reminds Maureen to keep doing the work of avoiding assumptions about Muslims in America and, more generally, anyone else she encounters in life. It is a simple but significant point, a big life question.

Conclusion

In this chapter, I have used *See Something, Say Something* as a case study of "stream if you want" humanization that *also* constitutes the work that Muslims might already want to do regarding big life questions *within* Muslim communities. The podcast is primarily for Muslim publics—or perhaps counterpublics—yet it also benefits members of dominant publics in ways that programming meant specifically for them may not. I want to emphasize that my purpose is not to dissuade people from engaging in community-building across local publics and counterpublics through IRL work. Rather, I write to show the potential of "stream if you want" digital Islam as a *complement* to other forms of humanizing outreach—and perhaps even to suggest that the "stream if you want" approach could work well IRL, too.[26]

One of Ahmed's initial goals in seeking digital connections with other Muslims was to build community among those who had questions about "common understandings of being Muslim." *See Something, Say Something* is an extension of that goal, and its focus on diverse, intersecting Muslim identities and experiences creates learning opportunities for Muslims who, like him, seek community with those beyond their immediate circles. As my interviews with Alice, Megan, and Maureen demonstrate, the podcast also creates distinctive learning opportunities for non-Muslims, even if—and perhaps because—that is not its primary objective.

Podcasts, as instances of digital Islam, are especially conducive to creating such varied opportunities simultaneously. The barrier to entry for podcasts is very low for listeners. They are available on demand, typically at no cost, and are therefore accessible to a wide variety of publics. Unlike forms of media that require watching or reading, people—in our case Muslims or non-Muslims—can engage podcasts as they go about other activities, discretely listening to others who may share their values, challenge their values, or open their eyes to worlds they had not imagined.

As a podcast, *See Something, Say Something* is an especially interesting example of the Humanizing Potential of Digital Islam because it is crowdfunded, offering a model for projects in which people can participate through financial support without the same kind of burden in time and energy as IRL humanizing work requires. As Ahmed explains in his pitch on Patreon, a popular crowdfunding platform, most of the financial support people provide goes to producing the podcast; some funds go to paying his bills, which feels like a fair arrangement given that the podcast is professional work in the public service. It is not volunteer service. With greater investment in instances of digital Islam like *See Something, Say Something* my hope is that IRL engagement with different publics could become an activity that is less a necessity and more a source of nourishment for Muslim communities in the United States.

CHAPTER 5

Latinx Muslim Digital Landscapes:

Locating Networks and Cultural Practices

Madelina Nuñez and Harold D. Morales

Introduction

For his 2005 *Los Angeles Times* article titled "Embracing Islam, Praying for Acceptance," journalist H. G. Reza interviewed several individuals who identified as Latino Muslim, including Richard Silva who embraced Islam in 2002. During this interview, Silva related that many of his family members and friends were "baffled" by his new religiosity: "They ask why I want to change my culture. I tell them I'm changing religion, not culture. I still eat tortillas."[1] Categorical divisions between religious and cultural identities within Latinx Muslim communities are diverse, complex, and emplaced. In addition to about a dozen communities that meet in cities with large Latinx and Muslim populations, Latinx Muslim discourse has proliferated within growing and changing cyberspaces. Latinx Muslim cyberspaces have complex relations to ethnic, religious, gendered, and city spaces. Attention to the categorical divisions made between religion and culture—and between different kinds of spaces by both Latinx Muslims and the researchers who work with them—allows for more nuanced engagements beyond those focused solely on issues of "convert identity."

Today, Muslim communities in the United States are continuously growing. A Pew Research Center report estimates that by 2040, Muslims will be the United States' second-largest religious group.[2] Individuals who identify as or are identified as Latinx have been embracing Islam since the 1920s for various reasons. As the overall Muslim population in the United States continues to expand, the Latinx Muslim population is also expected to grow alongside it. According to a survey of Latinx Muslims published in 2017, over 93 percent of the participants were not raised as Muslims. Most chose to embrace Islam for its theological, ritual, or aesthetic appeal. Many cited theological beliefs, the communal character of Islamic prayer, and the beauty of the Qur'ān when recited out loud as principal reasons for their conversion. The individuals or relationships that first introduced participants to Islam also played a significant role: many first learned about Islam through a friend, relative, future spouse, colleague, or mediated interlocutors. Finally, space seems to have played an important role in these decisions as well. Cities, homes, workspaces, school campuses, media (pamphlets, newspapers, books, radio, television, and the internet) were also cited as inspiring *shahādah* (the proclamation of faith). Questions regarding why Latinxs are choosing to embrace Islam have garnered quite a bit of journalistic attention and an increasing amount of scholarly inquiry as well.[3] Even so, most scholars have largely located Latinx Muslims within "official" sites, including mosques and Islamic centers, journalistic productions, and, more recently, organizational websites. The result has been an overemphasis on issues around conversion and identity.

This chapter traces the interplay between identity and community formation by engaging diverse Latinx Muslim activities within different cyberspaces. We begin with a brief chronology from the 1990s to 2017, in which we describe early activities within listservs, AOL (America Online) chatrooms, institutional websites, and a digital newsletter. Scholarly engagements with interlocutors in these "official" or "traditional" sites, we argue, have focused primarily on issues of conversion and identity, and as such have inspired particular categorical or conceptual divisions between religion and culture and between individuals and the spaces they inhabit. The second part of this chapter therefore explores more recent activities within new cyberspaces on social media, cloud file sharing, streaming platforms, and video conference rooms, with a particular attention to Latinx Muslim foodways (*halāl*, Latinx food) online. We conclude by outlining the overall limitations of engaging Latinx Muslims primarily within "traditional" spaces, pointing to other possible trajectories for future scholarship.

La Alianza Islámica

Some of the earliest references to Latinx Muslims in the United States date back to the 1920s. These include ethnographic accounts of industrial farms in California, where workers from Mexico and the Indian Punjab sometimes came into contact with one another, as well as in Ahmadi newsletters listing "converts" with surnames likely from Latin America.[4] In a 2010 article, "Early U.S. Latina/o-African-American Muslim Connections: Paths to Conversion," Patrick Bowen documented other possible references to individuals embracing Islam through the Moorish Science Temple of America, the Nation of Islam, Five Percenter Nation, the National Party of North America, and other groups. The first communities of Latinx Muslims emerged in the 1970s through the Bani Saqr—about which not much is known—and in the 1980s through the work of La Alianza Islámica.[5]

Several of the Alianza's early members had been a part of other Islamic and non-Islamic liberation movements and organizations. Three of its cofounders, Yahya Figueroa, Rahim Ocasio, and Ibrahim Gonzales, converted to Islam at a time when they were seeking for a spiritual core to their social justice work. The Alianza thus engaged in *da'wah* (the propagation and teaching of Islam) and justice activism as two sides of the same coin which they deployed within their Latinx communities located in the barrios of New York. Over time, the Alianza's leadership became weary of new forms of potential "spiritual colonization" by African American and immigrant Muslim communities. Within this context, Al-Andalus (sometimes referred to as "Islamic Spain") served as an inspiration for self-determination, offering a powerful narrative for framing Latinidad (Latinx ways of being) as rooted in Islamic culture and civilization.

In several interviews and self-published works, leaders from the Alianza affirmed that the group was born of struggle: an attempt to resist European and US colonization, as well as non-Latinx Muslim spiritual colonization, to shape their own self-determination and to develop their own interpretive authority and spaces. The storefronts they were able to procure served as economic, social service, and spiritual hubs for their work and lives. Their efforts were aimed primarily at improving the lives of their Latinx communities that had been ravaged by systems of oppression, including income, housing, and food insecurity; the proliferation of drugs and the racist war on drugs; the AIDS epidemic and other health disparities; and the pervasive lack of quality education capable of offering alternative realities to these disparities. The spaces that the Alianza worked within were thus complex and varied: racial/ethnic, colonized, liberationist/activist, economic, spiritual/religious, and urban/barrios. When the organization's doors in New York closed in 2005, its leaders decided not to shift to online platforms. In a 2016 interview, Rahim Ocasio argued that the work they were doing with "broken people" (i.e., psychologically and economically colonized people) could simply not be replicated within virtual spaces.[6] In between the birth, dissolution, and rebirth of the Alianza in 2017, numerous Latinx Muslim organizations emerged, including PIEDAD, LADO, LALMA, IslamInSpanish, and several others—each with its own distinct approach to emerging cyberspaces.

PIEDAD

Khadijah Rivera founded PIEDAD in 1987 as a solidarity group for women who had embraced Islam. Named after the Spanish word for "piety," PIEDAD also served as an acronym for *Propagación Islamica para la Educación de Ala el Divino*, "Islamic Propagation for Education on and Devotion to Allah the Divine." The organization began in New York and subsequently established offices in Florida, Chicago, Georgia, Illinois, and New Jersey. Most of its members were Latinx women who married men who had immigrated to the United States from Muslim-majority societies. The group helped to support its members as they navigated difficult questions that involved categorical divisions between religion and culture/ethnicity. These debates involved a range of issues, including whether veiling (and religious dress more broadly) is a religious or cultural practice; Islam's impact on culinary and eating practices; and the permissibility of Latinx Muslims attending their family's Christmas gatherings.

Like La Alianza Islámica, PIEDAD's mission also included educational and *da'wah* programs. Unlike the Alianza, however, PIEDAD (like most other Latinx Muslim organizations) did not have the resources to obtain a physical space of its own. Instead, PIEDAD typically held meetings at homes, Islamic centers, mosques, and cyberspaces. The group also maintained a toll-free number, 1-800-44-ALLAH, through a collaborative effort of its chapters in order to provide a channel through which anyone could access the group's educational and *da'wah* services. Interested individuals or recent converts/reverts could talk to and learn about Islam from a PIEDAD member and set up a face-to-face meeting. PIEDAD's phone service was eventually replaced with a more cost-effective, basic blog that provided basic information on Islam and updates on the organization's events while also serving as an archive. Eventually, PIEDAD developed a simple website that had a few informational articles but was used mostly for connecting people through email addresses. In the early 2000s, its website was replaced with a professionally designed site by Iman Studios, which allowed for massive amounts of information in various formats (including YouTube videos) to be uploaded or embedded without much training in web design or coding.

On November 22, 2009, Khadija Rivera passed away. On the *Suhaib Webb .com* virtual mosque, one participant posted in her honor:

> she not only fed empty stomachs, she touched hearts, of the fallen and downtrodden. she not only believed in what she said, she had set an example of mutual respect and dignity for those who have lost it in the eyes of the world. I pray and hope that Allah Almighty has honored her with the best of rewards and saved her from hellfire.[7]

Following in Rivera's footsteps, Nylka Vargas began leading the group from New Jersey, working closely with the North Hudson Islamic Center and the annual Hispanic Muslim Day hosted there. Although PIEDAD's blog was never updated following Rivera's passing, it remains as an immaculately preserved archive. The group's last Facebook entry dates to 2013. Its website subsequently went untouched for several years until it was stripped down, like a crumbling archive; in 2021, its hosting expired and is now defunct.

LADO

Virtual chat rooms emerged in the 1990s, providing an alternative space where people—many without an existence outside of these cyberspaces—could develop specialized enclaves and discuss a variety of topics including religion.[8] It was in one of these chatrooms that the three cofounders of the Latino American Dawah Organization (LADO), Juan Alvarado, Samantha Sanchez, and Saraji Umm Zaid, met and began working together. As their group grew, the trio established an email news list, solicited requests for Islamic literature in Spanish to both its members and larger Islamic organizations, and shared any materials they received with their virtual community. In 1997, they named their group the Latino American Dawah Organization, or LADO, embracing slogans such as "Puro Latino! ¡Puro Islam! ¡A su LADO!" ("Fully Latino! Fully Islamic! At your side!"). Like PIEDAD, the group concluded that "a website would be the most cost-efficient way of offering free information about Islam."[9] Using a personal AOL homepage, LADO was able to initiate *The Latino Muslim Voice*, the longest-running and most prominent newsletter by and on Latinx Muslims. Its articles included Qur'ānic quotes of the month, discussions on doctrinal issues, news events on Islam and Latinx Muslims, and announcements for (and coverage about) organizational programs, poetry, songs, recipes, and other cultural exchanges.

In 2001, Juan Galvan joined LADO remotely from his home in Texas. While searching for other Latinx Muslims, Juan came across LADO's website, joined the group, and eventually became its director. Galvan's skills in management information systems proved to be a pivotal catalyst in the development of LADO's online presence and that of several other Latinx Muslim organizations which he designed and maintained. Galvan procured the now dominant *LatinoDawah.org* domain name, initiated an ongoing online census of Latinx Muslims, and collected reversion stories with Sanchez on *HispanicMuslims.com*. The website has since been replaced by the book *Latino Muslims: Our Journeys to Islam,* which is available on Amazon in both print and digital formats.[10] Over time, LADO was endorsed by both the Islamic Society of North America (ISNA) and the Islamic Circle of North America (ICNA), was featured in various news media outlets including the *Islamic Horizons* magazine, established relationships with various other Muslim organizations across the United

States, and produced a Yahoo Group with limited editorial involvement. In January 2002, LADO overhauled its website and eventually included a Spanish-language version.

By the 2010s, LADO's flagship website was receiving almost 90,000 visits per month and consistently dominated search engine queries for "Latino Muslims" and "Hispanic Muslims."[11] For many years, LADO's site served as a hub and gatekeeper to publicly accessible information on and by Latinx Muslims. Over time, LADO became one of the most widely recognized and well-connected Latinx Muslim organizations in the United States, and continues to play a prominent role in the public sphere. Despite the group's online prominence, Galvan continues to stress that it is not a "virtual or online community." Instead, he describes the mosque as the "center of Islamic life" and LADO's website as nothing more than a tool.

LALMA

The Los Angeles Latino Muslim Association (LALMA) was founded in 1999 as a Qur'ān study group by a small collection of individuals that included its current director, Marta Galedary. It presently meets at *Masjid Omar Ibn al-Khattab*. In its early years, much of LALMA's Spanish-language literature on Islam was downloaded from a website in Spain: *VerdeIslam.com*. LALMA used many of its documents for its own study sessions, including works by the famous medieval Persian philosopher, theologian, and mystic, al-Ghazālī (1058–1111 CE). During these formative years, access and dial-up speeds proved to be prohibitive, so one document was downloaded at a time before being printed, photocopied, and distributed among members who congregated on Sunday mornings at the mosque.

Beyond its Sunday morning study sessions, LALMA continues to participate in interfaith dialogues, maintain information booths at LA's Fiesta Broadway and other public events, and host carne asadas at Elysian Park overlooking Dodger Stadium. In addition, the group sponsors weddings, baby showers, and presentations where the members share *hajj* experiences, and coordinates *shahādah* and potluck celebrations that often include combinations of Arab and Mexican food platters. After taking *shahādah* (the testimony of faith), new members were previously given a physical three-volume copy of Muhammad Asad's translation of the Qur'ān, which included some Arabic calligraphy and Arabic text, Spanish transliteration, and Spanish translations along three columns on each page with a corresponding Spanish-language commentary at the bottom. Today, new members are instead emailed a digital PDF copy which only includes the Spanish text of Asad's original translation and commentary.

LALMA has recently undergone several additional changes. It has become increasingly active with the interreligious faith-based activist organization, PICO California; its acronym now stands for La Asociación Latino Musulmana de América (the Latin/o American Muslim Association) to reflect its transnational connections to Latin America; and its website, *LALMA.net*—which was initially primarily in English before transitioning to bilingual—is now exclusively in Spanish since the majority of the group's membership speaks only Spanish.

IslamInSpanish

The IslamInSpanish group was founded by Mujahid Fletcher in the aftermath of September 11, 2001, and the increased media attention on Muslims and Islam that put him in the public spotlight. Determined to increase the number of "quality" multimedia information on Islam in the Spanish language, he and others founded IslamInSpanish as a 501(c)(3) in order "to become the trusted source of Islamic Multimedia resources and products to educate Latinos in the Spanish language worldwide."[12] The group has produced over 500 audio books and 250 videos. Like other organizations before them, IslamInSpanish also emphasizes a connection with Islam in Spain and celebrates Islamic influences on Latinx culture through its digital media productions. The group relies primarily on its *IslamInSpanish.org* website, as well as its independent YouTube and SoundCloud channels. One of its videos titled "Raices Islamicas en la Cultura Latina" ("Islamic Roots in Latino Culture") was published in 2011 and has been viewed nearly 1,200 times. Another video, "Scientific Miracles in the Quran," garnered 39,328 views and 488 comments. By 2015, IslamInSpanish maintained nearly 170 videos on YouTube, 128 audio tracks on their SoundCloud site, and weekly live streams of its Friday sermons.

Given this reliance on services like YouTube and the usage data it makes available, the group's cyberspaces are envisioned as platforms for spotlighting the historical-cultural connection between al-Andalus, Spain, and Latinidad. These historical and cultural networks are displayed visually through images of the Alhambra in Granada, the Mosque of Cordoba's interior grid of red and white double horseshoe arches, and a mural by artist Brandon Berrios featuring Andalusian geometric patterns. The "Islamic Roots in Latino Culture" video similarly highlights several Islamic contributions to Latinx culture and the development of a *convivencia* (coexistence) celebrated as an instance of successful religious pluralism or at the very least of tolerant policies and practices. Like many other Latinx Muslim cyberspaces, the video contains lists of Spanish-language names and words that have roots in Arabic, including the terms "azucar y arroz" ("sugar and rice").[13]

Up until the mid-2010s, Latinx Muslim cyberspaces were, in fact, dominated by theological texts and references to the Islamic roots of Latinx culture. The IslamInSpanish group's name itself highlights a prominent feature of most Latinx Muslim activity online: the use of "Spanish language," in all its forms, as a signifier for both Latinx culture and its Islamic roots. Significantly, the group is the only organization to procure its own physical space since La Alianza Islámica. Through its center in Houston, IslamInSpanish has nurtured a physical community while developing multimedia for its various cyberspaces at a dizzying pace. Given these multifacted, coordinated efforts, it is well positioned to expand its presence and influence beyond its current physical and virtual borders.

Organizational Developments from 2010 to 2020

In 2015, IslamInSpanish held a grand opening for their new Islamic Center in Houston, Texas. Yahya Figueroa marked the occasion with an open letter titled "A Lifetime of Reclaiming Our Islamic Heritage," which was distributed widely on email, Facebook, and other cyberspaces. Less than two weeks later, this letter and several articles were posted as entries on the newly minted La Alianza Islámica blog at *AlianzaIslamica.org*. A month later, another dozen posts were published on the website, effectively reestablishing the group—but this time almost exclusively within cyberspace.

In addition to the revived Alianza, PIEDAD, LADO, LALMA, and IslamInSpanish, several other Latinx Muslims groups have emerged in recent years. This includes the Latino Muslims of the Bay Area, the Chicago Association of Latino American Muslims, Hablamos Islam out of New Jersey, the Tri-State Latino Muslims in the East Coast, the Atlanta Latino Muslim Association, and the Ojalá Foundation in Chicago, among various others. These new organizations are as fractured as they are numerous. Though most of these groups also promote connections between Latinx culture and its Islamic roots, the very terms "Latino" and "Muslim" remain highly contested even within Latinx Muslim discourse. On social media feeds some contributors are critical and others are supportive of the use of the term "Latinx" over "Latino." On another online forum, an anonymous user made the following comment regarding the signification of Latinidad for uniting all the different Latinx Muslim groups: "Our meetings usually got stuck around food [and] what cultural dishes would be most appropriate. . . . We have to have rice and beans, but what style beans? Black or Pinto Beans? Central American style, Caribbean style or Mexican Style"[14] In fact, various attempts have been made to overcome ethnic and religious differences among these diverse communities. A prominent example is the League of Latino American Muslim Organizations (LLAMO), whose website emerged in 2010.[15] Despite its organizer's vision, however, LLAMO never became more than a mission statement and website because its constituent groups could not agree on how to consolidate their resources and develop an authoritative body for its administrative management. LLAMO's short-lived and now stagnant representation in cyberspace therefore offers a poignant reminder that a unified Latinx Muslim community continues to exist more as a disparate set of online visions than as an offline, "real world," lived experience.

By locating Latinx Muslims within organizational spaces, whether online or offline, scholars are continuously forced to wrestle with questions regarding collective authority, hierarchical resource distribution, failed unifications, fractures, and conflict. We propose instead that by working with Latinx Muslim networks outside of official organizational spaces, a new set of questions become available for scholarly inquiry, including those regarding Latinx foods and foodways.

Ḥalāl, Latinx Foods, and Foodways

The issues that exist within the spectrum of "Latinx" and "Muslim" become ever more critical as these communities grow, interact, and collaborate. Even so, most scholars who have worked with Latinx Muslims have largely located the group in organizational spaces. Though much of this work includes cyberspaces in addition to physical ones, both locations are nevertheless primarily limited to "official" organizational institutions—and this approach has had significant consequences. One outcome of this narrow framing has been the myopic focus on issues of identity, conversion, and conflict. Scholars have yet to fully examine or substantially engage other possibilities, such as the foodways of Latinx Muslims. This area of study is of particular interest since much of traditional Latinx food includes the use of ingredients that are Islamically *ḥarām*, or forbidden, such as pork.

The presence of *ḥalāl* food in the United States is on the rise. In 2016, sales of *ḥalāl* food in grocery and convenience stores increased 15 percent from 2012, and the overall sales of *ḥalāl* food in these spaces reached 1.9 billion dollars.[16] *Ḥalāl*, meaning permissible, encompasses many areas of life outside of cuisine. For many food items, the Qur'ān clearly delineates the distinction between *ḥalāl* and *ḥarām*: "People, eat what is good and lawful from the earth . . . [God] has only forbidden you carrion, blood, pig's meat, and animals over which any name other than God's has been invoked" (Qur'an 2:168).[17] According to the Qur'ān, Muslims must eat foods that are both *ḥalāl* and *dhabīḥah* (ritually slaughtered). As Robinson notes, "For meat to be considered *ḥalāl*, Qur'ānic law requires that the animal be killed in a specific way: God must be invoked and, to avoid prolonged suffering, a carotid artery and the trachea must be cut with a sharp knife."[18] These ritual prescriptions, including the draining of the animal's blood and invoking the name of God during slaughter, are what distinguishes *dhabīḥah* meats as permissible (*ḥalāl*) for consumption.

As Latinx food often includes *ḥarām* items such as pork, the narration surrounding the creation of *ḥalāl* Latinx food becomes particularly important. After all, food not only is a reflection of community but also serves as a source of cultural memory. In her printed cookbook *My Halal Kitchen*, Yvonne Maffei is explicit in linking her food's relationship to her own cultural memories. As a half Sicilian, half Puerto Rican writer from the Midwest, Maffei mentions that due to her mother's Puerto Rican origin, "meals with her side of the family were abundant with arroz con frijoles, pasteles wrapped in banana leaves, and sweet guava and coconut desserts . . . these experiences connect good food with the people I cherish most."[19] The memories that are developed, and maintained, through food tie Latinx individuals to a greater imagined community of Latinidades (a shared sense of Latinx identity). In this sense, food becomes a medium used to further explore and define Latinx Muslim identity and relationships with Muslims, non-Muslims, and the self. According to Maffei, "I discovered that I was in the middle of two worlds . . . my goal is to bridge the gap between the two worlds in which I live."[20]

The bridging that Maffei describes may also be understood as a border crossing—an embracement of the borderlands between dichotomous understandings of "Latinx" and "Muslim." Through food, namely *ḥalāl*, Latinx foodways, Latinx Muslims are traversing these liminal spaces and finding ways to confront binary thinking around these communities.[21] For Latinx Muslims, food confronts the binaries that underlie communal friction. As Hjamil A. Martínez-Vazquez argues, "Most of the food they [Latinxs] eat is either made with a base in lard . . . since we cannot eat that, they [family and friends] just stopped preparing it because they wanted to avoid confrontation . . . it was better to avoid it."[22] The ability to learn and embrace the concept of *ḥalāl*, Latinx food as not only a possibility but a means of cultural expression becomes critical. An examination of *ḥalāl*, Latinx online food spaces therefore helps us understand both individual eating habits and the continued sharing of these foods communally, both online and offline.

Latinx Muslim Food Blogging

This chapter began with a quotation from Silva, a recent convert, or revert, to Islam who stated, "I tell them I'm changing religion, not culture. I still eat tortillas." Yvonne Maffei not only still eats tortillas, she also teaches others how to cook up something delicious to put inside. She has abundant recipes for beef tacos, lime chicken tacos with tomatillo salsa, and even chicken tikka masala tacos. These particular recipes can be found on her website, *myhalalkitchen.com*, which she launched in 2008 before the eventual release of a 2016 cookbook under the same title.[23] Maffei and her *ḥalāl* kitchen have garnered 1.5 million followers on Facebook and nearly 40,000 followers on Instagram as of 2021. "Thank you," she says on the website, "for joining me here to learn how to make *any* type of global cuisine *Halal*." Maffei has gained a significant following—and developed a distinct space for her food and community—through the development of her own popular online platform.

Although there are a host of Latinx Muslim food bloggers who have not developed—and will not develop—Maffei's level of engagement, they are nevertheless impacting the sharing of (and discussions around) *ḥalāl*, Latinx foodways. One such individual who lacks a dedicated platform but is still making significant contributions is Anisa Abeytia. A "third-generation Mexican American," Abeytia embraced Islam in 2007. Nine years after she embraced Islam, she wrote "Curries, Tajeens, and Moles," an article that explores her relationship to and with Islam through a discussion of foods.[24] "Food was one of the ways I was first introduced to Islam," she asserts. While viewing food as a source of comfort, she describes her introduction both to Islam and to certain foods as a shock to the palate. For Abeytia, everything in the early stages of her journey to Islam, including the foods she ate along the way, was new and strange to her. Not only did she experience this discomfort within herself, but she reflects on how those around her, both Muslim and non-Muslim, were also surprised by a perceived collision of different worlds. "I sensed that I made people as uncomfortable as they made me," she admits about her journey toward Islam and into Islamic communities as a third-generation Mexican American, raised in the United States and accustomed to "a standard American diet."[25] Her time cooking in her kitchen became her means of navigating these shocks to the system. As she states, "[food] turns something novel and strange into something intimate."[26] She concludes her article by sharing eleven of her own recipes, including "The 'Shehabi' Burrito," "Chicken Marinated in Charmula with Mango/Papaya Salsa," and "Flan with Cardamom, Honey, and Pistachios." Through recipes, Abeytia aims to translate multiple worlds to others who may have a positionality at the intersection of "Latinx" and "Muslim" in the United States. She does this in order to help herself and others embrace what may seem at first uncomfortable.

While Maffei and Abeytia are food bloggers, they are in fact *ḥalāl* food bloggers. To be even more precise, they are Latinx Muslim *ḥalāl* food bloggers creating *ḥalāl*, Latinx recipes. These layers of increasing specificity are important since they reflect not only an appreciation of *ḥalāl*, Latinx foods but also contribute to the digital culture of food blogging as a whole. As Jennifer Lofgren notes, food blogs are critical culture makers and definers: "Food blogs have demonstrably revitalized an interest in recipe sharing among 'ordinary' people and provide a useful case study for understanding how our online and offline lives have become intertwined and showcase the Internet as a part of everyday life."[27] This focus on the ordinary and everyday practice of individuals has been a subject of particular interest to researchers, especially those interested in foods and the power and meaning these cuisines possess.

Food blogging has been described as establishing and creating "a role in inscribing the self with a sense of place, belonging and achievement."[28] Latinx Muslim food bloggers express these sentiments of belonging through the creation and sharing of *ḥalāl*, Latinx food in the everyday. This is an important point of emphasis, since the creation of a sense of place, both online and offline, is critical to the development of both self and communal identity. These autonomous choices, mirrored through the deployment of social media in the digital landscape, become even more important when we further recognize that the active agents in these digital creations have predominantly been Latinas. Meredith Abarca notes that "recipes are individual authorities . . . [and] in the act of piecing together recipes and creating new ones, women take authorship of their creation."[29] This is certainly the case with Latina food bloggers who are active culinary innovators—a form of power and artistry in and of itself. Through the sharing of their creative genius via the medium of food blogging, these women claim authority and further autonomy. As the mainstream media and academic literature often depict women's autonomy and their practice of Islam in other spaces and places, Latinx Muslim women food bloggers are actively exercising their cultural authority and creative talents through the online distribution of these recipes.

While these *ḥalāl*, Latinx recipes have their origins in negotiations of the self, they may also be derived from the broader context of social interactions. Through the act of food blogging their personal recipes, Latina chefs are inviting visitors to their websites to reproduce these foods in their own homes in order to establish what Meredith Abarca calls "communities of practice."[30] These shared practices establish a collective sense of self, place, and identity, formed through the everyday practices of creation, sharing, and, of course, eating *ḥalāl*, Latinx food online. As Jennifer Cognard-Black and Melissa A. Goldthwaite assert, "A recipe is both a handbook and a shared act of creation."[31] Like Maffei and Abeytia, we invite you to create, and share, whatever you decide to fill your tortillas with.

Taco Trucks at Every Mosque

Locating as well as establishing a shared sense of place is a critical act for Latinx Muslims. To this end, Taco Trucks at Every Mosque is an innovative initiative focused on bringing Latinx and Muslim communities together through the sharing of *ḥalāl* tacos. The campaign has gained traction across the country, garnering considerable media attention in the process.

Significantly, the initiative manages to share *ḥalāl*, Latinx foods while simultaneously creating a unique space and place for Latinx Muslims and for a Latinx Muslim collective identity. This placemaking manifests in digital landscapes throughout social media as much as it does in the physical landscapes and communities around *masjids* (mosques).

Taco Trucks at Every Mosque was established during the Trump era, as Latinx and Muslim communities were both faced with heightened xenophobia and racism. The need to solidify a shared sense of space and place was made clear during this time as the Trump administration's rhetoric and policies focused on marginalizing and dehumanizing racialized others. The project was launched in California by co-organizers Rida Hamida and Ben Vasquez in response to comments by Marco Gutierrez, founder of "Latinos for Trump," in a live interview on MSNBC: "My culture [Mexican] is a very dominant culture. It's imposing, and it's causing problems. If you don't do something about it, you're going to have taco trucks on every corner."[32] These anxieties over the loss of "American" space to racialized others rang out loud and clear. In a clever strategic rejoinder, organizers Hamida and Vasquez aimed to feed these same anxieties by fulfilling Gutierrez's prophecy of the threat of taco trucks on every corner. Going further, they also wanted them in front of every mosque, another space that triggers the xenophobic and racist fears of the loss of "American" space. Before becoming president, in 2010 Donald Trump offered to pay a reported six million dollars to halt the construction of a proposed Islamic Center near "Ground Zero" in New York City: the site of 9/11 and a key touchstone for American Islamophobia.[33] This heated public rhetoric should be read alongside a wide range of anti-immigrant and anti-Muslim campaigns. This includes what has come to be known as the "Trump Wall," a campaign proposal to build a physical barrier along the US-Mexico border, as well as Presidential Executive Order 13769 "Protecting the Nation from Foreign Terrorist Entry into the United States," otherwise known across the country as "The Muslim Ban." These discourses reveal a rampant fear that the "American" landscape is at risk of being lost to Latinx and Muslim spaces.[34]

The creation of a distinct Latinx Muslim sense of space, place, and belonging in digital and physical landscapes is a critical practice of resistance. In our view, the reclamations of identity via technologies of food, coupled with the strategic use of cyberspace, constitute forms of resistance against nationalistic forms of erasure. Latinx individuals have long been subjected to the state's history of dismissing the profound impact that Latinx communities have on landscapes. The American national project has, in fact, pursued an active erasure of Latinx peoples from land and space—and the entire "colonization process, an obviously spatial process, has had ongoing ramifications, and [Latinx and] Chicanx have felt and observed them to this day."[35] In this context, Latinx writing, particularly Chicanx writing, has been understood as a technology for "decolonizing the social imagination" by undoing dichotomous and binary socially constructed understandings of the self.[36] We interpret Latinx Muslim food creation and sharing, in all its various forms, through this same lens. In this sense, *ḥalāl*, Latinx food can be understood as a technology for undoing the socially constructed and binary borderland between "Latinx" and "Muslim." As its name suggests, Taco Trucks at Every Mosque asserts that the foods and peoples of Latinx, Muslim, and Latinx Muslim communities can lay claim to a sense of belonging. The campaign champions Latinx Muslims as an integral part of the American landscape—a critical assertion in a country where the state perpetually looks to deny racialized others a sense of space and place.

The Taco Trucks at Every Mosque initiative provided Muslims the opportunity to break the fast during the month of *Ramaḍān* with a perceived novelty: *ḥalāl* tacos. Latinx non-Muslims who were perhaps unfamiliar (and even uncomfortable) with Islam were encouraged to join communally with Muslims through the comfort of a familiar meal. For Latinx Muslims, Taco Trucks at Every Mosque served as a vehicle to unite communities together in a shared space—events they captured and circulated throughout various digital media. In doing so, they sent a clear message that Latinx Muslims and *ḥalāl*, Latinx foods are here to stay. A virtual campaign utilizing *#TacoTrucksatEveryMosque* on social media was a call to create space for Latinx Muslims, *ḥalāl*, Latinx food, and Latinx Muslim collectivism in cyberspace. This campaign has been particularly successful on Twitter and Instagram, with reports, photos, and tacos shared across the country. "Taco Trucks at Every Mosque is a project that will continue to grow and expand," Vasquez declared. "Not only will it expand geographically, but the program will grow into deeper conversations."[37] Those "deeper conversations" will be rooted in a decentralized collectivism as all of these communities begin to gain a further sense of place and belonging beyond traditional religious spaces—including in parking lots and hashtags. The visuality of the campaign remains salient as the media coverage continues and the social media hashtag gains new posts and photos. In these digital spaces, followers and onlookers alike are able to see Latinx Muslims, perhaps for the first time. As a result, Latinx Muslim sense of place and space has started to be established on every corner of the internet, making real Gutierrez's prediction, "You're going to have taco trucks on every corner."[38]

Conclusion

While Latinx Muslims have been part of the social fabric of the United States and the wider Americas for generations, a broader awareness and understanding of Latinx Muslim networks and cultural practices have emerged in tandem with the development of internet technologies. Diverse cyberspaces, both "official" and "unofficial," now provide vital alternative landscapes for Latinx Muslims. For those who live outside of major city centers, and therefore often suffer from isolation, these cyberspaces provide vital spaces for community-building and social networking. It is through these digital landscapes that Latinx Muslims are creating their own sense of space and community and, in the process, actively contribute to the development of distinct Latinx Muslim identities.

Scholarship on Latinx Muslims has increasingly paid attention to the role that space in general and cyberspace in particular play in the development of lived realities. This work has yielded important insights regarding how ethnic identity and Islamic authority are often reframed within digital media.[39] Another important insight regards the ways in which numerically small Muslim communities like Latinx Muslims navigate their marginalization within more expansive social networks (in this case within broader US groups, Latinx groups, and Muslim American groups). In some ways, internet technologies have democratized authority and expanded access to public discourse. At the same time, they have presented severe challenges, given the internet's commodification, access inequities, government surveillance practices, and misinformation. Latinx Muslim organizations have benefited from new opportunities within diverse cyberspaces, while also experiencing acute challenges such as increased community fracturing, internal conflict, censorship, limited access, and a lack of digital proficiency.

How and where Latinx Muslims are located shapes the kinds of questions, answers, and assumptions scholars develop of their lived realities. Framing Latinx Muslims within mosque and organizational spaces (both offline and online) has produced invaluable scholarly insights into conversion and racial/ethnic identity, as well as important perspectives on the broader issues regarding cyberspace and the development of solidarity groups. However, not enough attention has been given to "nonofficial" spaces outside of organizational mosques and websites. In her 2018 monograph *Being Muslim: A Cultural History of Women of Color in American Islam*, Sylvia Chan-Malik argues that because religion is embodied, our scholarship must center on theoretical and methodological aspects of space: physical, gendered, and ethnic.[40] With this insight in mind, scholarship on Muslim communities needs to pay increased attention to the relationship between space and embodiment, and how these dynamics shape specific interests and acts. As Sher Afgan Tareen illustrates, engagements with issues such as gender and Islamic authority are too often overdetermined by scholars who engage Islamic religious spaces through a religious studies legacy informed largely by an American white-settler Protestantism that locates Christian religion primarily within texts and church spaces. The result is a field of Islamic studies that focuses almost exclusively on the Qur'ān, commentaries on the Qur'ān, and on practices within mosques. By comparison, when we locate Islam within domestic spaces or private Islamic schools in the United States, argues Tareen, issues of gender and Islamic authority take a markedly different direction.[41]

Though these issues are of vital importance, we maintain that significant lacunas emerge through engagements limited only to official mosque and organizational spaces offline and online. In particular, we assert that locating Latinx Muslims primarily within these spaces has overdetermined the questions we ask and theories we develop about their everyday, lived realities. As we have seen in the case studies explored in this chapter, there are many questions that Latinx Muslims ask themselves and the larger community that go far beyond the initial inquiry, "Why do Latinxs convert to Islam?" For Latinx Muslims, the *shahādah* is only a first step. It is in the everyday lived experience and practice of Islam, where Latinx Muslims begin to ask deeper (and more difficult) questions of themselves and of their communities. Quotidian questions such as "where can I find others like myself," "puedo leer el Corán en español (can I read the Qur'ān in Spanish)?," and "how can I make my favorite tamales *halāl*?" point to the critical, everyday issues prevalent in these emerging cyberspaces. These digital platforms not only provide spaces where Latinx Muslims discover the freedom to ask and explore new questions, they also open up a distinct space and place for the experience of a Latinx Muslim collective identity. This placemaking manifests itself in social media as much as it does in the physical landscapes and official websites of communities and their public *masjids*. Thus, if we limit our critical and creative attention to "official" cyberspaces—the digital media of legally and institutionally recognized organizations—we are likely to overlook the borders where Latinx Muslim food creation and sharing meet with *halāl*, Latinx food. Going beyond a narrow focus on why Latinxs convert to Islam, the exploration of offline and online foodways offers a powerful counternarrative to the socially constructed and overly binary borderland between "Latinx" and "Muslim." We invite you to take a seat at the table in these landscapes, for it is in these everyday gatherings where community and identity are most fully experienced and enjoyed.

CHAPTER 6

Revisiting Digital Islamic Feminism:

Multiple Resistances, Identities, and Online Communities

Sahar Khamis

Introduction

With its transnational, borderless, and inclusive nature, the internet ushered in a new dawn for many religious communities around the world. The global Muslim community, or *ummah*, is no exception.[1] The availability of new digital media, with all their unique potentials, opened alternative pathways in the realms of political participation, civic engagement, religious education, and self-expression.[2] This is especially true in the case of marginalized groups, which have traditionally enjoyed less power and, therefore, had less access to the tools needed to amplify their voices and to make their needs, demands, and grievances heard.[3] Muslim women are no exception. This chapter investigates the dynamics of transnational gendered Muslim communities in cyberspace, shedding light on how these faith-based, digitalized groups of Muslim women, both at home and in the diaspora, are creating, negotiating, affirming, and challenging hybrid feminist identities via new media technologies—in particular internationally accessible and technologically enabled social media platforms such as Facebook groups and Twitter campaigns.[4]

This qualitative, feminist study provides an overview of the plethora of online activities which different generations of Muslim women from around the world—representing varying interests, ideologies, religious orientations, and backgrounds—engage in. They do so through participation in a wide array of gendered online communities, activities, and initiatives. My approach relies on a critical analysis of a number of Muslim women's online groups and campaigns. I examine their goals and objectives by spotlighting examples from the posts of some of these groups and contextualizing the depicted discourses within broader transnational, social, political, and religious frameworks.[5] By engaging in a deep analysis of the various push-and-pull mechanisms (and the competing influences) impacting these groups, as well as the dynamics they engage in, this study unpacks the complexities, hybridity, and ambivalences of the multifaceted Muslim gendered identities manifested in cyberspace. My analysis reveals three main functions under which these various activities can be classified, namely: exercising resistance, expressing identities, and extending solidarity and support. To illustrate these discrete functions, I spotlight case studies from various groups and campaigns which have been launched by Muslim women online.

In investigating the dynamics of these interrelated and intersecting processes, this study pays close attention to the complex phenomenon of "Islamic feminism."[6] My analysis explores how different groups of Muslim women define the concept of feminism according to their own realities, identities, and experiences—and how they use social media platforms to express their shifting gendered subjectivities and activisms, and to meet their various religious, social, cultural, and professional needs. In doing so, I argue that these groups are creating and reflecting, as well as redefining, the growing phenomenon of multifaceted digital Islamic feminism, with all its complexities and intricacies. This chapter also demonstrates how this online engagement simultaneously contributes to the equally complex process of producing "third spaces of digital religion,"[7] exemplified in the immense diversity of digital, feminist "third spaces on social media."[8]

Exercising Resistance Online: Raising Voices and Pushing Boundaries

Muslim women globally use the internet not just as a window to see the rest of the world, while being seen by the rest of the world, but also as a tool, or even a *weapon*, to fight back against the many attempts to sideline them, profile them, stigmatize them, and silence them. Their efforts to deploy digital media as a platform that gives "voice to the voiceless,"[9] helping them to amplify and spread their messages, became particularly important in the midst of the surging tide of Islamophobia worldwide, including in the United States.

Islamophobia can be defined as "an exaggerated fear, hatred, and hostility toward Islam and Muslims that is perpetuated by negative stereotypes resulting in bias, discrimination, and the marginalization and exclusion of Muslims from social, political, and civic life."[10] Its spread has prompted "an increasingly visible 'backlash' against Muslims across Europe and the United States."[11] Islamophobia has been steadily on the rise in the United States after the terrorist attacks of 9/11, but it became exponentially worse after President Trump came to office in 2016. During his presidency, some of the most prominent Islamophobes launched their campaigns online, using the internet to spout hatred and fuel anger and discrimination against immigrants and minorities in general, and Muslims in particular.[12]

In 2016, Republican presidential nominee Donald Trump insinuated that Ms. Ghazala Khan's religion might have stopped her from speaking at the Democratic National Convention, when she stood beside her husband, Mr. Khizr Khan, on stage. Soon after, Ms. Khan stood up for herself and spoke out in a televised interview, explaining that she remained silent only after seeing a displayed photo of her martyred son, a Muslim American fallen soldier, which made her very emotional.[13] In response to this incident, other Muslim women started a far-reaching Twitter campaign using the hashtag #CanYouHearUsNow to show just how powerful, strong, vocal, and outspoken they are, exhibiting clear examples of their successes and achievements in various professional fields. In other words, they effectively, and powerfully, countered and *resisted* the distorted stereotype of the silenced, oppressed, and marginalized Muslim woman by making their *voices* heard, loudly and clearly, through this Twitter campaign.[14]

Many of the tweets in this massive campaign went viral on Twitter, spilling over into mainstream media. Here are a few examples, among many.[15] A tweet from the Washington DC-based group *Karamah* (Muslim Women Lawyers for Human Rights) proclaimed: "Today we raise our voices for Muslim women around the world who empower their community #CanYouHearUsNow."[16] American Muslim activist Hind Makki, commenting on a photo of eighty American Muslim women speakers at the ISNA (Islamic Society of North America), declared, "Check out all these Muslim women speakers NOT silent at a major American Muslim conference #CanYouHearUsNow." In a post displaying an image of Wonder Woman, Faiza N. Ali tweeted: "I'm an organizer, activist, public servant fighting 4 dignity & respect. Pretty much Wonder Woman #CanYouHearUsNow." Rim-Sarah Alouane provocatively asked, "@realDonaldTrump I'm a #humanrights scholar, trying to make sure rights and freedoms are protected. What do you do? #CanYouHearUsNow." And Dalia Mogahed, the coauthor of the book *Who Speaks for Islam?*, asserted: "Muslim women 'not allowed to speak?' I gave a @TEDTalks and got a standing ovation #CanYouHearUsNow."

In commenting on this influential online campaign, some mainstream media outlets described it as a powerful and effective effort to showcase the diverse voices, talents, and successes of Muslim women who—as journalists, activists, academics, and more—demonstrated how they regularly speak out to make the world a better place.[17] The campaign was also praised for helping Muslim women take back their own *narratives*—especially at a time when their perceived "oppression" under Islam is weaponized as a means to implement discriminatory policies and when they are the most frequent targets of hate crimes and bias incidents. The public impact of this campaign also revealed how social media democratize voice share if used properly: amplifying voices often ignored by mainstream media while, at the same time, encouraging reporters and journalists to pay attention and communicate accurate stories.[18] Other media outlets commended Muslim women for amplifying their voices, broadcasting their strength, and, most importantly, reclaiming the narrative from Trump while exposing his Islamophobic, sexist, and misogynistic rhetoric in a simple, agile, effective, and powerful manner.[19] This dynamic illuminates the double-edged sword of social media when it comes to the complex phenomenon of Islamophobia: it provides platforms to spread it and the tools to counter it at the same time.[20] Muslim women exercise *agency* online when they effectively utilize the opportunities made possible in cyberspace to *resist* misrepresentation, stereotyping, profiling, and marginalization.[21]

Another salient example of Muslim women's strategic use of digital media platforms for resistance emerged with France's 2021 decision to ban girls under eighteen years of age from wearing the *ḥijāb* (the Islamic headscarf) in public and prohibiting mothers wearing the *ḥijāb* from accompanying their children on school fieldtrips.[22] These decisions are just the most recent actions by the French government, among a long series of past legal maneuvers aimed at restricting the *ḥijāb* in France.[23] This previously included banning the wearing of the *ḥijāb* in public schools in France; banning the *burkini* (the modest, religiously compliant swimwear worn by some Muslim women); and the banning of the *niqāb* (the full-face covering) by law in 2010—an action which was subsequently critiqued by the UN Human Rights Commission as an unjustified decision that disproportionately targets the minority of Muslim women who wear it, thereby violating their rights of religious freedom.[24]

Commenting on this latest decision by the French government, New York American Muslim activist and organizer Linda Sarsour tweeted, "I need all the folks that express outrage at Iran for forcing Muslim women to wear *hijab* to express the same outrage at France for banning girls under age 18 from wearing *hijab* & their moms who want to go on school trips." Other Muslim women supported Sarsour's position with additional tweets such as "I know this ban hasn't been passed into law yet, but the fact that a majority of the French Senate voted in favor of the ban preventing women under the age of 18 from wearing *hijab* is telling. Praying for my *hijabi* sisters in France." Similar comments from American Muslim women criticized what they described as French "hypocrisy" and "double-standards," highlighting the sharp contrast between the principles of "equality, liberty, and justice," upon which modern French society is allegedly built and which it prides itself on, and the harsh and unequal treatment of religious monitories in France, especially Muslim women. These critiques pointed to the constant efforts and singular obsession on the part of the French government to "regulate and police their bodies," including suppressing their right to dress in a way which matches their religious values and beliefs.[25]

Interestingly, in response to these new discussions and debates, related posts about past issues—such as the previous *burkini* ban in France— surfaced once again in some online groups. This included, for example, the closed Facebook group, "Sisters Uncut-South East London." A post from August 26, 2016—originally composed in response to the *burkini* ban in France—was reposted on this group's page under the heading, "As Muslim Sisters with Sisters Uncut, we send love and rage to our sisters in France." The post expressed a strong message of resistance to multiple forms of repression:

> The #burkini ban isn't an isolated incident. It follows in a long tradition of policing, controlling and politicizing the bodies of women, and, in particular, the bodies of black, brown, and Muslim women. As Muslim Sisters within Sisters Uncut, we send love and rage to our Sisters in France. In the face of continued Islamophobic, racist, and misogynistic actions everywhere, we would like to offer a reminder that true solidarity with our Muslim sisters everywhere starts with listening. It starts with recognizing that Islamophobia is not just something that happens when four armed men force a woman to remove her clothes on a beach in Nice. It starts with understanding that in the UK there has been a 326% rise in hate crimes against Muslims since 2015 (and that this, as ever, is targeted at black, brown, and visibly Muslim sisters).[26]

This powerful statement highlights the necessity of gendered resistances to multilayered (and multiple) forms of oppression inflicted upon Muslim women globally along the intersectional (and intersecting) identity markers of gender, color, race, class, and religion. This is especially apparent in the case of the visibility of Muslim identity among women who decide to wear the *ḥijāb*, the *niqāb*, or the *burkini* in public. What is evident here is the existence of intersectional layers of identity—such as being Muslim, female, and Black—that oftentimes create equally intersectional, multiple layers of oppression which, in turn, triggers a plethora of resistance tactics and strategies.[27] The "third space" created via various social media platforms provides an ideal arena of contestation where these tug-of-war, push-and-pull mechanisms can be exercised, amplified, and proliferated to a diverse, transnational audience—inviting new players and facilitating innovative dynamics within an interconnected, ongoing cycle in cyberspace.[28]

Expressing Diverse Identities: Blending Tradition and Modernity

One of the many ways that modern Muslim women strive to express their diverse identities in cyberspace is through blending tradition and modernity.

The booming world of internet fashion offers a good example of the crossover between these categories. Since the way we dress always speaks volumes about who we are, providing a mirror that reflects our identity, a young generation of Muslim women around the globe now utilize the borderless, transnational, internet-based modes of modern communication to prove to themselves, and to the world, that modesty and elegance are not mutually exclusive—and that faith and fashion can, indeed, go hand in hand.

Echoing the concept of "fashionista," a fashion icon and role model, especially in the digital sphere, the term "*hijabista*"—which, as Waninger explains, combines the terms "*ḥijābi*" and "fashionista"—refers to "a Muslim woman who dresses 'stylishly' while still adhering to an array of 'modest' apparel that coincides with Islamic dress code."[29] Combining modesty with fashion in the online sphere, Muslim women *hijabistas* have become very popular among young Muslim women in recent years, setting a new global trend. In effect, these "influencers" play a significant role as "fashion public opinion leaders" and "fashion agenda-setters." As role models, they set the agenda for other young Muslim women who are keen to dress both modestly and stylishly. Some Muslim women social media influencers today have hundreds of thousands, if not millions, of followers online—a vast audience of mostly young Muslim women who interact on digital platforms such as Twitter, Snapchat, YouTube, and Instagram.[30] Prominent online *hijabistas* effectively serve as the go-to sources for *ḥijāb* fashion, demonstrating various styles of the *ḥijāb*, giving useful fashion tips, and, most importantly, providing modest fashion inspiration for other young Muslim women.[31]

One of these young *hijabistas*, twenty-five-year-old Abrar Al-Heeti, explains in a 2019 article how the internet has helped her feel comfortable in modest clothing by connecting her to a large global community of like-minded young Muslim women who have also decided to combine modesty and elegance, celebrating both faith and fashion. She describes how she was initially on her own when figuring out how to wear her *ḥijāb* in a stylish way that reflected and expressed her identity. It was not until the rise of modest fashion social media sites, she notes, that she felt she was starting to receive some support and inspiration. According to Al-Heeti, social media accounts and blogs opened up a whole new world of *ḥijāb* fashion and, in the process, made wearing the *ḥijāb* a personal expression for Muslim women. Commenting on this point, she asserts, "Muslim fashionistas like me once felt isolated. But influencers have given us a safe haven."[32]

Despite its glamor, wide appeal, and lucrative economic rewards, this new trend of digital *hijabistas* is not a "one size fits all" phenomenon, nor it is free of tensions and controversies. As Kavakci and Kraeplin found in their research on *ḥijābi* social media personalities, "the digital realm allows for opportunities for multiple constructions of self."[33] This was reflected in the hybridity of the three famous *hijabistas* they studied who "revealed both an Islamic religio-cultural identity and a fashionable Western identity, at times emphasizing one more than the other, at times combining the two in unorthodox ways."[34]

This, in turn, triggered equally hybrid and mixed reactions from diverse Muslim communities online, depending on gender, generation, religious orientation, and geographic location, among other factors. The younger, more cosmopolitan, female internet users in the diaspora mostly expressed admiration and fascination; by contrast, older, more conservative, religiously orthodox internet users, especially those outside of the Western world, mostly criticized these new stylish fashion icons and their Western-influenced styles as the antithesis of modesty and religiosity. As Kavakci and Kraeplin aptly conclude, however, in every case these new negotiated identities are reflective of "the experience of duality or multiplicity that confronts *hijabis* with an active online presence."[35] Despite all the controversies, tensions, and push-and-pull dynamics, there is no question that these new digitally savvy *hijabista* influencers are setting the pace and establishing the pattern for a new phase in the representation of multiple, hybrid Muslim feminist identities. In doing so, they are simultaneously triggering wider debates, both online and offline.

Beyond the world of Muslim women's fashion, another interesting example of an effort to express and assert Muslim women's diverse and hybrid gendered identities in cyberspace was the launch of the annual global campaign #MuslimWomensDay on March 27, 2017.[36] This idea was introduced by a young American Muslim feminist and activist, Amani Al-Khatahtbeh, in response to the Muslim Travel Ban as a way to amplify Muslim women's voices and to boost the visibility of their obscured, or misrepresented, identities. It is worth noting that Amani is the founder of a group blog called "Muslim Girl," which subsequently became an online magazine and a foundation dedicated to increase Muslim women's media representation and visibility, providing them with a safe space to reclaim their narratives and to amplify their voices.[37] A number of Muslim women, representing different backgrounds and identities, used the #MuslimWomensDay on Twitter in 2017, to propagate their narratives of diversity, often coupled with visuals such as attractive selfies. For example, a group of Black Muslim women tweeted a photo of themselves with the caption, "We are different shades of melanin. We are veiled and un-veiled. We are BLACK. Please don't erase us. Happy #MuslimWomensDay."[38] Another woman tweeted a selfie alongside the caption, "About time we got a #MuslimWomensDay. Perhaps it's a step towards being heard inshallah. #TraditionallyUnsubmissive #Muslimah."[39] In both of these tweets, women were pictured wearing *ḥijābs* as a way to assert their Muslim identities and to fight the pervasive idea that Muslim women lack agency.

On its fifth anniversary in 2021, #MuslimWomensDay provided another excellent opportunity for many Muslim women from different walks of life to represent their diverse identities through a number of tweets and posts on a number of social media platforms, including Twitter, Facebook, Snapchat, and Instagram. Many of these posts also combined text with visual imagery—photographs, selfies, videos—marking another example of how Muslim women utilize the digital sphere to amplify their messages and share them with a widely diverse global audience—expressing and negotiating their individual identities while challenging the commonly held misconceptions and stereotypes clouding their lived realities and varied experiences. A typical example of the kinds of sentiments expressed during this 2021 global campaign is an article titled "Muslim Women Should Look to the Past to Find the Empowerment We Need Today," written by Mariam Khan, the editor of *It's Not About the Burqa*. The article urges contemporary Muslim women to follow the examples of strong, resilient Muslim women leaders from the past who can serve as role models for all women today. Khan remarks, "Muslim women are constantly being told that we don't and have never had any agency. To counter this, we need to hear and tell the stories of our forbearers."[40] She goes on to assert, "These Muslim women existed before feminism even began in the West. They've taught me I can be a feminist and a Muslim woman and empowered and so many other things, because so many Muslim women before me have been."[41]

This is certainly a forceful response to the false claim that Islam and feminism are mutually exclusive and, therefore, incompatible. That theme was also emphasized by Amani Al-Khatahtbeh in a number of tweets marking this day, along with a video in which she exclaimed, "It really pisses me off that people think the words 'Muslim' and 'feminist' don't go with each other."[42] Other postings from this 2021 global campaign included a tweet from a young Muslim woman, Shahed Ezaydi: "A happy #MuslimWomensDay to all Muslim women everywhere! We are constantly sidelined, silenced, and excluded, so today is a day to listen and pass the mic to Muslim women." Similarly, another Muslim woman, tweeting as "King Marwa," declared, "Happy #MuslimWomensDay. Being a Muslim woman means everyone around you has ideas about who you are and what you believe in. I encourage you to speak to a Muslim woman and understand where we come from and OUR beliefs. Not the lies the media and false sources like to give. It is OUR narrative." This tweet was coupled with a drawing of a *ḥijābi* Muslim woman carrying a sign that stated "Muslim Women Do Not Need Saving."

Significantly, the 2021 #MuslimWomensDay global campaign was launched under the theme of "healing, resilience and renewal." This special focus highlighted the importance of empowering Muslim women's voices and listening to their stories as they reflected on their experiences navigating the Trump era and the Covid-19 pandemic, both collectively and individually.[43] The campaign also included the first-ever "digital summit," hosted and organized by the "Muslim Girl Foundation." This event was designed to bring together prominent allies from the media and entertainment industry, along with public figures, influencers, and activists on the frontlines of creating Muslim youth culture in the digital era, to engage in online conversations on diverse representations, social impact, and alliance-building.[44] What is clearly evident from all these examples is the emergence of a heterogeneous, virtual *ummah* that mirrors the transformation, hybridization, and negotiation of Muslim gendered identities as they constantly oscillate between tradition and modernity.[45]

Extending Solidarity and Support: Gated Online Communities

In our book *Islam Dot Com*, Mohammed El-Nawawy and I conducted an in-depth textual analysis of the threads in the discussion forums of three of the most popular, mainstream Islamic websites (www.Islamonline.net, www .Islamway.com, and www.amrkahled.net) to examine the multiple Muslim identities displayed in these online platforms and the complex factors behind their construction. Our research also compared the degrees of uniformity and divergence manifested in some of these online forums, as well as the reasons behind these differences.[46]

One of the websites we examined, www.Islamway.com, included a discussion forum in English and another one in Arabic, both under the name "Islam Way Sisters Discussion Forum." Access to both of these forums was restricted to Muslim women only. In effect, this exclusively female online space allowed for the creation of a type of "Islamic feminism" or "Islamic sisterhood" that enabled the discussion of women's issues, family issues, and domestic issues within a gated, gendered online community.[47] It provided a *safe space* for Muslim women to vent, open up, and share their private experiences, not just as members of the same faith community but also as mothers, wives, sisters, and daughters, among other gender-based identities.[48] Our analysis of this particular website revealed how the discussions and deliberations in both the English and Arabic discussion forums increased the degree of uniformity, solidarity, and cohesion between the female Muslim participants who shared a "collective identity," united by both gender and faith identity markers as members of the same Muslim *ummah*.[49]

The online deliberations in some of the other discussion forums we explored in the book widened the gap and demarcated the boundaries between "divergent identities," as in the case of some online discourses between Muslims and non-Muslims, as well as between different categories of Muslims, such as Sunnis and Shi'a. By contrast, the interpersonal exchanges on "Islam Way Sisters" discussion forums were characterized by a high degree of consensus.[50] Even so, it was oftentimes an emotionally triggered consensus, which lacks the principles of rational-critical deliberation that Habermas identified as part of his ideal conception of the public sphere.[51] The exchanged discussions in this gated, gendered online community ranged from seeking advice on spiritual and religious matters (such as questions by recent converts to Islam about the specific details of daily religious rituals); to intimate questions about family affairs (such as adapting to an intercultural marriage situation); to requests for help, guidance, and emotional support in the face of a difficult and challenging situation (such as falling in love with a non-Muslim man). In every case, the Muslim sisters in the Arabic and English discussion forums of "Islam Way Sisters" provided unwavering emotional, spiritual, religious, and social support, while avoiding judgment, criticism, profiling, and stigmatization.[52]

Another group that works to build solidarity and community-based support online along gendered and religious identity lines is "Surviving *Hijab*." The founder of this closed Facebook group defines its mission as follows:

> Ladies—this is just for all the beautiful ladies out there who have taken the (very difficult) decision to wear the *hijab* for days, months, or years now, and are still battling with the decision, or have given in and given it up. There is a crazy trend going around, but we don't seem to be affected, right? I'm guilty, and I can't deny it. I'm finding it hard and harder every day, especially when I see, and observe, the most faithful of girls take it off, and it could happen to anyone of us any minute, any day. So, since nobody likes to go through it alone, I have decided to create this group to urge those who are veiled (and those who are considering it in these hard times) to continue holding on to this hard *ibada* [religious ritual], despite the hardships, in order for us to motivate each other, push ourselves to hold on, and, perhaps, even become better veiled Muslim women. I sincerely need your help, and feel free to invite your friends, even those who might have taken it off, regret doing so, and wish to come back.

This description of this group's goal and the purpose behind its creation is an optimal example of the function of "community building" and "solidarity strengthening" among Muslim women transnationally. In this case, "Surviving *Hijab*" embraces the wearing of the Islamic headscarf as an important Muslim practice. Unlike many of the other groups where the posts are predominantly in English—except when quoting from *āyāt* (verses from the holy Qur'ān) or *ḥadīth* (sayings of Prophet Muhammad)—the posts in this group were in both English and Arabic. This bilingual format is an interesting feature which allows more women to join in and encourages them to take part in discussions and conversations online. This group also integrates visual materials in posts, mostly photos that women share of themselves after deciding to wear the *ḥijāb* or images of some of their close relatives and friends who have embarked on this journey. Some good examples of such posts in Arabic included the following: "This is a photo of my 14-year-old daughter on her first day wearing the *hijab*. Please show her some love and support" and "This is my first day wearing the *hijab* and going to work. Please let me know what you think of my new look! Wish me luck, power, and strength!" The combination of both the visual and the textual and the group's transnational outreach and bilingual features are powerful strategies that help increase this group's effectiveness in performing solidarity and promoting community-building on a broad, global scale.

Muslim women converts, who often refer to themselves as "reverts," also participated in this closed Facebook group—albeit in smaller numbers—to seek support from life-long, *ḥijāb*-wearing Muslim women. "Salaam Sisters. I'm a new convert to Islam from Australia, and I'm still hesitant about taking the step of wearing the *hijab*, although I really want to do it. I would highly value your support please," announced one woman in a post. In a similar fashion, another said, "I'm a new Muslim revert from Germany. I just took my *shahadah* [proclamation of faith] last month. Despite the racism and discrimination against Muslims here in Europe, especially Muslim women who wear the *hijab* in public, I decided to take this life-changing step today. Alhamdulilah [thank God]. Here is my photo! Please keep me in your *du'aa* [prayers]!" The responses from the group's members to these posts, and others like them, included a mix of prayers, encouraging statements, and comments of admiration and moral support, such as "May Allah bless you, dear sister!"; "*Mabrouk*! [Congratulations!]"; "Insha'Allah [God willing] God will make it easy for you. Hang in there!"; and "We are here for you, we are all your sisters, and we support you every step of the way." As in the case of "Islam Way Sisters," the "Surviving *Hijab*" Facebook group demonstrates a high degree of emotional support along religious, spiritual, and gendered lines. This group's solidarity also crosscuts the social domain, leaning more toward uniform consensus but lacking any form of critical, rational deliberation.[53]

An array of additional online groups created along gender and faith lines illuminate additional dimensions of community-building and identity-construction in digital spaces. Another closed Facebook group, "Monthly Sisters' *Halaqa* (religious study circle)," focuses on enhancing Muslim women's spirituality and educating them about their religion and its principles using varied tools and techniques. This includes Qur'ān study and recitation groups, watching and sharing religious lessons, and engaging in fun religious learning activities, such as taking online quizzes.

The closed Facebook group "Muslim American Women in Media" was explicitly created for the purpose of providing professional help and support to young Muslim women who have decided to pursue a career in the field of media and journalism. This online community provides professional advice, guidance, resources, and networking to help beginners fulfil their career goals and find their dream job. Often, this is achieved by putting them in touch with more experienced and established professionals in the field of media and communication. One of the main goals of the group is to ensure that Muslim women have better media representation, increased visibility, and more prominent representation. This reminds us of the importance of amplifying women's *voices*, using a variety of digitally mediated tools.[54]

Other gendered, gated groups were created based on other criteria, such as geographic location. This includes "East London Muslim Sisters,"

"Sisters Uncut-South East London," "Muslim Sistas, Farmington, Michigan," "East Michigan Muslim Sisters," "Muslim Sisters Association-London," and many others. The purpose of these types of gated Facebook groups is to provide "local" community networking—supporting Muslim women by helping them to identify and utilize local resources, especially faith-based, or faith-specific, resources. Requests for "a female Muslim doctor in this area," "the closest Islamic school to this community," or "the best, and nearest, *halal* food market" are just a few examples. Interestingly, in certain online groups more specific identity markers were sometimes added to the geographic location. The closed Facebook group "Muslim Moms of Maryland," for example, adds the criteria of "motherhood" to geographic location, creating a more channeled and focused mission for this group. This online community frames its mission as raising Muslim children in a non-Muslim society and tackling its particular challenges, such as bullying in schools which impacts Muslim children to an alarming degree, finding good Muslim studies' home tutors, locating the best Qur'ān teachers in the area, and many other locally based, motherly focused requests.

Other groups narrow the topical focus even further. "Young Muslim Moms of Montgomery County, Maryland" determines the age and generation of the mothers and their children in addition to specifying the group members' geographic location more narrowly to produce more targeted results. Typical posts in this group focus on "finding a good Muslim nanny," "finding a reliable part-time Muslim babysitter," or "locating the nearest store to buy *halal* food and baby food." "Muslim Sisters United" is yet another closed Facebook group, which is generationally and locally based. It describes itself as "An organization for young Muslim sisters, youth who are 12 years and up, who would like to engage in community and charity work in Montgomery county, Maryland." Here again, the granular focus on a specific age group and geographic location helps to maximize the benefit of this group and to enhance the collaboration and coordination between its members.

Three interesting points are worth highlighting here. First, many online groups like "Muslim Sisters United" are indicative of a pervasive emphasis on charity and philanthropy in Muslim communities, especially the American Muslim community, in the aftermath of the Covid-19 pandemic. Muslim women, and particularly American Muslim women, play a vital role in this domain of charitable work, a great example of "putting faith in action." The internet certainly helped to coordinate, organize, and expand such efforts—a reminder of its critical role in aiding women's activism.[55] Second, while cyberspace has certainly played an important role in terms of enhancing and expanding globalization, all these cases illustrate how it also enhances and aides "localization"—an equally important, yet mostly overlooked and understudied, aspect in internet-related research. Third, a micro-level analysis of these various layers of identity markers and their segmentations and divisions into categories and sub-categories—based on geographic location, coupled with other factors such as motherhood, marital status, and age—reveals how this growing phenomenon of creating "mini virtual *ummahs*" in cyberspace plays different roles and serves multiple functions within the complex social fabric of everyday Muslim life.

Conclusion

This chapter has documented some of the innovative and creative strategies that Muslim women are using to engage in three interrelated and ongoing functions: creating resistances, constructing identities, and building communities in new digital spaces. The findings of this study clearly illustrate a unique amalgamation of multidimensional activities in cyberspace, signaling both the complexity and hybridity of these new digitalized mediated spaces, on one hand, as well as the identities and agencies competing within them, on the other.[56] My analysis also clearly reveals the crossovers, intersections, overlaps, and divergences between these multiple identities and voices, both online and offline, while reminding us of the participatory possibilities which are available for Muslim women in the domain of online culture.[57] All the activities and initiatives that these Muslim women have been engaging in are reflective of their own dynamically shifting realities as gendered and mediated beings who are capable of utilizing new media technologies to exercise their resistances, express their identities, and extend their solidarity and support to each other.

This research highlights the new potentials and possibilities opened up to these diverse groups of Muslim women with their adoption of new digital platforms for communication in cyberspace—alternative spaces that were simply not available in the past. In her study of the power of social media activism, Goehring reminds us that hashtags "are not merely tools for slacking activists."[58] Rather,

> Combined with their use on the Twitter platform, in which one is encouraged to make and foster connections with other Twitter users globally, hashtags emerge as powerful tools utilized to educate, critique, and express solidarity. With regard to Muslim women, they have been used to question, critique, react against, and affirm the multiplicity of identities expressed through any number of identifiers.[59]

The case studies in this chapter confirm these insights, illustrating how the numerous gendered activities and activisms of different Muslim women, both individually and collectively, skillfully utilize hashtags and other digitally enabled tools and techniques to strategically execute multiple functions.

In addition, Goehring highlights the fact that in participating in social media networks, "a user is connected to a global community of other users through a platform that encourages connection between its users. By creating open spaces in which one has the capacity to engage in sharing information with other users, social media offers a fruitful space for conversation regarding certain topics such as identity."[60] The results of my own research confirm the need to acknowledge the crossovers and overlaps between the different categories of digital feminist Muslim agency and activism in cyberspace and the three main functions under which they were classified in this study: exercising resistance, expressing identities, and extending solidarity and support.

For example, we can argue that the wide array of online activities included under the banner of #MuslimWomensDay online campaign do not just offer significant platforms for Muslim women's self-expression that increase the visibility of their gendered, feminist, Muslim identities. They also provide salient examples as to how modern Muslim women are deploying new social media tools as effective weapons to push back against their misrepresentation and to resist their silencing, profiling, stigmatization, and marginalization. Likewise, I argue that groups like "Islam Way Sisters," "Surviving *Hijab*," and "Muslim Moms of Maryland" provide ideal examples of how Muslim women are using social media to build gendered online support communities while simultaneously expressing their rich identities and sharing their varied experiences. In doing so, these virtual communities are creating and reflecting different shades, styles, and degrees of "Islamic feminism"[61] in the digital age through constantly engaging in the complex, interconnected dual processes of the "Islamization of feminism and the feminization of Islam."[62]

In unpacking these interrelated and intersecting phenomena, this chapter has illuminated Muslim women's engagement in the creation of new mediated, hybridized, gendered identities. These feminist positions of "in-betweeness" in cyberspace crosscut the boundaries between localization and globalization, tradition and modernity, the online and the offline, the private and the public, the national and the international, the social and the political, and the secular and the religious. Moving forward, it is only logical to predict that as the number of young, educated, technologically savvy, and digitally empowered Muslim women continues to grow, both at home and in the diaspora, so too will their multiple usages of internet-enabled platforms. The expanding opportunities enabled by digital media, in turn, will allow Muslim women to raise their voices, amplify their messages, exercise their resistances, and build their support communities. By doing so, they will continue to shape their changing identities and hybrid narratives within the equally dynamic and hybrid world of cyberspace.

CHAPTER 7

#MuslimGirlWoke:

A Muslim Lifestyle Website Challenges Intersectional Oppression

Kristin M. Peterson

Introduction

In a reflection article about the first ten years of the online magazine *Muslim Girl*, founder Amani Al-Khatahtbeh explains that the overall goal of the website has always been to counteract dominant stereotypes by creating an online community for Muslim women to share their own complex identities. Al-Khatahtbeh created the lifestyle magazine when she was just seventeen years old and living with her Jordanian immigrant parents in New Jersey.[1] Rather than simply responding to the latest anti-Muslim political statement or policy coming from Western countries, Al-Khatahtbeh explains that *Muslim Girl* "is and always will be defined by the women who make it up, our own MG generations of contributors and team members weaving different walks of life into a new DNA that defies the media-programmed image of the 'Muslim Girl.'"[2] The posts shared on the website are driven by the intersectional identities of the contributors and the concerns related to social injustices beyond religious identity, such as racism, sexism, homophobia, and colorism.

When *Muslim Girl* began as a group blog in 2009, the cultural and political landscapes looked very different. There were very few portrayals of Muslims in American popular culture—excluding the violent terrorist trope—and *ḥijāb* (headscarf) wearing Muslim women were not seen in cultural spaces like fashion runways, lifestyle magazines, advertisements, or sporting events. At the same time, the site developed into a collective space to share advice and experiences on daily issues. Al-Khatahtbeh writes in her memoir, *Muslim Girl: A Coming of Age*, that she wanted to create a community with other Muslim girls who "wanted to have conversations that were directly relevant to our Muslim lifestyles in today's society."[3] Girls would post questions about Islamic teachings as they related to daily practices like health, nutrition, fashion, and beauty. Although they were discussing daily practices, the overall goal "was always to increase our media representation and reclaim our narratives."[4]

Al-Khatahtbeh and the other contributors to *Muslim Girl* reflect the website's intended audience of young Muslim women who have grown up with a hybrid, third culture experience. Many are like Al-Khatahtbeh, children of immigrants who moved to Europe and North America. The articles on *Muslim Girl* point to these hybrid interests in Islam and cultural traditions, along with American popular culture and lifestyles. The magazine's articles also showcase an interest in progressive political causes, rooted in Islamic teaching and intersectional feminism. Although the articles on *Muslim Girl* address a variety of global issues, the site features English content that is mainly focused on Muslim experiences in North America.

Since *Muslim Girl's* beginnings, American culture and politics have shifted drastically. Muslim women are increasingly a touchstone of larger social debates about immigration, foreign policy, and the role of religion in public. At a time when policies and hate crimes target Muslim women, images of Muslim women circulate as icons in progressive spaces. *Ḥijābi* women are also increasingly prominent in TV shows, on magazine covers, in fashion spreads, in the Olympics, and in politics. Al-Khatahtbeh rightly says in her book that "*Muslim Girl* blew up" since 2015, as countless media outlets in the United States, as well as some international news sites, featured the website and Al-Khatahtbeh's activism.[5] However, Muslim women like Al-Khatahtbeh remain critical of this public relations strategy to make Muslim women more "palatable" by focusing on the bodies that can be "reprinted, sold, contorted to fit the only cool narrative society can accept."[6] Rather than create images and stories that fit into this palatable media narrative, *Muslim Girl* is designed to be an "alternative media channel" where the writers can express who they are "unapologetically."[7]

In this chapter, I build on previous studies that explored the influence of teen girls' cultural spaces—such as lifestyle magazines, fashion trends, zines, and blogs—in developing the political consciousness of young women. Through an analysis of a selection of articles from 2015 to 2019, I explore how *Muslim Girl* is a significant site for the formulation of the political disposition of Muslim American women and the development of an awareness of how the identities of Muslim women intersect with the experiences of other marginalized groups. My analysis of over 200 articles illustrates two significant ways that *Muslim Girl* has shifted to addressing more political and intersectional feminist concerns. First, the majority of *Muslim Girl* articles focus on political issues as compared to coverage of lifestyle topics, popular culture, and religious teachings. Second, the content of the magazine's articles illustrates a clear shift from 2015 when Donald Trump was a far-off candidate to deep into the Trump administration of 2019. The earlier articles focus more exclusively on political topics that affect Muslim Americans from Middle Eastern or South Asian backgrounds, such as foreign affairs, immigration issues, public discrimination, and anti-Islam policies like travel bans or surveillance programs. Beginning in 2017, *Muslim Girl* published more articles that address the ways that Muslim experiences intersect with other forms of oppression based on race, gender, class, or sexuality. This emphasis on more expansive political topics demonstrates how digital media provide hybrid and interstitial spaces for Muslim youth to cultivate a larger community, seeking to deconstruct larger structures of oppression, such as white supremacy, colonialism, and patriarchy.

Politics within Girls' Media Spaces

Muslim Girl is part of a larger tradition of young women developing their awareness of larger political concerns within cultural spaces that are often disregarded as frivolous, such as lifestyle magazines, fashion trends, zines, and blogs. For instance, Angela McRobbie conducted one of the first studies of fashion and music magazines for teen girls in the UK. Although these magazines reinforce ideologies of the perfect woman, who is thin and attracts a cute boyfriend, the young readers negotiate these ideals of feminine perfection.[8] These magazines cultivate an independence in the teen girls so that they are interested in fashion and beauty but "these interests are no longer pursued simply to impress boys, but they are about self-image and self-satisfaction."[9] McRobbie was one of the first cultural theorists to seriously consider the agency that young women display when they negotiate how these images of beauty, femininity, and romance relate to their own lived experiences. Although this negotiation process is present in the variety of articles on *Muslim Girl* that examine the traditional lifestyle topics of fashion, beauty, and diet, the website also spotlights articles about other aspects of these issues like body image, colorism, eating disorders, and the environmental impact of fast fashion.

Along with lifestyle magazines, fashion itself is a productive space for the negotiation of identity and community. In her book on fashion and cultural studies, Susan Kaiser argues that fashion enables individuals to examine their various interconnected subject positions. Fashion, according to Kaiser, "highlights the multiple intersections and entanglements among gender, race, ethnicity, national identity, social class, sexuality, and other facets of our identities."[10] Fashion is a significant space in which individuals can address their multiple identities and positions. The choice of what to wear is an agentive act situated within larger cultural and institutional forces. For Muslim women in particular, the choice to wear both modest and stylish, fashionable clothes is a significant act of displaying one's intersectional identity, religious conviction, and agency. Annelies Moors and Emma Tarlo assert that fashion has political potential for young Muslim women in Western countries, where their voices are often silenced. As they explain, "Through their visual material and bodily presence, young women who wear Islamic fashion disrupt and challenge public stereotypes about Islam, women, social integration and the veil even if their voices are often drowned out in political and legal debates on these issues."[11] Muslim women use modest but creative and stylish fashion to visually contradict pervasive stereotypes of the backward and oppressed Muslim woman. However, Amani Al-Khatahtbeh's advocacy work, along with the contributions on *Muslim Girl,* often resists performing this palatable representation of stylish and modern Muslim women. Instead, the content on *Muslim Girl* is intentionally not meant to be easily digestible by a non-Muslim audience, as the women unapologetically address the messiness of their intersectional experiences.

In her foundational work on girls' media production, Mary Celeste Kearney discusses how teen girls in the United States use media spaces to respond to the ways that their concerns are ignored or misconstrued in mainstream cultural spaces. Kearney explains, "many girl media producers rely on the practices of appropriation and *detournement* to reconfigure commercial cultural artifacts into personalized creations that speak more directly to their concerns, needs, fantasies, and pleasures."[12] Kearney documents how young female creators engage with zines and independent magazines to both speak back to how they are misrepresented and discuss serious social concerns, like sexual harassment, mental health, eating disorders, and STDs that are rarely discussed in commercial magazines.[13] *Muslim Girl* has a similar dual focus on critiquing the ways that Muslim women are misrepresented in mainstream American media and popular culture while also addressing resonant and pressing issues that are relevant to the daily lives of Muslim girls.

Digital Media and Feminist Politics

With the expansion and malleability of digital media spaces, feminist scholars of girls' media production have shifted their focus to the political potential of blogs and social media to enable the creative articulation of marginalized identities. Anita Harris focuses on how what she terms "online DIY cultures" serve as sites "for expression and dialogue about political and social issues in light of youth marginalisation from and disenchantment with formal politics."[14] These online DIY (do-it-yourself) cultures address political topics to raise awareness but they are "not conventionally political."[15] *Muslim Girl* similarly features articles on a variety of social issues, and the sharing of these articles serves as a method of consciousness raising and promoting offline action. As Harris explains, these online activities are important spaces for the development of "counterpublics" or "forums for debate and exchange of politically and socially engaged ideas by those who are marginalised within mainstream political debate."[16] Over time, the topics discussed in *Muslim Girl* have expanded to incorporate not only the experiences of Muslim women but also broader issues related to compounding marginalization based on race, class, sexuality, or gender identity. As Harris illustrates, online activism is an avenue for young women to develop a political sense of self and to negotiate their position within a changing landscape of activism and digital media.

Muslim Girl is a clear example of how online DIY culture can enable Muslim women to move beyond simply embracing the trappings of Western culture—such as fashion, consumption, and popular culture—by instead offering a critical perspective on the hybrid experiences of Muslims living in North America and Europe. For instance, when mainstream news sites and feminist blogs were covering Mia Khalifa, a Christian Lebanese porn actress who wore a headscarf in her videos, *Muslim Girl* published an article that rejected the assumption that viewed this as a liberating gesture. As Amani Al-Khatahtbeh argues in her book, "*Muslim Girl* became one of the only sites to offer a critical analysis of Mia's success, garnered by what we argued was using a religious garment as a prop to portray colonial sexual fantasies."[17] In effect, the contributors to *Muslim Girl* want to avoid reinforcing one-dimensional stereotypes of Muslim women as either oppressed by Islam or liberated by Western culture. Instead, they aim to build a space to share their daily experiences of various forms of oppression in an effort to raise awareness and deconstruct institutional forms of power.

In a similar vein, Jessalynn Keller's work on the feminist blogosphere among young women in North America explores how online blogs create forums "where young people can explore contemporary feminism and articulate their own perspectives about what it means to be a young feminist."[18] Digital spaces enable young women to develop their political agency as they produce blogs and other creative projects, and this creative work has political potential as girls discuss and debate topics that are relevant to their own lives rather than the topics that are addressed in mainstream political spaces or even feminist activism among older generations.[19] This focus on the activist work that young women do in online spaces like *Muslim Girl* leads to a shift in thinking so that girls and young women are seen as "active agents, cultural producers, and citizens rather than passive victims and cultural dupes in the online world."[20]

While *Muslim Girl* is a space for the representation of the experiences of Muslims that goes beyond one-dimensional tropes of Muslim women as oppressed victims or as objects of Orientalist sexual fantasies, it is also a platform to articulate an intersectional positionality and to raise awareness of the political issues that impact individuals who fall outside of the concerns of white, Western, progressive feminism. In her memoir, Amani Al-Khatahtbeh reflects on her feelings of not fitting into the normal white standards of American femininity. She discusses this sense of double consciousness as she grew up in a post-9/11 America where Muslims always had to prove their humanity.[21] As Alexandra Magearu explains, this racialization of Muslims creates feelings of disorientation and objectification that become internalized in how people understand their own value.[22] Magearu asserts, "disorientation has serious affective consequences registered as physical and psychological stress which not only reduces the body's movement and what it can do in the world, but also diminishes the sense of self."[23] Digital media projects in sites like *Muslim Girl* provide a platform for the participants to "re-orient" themselves and demonstrate their inherent value while also addressing the intersecting forms of oppression and compounding feelings of inferiority.

Methods

In order to examine how *Muslim Girl* addresses political issues and intersectional feminist concerns, I conducted an analysis of the content of 220 online articles from December 2015 to September 2019. I focused on the time frame between the announcement of Donald Trump's presidential election campaign and the first years of Trump's presidency. Within this nearly four-year time frame, I chose nine dates to examine twenty to twenty-five articles. Some of these smaller segments were selected around certain key political moments, but some were randomly chosen. Time frame one was timed to start on December 5, 2015, around when Trump first announced his candidacy for president. Time frame two fell in the middle of the campaign in March and April of 2016. Time frame three covered the time between Trump's election and before the inauguration in December 2016. Time frame four was in the early months of Trump's term in March 2017. The remaining time frames were random dates spread out through Trump's administration, from July 2017 to September 2019.

A student assistant and I coded the articles based on whether they fit into one of the following topics: politics, religion, culture, and lifestyle. I used a wide definition of politics, including elections and public policy, along with foreign affairs, identity politics, and social justice concerns.

The religion posts covered themes such as inspiration, prayers, reflections on the Qur'ān, and Islamic teachings on personal topics. Culture articles discussed the arts, music, film, photography, TV shows, and entertainment media. Lifestyle topics included fashion, makeup, nutrition, household products, and recipes. Instead of organizing the website into subsections for the various topics, each article on *Muslim Girl* was coded with a hashtag, such as #MuslimGirlWoke, #MuslimGirlLife, or #MuslimGirlBlessed. After coding all the articles, I then highlighted those that addressed issues related to intersections outside of Islam, such as critiques of white, Western feminism, racism, colorism, sexual identity, reproductive rights, indigenous issues, colonialization, climate change, and sexual assault and harassment. These articles will be discussed in detail in the "Analysis" section.

In analyzing these materials, I employed a grounded theory approach and feminist methodology to highlight the main political issues and social topics discussed in the magazine articles. Instead of approaching the *Muslim Girl* articles with a clear idea of what they would discuss, grounded theory enables researchers to uncover the concepts and theories within the data.[24] Furthermore, the combination of grounded theory and feminist methodology places the spotlight on the topics discussed by the contributors to *Muslim Girl*. As Orit Avishai, Lynne Gerber, and Jennifer Randles discuss, feminist methodology and grounded theory "encourage us to privilege our respondents' voices and modify received theory when it cannot fully account for new empirical discoveries."[25] Although I did intentionally select this time frame because it coincided with larger political and social events, I did not approach the data with preconceived ideas of how this larger context would influence the topics discussed on *Muslim Girl*.

Findings

After gathering data on 220 articles on *Muslim Girl*, two key findings were notable: political issues were the most discussed topics on the site, and there was a clear shift in the types of political stories from the 2016 election campaign to the Trump administration in 2019. First, political issues were discussed in 109 articles (50 percent). This was far more frequent than forty-two religion articles (19 percent), forty-nine pieces on lifestyle topics (22 percent), or twenty articles on culture (9 percent). It is notable that an online magazine about the daily experiences of Muslim girls focuses around half of its articles on political topics. *Muslim Girl* covers a range of political issues from anti-Islam harassment in public spaces to specific political policies that harm Muslims, such as the proposed Muslim registry, the travel ban, surveillance programs, and the terror watch list. Several writers discuss experiences that are specific to Muslims, such as bad TSA and airport encounters, hate crime attacks, and having a headscarf removed. While the

TABLE 7.1 Shifts in political coverage

Time Frame	No. of Political Articles	Examples of Political Topics Discussed in Articles
December 5–16, 2015	20 out of 25	Public harassment; hate speech; TSA experiences; the bombing of a mosque
March 30–April 13, 2016	14 out of 25	Hate crimes and Islamophobic policies in the United States; experiences of Palestinian women in Israeli prisons
December 17–23, 2016	18 out of 25	Trump's proposed Muslim registry; Muslims kicked off flights or discriminated against at airports; a KKK hate crime plot against Muslims; pulling off *ḥijābs* in public; *burqa* bans; political situations in Turkey and Syria; famine in Yemen
March 10–23, 2017	9 out of 25	War in Syria; EU rules on religious symbols in the workplace; the banning of electronic devices on certain flights from Muslim countries; experiences of Latina Muslims
July 9–23, 2017	11 out of 25	Boycott, Divestment, and Sanctions movements in the United States; Palestinians killed in protest; an advertising campaign against Islamophobia; discussion of the travel ban's impact. *Intersectional articles*: queer Muslims; Latinos in the United States; slavery in the United States
February 1–March 5, 2018	9 out of 25	Harassment of a contestant on France's *The Voice* over support for Palestine; a Pakistani feminist icon; gun violence and terrorism. *Intersectional articles*: the misrepresentation of feminist issues by focusing only on white women; Latina Muslims; Black History Month in the United States
October 1–21, 2018	14 out of 25	*Intersectional articles*: male victims of sexual assault; indigenous people; immigrants; reproductive rights; colorism; Black Muslims; sexual crime; child-friendly workplaces
May 8–31, 2019	3 out of 25	Trump's policies on Iran; Palestinians living in the diaspora; abortion bans in US states *Note*: This time frame overlapped with the month of *Ramaḍān*, so the majority of articles focused on religious inspiration for *Ramaḍān* or lifestyle tips for health and wellness during the month of fasting.
August 30 – September 17, 2019	11 out of 19	Remembering 9/11 as Muslim Americans; the terror watch list; foreign policy in Afghanistan. *Intersectional articles*: climate change; African Muslim immigrant elected to a city council

reflection articles on personal experiences are highly resonant on *Muslim Girl*, the political articles also address foreign policy and international issues related to Saudi Arabia, Turkey, Yemen, Iraq, and Iran. Furthermore, several articles discuss the Palestinian-Israeli conflict with a focus on the Boycott, Divestment and Sanctions movement and the experiences of Palestinian refugees. Finally, some of the articles discuss general political topics like elections, gun violence, poverty, and sexual crimes against women.

The second major finding that emerged in the data was that there was a shift in the overall political discussions on *Muslim Girl*. During the presidential campaign and then immediately after the election of Trump, the political articles focused on issues that primarily impact Muslim Americans of Middle Eastern or South Asian descent, such as Islamophobia, public harassment, immigration, refugees, or foreign policy. While Muslims of other backgrounds are also impacted by these issues, the articles are mainly framed around the Middle Eastern and South Asian immigrant experiences. From the summer of 2017 onward, however, the discussion shifted notably to address more intersectional feminist concerns, such as how Muslim experiences overlap with and run parallel to anti-Black racism, GLBTQ issues, and the experiences of Latinos. Table 7.1 elaborates on the various political articles in *Muslim Girl* during these time frames.

Muslim Girl Article Topics

Analysis of Key Themes

Feminist studies demonstrate the ways that cultural spaces such as lifestyle magazines, fashion, blogs, and zines cultivate the political agency of young women. Muslim women engage with digital spaces like *Muslim Girl* to speak back against the ways that their bodies and experiences are often misrepresented in mainstream media and white feminist spaces. At the same time, *Muslim Girl* develops the political agency of these young women to engage in larger political causes. The shift in political coverage, documented by the data in Table 7.1, illustrates the way that this political consciousness raising has spread beyond the concerns of Muslim American women from Arab and South Asian backgrounds. The data illustrate a clear change from this narrow focus to a wider concern with how the experiences of Muslim women intersect with other forms of oppression. This shift is also visible in broader social activism, as young Muslim Americans are more engaged in movements around racial violence, prison reform, immigration rights, reproductive justice, LGBTQ issues, climate change, and anti-poverty initiatives.

The notable expansion of coverage in the *Muslim Girl* articles supports an argument that the interstitial and flexible nature of digital media encourages young Muslims to engage with intersecting experiences of oppression and to network with others to deconstruct institutional power structures. In a similar way to how young women and other marginalized groups found modes of expression in creative cultural spaces like music, zines, fashion, comics, or artwork, these young Muslim women are also expressing their intersectional experiences in written articles and imagery. Digital media expand the potential of these creative voices by providing more open and malleable spaces, like *Muslim Girl*, for a variety of voices to share their experiences. Digital media also encourage more networking, as points of connection can be made over different identity markers. For instance, a young Black woman may come across a *Muslim Girl* article about anti-Black racism through a link on social media and then learn more about the experiences of Muslim women. While social media can create isolated silos, there is also the potential for the networking web of digital media to allow individuals to branch out and learn about issues that intersect with their own personal experiences. The specific topics discussed on *Muslim Girl* indicate the plethora of interconnected issues that diverge from the concerns of Muslim women.

Intersectional Feminist Critiques

Several articles on *Muslim Girl* reflect on the narrow definitions of feminism that often exclude any form of intersectionality. For instance, Rabia Ali[26] writes a brief critique of the limitation of the pink pussy hats that were made popular at the January 2017 Women's Marches, asserting that "the pussy hats are a reminder that we are far from including all races and genders in the pro-feminist conversation."[27] Another post by Aisha Saleh, entitled "What Feminism Means to Me," offers a series of statements on feminism that includes references to intersectional causes related to racism and poverty. "Feminism is NOT the gains of the white woman at the expense of the brown woman's voice," Saleh writes. "Feminism is NOT a t-shirt that celebrates feminism at the cost of a child's humanity in a sweatshop factory."[28] These statements emphasize that for feminism to be truly about justice for all, it cannot prioritize the rights of white, wealthy, straight women above the rights of others.

Racism and Colorism

A larger portion of the magazine articles that address intersectionality focus on the experiences of Black Muslims with anti-Black racism in American society and Muslim communities. In an article on the 2018 March for Black Women, Vanessa Elshamy, who identifies as a white woman, argues for the need for political spaces for Black women to organize and address their specific experiences of intersectional oppression. She explains, "The

March for Black Women is specifically for BLACK WOMXN to attest to the daily struggles they face because they happen to be Black AND female."[29] Elshamy argues that feminism should not privilege white, straight feminist issues while downplaying the concerns of Black women. Another article in *Muslim Girl* examines the intersectional experiences of nonwhite women in sports by focusing on the racism and sexism that Serena Williams frequently experiences in her tennis career. The author argues that when Serena got angry at a referee during a match, her race and gender worked together as people judged her as overly emotional, irrational, and disrespectful, especially when compared to white male athletes.[30]

Furthermore, several articles call attention to the prominence of racism and colorism within Muslim American communities. Sarah Ahmed, a South Asian Muslim American, calls on fellow Muslims to recognize the importance of Black History Month, especially in the face of a racist society. Ahmed writes, "the harsh reality is that to be seen as full, respectable human beings, Black people have to work twice as harder, and constantly prove they aren't their stereotypes."[31] Additionally, Ahmed argues that Muslims of other ethnic backgrounds must support Black Muslims who are doubly persecuted for their race and religion. In her words, "I say this as a South-Asian, Muslim immigrant. We need to work on our biases, and we need to fight for equality and not only when it affects us. Just because we are marginalized doesn't mean that we are incapable of being prejudiced."[32] Ahmed's reflections point to the fact that an intersectional feminist approach recognizes how experiences of prejudice among Muslims overlap, but also that certain experiences of oppression are compounded based on factors like gender, race, or sexuality.

Some of the most impactful articles are those written by African American Muslims addressing their daily experiences of racism and colorism, oftentimes within Muslim communities. Leah Vernon discusses how the experiences of Muslims of African descent are often ignored in mainstream representations of Muslims, which usually focus on thin, light-skinned, Middle Eastern women. Furthermore, Vernon and other Black Muslims experience prejudice in Muslim American spaces like mosques and businesses. She argues that some Muslims of Arab or South Asian descent embrace American racism: "There's a superiority complex that a Middle Eastern Muslim is better, more authentic and that anyone else is a 'copy' or 'unauthentic.' In my experience, too many Muslims play into the stereotypes of African-Americans: that we are lazy, less educated, promiscuous and aggressive."[33] By appropriating these racist stereotypes, she insists, Muslims ignore the foundational religious teachings about the inherent equality of all people.

In an article about the importance of Black spirituality, Amal Matan writes about how Black Muslim women face discrimination because of their religion, race, and gender, but are often not accepted or valued in Muslim spaces. "To be Black, and Muslim is truly a difficult thing," Matan asserts. "To believe and to believe on your own accord, while actively being pushed out and away from these spaces you are entitled too, is painful. It's really to the detriment of Muslims everywhere that Islamic leadership continues to aspire to whiteness, and colonial power."[34] Matan critiques Muslim Americans who are so concerned with fitting into American culture and being overly respectful that they embrace a white supremacist interpretation of Islam. In order to root out white supremacy within Muslim spaces, Matan calls for a focus on Black spirituality, which she defines as "a reassertion of belief in that Blackness is included in the core of humanity; that Black people are human and worthy of, and afforded the full freedoms of personhood."[35] In her assessment, a religious space that promotes the inherent value of Black lives is essential in order to support and heal the souls of Black Muslims.

Muslim Girl serves as a site for non-Black Muslim contributors to call out their fellow Muslims for prejudicial behaviors and beliefs toward African and African American Muslims. At the same time, the contributions from Black Muslims provide deeper reflections on how these experiences of oppression impact their own consciousness. These articles discuss the specific experiences of oppression that Black Muslim women face but, at the same time, the writers bring to the surface the ways that white supremacy, patriarchy, and the enduring legacy of colonialism have negative impacts on all Muslim women. An awareness of the interconnection of these forces also illustrates how these dynamics are often used to pit marginalized groups like Arab Muslims and Black Muslims against each other.

Latino Muslims

While Black Muslims have long been a significant section of the Muslim American community, Latino Muslims are a growing portion of the population that *Muslim Girl* often discusses.[36] Among the articles that I examined for this chapter, four highlight the particular experiences of Latino Muslims. Two feature videos that examine the reasons why Latinos are converting to Islam. These videos do not address structural forms of oppression like the articles about African American Muslims do. Instead, they focus on how Latinos are a growing movement within American Islam,[37] or they explore specific experiences of public harassment and stereotypes.[38] In general, the pieces on Latina Muslims spotlight misconceptions and stereotypes of Muslim women. Unlike Black Muslims who are often not seen as authentic Muslims because of their skin color, Latina Muslims emphasize how they are typically confused for Arab or South Asian Muslims.

In one article, a Latina convert, Breonnah Colon, comments on how she is often asked why she converted to Islam or other questions about common misconceptions of Muslim women, particularly Latinas, who convert to Islam. For instance, there are widespread assumptions that women only convert to appease their Muslim husbands, perpetuating a stereotype that Muslim men are controlling women. She also reflects on how people assume that she is Arab and speaks Arabic or ask why she wears the headscarf.[39]

Although these questions are ignorant and point to deeper prejudicial attitudes, the experiences that Colon documents are not as pernicious as what some of the Black Muslims describe as being treated as subhuman in Muslim communities. In another article, Breonnah Colon reflects on her conversion to Islam and some of the particular challenges of practicing the faith like wearing the headscarf. She describes how as a Latina, growing long hair is significant to her identity—but that wearing the *ḥijāb* is an act that humbled her.[40] Her reflections emphasize the spiritual aspects of wearing the *ḥijāb* and are not focused on public harassment or discrimination.

Overall, these videos and articles on Latino Muslims are feel-good pieces that promote the positive aspects of Islam and avoid addressing the underlying structural forms of oppression. Furthermore, Latino Muslims are portrayed as being saved by Islam. This is distinct from the African American Muslims who work to celebrate the importance of Black spirituality and African history as part of the Muslim American community.

Colonization and Indigenous People

A few magazine articles address issues related to the rights of Indigenous people, as well as the effects of colonization. In a piece about Columbus Day, *Muslim Girl* contributor Uyala Yousaf presents the many reasons why Christopher Columbus should not be celebrated. Driven by the colonialist ideals of destruction and dominance, she asserts, Columbus was responsible for the death of indigenous people through disease and violence, as well as their enslavement and forced conversion to Christianity. While this article does not mention Islamic values or Muslims per se, the author clearly articulates a need to celebrate Indigenous People's Day.[41] In another piece, Imaan Asim makes a direct connection between the Western project of colonization and capitalism and the destruction of the planet. She writes, "Our Earth is dying. Yes, large corporations, White settlers and governments in charge are largely to blame."[42] While these articles do not explicitly mention Islam, they demonstrate the ways that *Muslim Girl*'s contributors take a wide-angle view on a range of social injustices in the world to spotlight the ways that dominant ideologies such as white supremacy, capitalism, patriarchy, and colonialism are interconnected.

GLBTQ Concerns and Reproductive Rights

While *Muslim Girl* frequently covers issues of sexism that impact young Muslim women, the website has also expanded the coverage of topics that relate to sexuality in terms of the experiences of queer Muslims and concerns over reproductive rights. For instance, one article chronicles the years of physical and mental suffering that a young Muslim man went through because of being gay. Although he faces harassment and discrimination from Muslims and non-Muslims alike, his faith remains important. The author, Zarina Iman, writes, "He acknowledges that he is probably unwelcome at his local mosque, though he prays five times a day and continues to be a practicing Muslim."[43] This article documents the struggles that Muslims face because of their sexuality.

In another anonymous post, the author describes growing up as a queer Muslim and feeling like an outsider: "The thought of being queer and Muslim was never spoken of in both communities, so I always thought I could only be one and not the other."[44] The author discusses how they struggled to find a Muslim space that would accept their queerness, before eventually coming to the realization that a Muslim's relationship with Allah is individual and private. Eventually, the author found other Muslims, "who reconciled with both identities, learned to unlearn cultural condemnation presented as religious values, and unapologetically combated Islamophobia in mainstream communities."[45] It was essential for the author to find spaces where one's intersectional identity is celebrated and not condemned.

Finally, a few of the articles on *Muslim Girl* address current feminist causes around reproductive rights. One of the articles examines the Trump administration's policy of denying the right to an abortion to women detained after trying to cross the border. The author, Aisha Saleh, argues that these decisions are part of a larger project to strip all detained migrants of their rights as human beings.[46] This article does not address Islam or discuss Muslim women, but it is a clear example of how these political issues of reproductive rights and immigration have a wider impact. Another article offers a clever argument against how some Americans, both conservatives and progressives, use *sharī'ah* law as a stand-in for a regressive approach that would deny women autonomy, especially in terms of reproductive choices. The author asserts that this use of *sharī'ah* not only misunderstands Islamic legal traditions but also ignores the ways that patriarchal interpretations of Christianity promote these abortion bans. The author goes through the teachings of what the Qur'ān actually says about abortion and women's rights to prove that these abortion laws are rooted in misogynistic interpretations of Christianity. For instance, she discusses how one passage in the Qur'ān (17:31) condemns infanticide, especially of female children. While the act of abortion is not discussed in the Qur'ān, she notes, Islamic laws generally view the abortion of a fetus at 120 days to be wrong, although exceptions can be made, and the woman who has an abortion does not face severe punishment.

Conclusion

From the early days of *Muslim Girl* as a group blog among teenage girls, the online lifestyle magazine has always strived to counteract stereotypes and, more importantly, to provide a supportive community for Muslim women to critique the ways that their lives are misrepresented in mainstream news media and popular culture. The identities of Muslim American women in the twenty-first century have been deeply tied to political concerns, as they have come of age during a period when their lives have been a touchstone of issues related to immigration, international affairs, and discrimination. In 2016, the content on *Muslim Girl* focused on issues that directly impacted Muslims, such as travel bans, surveillance, public harassment, and foreign policy. As the Trump administration and Republican policies expanded to having a wider impact on other marginalized groups, the coverage of *Muslim Girl* also broadened to include wider concerns related to the experiences of African American and Latino Muslims as well as queer Muslims. The authors address intersecting forms of oppression in pieces on reproductive rights, immigration, climate change, indigenous rights, poverty, and institutional racism. Rather than focusing exclusively on how Muslim women are impacted, these articles address how dominant forces of oppression influence a wider community.

Although digital media have been shown to solidify divisions and entrench political beliefs, *Muslim Girl* illustrates how the hybridity and flexibility of digital media develop communal connections from across different marginalized perspectives. The open space of *Muslim Girl* encourages contributors from a variety of backgrounds and experiences to share their perspectives, and the fluidity of the site allows for a mixture of writing styles, topics, and opinions. All the articles are equally accessible on the site, so readers are exposed to a mixture of viewpoints. Moreover, the networking web of digital media allows readers to find points of connection as well as entry points that expand beyond Muslim American lives. *Muslim Girl* illustrates how issues that seem to only impact Muslim women expand out to touch on larger concerns like racism, socioeconomic issues, reproductive rights, criminal justice reform, climate change, colonialism, gender justice, and sexuality. In doing so, the content on *Muslim Girl* raises the political consciousness of Muslim women to larger forces of oppression. At the same time, digital media enable the circulation of these articles to wider audiences, creating a greater understanding of the experiences of Muslim women. These online connections promote wider coalition building and political activism in offline spaces as people become more aware of their interdependency in the collective struggle against the same forces of oppression.

Part III

Piety and Performance

CHAPTER 8

The Digital *Niqābosphere* as a Hypermediated Third Space

Anna Piela

Introduction

In this chapter, I discuss a story self-produced by a *niqāb*-wearing woman who inhabits an online space that I have called the "digital *niqābosphere*." I use this term to refer to a digital space that consists of individuals and groups invested in the idea of wearing the *niqāb* who create, discursively and performatively, interconnected third spaces across multiple digital media platforms, where they develop, perform, adjust, and negotiate their hybrid religious and gender identities in relation to the practice of *niqāb* wearing.[1] These digital spaces facilitate the creation of shared discourses and aesthetics of the *niqāb* that underpin the production of global, mediatized alternative religious narratives and counterpublics.

To date, the existing literature has not amply addressed *niqāb*-wearing women's efforts aimed at fostering their pious lifestyles online, even though some of these women are active on social media commenting on a wide range of social and political issues. Instead, academic study of *niqābi* women's voices on social media is primarily focused on non-organized women who are not involved in public-facing activism. For instance, Nisa analyzes internet usage among local *niqāb*-wearing, mostly Salafi Indonesian women and demonstrates how they create and maintain digital subcultures of piety and run online businesses which enable them to engage in "pious projects of self-shaping and learning."[2] My earlier work details the role of Islamic online communities of learning for converts who prepare to adopt the *niqāb* and the discussions about *niqāb*-wearers' self-portraits that demystify the *niqāb* and its implications on secular digital forums.[3]

Access of *niqāb*-wearing Muslim women to traditional media platforms is limited.[4] As a result, they are able to influence narratives produced in print and broadcast media in ways that remain in dialogue with dominant frames prescribed for them: usually in response to a "*niqāb* controversy," where their voices are grudgingly included and subsequently often drowned out by the *niqāb*'s detractors.[5] This chapter traces ways in which *niqāb*-wearing women engage with, respond to, and challenge hegemonic representations of *niqāb*-wearers in the West within the digital *niqābosphere*. This abstract space extends to photo-sharing sites, text-based discussion forums, and social media groups and other online spaces that form an interwoven network characterized by a striking consistency: the discourse that circulates in these interconnected spaces suggests that despite challenges involved in being visibly Muslim in the West, wearing the *niqāb* is a beneficial practice at the psychological and spiritual levels. The narrative that a Muslim woman is only able to reach maximum growth potential when in harmony with her religious values, here represented by the *niqāb*, is keenly articulated here. The degree of "success" is related to the ability to integrate piety with intellectual and material aspirations, rather than achieving a celebrity status or financial gains. Some *niqāb*-wearing users are simultaneously prolific digital content producers, who build personal brands based on tailoring their message for various audiences.[6]

Performing identity work collectively in "hypermediated religious spaces"[7] allows the creation of "networks of actors and actions that involve media platforms as well as physical spaces."[8] This requires interpreting multilayered online communication as "diverse communicative networks with nodes of linkage."[9] The concept of "third spaces of digital religion," developed by Hoover and Echchaibi,[10] who drew from Bhabha's extensive theorization of "the third space," is related to hypermediated religious spaces.[11] Third spaces of digital religion have been described as "religious venues approached by believers as if they are authentic spaces of religious practices."[12] This concept assists with examining the "lived religious practices of actors as they negotiate their way of being religious within the digital realm."[13] The main characteristics of these spaces are the articulation of hybrid religious identities, the creation of shared aesthetics, and the enablement of alternative and non-mainstream religious narratives.[14]

In this chapter, I spotlight the case study of Rivka Sajida—a prolific digital media influencer who expresses her complex, intersectional identity as a Muslim woman while publicly performing her piety through the wearing of the *niqāb*—to demonstrate how an intricately woven digital storied self, shared across hypermediated spaces, becomes a foundation for the articulation of a hybrid religious identity, a shared aesthetics of the *niqāb*, and an alternative religious narrative.

Hybrid Religious Identities and Associated Non-Mainstream Religious Narratives in the Digital *Niqābosphere*

Hybrid cultural identities have been studied extensively by postcolonial theorists who consider them in the context of diaspora and ethnic cultures.[15] For example, Brah argues that the relationship between the local and the global that constitute diasporic identities always varies since these identities are "constituted within the crucible of materiality of everyday life; in the everyday stories we tell ourselves individually and collectively."[16] From this perspective, the relationship between hybridity, materiality, and storytelling comes into focus. Hybridity in this context is living with and through, not despite, difference.[17] New subject positions are able to emerge within this "third space" which, in turn, "displaces the histories that constitute it, and sets up new structures of authority, new political initiatives, which are inadequately understood through received wisdom."[18] According to Bhabha, this third space is a place where authority is negotiated, translated, and reinscribed, leading to unexpected forms of agency and resistance.[19] It is "where the negotiation of incommensurable differences creates a tension peculiar to borderline existences." The concept of third space can be applied to theorizations of the online space in order to throw light on the formation of religious communities that produce new aesthetics, new forms of authority, and inevitable tensions, allowing an "engagement with technology, practice, and lived experience."[20]

The "storied identity" concept in the digital context describes people's attempts to "create coherence amidst the fluidity of the internet."[21] This coherence is particularly important for those performing hybrid, bricolage identities that involve constant meaning-making. Identity becomes a "production," "never complete, always in process."[22] People "select, assemble, and present a sense of self" by drawing from various resources, such as affiliations, personal history, social connections, or artwork.[23] While striving to unify different aspects of identity, they inevitably remain in-between, in the liminal space of hybridity.[24] Individuals may assemble their religious narratives (which are fundamental for self-expression) using an array of global and local elements, combining references to online and offline practices, connections, choices, and experiences. Inevitably, they integrate highly individualized and community-oriented narratives while attempting to present a coherent "story of the self."

It would be incorrect, however, to assume that the ostensible freedom of expression the internet affords creates a natural setting for non-mainstream, alternative religious narratives. Sometimes it may be unclear what constitutes non-mainstream narratives anyway—it depends on where we locate the notion of "mainstream." In the case of the Muslim women who wear the *niqāb*, non-mainstream narratives can take multiple forms: focusing on piety-motivated *niqāb* adoption that contradicts mainstream Western perceptions of the "oppressed" *niqābi*, emphasizing women's religious authority that contests mainstream views of hierarchically structured religion in which male perspectives continue to be the authorized ones, embracing unusual/nontypical concerns and alliances, or formulating religious practices which bring together theologies commonly perceived as incompatible. Some narratives combine all these elements at once. Through an analysis of Rivka Sajida's digital media content, I demonstrate how through the performance of storied, hybridized identities she is able to attract and navigate different audiences, challenge preconceptions, and engage in *da'wah* (proselytization, attracting new believers to Islam).

Rivka Sajida's Noncomformist Articulations of a Hybrid Religious Self

Rivka Sajida is the author of "A Day in the Life of a Disabled Niqabi"[25] and "Deen Talk!" vlogs.[26] On her Twitter profile page, she briefly introduces herself as a "Jewish revert to Islam, feminist, and religion scholar. I'm loud and opinionated and goth; nice to meet you."[27] She publishes her content on her own YouTube channel, Facebook page, Twitter, Instagram, and review blogs. She also runs an Etsy business selling "Islamic Art, *hijab* pins, and items to help reverts to Islam, as well as jewelry, art, and a few odds and ends. Plus some Islamic clothing, too."[28] On YouTube, she has 3,570 channel subscribers and over a hundred uploaded videos which vary in length between thirty-three seconds and thirty-seven minutes. Her most popular video (37,000 views) is a *niqāb* review.[29] Her videos tend to be shot indoors, in either her bedroom or her living room. Sometimes she can be seen outside in her yard or, occasionally, in a public space like a shopping mall. Usually, she wears the *niqāb* while filming but sometimes she appears with her face uncovered. In some videos she is with a woman who she refers to as her co-wife, which suggests that she is living in a polygamous marriage; she openly identifies as a queer, polyamorous Muslim.[30]

Prior to embracing Islam, Rivka Sajida identified as Jewish (her mother was Jewish and father was from a Roman Catholic background). This makes her nontypical, as 77 percent of converts to Islam in America are former Christians, 19 percent are former atheists or agnostics, and only 4 percent hail from other faith backgrounds such as Judaism or Buddhism.[31] The theme of her Jewish background is quite pronounced throughout her digital media content. The name she uses in the *niqābosphere*—Rivka Sajida—is a clear example of her hybridized ethno-religious identity. She writes in the blog post from September 26, 2016: "To introduce myself, I'm Paige but I will probably sign as Sajida, which is a part of my Muslim name (the first part being Rivka, from my Hebrew name)."[32] Interestingly, what she considers as her Muslim name includes her Hebrew name but not the English one (Paige). The logic behind this decision is explained in her YouTube video "My Revert Story," dated May 29, 2018:

> I grew up in a mixed religion home, and my mom was a Reform Jew. And my dad was a "failing" Catholic, meaning he didn't even go to Mass on Easter or Christmas or anything, he was agnostic. . . . I practiced major Jewish holidays, and I practiced the four major Christian holidays with my family, that's just kind of the culture I was born into, you know, we practiced Easter, at the same time that we practiced Passover, we practiced Christmas at the same time that we practiced Chanukah, you know, and it's just kind of how it was. . . . You know, I think that really, really helped. And I think that really helped form my opinion toward religion, and *inshaa'Allah* [God wiling] I want to raise my children in such a way so they can be respectful of all religions. Because, you know, their family is going to have all of this different stuff going on. But I was raised to be very open minded. I was told I could choose whatever religion I wanted. And so I was really fascinated with religion from young age.[33]

This narrative of the past reveals how Rivka Sajida was socialized into embracing hybridized identities from a young age, which likely facilitated her later ability to blend different influences and philosophies. Although it is not mentioned explicitly, the story of how she became a Muslim supplies a sense of continuity between her past and present. It was the Jewish part of her identity (which is also probably what marked her as different in the school setting) that brought her closer to bullied Muslim students and, through them, to Islam:

> My first real exposure to Islam was in high school, there were these three sisters and their brothers. They moved to where I am in the United States from Jordan. And people were just so mean, you know, high school kids, they said to those sisters, you know, you're terrorists, things like that, *astagfirullāh*! [I ask Allah forgiveness]. And I stood up for them. And I was like, "You can't say that to them. That's not okay." So we became really close friends really quickly. And we talked a lot about how Judaism and Islam are really similar. I remember one conversation in particular, where we were eating lunch. And we were talking about Judaism, what we're allowed to eat or not allowed to eat. Not that I kept kosher, because my house didn't do that. But we were discussing the dietary rules. And they're like, wait, you can't eat pork either! And it was just this crazy moment where it was just like, whoa!. . . . And so it was this really great, amazing bonding moment, where we realized, you know, we're really the same. You know, it doesn't matter if you're Jewish, or if you're Muslim, our beliefs are so similar.[34]

In Rivka Sajida's story, it was not a long leap from Judaism into Islam because the main difference was accepting Muhammad as a prophet, which she had already done at this point. In her online discussions of modest clothing, she talks about modesty rules not just in Islam but in Christianity and Judaism (where they are called *tzniut*). She sometimes makes references to the Jewish-style headcovering (*tichel*) in her blog; she shares, for example, that according to Jewish custom she started covering her hair (but "*ḥijāb* style" rather than adopting the Jewish-style *tichel*) after she got married, while she still self-identified as Jewish. Examining other similarities, in her blog post "Yemeni Style" from September 6, 2018, she points out that in Yemen both Muslim and Jewish women tend to wear the *niqāb*.[35]

Theological and Ideological Bricolage

On social media, narratives are necessary to communicate individual identities. As Khamis, Wang, and Welling remind us, "social media is driven by a specific kind of identity construction—self-mediation—and what users post, share and like effectively creates a highly curated and often abridged snapshot of how they want to be seen."[36] By deploying different social media platforms and focusing on a variety of issues, Rivka Sajida constructs a highly versatile, complex subjectivity that juxtaposes a range of non-normative identities commonly imagined as contradictory: Jewish-Muslim, Muslim-Queer,[37] Muslim-Feminist,[38] and Orthodox-Sufi.

Rivka Sajida's theological bricolage, as illustrated here in an extract from her blog, implies that traditional religious boundaries may not always apply:

> I consider myself a Queer, Feminist Theologian with major Orthodox leanings. My Islamic theology looks to be a mix of Salafism and Sufism, and my ideas are out-of-the-box when it comes to Queer application of theology within Islam and Abrahamic religions as a whole.[39]

This deconstruction of boundaries—and consequently of academic typologies of progressive versus conservative Muslims—has been noted by Zebiri in her study of British converts to Islam.[40] Zebiri describes an "idiosyncratic mosaic" of converts' views where, depending on the issue or context, one person's opinions could be simultaneously conservative and progressive.[41] This may also be bolstered by the fact that converts do not have their parents' religious communities to contend with and are free to simultaneously draw from, or even adhere to, different theological traditions. I observed the same phenomenon in my earlier work on theological positions which emerged from interpretive discussions of Muslim women in online groups.[42] Rivka Sajida's example demonstrates that the intensity of religious practice, often ascribed to converts as "the zeal of the converted," does not necessarily have to be channeled through orthodoxy but may instead be expressed through various social justice concerns and hybridized, collective personal practice.[43] In this way, the intensity of conviction may translate into a radical project of self-discovery. Thus, Islam may be the language that provides a safe space for experimentation within hypermediated religious spaces characterized by a high degree of liminality where alternative discourses engage mainstream narratives.[44]

In the "Women and Islam, Part 3: Feminism" YouTube video dated October 25, 2017, Rivka Sajida unabashedly describes herself as a feminist.[45] Instead of plunging into the discussion of her understanding of feminism in Islam, she first attempts to deal with misconceptions about feminism, which she encounters "both inside the *Ummah* [the Muslim community] and outside the *Ummah*, in the larger society." She defines feminism as "the active pursuit of equality between men and women and all genders." In her explanation of how feminism has transformed over time, she refers to the second and third waves of feminism which she sees as a setting for the "battle of the sexes." This, she asserts, no longer applies to "modern day feminism." As fourth-wave feminists, she and her friends "work on intersectionality which encompasses equality regardless of race, religion, socioeconomic status, sexuality . . . but we're still under the label of feminism." In contrast, feminists of her parents' generation have this

> misconception that you can't be religious and a feminist, you can't be Muslim and a feminist, you can't be a traditional woman like a housewife or submissive to your husband or anything like this if you are a feminist . . . [that kind of feminism] mostly focused on white women and so it really did a disservice to all women of color and to women that weren't Christian.

She recounts an experience when she

> was approached by a sister and she was like, can you please help explain to these people what the *niqāb* is and why you wear it? Because they were saying that if you are a feminist, you can't wear a *niqab*. Well obviously I'm a feminist and I wear a *niqab*, [name], she wears *niqāb*, and my friend [name], she wears *niqāb*. This is ridiculous. So these women were older than my friend and they were from the third wave of feminism. So I had to explain what equality is as freedom of choice.

Rivka Sajida cultivates her identity as a scholar of Islam by introducing herself as an alumna of a BA program in comparative studies and a student in an MSc program in Islamic theology. By invoking these credentials, she emphasizes her own religious authority—a status she then deploys in her vlogs. In the same way that she challenges theological boundaries, she questions the common perceptions of what it means to be a feminist; her identity as a queer Muslim helps her position herself as a "descendant" of earlier feminist movements who has simultaneously transcended the binaries and biases that characterized them.[46] She situates those movements in the past, while claiming a feminist identity without any qualifications. In the process of making sense of this loaded term, and the debates over its definitions and boundaries, she challenges the understanding of the category of feminism as immutable and exclusionary.[47]

The Shared Aesthetic of the Digital *Niqābosphere*

Rivka Sajida's platform in the digital *niqābosphere* allows her to talk about her passion for Islam, raise awareness about "invisible" disabilities that affect Muslims, and channel her creativity. She not only models and reviews different kinds of *niqābs*, *burqas*, and *jilbabs* (all of which she collects) but sews her own clothing too.[48] Through her material creations and adoption of a particular sartorial style, she successfully propagates an unusual aesthetic of the *niqab*—and Islamic traditional clothing more widely—that both challenges their hegemonic representations as stern, cheerless, and puritanical[49] and differentiates them from "hip, colourful bricolage that some young Muslim women in the West (and elsewhere) engage with."[50]

At the material level, Rikva Sajida situates herself between the locality of her home community and the global dimensions of her appeal. She often provides a public glimpse into her private life, introducing her friends and her co-wife in the videos shot at home. Her collection of Islamic outfits reveals a fascination with the diversity of styles from different Islamic cultures: in her videos, she wears not only the "traditional" black *niqāb* but also both simple and richly ornamental Afghan *burqas*, Algerian and Yemeni style *niqābs*, Iranian *chādors*, Malaysian surgical-mask-style *niqābs*, and a Bedouin chain-link *niqāb* in her favorite pinks, blues, burgundy, and fuchsia colors.[51] Demonstrating her ability to bring together diverse cultural

FIGURE 8.1 *Rivka Sajida on YouTube, screenshot from video, "Review: Mantilla Transformer* Jilbab *by ScarfTurbanHijab!" (https://www.youtube.com/watch?v =LqQzyXzJpaA&t=102s (1:42)). Accessed February 24, 2021.*

artifacts in her quest for creative modest clothing, Rivka Sajida models a *jilbab* adorned with a Spanish-style mantilla (a lace headscarf) which she styles in different ways over her head and face in a YouTube video dated April 7, 2019 (Figure 8.1).[52] She tells the viewers that she made a custom order for the *jilbab*, requesting the mantilla detail based on her own idea for adorning the outfit.

The wide range of cultural traditions from which she draws situates Rivka Sajida's personal aesthetic as an alternative voice in the conversation about the place of face-covering practices in Muslim communities globally. By explicitly identifying the styles of her garments as cultural artifacts from across the world, she challenges the normative, binary discourse that portrays Muslim womens' clothing as a Saudi/Arab cultural imposition rather than a personal religious practice or, conversely, a legitimate religious dress versus insufficiently modest cultural sedimentation.[53] By stepping away from this reductive framing, and by resisting the undergirding logic of the "Islam versus culture" framework, she opens up possibilities that allow different aesthetic interpretations of the notion of modesty.[54]

Building Strategic Relationships with Audiences

While Rivka Sajida regularly uploads Islamic clothing tutorials and product reviews, her "Deen Talk" vlog was gradually eclipsed by "A Day in the Life of a Disabled *Niqabi*" series that commenced in 2017. Rivka Sajida is a self-described part-time *niqābi* who lives with an "invisible disability" known as Ehlers-Danlos syndrome, which affects her mobility. While her condition is mostly hidden, sometimes she has to walk with a cane or, when the joint pain is at its most severe, use a wheelchair. Her reflections on living with a disability as a (new) Muslim run through many online videos, not just those specifically dedicated to this topic. For example, in a "Deen Talk!" episode titled "Mental/Physical Illness, Disability, and Ramadan" from May 26, 2017, she describes how she has had difficulty fasting all her life.[55] Previously a practicing Jewish woman, she suffered during the Yom Kippur fast (which lasts for twenty-five hours). In the episode, she recounts her dilemmas over whether she should fast during *Ramaḍān* since she is taking various medications to manage the pain that results from her condition. Upon consulting an unnamed female Muslim scholar who advised her not to fast as she was exempt due to illness, Rivka Sajida confesses she still felt upset about not fasting due to being unable to join the *ummah* in this annual spiritual practice. She observes that there is a societal stigma whereby only visually observable conditions, like "throwing up . . . or breaking a leg," qualify a Muslim for exemption from fasting, whereas invisible conditions, including in particular mental health conditions "such as depression or eating disorder," are not considered "real" by the community generally. She talks about suffering from mental health issues and calls for recognition of the need for non-stigmatizing treatment of mental health conditions. She also recalls conversations with fellow Muslims who face a dilemma whether to fast despite their own medical conditions—thereby risking relapsing into sickness (due to not taking medication as part of the fast or the fasting itself in the cases of eating disorders) or facing the social stigma for not participating in the communal ritual. Rivka Sajida then advises that individuals in this situation ought to either feed another person who is poor and hungry to make up for the lost fast or improve their spiritual practices (e.g., via more punctual prayers or a more engaged reading of the Qur'ān). In doing so, she argues, the bodily and spiritual dimensions of *Ramaḍān* are retained while accommodating a variety of conditions that make fasting difficult (if not dangerous).

Rivka Sajida's sensitivity to people living with special needs is a theme running throughout her social media content as such needs tend to shape people's Islamic practices. In one of her reviews, dated February 18, 2019, and also published as a text blog entry co-produced with a D/deaf friend, she points out that the style of *ḥijāb* they were reviewing (a "cap-style" *ḥijāb*) was a great choice for someone wearing hearing aids as it did not cause "rustling sounds or feedback (electrical ringing)."[56] In a similar fashion, in one of her "Deen Talk!" episodes titled "Helping Our D/deaf Brothers and Sisters This Ramadan" (dated May 4, 2018) she signs throughout the entire video.[57] Going further, she suggests having sign language interpreters during communal events such as *ṣalāh* prayers, *khuṭbah*s, and *ifṭārs*.[58] These observations were inspired by her Muslim friends living with impaired hearing who have not had a chance to learn to pray. She laments that they are excluded from the Muslim community because others do not take the time to accommodate their needs. Viewers commenting on the video suggest that she turn on the closed captioning function as her hands sometimes appear outside of the frame. This exchange demonstrates that in order to gain popularity on social media, the content author needs to frequently provide content on issues that capture the attention of different audiences in an engaging way across a variety of platforms. To that end, Rivka Sajida diversifies her advocacy by making different recommendations on her blog and YouTube channel, while constantly improving her delivery based on audience suggestions. By drawing attention to special needs of D/deaf Muslims, her content engages educational qualities appreciated by the audience. Commenters thanked her for "educating them on the topic" as they "never considered what their fellow deaf Muslims must endure."

Rivka Sajida primarily uses YouTube to update her subscribers on developments in her life, with a particular emphasis on how she negotiates various health issues while simultaneously living out her adopted faith in a Midwestern city as a new Muslim. She shares the following reflection in one of her "A Day in the Life of a Disabled *Niqabi*" videos, dated February 2, 2019: "So it can be really, really difficult and really strenuous but *alhamdulillāh* you know, I have this platform, I have YouTube, I have Facebook I have Twitter, I have Instagram and *alhamdulillāh Allah taʿala* [Thanks be to God, Allah the most high] is allowing me to, to bring knowledge to people and awareness about those things."[59] Later in the same video, she says, "My *iman* [faith] has been more up lately *alhamdulillāh*, so I'm really excited to bring all these things [updates] to you guys." This informal, laid-back form of address, coupled with frequent references to communications with her subscribers/ fans, suggests a sense of familiarity and reciprocity. Upon a more detailed examination of the videos and comments, it becomes clear that people often express concern for her. Rivka Sajida, acknowledging those concerns, regularly updates her viewers on her own health issues. This highlights that beyond simply gaining the attention of audiences, fostering an interactive dialogue with them is required in the process of online community-building.

Founding Daar ul-Gharib: A Culmination of Hybrid Identities, Non-Mainstream Narratives, and Shared Aesthetics

As the Covid-19 pandemic struck, and access to in-person worship became severely restricted, the social and cultural capital that she had developed among her communities of followers enabled Rivka Sajida to organize more formally. In order to negotiate the looming physical alienation prior to *Ramaḍān* 2020, she decided to establish an online mosque on a Discord server which she called *Daar ul-Gharib* (Home of the Stranger)—a reference to the pervasive exclusion experienced by nonconformist Muslims. As I asked her about how she was dealing with the challenges of the lockdown, she enthusiastically described her new project:

> Right before the pandemic started, I had made *niyyah* [intention] to attend *Jummah* [Friday] prayer each week. Obviously, this didn't happen. As Ramaḍān approached, I had inspiration from *Allah subḥānahu wa taʿālā* [Allah glory to Him the most high] and I created a virtual *masjid*, *Daar ul-Gharib*, for Queer Muslims (mostly femme and nonbinary), who already are generally isolated in the larger Muslim community. *Alhamdulillāh* [praise be to God] this has helped us all have a home even if we can't congregate physically! The *masjid* I started is hosted on a Discord server. This allows us to hold *iftar* [the breaking of the fast] hangouts, and, *inshaa'Allah* [God willing] hold a virtual party for Eid. . . . We hold congregational prayer daily, as well as Qur'ān reading and classes.[60]

The following statement demonstrates how the new online mosque, and her leadership role within it, consolidates her identity production:

I think that this is what *Allah ta ʿālā* was leading me to all along. I've always felt in my studies that He was leading me to Queer Theology, but I never would have thought He would lead me to be, essentially, a woman *imam*! A few years ago I would have laughed at the idea. We plan and Allah plans, but He is the best of planners.[61]

By using the title of a woman *imam*, Rivka Sajida officially takes a position in the debate on female religious leadership in Islam.[62] While female prayer leadership is especially controversial in mainstream Muslim communities,[63] in nonconformist communities such as those of queer Muslims, the conversation transcends this issue and addresses the need to affirm nonbinary individuals' leadership.[64] Rivka Sajida's sermons (available on YouTube[65]) display a format similar to traditional sermons; coupled with her prayers in Arabic, they reflect a claim to authority and continuity with the Islamic tradition writ large.[66] At the same time, however, by reenacting these elements she simultaneously recreates and renegotiates them simply by virtue of being a queer Muslim woman.[67] In her words:

> This year I'm focusing on prayer and in providing others with ways to perform *ʿibādah* [worship], as well as providing information and education. I've been giving *khuṭbahs* [sermons] and answering questions from members of my *masjid*. . . . I have switched my focus from my "everyday" job to my job in leading the *masjid* I created, as I figure this is where my focus should be during Ramadan.[68]

The earlier production of religious content for her vlog prepared Rivka Sajida for the complex role of *imam* as much as her formal academic study of Islam. Not only did this digital media work allow for the building of a community of followers, it also constituted a training of sorts in public speaking. These skills allowed her to communicate a particular affect based on accessibility, intimacy, and directness—a message and medium that other believers needed and responded to, especially in the context of the pandemic that limited social interactions. The *Daar ul-Gharib* mosque provides a powerful sense of belonging, connection, and healing. As an embodiment and expression of a redefinition of the traditional community of faith, and the culmination of Rivka Sajida's hybrid identities and non-mainstream narratives, it offers a clear example of a third space of digital religion in practice.[69]

Conclusion

The storied, hybridized identity that Rivka Sajida has produced in her corner of the digital *niqābosphere* opens up many avenues that might otherwise be closed to her because of her intersecting marginalized identities. Her lived experience speaks to bell hooks's famous quote: "more than a site of deprivation . . . [marginality] is also the site of radical possibility, a space of resistance."[70] Within this virtual space, she is able to cultivate a subjectivity that allows for the flawless blending of ostensibly disparate commitments and affiliations.

Rivka Sajida's non-mainstream religious narratives manifest themselves in her digital content which she orients to various axes that shape her life. Her experience of both physical disability and religious expertise situate her as a powerful advocate for other Muslims living with disabilities. Comments under her videos indicate that she successfully manages to raise awareness in the Muslim community of special needs related to disability and creative ideas about how to meet them. Simultaneously, Rivka Sajida's other videos—including reviews of Islamic clothing and *ḥalāl* cosmetics also embedded on her blog—are performing a different role, one that allows her to respond to the needs and interests of her target audiences.[71] While none of her videos speak specifically to her experiences as a Jewish convert to Islam, she makes passing references to her Jewishness in her online content to highlight that there is no conflict between her ethnic background and faith. By juxtaposing her wide array of identities across different platforms she effectively constructs a complex personal brand; the appeal of her profile is based on a multilayered, responsive public identity. What is particularly striking about her narrative is that she very rarely addresses the *niqāb* as a discrete topic. Although it is almost always present in her content, she positions it dialogically with other aspects of her identity such as her disability, ethnic background, or feminism. Whether that is intended or not, the *niqāb* she wears is demystified by Rivka Sajida's ordinary concerns and the mechanics of her everyday life.

I have argued in this chapter that the narratives and identities of Rivka Sajida are non-mainstream in that they resist the ubiquitous negative and skewed representations of *niqāb*-wearing women through their multilayered self-mediation. Through hybridization, she opens the avenue to engaging different audiences and creating spaces of resistance to exclusionary practices within both non-Muslim and Muslim communities. This is particularly poignant in her endeavor to lead an online mosque. By performing her Muslim identity and piety in digital media platforms, she has discovered new pathways to continuous self-reinvention. In demonstrating how articulations of piety are enmeshed with social justice concerns in Rivka Sajida's narratives, this chapter responds to the call of Schielke who argues against a bias in research on Islam and Muslim that privileges identities of people who consciously present themselves as pious Muslims—especially in circumstances where they intentionally perform these identities (in mosques or study groups, for example)—but neglects the wider matrix of interests, commitments, and contexts in which these individuals function.[72]

The digital *niqābosphere* represents a new "counter-public,"[73] which challenges the pessimistic view of the public espoused by Adorno and Horkheimer who believed that contemporary mass media rendered audiences passive and uncritical of the ideologies that popular culture promoted.[74] By contrast, the narratives I have analyzed resist and challenge domination by establishing discursively connected public spheres, rich in visual and textual data. Both these types of data are particularly important in resisting mass-mediated, dominant representations of the *niqāb* and the Muslim women who wear it. The digital *niqābosphere* facilitates such activity by facilitating the creation of tailored, grassroots political interventions. Notably, the interactions between *niqābis* and their audiences challenge Habermas's somewhat downbeat idea of separated counterpublics "[on] the Internet [which] remain closed off from one another like global villages."[75] This suggests a potential for interconnectedness, even if tentative and temporary, between seemingly disparate groups.

The digital *niqābosphere* offers a rare chance to interact with a *niqābi* to many people who otherwise would not have this opportunity. For the women themselves, these settings facilitate mobilization around shared values, beliefs, and experiences. In virtual spaces, Muslim women are able to deploy storied, hybridized identities based on narratives describing the experience of "full *niqāb*-wearing" as piety-driven and overwhelmingly positive; this stands in contrast to the indictments of the *niqāb* in the mass media. It is notable that geographical dispersion does not impact the readiness of these women to connect with each other. As Downey and Fenton argue: "[The counterpublic] offers forms of solidarity and reciprocity that are grounded in a collective experience of marginalization and expropriation, but these forms are inevitably experienced as mediated, no longer rooted in face-to-face relations, and subject to discursive conflict and negotiation."[76] Digital networks connect urban women with rural ones; they may also transcend sectarian, racial, language, national, and cultural divides. Rivka Sajida's example illustrates the multiple ways in which some *niqāb*-wearing women are able to translate issues and concerns across such lines. The phenomenon of social media personalities such as hers is driven by the "extent to which social media proceeds without the gamut of gatekeepers that otherwise determines and limits content flows; audiences increasingly predisposed to 'ordinary' people in the spotlight; and a cultural economy that contours almost everything (including conceptions of the self) along consumerist lines."[77] Ultimately, the social media processes described in this chapter do not occur in a vacuum. Instead, they are located within a complex matrix of materiality, institutions, and technologies, interpolating physical objects, social structures, performances, authority, belonging, and continuous innovation.[78]

CHAPTER 9

Islamic Meditation:

Mindfulness Apps for Muslims in the Digital Spiritual Marketplace

Megan Adamson Sijapati

Introduction

This chapter describes and analyzes three digital sites that offer guided meditations curated by and for Muslims: *Sakeenah*, *Sabr*, and *Halaqah*. My analysis offers thick descriptions of these mobile apps, which first appeared in the online "meditation marketplace" in 2020 and 2021, and identifies resonant themes and questions that I believe are fruitful for the study of religion in digital landscapes and for mapping the shifting contours of lived Islam.[1] Today's industry of online meditation and mindfulness products is highly profitable, as meditation—and, more broadly, "mindfulness"—has in recent decades been embraced and normalized in contemporary, cosmopolitan life as a key part of health and wellness. The guided mindfulness and meditation practices found on the most popular mainstream apps, however, tend to be assemblages of meditation styles modeled upon Buddhist mindfulness and yogic somatic practices, despite the frequent absence of clear markers of these religious foundations.[2] In contrast, the Muslim-created apps I discuss here, while mirroring similar styles of meditation to those in the mainstream meditation marketplace, offer guided meditation practices imbued with the cultural, theological, and epistemological frames of Islamic piety. This, I suggest, is a noteworthy development in both the meditation marketplace and contemporary Muslim piety. These apps demonstrate Muslim efforts at carving out distinctly Muslim spaces, not just within the digital meditation marketplace but also apart from the already well-established genre of Muslim religious apps. In my view, these new developments warrant close examination as a distinct genre in the growing academic study of religion in cyberspace.

Until 2020, there were no apps exclusively designated for "Muslim meditation" or advertised as meditation *for* Muslims among the myriad offerings on Google Play and iTunes. While a few guided and self-styled "Sufi meditations" (*dhikr*) were available on the widely used meditation app *InsightTimer*, other popular meditation apps such as *Headspace* did not feature meditations with a specific religious affiliation.[3] The content on Islamic religious apps such as *MuslimPro* and *IslamiCal* included Qur'ān recitations, *ḥadīth*, prayer times, and *duʿāʾ* but nothing resembling guided meditations.[4] However, by summer 2020, as people's lives migrated to being more virtual to a degree unimaginable before the Covid-19 pandemic, the meditation app landscape expanded exponentially in a variety of ways. In fact, two million more mental wellness app downloads were recorded in April 2020 than in pre-pandemic January of the same year.[5] As part of this sudden and rapid development, the meditation app marketplace shifted to include new "Islamic" modes of meditation. Now guided meditations designed by and for Muslims, and marketed as such, can be downloaded from Google Play or Apple's App Store.

In delivering to Muslims guided meditations and tools for mindfulness that are compatible with multiple forms of Islamic piety, these sites provide Muslims with alternatives to the mainstream meditation offerings online that, as I have argued elsewhere, are not as "secular" or "cross-cultural" as they present themselves to be.[6] The introduction of Islamically framed versions of guided meditations on the new apps *Sakeenah*, *Sabr*, and *Halaqah* allows for the participation in, and performance of, app-based meditation as a form of Muslim piety that is free of the subtle (and sometimes not so subtle) references to Buddhist and Hindu principles that undergird most meditations offered in the mainstream meditation marketplace.[7] In this way, *Sakeenah*, *Sabr*, and *Halaqah* construct a digitally based mode of Muslim piety through an Islamically inflected, innovative, and distinctly modern ritual performance—firmly situated in both Islamic tradition and the contemporary wellness industry.

Sakeenah

Sakeenah (from *sakinah*, an Arabic term meaning "tranquility, peace, serenity") is an app launched and copyrighted in 2020 by Muzmind FZ-LLC, based in Dubai. The *Sakeenah* website claims it is "in the business of creating happiness for people"[8] and describes the app as providing techniques bundled together in a cohesive, easy-to-use product designed to address mental health issues facing Muslims today. As the website explains, its content and approach:

> are a marriage of religion and modern sciences serving the 475 Muslims struggling with mental health issues. By featuring Mindfulness & Meditation created by scholars, qualified experts and life coaches, Sakeenah assists with emotional, mental and spiritual well-being. This content is a mixture of modern mindfulness techniques with backing/ references from Quran and Hadith that would create an emotional connection for a Muslim, getting them through a particular state of mind, call it anxiety, depression, etc. [sic].[9]

On Google Play and the iTunes App Store, *Sakeenah*'s description adds that it is "a mindfulness and meditation app for Muslims" and addresses its Islamic character more directly:

> A Muslim's state of Mindfulness is to be in the continuous full knowledge that Allah is Aware [sic] of him or her, inwardly and outwardly. It is a complete state of conscious self-awareness in one's relationship with Allah in the heart, mind, and body.
>
> The basis of mindfulness in Islam is our knowledge that Allah is always watching us at all times and, as a consequence, we develop greater attention and care for our own actions, thoughts, feelings, and inner states of being. As Allah said, "Remember that God knows what is in your souls, so be mindful of Him."
>
> Modern life involves a daily bustle of noise, distraction, and information overload. Our senses are constantly stimulated from every direction to the point that a simple moment of quiet stillness seems impossible for some of us. This continuous agitation hinders us from getting the most out of each moment.[10]

These claims connect *Sakeenah*'s Islamically inflected meditations on the app with a foundational theme of mainstream mindfulness: the continuous "agitation" that people experience in modern-day life, and during stressful times in particular, is best alleviated through a stilling of the mind that comes through a focus on the present moment. Here, *Sakeenah* offers the solution in an Islamic rendering, describing the "conscious self-awareness in one's relationship with Allah in the heart, mind, and body" that the app will help cultivate.

The app's website features an image of a woman in *ḥijāb* (headscarf) meditating with eyes closed, smiling, her hands on her knees with index fingers and thumbs touching—a bodily posture and hand gesture commonly seen on mainstream meditation apps but not typically associated with Islam (Figure 9.1). Beside this image is written, "Mental Wellbeing Solutions in light

FIGURE 9.1 *An image from the* Sakeenah *app's website (https://www.sakeenah.io/).*

of Quran, Hadith, and Islamic Literature." Below that are brief descriptions of the app's content listed under green, one-dimensional images of a lotus flower; a hand with the thumb and index finger touching and the palm facing upward; and a *yin–yang* symbol.[11] This use of non-Islamic symbols is striking, suggesting the app's creators believe *Sakeenah* may appeal more to Muslim users (or investors) by incorporating ambiguous—but highly marketable— signifiers of "Eastern" mysticism and spirituality. Below these symbols is a diagram of the company's planned development phases over the next two years, as well as short bios of key team members: four men (who appear to be either Arab or South Asian) shown in black-and-white headshots. Their biographies list degrees and professional backgrounds in marketing, mobile app development, and revenue streaming. No mention is made, however, of the developers having any experience in the research, teaching, development, or practice of mindfulness or meditation, nor are there descriptions of their *maḏhab* affiliations or educational lineages.[12] Whether intentional or not, this sparsity of information—coupled with the visual deployment of authority that is male and tech-savvy but not attached to any specific cultural group, teaching lineage, or expertise in jurisprudence (*fiqh*)—works to minimize any particular Muslim identity that might otherwise be associated with the app. Alternatively, downplaying, or de-linking, the sources of the meditation practices from any specific Islamic institution or school of thought could be an intentional, strategic move to broaden the app's reach and appeal to Muslims from a diverse range of backgrounds.

The *Sakeenah* app is visually decorated with images of Islamic art and sacred sites. Upon opening the app a message appears with the user's name, saying, "Salaam, welcome back [user name]! Let's bring that smile on you, *Inshah'Allah* [God willing]. Pick a category and let's get started."[13] Users choose their preferred background color and meditation practices are labeled with colorful pictures of iconic mosques, Qur'ānic calligraphy, or geometric designs. The user then personalizes their guided meditation based on duration, topic, or their internal condition (such as anxiety). The seven-day course titled "Anxiety" offers short meditations titled "Don't fall in hopelessness," "He is *Saami al Baseer*,"[14] "Allah is *Arahman & Araheem*,"[15] "Allah is in Control," and "The Art of Pausing." Each link offers an audio track that guides users through a meditation practice on that specific topic.

Another example is a practice titled "[The] Concept of Meditation in Islam." The following is an excerpt of the accompanying audio track:

> Assalamu Alaykum [Peace be upon you]. I would like to explain an Islamic practice that really is at the core of Islamic spirituality, yet unfortunately nowadays is not really given the attention, focus and honor that it deserves.
>
> When we think of meditation we think of a monk, or a Zen master, someone sitting peacefully with eyes closed in a state of bliss, but what relation does meditation have with Islam? Meditation is quite simply the art, the practice, the experience of being still. It's about surrendering. Surrendered at the most fundamental levels of our existence.
>
> Meditation is about completely letting go and aligning and immersing oneself in the divine presence of Allah the almighty. We are constantly doing, we are continually asserting will, asserting self. In meditation we learn to simply be.
>
> Is meditation necessary in Islam? Absolutely. There is no way to attain that state of surrender and mindfulness without practicing it. And we know that Prophet Muhammad, peace be upon him, spent days in meditation. Not just for an hour or two, but for days at a time. And it was in that state of surrender, or presence, that he was given revelation. Meditation is about tearing away the filter that is created by our ego, our identity. *Fikr* [observation, concentration] is a *Siraj al-Qalb* [a lamp of the heart].[16]

By invoking the stereotypical meditator as an "Eastern" Zen monk figure, and then countering that with the claim that the quintessential meditator can also be a modern-day Muslim, and by locating the root of meditation in surrender to Allah and working with the *nafs*—both key inflections of Islamic piety—*Sakeenah* asserts that meditation should be properly understood as a fundamental expression of Islamic piety.[17] The app goes even further to assert there is "no way to attain" the state of mindfulness and surrender without the practice of meditation. This claim positions meditation as a performance of individual piety alternative to (and beyond the parameters of) the mosque, the family, or traditional Islamic communities such as study groups or Sufi *dhikr* circles. Instead, this expression of piety as a practice of "presence" and surrender (the literal meaning of "Islam") is a solitary experience that can be performed anytime and anywhere, requiring nothing more than a mobile device.

Sabr

Sabr (from *ṣabr*, an Arabic term meaning "perseverance" or "active patience") was launched in October 2020 and copyrighted by Deen Academy, LLC. Like *Sakeenah* and *Halaqah*, some of its guided meditations and mindfulness courses are free and others are unlocked with a Premium subscription.[18] On the iTunes Store the app is listed in the "Health and Fitness" category with the description "A Guided Meditation App For Muslims: Sleep more. Stress less. *Bismillah* [In the name of God]. Improve your Relationship with Allah."[19] *Sabr*'s website explains that "Life can get tough at times. With the hustle and bustle of work, the variety of distractions, informational overload, and yes . . . the pandemic, finding time to reflect and slowdown [*sic*] seems almost impossible."[20] A YouTube video on the landing page of *Sabr*'s website states that

> 25% of adults experience some type of mental illness, and with mental health issues across the country increasing, meditation is more important now than ever before . . . while there are many guided meditation and mental health apps in the market such as *Calm* and *Headspace*, the need for an Islamic one is more important now than ever before.[21]

Sabr positions its product as meeting this need—a lacuna, it emphasizes, that has only increased during the Covid pandemic era.

The *Sabr* website features brief bios and photos of its twenty-one teachers. On the app itself, only the instructors' names are listed alongside the meditations and courses they lead. Notably, this downplaying of individual personalities and identities is in stark contrast to other mainstream meditation apps whose advertisements spotlight meditations led by celebrity meditators and teachers. Most of *Sabr*'s instructors hold advanced degrees either from academic institutions in the United States and the United Kingdom or from Islamic academic institutions in the Middle East, South Asia, and the United States. A number of them are based in New Jersey. Its founder is Subhaan Ashrafi,[22] who reportedly came up with the idea for *Sabr* after encountering Muslim youth with mental health struggles through his sports show on YouTube and realizing the increased importance of mental health and self-care during Covid-19.[23] *Sabr*'s establishment was supported by a LaunchGood campaign in the summer of 2020.[24]

Sabr has three categories of guided audio track practices. The first is "Guided Meditation" (*murāqabah*), which the app describes as "Research-backed guided meditation sessions through an Islamic Lens. We are working with Muslim therapists and professionals across the globe to curate this material. Alhamdulillah!" The other modules are "Spiritually Uplifting Courses" and "*Nasheeds*" with, the app emphasizes, "AMSR soundtracks," a common feature of guided meditations in the broader meditation app landscape.[25] *Sabr's* visual design uses stock photographs of nature scenes: palm trees at sunset, deserts at dusk, northern lights, empty beaches. Most of the app's guided meditations include a sonic backdrop of low-volume ocean waves, but the specific content and style of its meditations and courses vary by teacher. The meditations tend to interweave instructions for breathing and somatic awareness, segments of *du'ā'*, excerpts of Qur'ānic verses (*āyāt*), and motivational phrases. Within any particular meditation the user can mark "favorites" by pressing a heart symbol in the upper right corner, which then makes it accessible on the user's "profile" tab. That is the extent of the customization allowed, however. The teacher leading most of the app's meditations is Wali Khan, whose bio picture displays a man in a tracksuit embroidered with "RN, BSN, Trauma" and a stethoscope around his neck—a depiction perhaps meant to highlight the app's medical-scientific claims to improve mental health.

A resonant example of a meditation on *Sabr* is a four-minute guided practice titled "I am Ready," which is one of three meditations grouped together under the title "You Can Do This" (Figure 9.2). The instructor for this module is listed as *Imam* Wisam Sharieff, whose bio on the *Sabr* website describes him as having studied at the Institute of Islamic Education in Elgin, Illinois, the Quran Academy in Pakistan, and under (unnamed) scholars

FIGURE 9.2 Sabr *app's opening page. Screenshot of the author's personal account.*

in Mecca and Egypt, as well as being a certified radiology technician.[26] He begins the guided audio meditation by saying, "Let's begin to heal. Turn the camera inwards. This moment, it's a new moment."[27] His narrative then shifts into first person as he says, "My breathing synchronizes with the universe around me. In this moment I am enjoying looking inwards and my focus is on healing my feelings, going within. . . . As I breathe in I bring in all the good around me."[28] The shift from third to first person creates a sense of the teacher becoming the meditator's own voice, guiding the listener through visualizations and imagined emotional and mental states. He then alternates between reciting parts of a *du'ā'* and giving first-person verbal somatic cues: "*Rabbanā ātinā fi ad-dunyā ḥasanatan* . . . as I breathe out, I allow all the pressure and worries to release . . . *wa fi al-ākhirati ḥasanantan wa qinā 'adhāba an-nāri.*"[29] He continues to lead the meditator through the relaxation of the body, saying, "my palms are open to receive . . . I am ready to trust myself and my inner guidance system to lead me to truth . . . I am ready to be a great listener. To myself and those around me . . . I am ready."[30] These self-affirmations continue, encouraging the meditator to reflect on the good around them and to expect good things from God. He then says, "*ḥasbi Allah*" (God is sufficient) before taking a long pause. *Ḥasbi Allah* works here as a synecdoche, instantly invoking the *du'ā'* "*ḥasbi Allah lā 'ilāha 'illā hu 'alayhi tawakkultu*" ["Allah is sufficient for me, there is no god but Him, I place my trust in Him"] and the Qur'ānic verse from which it comes.[31] This phrase aims to create a connection in the meditator between Islamic sacred sources and a universal Muslim piety—echoing the app's foundational claim that all mindfulness is ultimately surrender to the reality that is Allah and that an embodied awareness of this ontological truth constitutes Muslim meditation.

The narration then returns to a style of guidance resembling common elements of mainstream meditations. The teacher instructs the meditator to develop a cosmic connection and breathe their negativity away, saying, "discarding negativity through the breath. . . . My breathing is synchronized with the universe. I am allowing myself to be calm . . . and graceful." Then, once again, he switches to a supplication: "Fill me with grace."[32] Here the focus is on the individual but in relation to the God—marking a significant difference from other mainstream (and especially Buddhist) style meditations which recognize no divinity and posit the individual as the agent creating the change in their internal condition. I argue that this feature of centering the divine in the meditator's experience of stillness and mindfulness, and hence their mental and emotional health, is one of the most distinct features of the marketing and teaching style of these new Muslim meditation apps. By shifting the agency for internal change from the modern, busy, individual meditator to God, Muslim meditation apps expressly reject the epistemological and ontological underpinnings of mainstream meditation apps.

Sabr, unlike *Halaqah* and *Sakeenah*, features a "Notifications" tab with hashtag messages that encourage users to try new features on the app. These are upbeat messages that range in style and content. Informal motivational notes encourage users to "Always remember! Allah LOVES you for your *Sabr*! It's going to be okay" and "Make Self-Care a Priority. Consider upgrading to premium to have full access to all courses, vocals, and meditations, *insha'Allah*!" Others include motivational quotes from influential American Muslims such as Shaykh Omar Suleiman and even non-Muslim writers such as Robert Collier, an early twentieth-century American author of self-help and New Age metaphysical books.[33] Other "Notifications" offer supplications such as "#JummahMubarak 'Ya Allah, grant us reflect from every difficulty. Ya Allah, bring happiness into our lives" or Qur'ānic verses preceded by the hashtag #SabrMotivation, such as "'Verily, with hardship comes ease' [94:5]" and 'And He is with. You wherever you are' [57:4]." These messages work to confirm the Islamic nature of these meditations, deploying the common social media app tools of hashtags and notifications to embed references to the Qur'ān or well-known Muslim authority figures in cyberspace.

Halaqah

Halaqah (an Arabic term meaning "circle" or, more specifically, an Islamic study circle) was launched and copyrighted in 2020 as "an Islamic meditation app" and is listed in the education section of Google Play and the iTunes App Store.[34] *Halaqah's* website promises users an opportunity to "Cope with Anxiety and Stress and Straighten your relationship with Allah" through "teaching people the power of mindfulness and prayer."[35] On the iTunes App Store, the description begins with a verse from the Qur'ān emphasizing the ease that comes with contemplative practice (here described as *dhikr*, or "remembrance"). It focuses on the mental and emotional health challenges endemic to being human and promises relief through its collection of curated remembrance practices:

> "Verily with remembrance of Allah do hearts find rest" [Qur'ān 13:28]. Anxiety, sadness, and stress. We all experience it in some form in our lives. But when we calm our mind and realign ourselves back to the source of all life, it brings us tranquility. *Halaqah* is your digital spiritual circle, with *dhikr* sessions and guided meditations, to bring tranquility and peace to your heart. We've created a collection of *adkhar* [plural of *dhikr*] that immerses you in a powerful collective experience that can remedy the symptoms of busy living, and also some guided mindfulness sessions to help you in your day.[36]

The website outlines *Halaqah's* origin story, describing that when one of the founders visited refugee camps in Turkey, Jordan, and Lebanon and witnessed people's trauma there he experienced acute stress and anxiety that were, in time, alleviated only through mindfulness practices. However, the site explains, "the mindfulness practices were lacking the spirituality of the Islamic circles he used to attend."[37] In response to this absence of spirituality, readers are told, *Halaqah* was specifically designed to help people, presumably Muslims, in all kinds of life situations, from refugee camps to upscale urban workplaces, through spiritually oriented meditation practices. *Halaqah* emphasizes that its meditations were created under the supervision of "mental health experts and scholars," which is a persistent theme on all three apps. Even so, there is no information given about the founders' "Islamic circles" (an affiliation with a Sufi order, for example), nor about the training of the mental health experts and scholars it claims created the app's meditations and *dhikr* sessions.

A January 2021 YouTube video advertising *Halaqah* features footage of Muslims—all young adults, with women in *ḥijāb* and men in both Islamic and non-Islamic dress—in a variety of urban settings and dramatized situations of stress. These scenes are then contrasted with scenes of the same people making *duʿāʾ* or sitting in tranquil settings such as a city park, leaning against a tree, with cell phone in hand and earbuds in, presumably listening to *Halaqah*. The narrator says,

> when we calm our mind with a daily dose of remembrance and reflection, it brings us tranquility and reminds us of our true purpose. *Halaqah* is a way to bring mindfulness and the rich tradition of *dhikr* into your life. So when you take part in any of the *Halaqah* sessions here, put your headphones on and be recharged by the remembrance and meditation.[38]

The message communicated here is that the *dhikr*s offered by *Halaqah* are a panacea for the range of internal turmoil experienced by busy, adult, urban Muslims—that healing and wellness only require them to step into a calm space, put headphones on, and participate through listening.

On *Halaqah's* website, cofounder Jubair Khan expands upon the place of meditation in Islam. He likens meditation to *dhikr* rather than *murāqabah* (meditation) or *fikr* (observation or concentration)—and then elides meditation and mindfulness and notes it is "rooted in science."[39] In his words:

> It's been a difficult year for everyone. . . . And with the world the way it is, we need Allah's remembrance now more than ever to bring us a sense of stability and calm. *Halaqah* is our small effort to do that. It gives you the opportunity to take part in the remembrance of Allah, and to be guided through your emotions with guided meditations.
>
> *Dhikr*, or the remembrance of Allah, is part of a rich Islamic tradition going back to the Prophet Muhammad himself, peace be upon him. It focuses the mind on the source of everything, Allah. You can say it's a type of Islamic meditation, but more powerful because of the spiritual element connecting you to Your Creator. Mindfulness is an ancient practice and now it's rooted in science.[40]

Halaqah's very name situates the app's meditations in the broader context of Islamic piety and ritual performance via an imagined gathering of users/viewers in a shared experience. Like mainstream meditation apps, it groups the meditations a user has completed and categorizes them as "My Halaqahs," which emphasizes individual choice. Although users decide which religious circles they step into, it is notable that they are not entering into a virtual community through participation since there is no interactive mode of connection with others on the app.[41] The *Halaqah* app labels groups of meditations with stylized color illustrations of a woman in a blue *chādor* (a style of *ḥijāb* common in Iran and parts of India); a man wearing an Emirati *thobe* with hands in position for *du ʿāʾ*; and various illustrated backgrounds such as silhouetted minarets, a crescent moon, a *muṣḥaf* (a written copy of the Qur'ān); and a Qur'ān stand. Guided practices are grouped in three categories: "Mindfulness," "Purification," and "Dhikr," and the user chooses to hear the meditation audio tracks in a "male voice" or "female voice" (not an option on *Sabr* or *Sakeenah*). Notably, and like *Sakeenah*, meditation practices are titled with the emotional/mental condition a user wants to either alleviate or cultivate, such as "motivation," "courage," "gratitude," "anxiety," "focus," or "sleep." Some modules are single meditations, while others are listed as a seven-day series.

An example of a *Halaqah* practice is its "Guide to Meditation" audio track: an introductory course in three segments aimed to teach "the basics of meditation and mindfulness" (Figure 9.3).[42] No information is provided

My Halaqahs

Featured course

Guide to
meditation
0 hours 13 minutes 30 seconds

In progress

Overwhelmed
9 min 37 sec

Motivatio
12 min 41 sec

Courses

Mindfulness
Mindfulness courses, to improve
your mental health
50 courses

Purification
Ancient and modern wisdom for
self improvement

FIGURE 9.3 Halaqah *app's opening page. Screenshot of the author's personal account.*

about the teacher or author. It begins with the *bismillāh*[43] and the narrator then speaks about mindfulness while birds chirp on an audio loop in the background: "the beauty of our *dīn* [religion] is that we are encouraged to reflect and ponder. . . . Today we'll learn the skill of observing our thoughts. Mindfulness is an ancient practice now rooted in science, which teaches us to become more aware."[44] He then gives cues for deep breathing and body awareness techniques, similar to those found in mainstream meditation apps, such as "be aware of your body's contact with your seat." He also instructs listeners to focus the mind upon sounds in the room and physical sensations in the body, and to redirect the mind's wandering thoughts to the rise and fall of the breath. The somatic dimensions of the meditations—the focus on the body as a means for stilling and focusing the mind—resemble techniques of both Sufi *dhikr* and meditations in the mainstream marketplace.

Halaqah's pervasive emphasis on science legitimating the practice of mindfulness is noteworthy. It suggests that the app's creators want to make clear they are not presenting meditation to Muslims as followers of contemporary, global consumer culture, but rather because meditation has objectively proven benefits. The message is that meditation is a supplementary form of Islamic piety objectively proven by modern science to be beneficial. In short, it is not any Islamic authority lending this app its legitimacy, but rather the invocations of the scientific evidence of the proven benefits of meditation for overall health and wellness.

Sakeenah, *Sabr*, and *Halaqah* and the Performance of Meditation as Piety

All three apps assert that the performance of meditation and mindfulness cultivate a stillness and calm needed for Muslims to face the emotional and mental strains of modern life. *Sakeenah*, *Sabr*, and *Halaqah* espouse the view that Muslims can practice meditation to improve mental and spiritual health. At the same time they each imply that for Muslims to practice these techniques in a way aligned with the *dīn*, the meditations themselves should be aligned with core principles of Islam: primarily that God, and not the individual self, is the source and facilitator of inner states of tranquility and mindfulness. An underlying message seems to be that *'ibādah* (ritual practices) and immersion in the *dīn* do not alone relieve Muslims from the difficult conditions of contemporary life such as stress, anxiety, depression, and insomnia because those very conditions limit one's ability to be fully present in their piety. These apps are not suggesting that meditation should replace prayer, but rather that if a Muslim's mental and emotional states are strained then their full potential—in both the *dīn* and *dunyā*—will not be realized.[45]

A central tenet of Islamic piety is *taqwā* (God consciousness). Although the term is not invoked directly on these apps, the meditations they provide are clearly informed by the goal of aligning an individual's present-moment consciousness of God with continual surrender to the divine will. It is implied across these apps that meditation can facilitate a deeper engagement with the key reservoirs for Islamic mindfulness: the *sunnah* (the example of the Prophet Muhammad) and the Qur'ān. The Prophet Muhammad's piety is invoked as a superior paradigm for what in contemporary society is understood simply as self-driven, self-regulated "mindfulness" and "meditation." Similarly, the Qur'ān conveys divine injunctions for (and guidance to) the practice of stillness and mindfulness that are ultimately rendered in Islamic idiom as "surrender"—a stark contrast to (and a more elevated form of) contemporary secular "mindfulness."[46] We have seen how these apps continuously invoke the example of the Prophet and the text of the Qur'ān as touchstones within their guided audio meditations. In doing so, they assert that the practice of mindfulness is not only found in Islam, it *is* Islam. Islam *is* mindfulness.

Sakeenah, *Sabr*, and *Halaqah* are notably devoid of sectarian markers and references to *fiqh*, *madhab*, *tarīqah* (a Sufi institutional order), or any single teacher, mosque, or institute. It appears these apps are strategically designed for a Muslim consumer who wants to participate in contemporary meditation and mindfulness but, at the same time, does not want the practices to be, or feel, un-Islamic. In the landscape of contemporary Islam, the stakes are high in debates about what practices are deemed authentically "Islamic" or "un-Islamic." Competing claims to what are (and are not) proper forms of Muslim piety often result in schisms and boundaries, exacerbating political and social dynamics that can minoritize and oppress. The definition of normativity—and what is recognized as *harām* (forbidden) or *shirk* (idolatrous disbelief)—can be a highly contentious matter. This intra-Muslim discourse is especially complex because of the manifold approaches to the Qur'ān and *sunnah*, coupled with the global diversity of ethnic, cultural, and political perspectives. By not linking (or intentionally *de*-linking) their Islamic references with specific "normative" institutions and established authorities, these digital apps reveal a logic of practice and an intended audience very different from the digital media productions of other Muslim groups. In a guided meditation on *Sakeenah*, references are made to Sufis, Sufism (*tassawuf*), and the Sufi practice of the "purification of the self" (*tazkiyah al-nafs*). For the most part, however, the language and concepts presented on these apps are devoid of any hint of sectarian or cultural markers that would situate a practice in a particular branch of Islam. By design, this gives an egalitarian, non-sectarian feel to these guided meditations and teachings, broadening their potential access and appeal to diverse audiences.

I suggest that what we see in these apps is something of a new Muslim vernacular, spurred by the evolution of digital technology that demands an ecumenical "language" which is comfortable for the broadest audience possible. This vernacular is ecumenical by virtue of its lack of references to normative institutions and established authorities—as well as a notable absence of the "influencer" marketing models that are at work in mainstream meditation apps like *Calm*, *InsightTimer*, and *Headspace*, wherein practices are often associated with popular (on the app) or famous (nationally or internationally) meditation teachers. This influencer model is certainly found in other Muslim digital media in cyberspace, where numerous Muslim teachers have transformed into religious celebrity figures who headline carefully designed and marketed digital "offerings" on multiple platforms (websites, IG, Twitter, Facebook, YouTube, TikTok).[47] *Sakeenah*, *Sabr*, and *Halaqah*, by contrast, present no ideal Muslim personality, nor anything that would situate the app's meditations in a specific Muslim culture, *maḏhab*, *ṭarīqah*, ethnicity, or nationality. Instead, their targeted audience seems to cast an extraordinarily wide net: English-speaking Muslims who are familiar with common *āyāt* and *du ʿāʾ* in Arabic and in possession of a mobile device.

Another distinguishing feature we see on these apps is that the distinctions between *fikr*, *dhikr*, and *murāqabah* go largely unaddressed. Instead, these practices are typically labeled simply as "meditation." Does this mean the nuances of terminology are not necessary for an app's practices to be useful—or for potential users to be "sold" on the product and willing to try it? It could be that the apps' creators minimize their use of these signifiers to attract an audience that might not be drawn to overtly religious meditation apps, but nonetheless would find digital resources that resonate with their religion appealing. Alternatively, it could be that these distinctions were just not considered in the production of the meditation audio tracks, and that "secular" meditations were used as the default models—with references from the *sunnah* and Qur'ān added only later. In a similar fashion, although these apps emphasize that their guided meditations blend Islamic principles with modern science, they offer scarce detail about precisely what this means. This is another feature they share with meditation apps in the mainstream marketplace. In fact, medical research is inconclusive as to "the effects of meditation programs in improving the positive dimensions of mental health and stress-related behavior,"[48] and little research exists on the effectiveness of meditation apps in particular. Even so, both mainstream and Muslim meditation apps are marketed as providing simple, affordable, and self-managed solutions to mental health and stress-related problems.

Sakeenah, *Sabr*, and *Halaqah* highlight the connection between their meditations and the achievement of states of mindfulness, emotional regulation, connection to God, mental health, and a better quality of life. These assertions all mirror to some degree a contemporary revival in Islamic psychotherapy and its embrace of Sufi *murāqabah* techniques for contemporary Muslims. Scholar, psychologist, and counselor Dr. Abdullah Rothman, whose research explores the "intersections of Islamic spirituality and mental health practice," is an example of someone whose public-interface work is reviving the Islamic science of psychology and bringing its tools for mindfulness to modern Muslims.[49] Rothman's work excavates the observations and techniques of Islamic Sufi scholar al-Ḥārith al-Muhāsibī (d. 857) for transforming states of the mind and soul for greater wellness. Rothman aligns al-Muhāsibī's methodological principles and psychological findings with the terminology of a twenty-first century, English-speaking Muslim audience by employing the now familiar Western notions of mindfulness and meditation.[50]

Another example is the Yaqeen Institute: a US-based nonprofit research center with an expansive digital reach. One of its digital infographics, "How to Be a Mindful Muslim," explains that "Islamic Meditation" is "a profound, forgotten tradition" and contrasts the mainstream marketplace meditations, which it calls "secular meditation," with Islamic meditation.[51] While the purpose of "secular meditation," the Yaqeen Institute explains, is mental strength and well-being, Islamic mindfulness adds to these "spiritual strength." Whereas the focus of "secular meditation" is "one's own heart and mind," *murāqabah* has "four aspects of focus": Allah, *shaitan* (evil spirits), the heart, and the mind.[52] The infographic lists the particular benefits of "Islamic meditation," which range from stress relief, to "easier presence" in prayer, to increased compassion."[53] The digital text cites classical Sunni scholars such as al-Ghazālī (d. 1111), al-Suyūṭī (d. 1505), and Ibn al-Qayyim (d. 1350) in its explanations of the methodologies and applications of mindfulness and meditation as developed in the Islamic tradition. In this sense, both Abdullah Rothman and the Yaqeen Institute seem to be articulating the historical and scholarly underpinnings of the "Muslim meditation" products that *Sakeenah*, *Sabr*, and *Halaqah* have created.

In ways that mirror the Yaqeen Institute's view of meditation, these apps position their Muslim meditations as a perfect blend of medical science and the religious knowledge embedded deep within Islamic tradition. While mainstream mindfulness-based therapy models blend Buddhist and Western psychology, other paradigms do exist in contemporary Islamic tradition for mindfulness-based therapy grounded in the "science" of Sufism. Since the 1990s, psychotherapy practices in the West have incorporated elements of Buddhist meditation for stress-reduction. In contemporary Islamic psychotherapy, "the application of classical Sufi understanding of human nature and mental and spiritual health issues has stimulated a new and dynamic discourse about the use of the Sufi practice of mindfulness."[54] Within a traditional Sufi *ṭarīqah* the normative meditative practice of *murāqabah* would be experienced under the direct leadership of a spiritual guide (*Shaykh*, *Shaykha*, *Pir*), "in order to avoid unpredictable unhealthy experiences such as *waswasa* (i.e., whispers, obsessions) disturbing or frightening experiences."[55]

By contrast, meditation practices on *Sakeenah*, *Sabr*, and *Halaqah* lead the individual user to meditation in the absence of context, community, or teacher support. The user experience on these apps is particularly solitary in comparison to the connectivity engendered in many mainstream meditation apps, where users can see how many other people are doing the practice at the same moment via an in-app user feedback section. On *InsightTimer*, for example, meditators can post about their own experience with the app's meditations, and these messages are time stamped and listed below the module's start button. There are also options for live sessions and direct question-and-answer exchanges with teachers. These devices create some sense of a virtual community or at least a loose network in a web of interconnected users. At the conclusion of a *Sabr* meditation, by contrast, the user can only navigate to additional online meditations; there is no visible tracking that displays how many others have completed these practices. In fact, none of these three apps offer a direct way to interact with other users and to share thoughts. Since there is no one to connect with, and no way to know if other users are doing the same practice, there is little possibility of a virtual community developing. This meditation in isolation marked a curious response to a time of enhanced isolation during the Covid-19 lockdowns. Perhaps the apps' practices are simply aimed at making the experience of solitude less lonely—with an underlying assumption that meditating in these digitally mediated and Islamically inflected ways is better than being entirely alone and under duress.

Conclusion

Sakeenah, *Sabr*, and *Halaqah* each offer Islamically inflected, digitally produced, guided meditations. Though these reflect similarities with other meditation apps in what I call the online "meditation marketplace," I suggest they constitute a new genre of digital media with specific cultural, theological, and epistemological frames of Islamic piety. These apps allow Muslim religious participation in the new wave of meditation and mindfulness, revive a tradition deep within Islam (even if the apps' methods and backgrounds are often obscure), and echo the wellness industry's promises of delivering improved mental health, emotional stability, and stress reduction. Placing these sites in the broader context of the meditation marketplace, we see the creators of these Muslim apps engaging in a reclaiming of meditation as an authentic Islamic practice but without explicit reference to any institutional or authoritative sources. Breaking with historical precedent, these apps seem to signal that Muslims need not be involved in an organized community or traditional Sufi *ṭarīqah*—or even have a personal spiritual guide—to engage in Islamic meditation practices. By promising a range of benefits for the body, mind, and spirit, these apps have carved out a new corner in the virtual meditation marketplace—providing an innovative, hybrid, portable, guided experience of Muslim piety, performed via the technological utility of a digital app.

CHAPTER 10

From Mecca with Love:

Muslim Religious Apps and the Centering of Sacred Geography

Andrea Stanton

Introduction

Mecca is the historical center and spiritual heart of the religion of Islam. Praying Muslims turn toward this nexus of sacred geography multiple times each day, and both historical and contemporary pious art and literature focus on it—especially the *Ka'bah* (the black cubical shrine at the heart of the Great Mosque in Mecca) and the key sites of the annual *hajj* pilgrimage. *Hajj* is one of the five pillars of Islam and is considered obligatory for Muslims who are financially, physically, and otherwise able to carry it out. This multiday ritual combines piety and performance, with pilgrims carrying out a complex set of prescribed ritual practices and spiritual exercises that begin and end with *ṭawāf*, walking around the *Ka'bah* seven times in a circular and counterclockwise manner. Historically, the inherent difficulty involved in *hajj*—long overland or sea journeys to Mecca that took months or years and cost considerable sums of money, coupled with the dangers of illness, accident, or attack in areas of political instability—meant that only a small percentage of Muslims were able to undertake the pilgrimage. Slightly more devotees made *'umrah*, however: the spiritually meritorious but non-obligatory "lesser pilgrimage" that involves most of the same ritual activities as the *hajj* but can be completed at any time in the year. In the modern era, Muslims have translated this long-standing pious love and reverence for Mecca into new modalities, with charter and commercial flights taking pilgrims for *hajj* since the 1950s, and religious tourism a linchpin of the Saudi government's Vision 2030 strategic plan—especially *'umrah*, which Vision 2030 aspires to grow to thirty million pilgrims annually, up from nineteen million in 2019.[1] Similarly, Muslims have embraced modern communications media—from printed books to film and now including social media and mobile apps—as a way to foster piety. Today, an array of websites, streaming media, and mobile apps focus on Mecca to support and further develop users' piety through affective relationships and religious observance, providing connective tissue that brings together online and offline experiences.

Religious studies research in the field of digital religion has grown dramatically since 2014, particularly in the area of religious apps. Although Islam-related mobile apps make up one of the largest groups of religious apps, to date there has been little research within the field of digital religion that documents these apps or analyzes their impact. This chapter surveys and assesses the large body of Islam-related apps that focus on Mecca. I argue that Mecca-focused religious apps deserve scholarly attention because of their proliferation on various app store platforms and because of their popularity with users, who appear to primarily be religiously active Muslims and download these apps in remarkably large numbers. I also contend that examining how Mecca figures in these apps helps to enliven and contextualize observations about contemporary Muslims' relationship with Mecca and delineate how apps might support both ritual practice and affective efforts at pious self-fashioning.

This research helps to fill two scholarly gaps. The first is the extant lacuna in religious studies literature on religious apps and their role in lived religion—an absence due in part to the evolving nature of the field. The second is the manifest lack of religious app research on Muslim and Islamic apps in particular; most existing religious studies scholarship on mobile apps focuses on Christian religious apps, despite the large global Muslim population and the proportionately high number of Islam-related religious apps. This project builds on Gary Bunt's work exploring early Islamic apps and their impact on religious authority and users' religious knowledge, particularly in relation to the Qur'ān.[2] It also draws on my own previous work on the Saudi Ministry of *Hajj* and *'Umrah*'s apps, which argues that religious apps can serve users' ritual and scriptural needs while also serving states' political or bureaucratic goals.[3] My analysis connects with ethnographic case studies, including Jacqueline Fewkes's work on American Muslims' use of *ḥalāl* food apps and Moch Fakhruroji's work on Indonesian Muslims' engagement with an app created by a popular religious preacher.[4] Ultimately, this chapter works to extend and contribute to this growing area of scholarship and to suggest areas for future research.

Methodology

This chapter utilizes a mixed-methods approach. First, it offers a broad content analysis that provides a quantitative overview and assessment of a substantial sample of Mecca-related apps available in Google Play, focusing on those available in English, Arabic, and Persian. A team of two graduate research assistants reviewed the top 220 apps available on Google Play that appeared in the results of searches for "Mecca" in English and Arabic between June and August 2020. Since United States' sanctions generally prevent Iran-based users and app developers from being able to access Google Play, the team also reviewed just under 100 Android-compatible apps from two Iran-based, globally focused app stores: thirty-three from Bazaar Android Market and sixty-four from Myket Android Store.[5] These two sets of apps provide a substantive sample of Mecca-focused apps available to Android users (and some iOS users). The team reviewed each app's description and the screenshots included in the app store, and opened a sample of the apps reviewed. They noted the developer, number of versions, the most recent update, and the system requirements. They also read the reviews and recorded the number, the average rating, and any salient reviewer comments. Finally, they tabulated the number of installations, whether the app was free (and its cost if not), and the app store category.

After this qualitative review, the research team classified and assessed each app according to its name; connection to Mecca; its main activity or purpose (e.g., broadcasting a *Ka'bah* livestream or offering a *hajj* and *'umrah* guide); the languages in which the app operates; the number of downloads (e.g., over 1000 or over 10,000); the average user rating and the number of ratings; and whether users provided many or few comments on the app store platform. They also noted the version number as a proxy for whether developers were regularly updating the app. Finally, the team recorded the app store category in which the app had been placed ("Entertainment," "Lifestyle," "Tools," etc.) and classified each app in accordance with its main purpose (livestream, direction of prayer (*qiblah*) finder, etc.), in order to better understand the prevalence of particular kinds of Mecca-focused apps and how they support users' understandings of Mecca. The findings and analysis from this work are detailed in the following section. In addition, this study highlights an example from each category of Mecca-focused app as an illustration and case study—and offers a qualitative analysis of each case study to help characterize the apps in each of the categories of Mecca-focused religious apps.

Theoretical Lenses

This project takes three strands of observations regarding Mecca and braids them together for a tri-part theoretical lens on the landscape of religious apps that focus on Mecca. First, it engages US historian of the Middle East and medieval Islam Richard Bulliet's argument that the fall of the original caliphate led to the increasing role of Mecca and the *hajj* in legitimating political leadership. The *hajj* did not initially serve as a source of legitimation for Muslim polities. Bulliet argues that the *hajj* started to play a role in statecraft during the medieval period, as regional sultanates sought political legitimacy outside the caliphate structure, since their rulers could not claim descent from the Quraysh tribe. The practice began with Ṣalāḥ ad-Dīn (1174–93 CE) and the Ayyubids, and continued with the Mamluks, who supported their claims to political legitimacy with three pillars: successful military exploits, providing good governance, and protecting Mecca and Medina. When the Abbasid caliphate fell to the Mongols in 1258, Bulliet argues, "pilgrimage to Mecca replaced the caliphate as the central unifying entity in Islam."[6] At the level of political statecraft, supporting the *hajj* became a key legitimator for early-modern states like the Ottoman and Mughal empires. At the level of popular culture, the importance of the *hajj* was signaled by the popularity of pious behaviors focused around honoring and celebrating those who had made the pilgrimage, like the addition of "*Hajji*" or "*al-Hajj*" as a title. Other ways of celebrating the *hajj* by honoring pilgrims, like the emergence of "*hajj* paintings" on the outer walls of pilgrims' homes, or "*hajj* certificates," illustrate the meaning attached to completing the *hajj* in Muslim communities across the Middle East and other regions.[7]

Significantly, focusing on the *hajj* also meant spotlighting Mecca—and Mecca seems to have been both a synecdochic stand-in for the *hajj* and important in its own right as a locus of political power. Bulliet focuses on the *hajj* as the key determinant of political legitimation: multiple states could claim to support the *hajj* by sending national caravans and delegations to Mecca. By contrast, only one state had control of Mecca. Perhaps this distinction is reflected in the title used by Saudi monarchs: *Khādim al-Ḥaramayn,* or protector of the two holy places, Mecca and Medina. This title both evokes the *hajj* and surpasses it, suggesting the preeminent role of Mecca as site of the *hajj*, locus of early Muslim history, and holder of the *Kaʿbah*, the direction of prayer. As Bulliet notes, from the late twelfth century, "The pilgrimage became the center of Islam, and the *Khadim al-Haramain* the most important Muslim figure, particularly for people in the Muslim South," whose communities came to Islam in the post-Abbasid era and thus "had never lived under a caliphate."[8] Here again, Mecca and the *hajj* were deeply intertwined: if the pilgrimage symbolized Islam and Muslim unity, so did the city and the idea of Mecca. This chapter suggests that the political and affective centrality of Mecca, as the site of the *hajj* and the direction of prayer, is today echoed in the number of religious apps that focus on Mecca: some spotlighting the *hajj* and *ʿumrah*, some focused on finding the correct direction for prayer, and others offering "Mecca livestreams" that feature the *Kaʿbah* in an act of religious synecdoche.

Second, this chapter draws from Pakistani British cultural critic and *Critical Muslim* editor Ziauddin Sardar's reflection on the history, politics, and pious centrality of Mecca for Muslims, past and present. Sardar, who worked for the *Hajj* Research Center at King Abdul Aziz University in Jeddah in the 1970s, argues that most Muslims have both an intimate and awe-filled relationship with Mecca, despite never traveling there in person. "It is a city that I, in common with almost all Muslims, have known all my life," he writes in *Mecca: The Sacred City*. Yet this is a particular kind of knowing, he asserts: most Muslims "will never see Mecca, and yet will have learned, perhaps even memorized, its geograph[ic location] from the moment they were taught to pray." The result, he suggests, is a relationship at once personal and universal: a "sense of personal attachment" and also a "love and devotion, a yearning and a dream that I share with more than a billion others." Sardar calls Mecca "the taproot of individual identity and the common link of an entire worldwide community."[9] He also describes how Mecca's centrality has been preserved in Muslim lived religion and material culture, like water from the *Zamzam* spring (the source of water that Muslims believe God provided for Hājar (Hagar) and 'Ismā'īl (Ishmael) after 'Ibrāhīm (Abraham) abandoned them in the desert); small pieces of discarded *kiswah* (the embroidered brocade cloth that covers the *Ka'bah*); and "before long anything remotely associated with Mecca—a relic, a book, a local product—was treated with veneration."[10] The proliferation of Mecca-focused religious apps, I argue, continues these historical practices of love and devotion to Mecca and of instantiating the veneration of Mecca through interactions with material objects—or, in the case of apps, through digital material objects.

Third, this chapter follows Saudi visual artist Ahmed Mater's argument that global Muslims focus exclusively on the pilgrimage dimensions of Mecca, ignoring or denying the contemporary city, an argument that connects with and builds upon some of Sardar's analysis. Mater—one of the most influential contemporary Saudi artists whose works reflect critically on national memories, histories, and politics—argues that Mecca exists for most Muslims living outside Saudi Arabia as an idea that includes only the sacred sites relevant for the *hajj*, and that Mecca's real existence as a living city not only has little appeal for them but is something they may actively work to ignore. "Rarely perceived as a living city," he asserts, "the idea of Mecca is unencumbered by the reality of its own inhabitants and historical developments. Yet inhabitants and all they entail are an inevitable and swelling reality"—certainly for residents and visitors. Mater suggests that for Muslims who do not live in or visit Mecca, the "prosaic truths" of modern life in Mecca "are diminished by a city that sustains its rarefied identity, perceived almost exclusively as a place of pilgrimage. In the collective consciousness, Mecca is no more and no less than the timeless, symbolic city." Hence, he suggests, the signs of ordinary life are unwelcome: "The denial of the real city is a denial of typical urban inconveniences like traffic, lack of public space, and the challenges of infrastructure."[11] Pilgrims, in Mater's view, do not want to experience ordinary life in an ordinary city.

Further, Mater argues, the denial of Mecca's ordinary reality by those who live outside Saudi Arabia is echoed in a different way by government planners and private-sector developers in Mecca. In his view, "Those who preside over the city's development are freed from the burden of practicalities. In this conceptual space, they dream wildly, implementing plans for massive, unfathomable transformation. This grand vision is proclaimed from giant billboards, in whose shadows the unacknowledged life of the city continues to be played out."[12] This chapter suggests that nonresidents' reduction of Mecca to its *hajj*-related elements and geography, coupled with their dismissal of the prosaic aspects of life there, may influence both the kinds of Mecca-focused religious apps developed, the version or vision of Mecca that they portray, and their relative popularity.

At the same time, as Mater and Sardar note, advances in the cost and reliability of air travel starting in the 1950s, which in turn led to the initial Saudi government impetus to expand the Grand Mosque and the pilgrimage areas, mean both that far more people have visited Mecca each year for *hajj* or *'umrah* than in previous eras and that the footprint and face of Mecca changed dramatically as a result. The increasing feasibility of travel means that more Muslims alive today have visited Mecca or know someone who has, regardless of where they live. And whether in terms of the expansion of the *Jamarāt* (the area of three stone pillars at which Muslim pilgrims throw pebbles as a symbolic act of rejecting the Devil), the creation of modern high-rise buildings, the bulldozing of old architecture, or the proliferation of gates and escalators around the Grand Mosque, the physical appearance of the pilgrimage and ordinary parts of Mecca have transformed considerably over the past seventy years, morphing significantly even from decade to decade within this period.[13] These changes have come in part to accommodate the great increase in the number of *hajj* and *'umrah* pilgrims, and in part due to political and economic influences: Saudi government efforts to remake Mecca in a more Wahhabi guise, coupled with the presence of "super-luxurious hotels, Rolex [watch stores and advertisements], Starbucks . . . and Burger King."[14] Muslims today, whether they have visited Mecca or not, are likely to be familiar with images of Mecca in its current state, at least in terms of the appearance of the Grand Mosque and the skyscraper hotel and other contemporary buildings that surround the *Ka'bah*. In a similar fashion, they are likely to envision the *Ka'bah* as a pristine black building with an immaculate covering, surrounded by women in black and men in white making *ṭawāf* on gleaming marble.

These "mind's eye" images of Mecca may add to the tension between the imagined pilgrimage ideal and twenty-first-century reality that Mater describes, while also erasing awareness of Mecca's earlier historical iterations. Further, the increased accessibility and lowered cost of print media (including newspapers, magazines, photographs, postcards, posters, and more), broadcast media (including television and film), and internet and social media (including digital photographs and streaming video, websites, and social media accounts on various platforms) have led to Mecca's increased visual presence over the past fifty to sixty years—or, at least, the Mecca of the *Ka'bah* and its immediate *hajj*-related environs. Stemming from Mater and Sardar's critiques, this chapter suggests that users of Mecca-focused religious apps are influenced by their expectations of seeing Mecca in its contemporary guise and by Mecca's greater visual preeminence, due both to increased visitor numbers and to its increased presence in the visual products of global print, broadcast, and social media. As a result, I argue, these apps reflect the idea of Mecca as outside of ordinary experience: as contemporary but timeless, with an immaculate *Ka'bah*, sophisticated cooling systems, efficient transportation, and high-tech pilgrim support and surveillance.

Together, these three analytical lenses offer a way to assess the landscape of Mecca-focused religious apps in terms of how much (and what version) of Mecca they portray; how and in what ways Mecca is connected to contemporary Saudi politics and to the monarchy and developers' vision of a modern city; and what pious actions or dispositions the apps' invocation of Mecca calls users to adopt.

App Store Categories

As Campbell et al. have noted, religious apps do not fit organically within app store categories where "developers must choose from a general list of utilitarian or secular classifications, such as Lifestyle or Reference."[15] Although this issue does not seem to inhibit users from finding and downloading religious apps, it is certainly apparent for Mecca-focused apps on the app store platforms reviewed for this study. On Google Play, Mecca-focused apps are categorized in a range of ways, and apps with similar functions may be placed in different categories. For example, livestream apps appear variously in "Video Players & Editors," "Education," "Lifestyle," and "Social." Pilgrimage-focused apps (which include ritual how-to guides, maps of Mecca and relevant offices, or other supports) appear in "Books & Reference," "Education," "Entertainment," "Lifestyle," "Social," and "Travel & Local." The appearance of similar apps in different app store categories highlights the challenge of appropriately positioning religious apps within secular app store categories.

Although Café Bazaar and Myket, the two Iran-based app stores, both have "Religion" categories, most of the apps from these sites reviewed for this study have been placed in other categories. The majority of the *qiblah*-finder apps, most of the pilgrimage guides, and some Mecca livestreaming apps are also categorized as "Religion." However, many others are not, suggesting that developers choose a different category, whether because they do not notice the "Religion" category option, do not consider it the best fit for their app, or think that it will not reach users. For example, *Ka'bah Buku Saku Umra Hajj Trip Planner*, an English-language app with over 500,000 downloads on Myket, is categorized in "Lifestyle." Similarly, several Persian-language *qiblah* finder and prayer time apps are categorized in "Tools," while a number of English-language *qiblah*-finder apps are categorized in "Lifestyle." While Café Bazaar and Myket are based in Iran and offer a "Religion" category, developers still place their religious apps in secular categories. In short, although religious apps do not fit smoothly into app stores' secular categories, this is not an issue for developers creating these apps nor for users downloading them.

Language and Positioning

Google Play appears to have the largest number of Mecca-focused apps, likely due to its sheer size and global reach. The apps operate across a wide range of languages; while Arabic and English dominate, app languages include a range of Asian, European, Middle Eastern, and African languages. The apps with the largest number of languages appear to have robust institutional support (as with the Saudi Ministry of *Hajj* and 'Umrah's *Manasikana*), rely on user content (as with *Hajj and 'Umrah Reviews*, which provides user reviews of particular pilgrimage services or experiences), or use a limited vocabulary (as with some of the prayer apps, like *Qibla Finder* on Google, which lists fourteen languages).[16]

Google Play dominates the Android app market globally and describes itself as reaching "over two billion active Android devices."[17] Although Apple's iOS App Store is often better known in the United States, Google Play has dominated the global market since 2015 in terms of available apps and total downloads. For example, in the first half of 2020, Google Play listed 30 percent more apps than Apple and almost three times the total downloads.[18] The next largest app stores, Windows and Amazon, list fewer than one million apps and are often excluded from app store download reports.[19]

The apps available from the Iran-based app stores showed a range of language diversity. Café Bazaar has both a Persian-language and an English-language interface. Searching the Persian-language interface primarily resulted in Persian-language apps, with a small number available in English and additional languages. Myket markets its English-language interface to a global audience of developers and users while also promoting stable downloads and mobile phone payment options for Iran- and Middle East-based consumers. It offers Mecca-related apps in languages from Russian to Urdu, with Persian and English predominating. While a small sampling, the Myket and Café Bazaar apps offer an important corrective to research focused exclusively on the major US-based app stores and a reminder of how geopolitics can influence app development, ease of purchase, and relative popularity.

Downloads and Usage

In order to gauge the popularity of particular apps and in kinds of Mecca-focused apps, this study examined the number of downloads and installations, user ratings, and user reviews. *Qiblah*-finder apps had the highest number of downloads, indicating users' high interest in this kind of app. The most downloaded Mecca-focused apps on Google Play were all *qiblah*- finding apps: one had over ten million downloads, eight had over five million downloads, and fifteen had over one million downloads. The Café Bazaar and Myket sample included one app with over one million downloads, highlighting the differential reach of the three app stores. Most apps on these platforms have fewer downloads, although they still found sizeable audiences. Forty-five Mecca-focused apps on Google Play had over 100,000 downloads and twelve had over 500,000 downloads—ten of which are *qiblah*-finder apps. Since *qiblah*-finder apps include at least one image of the *Ka'bah*, they also work visually to further emphasize to users the image of a Mecca reduced to its prayer or ritual aspects, as well as an idea of a Mecca disconnected from any specific state or government.

In terms of user comments, 144 of the apps reviewed for this study were identified as having "a lot" of user comments—approximately 45 percent of the total sample. Similarly, 242 apps received user ratings of 4.0 or higher—approximately 76 percent of the total sample. These two percentages indicate users' high satisfaction with most apps, as well as a relatively high level of engagement with the apps they download. Collectively, these numbers attest to the popularity of Mecca-focused apps and gesture toward the overall popularity of religious apps.

Research Findings: Key Categories and Analysis

The 220 apps reviewed in this study were categorized by the role that Mecca plays for them and by their intended purpose. Because these apps do not fit organically into app store categories, the research team placed Google Play's Mecca-focused apps into seven main categories: *qiblah* finder (83), pilgrimage guide (69), livestream (28), live broadcasting (5), call to prayer (4), virtual reality experiences of Mecca (5), and wallpapers (9). (Café Bazaar and Myket each also have a few apps that create Mecca-centered photo frames.) The first three are the most popular, comprising 82 percent of the Mecca-focused Google Play apps in this study. Some apps, like *vMakkah*—which acts both as a pilgrimage guide and as a virtual reality experience—blend aspects of multiple categories (Figure 10.1). It offers a customizable virtual tour of key sites from the *hajj* and the Prophet's Mosque in Medina, helping users "learn to perform" both *hajj* and *'umrah* via male or female avatars.[20] Developed by a Saudi Arabia-based company, the app operates

FIGURE 10.1 *Virtual pilgrims performing the* tawāf, *circumambulating or walking around the* Ka'bah *seven times at different moments during the* hajj *or* 'umrah *pilgrimages (*vMakkah, *Apple Store).*

in seven languages and has been updated regularly; with over 100,000 downloads and over 2400 user reviews, it is reasonably popular.

Most of the reviewed apps offer real-time engagement with location-based digital content from Mecca, including images, videos, and traffic patterns. Some spotlight Mecca; others interlace Mecca-focused content (like a *qiblah* finder) with content based on the user's location and location-neutral content. For example, Islamic Finder's *Athan* app, named after the Arabic term for the call to prayer, offers prayer time alerts; forty-five translations of the Qur'ān; a repository of religious supplications; step-by-step *hajj* and 'umrah guides; a *qiblah* finder and a nearby mosque finder; a *Hijri* calendar and calendar conversion; and a "prayerbook" option for tracking users' progress in completing their daily prayers.[21] The rich content that this and other apps offer suggests that they fit across multiple classifications within the typology of religious apps that Campbell et al. have developed. *Athan* offers content that fits within the "Prayer," "Ritual," "Devotional Worship," "Religious Utilities," "Focus /Meditation," and "Sacred Textual Engagement" classifications.[22]

Qiblah-finder and pilgrimage guide apps comprise over two-thirds of the Google Play app sample, suggesting their importance for both developers and users. They fit within Campbell et al.'s classification of "apps oriented around religious practice": those that offer support for particular religious rituals and activities. More specifically, the *qiblah*-finder and call to prayer apps support Muslims in carrying out the obligatory daily prayers. *Qiblah*-finder apps' descriptions emphasize their accuracy and ease of use, as with

Qibla Compass – Find Direction, a Google Play app with over one million downloads. "This Qibla finder app can be used anywhere in the world," it states, in order to find Mecca "with complete ease."[23] These *qiblah-finder* apps—which often include the call to prayer and prayer times, and sometimes a *Hijri* calendar—support users to engage in regular, correct, and meaningful ritual activity.

Pilgrimage guides make up the second-largest group of Mecca-focused religious apps. These apps support Muslims in carrying out the complex processes of *hajj* or *'umrah*, providing instruction on how to complete the steps of the rituals, guidance on navigating pilgrimage travel logistics, or supplicatory prayers. These are major ritual acts that can be categorized within Campbell et al.'s typology as acts of "devotional worship."[24] They do so in ways that echo some of Bulliet, Mater, and Sardar's arguments: emphasizing the centrality of *hajj* in Muslim ritual life, presenting Mecca as synecdochally reduced to the *Ka'bah* for the purposes of prayer, and fostering in users an attentive relationship to ritual and devotional Mecca that is both intimate and omnipresent. For example, *Mecca Live Wallpaper* is one of multiple apps that uses "Mecca" in its title but shows images only of the *Ka'bah* and Great Mosque, rather than the city as a whole. It promises users that looking at the app's wallpaper images will feel like seeing the *Ka'bah* in real life, eliciting similar emotional effects: "Visit the most wonderful place in the world that will make you feel tranquil and connected to [God]." It suggests further that this virtual experience is itself a kind of pilgrimage: "Pray with the rest of the Muslim world on a pilgrimage to this sacred city."[25]

Mecca Live Wallpaper has over one million installations and nearly 10,000 user reviews, indicating its popularity—and the appeal of Mecca wallpaper apps in general. The reviews are enthusiastic, with typical user comments suggesting deep emotional and spiritual engagement with the wallpaper images. Examples include:

- "I'm happy when I look at it, and every time we remember to make doa [*du'ā'*, or a supplicatory prayer] to get [to] this place"

- "Allah bless who[ever] introduced this app. Its cool to hearts and calm to souls."

- "Superb, it seems like I am [in] front of *kabbathulla* [the *Ka'bah* of God] love this app *Masha Allah* [an expression of respect and praise]"

- "This is beautiful because I'm [a] Muslim I'm crying"

- "Plss [Please] download this app [God] will bless you"

- "I Liked it sooo much When we open the android we can see Makkah [Mecca] it makes us remember about [God] and [M]akkah"

Collectively, these comments suggest how this and similar apps function as a kind of digital connective tissue joining users to the ritual and devotional practices associated with Mecca in the material world. By design, the process of viewing Mecca on a mobile app is transformed into an act of piety and devotional performance, blurring the digital and the material realms to draw users into a closer relationship with the sacred city.

This aspect of these Mecca-focused apps connects to one of the key characteristics of the livestream, live broadcast, virtual reality experiences of Mecca, as well as wallpaper, lockscreen, and photo frame apps: their ability to create an affective relationship with, or disposition toward, Mecca. In keeping with Mater's observations, the Mecca invoked in these apps is the Mecca of the *Ka'bah* and the other spaces of the *hajj*, not the sprawling modern city that stretches over 460 square miles and has over two million inhabitants in its metropolitan area. For example, *Mecca Live Screen Lock*, a Google Play app with over 500,000 downloads, offers various views of the *Ka'bah* and *matāf* (the marble-covered open area around the *Ka'bah*), including an image of the *Ka'bah* in front of the Abraj al-Bait skyscraper complex. This is a popular vantage point for *Ka'bah* photos: *Mecca Live Wallpaper* offers a similar one (Figure 10.2). The app description explains that it is "made for those who really want to go [to Mecca]" and that "when you start your mobile you will see the Holiest place of the world."[26] As with many apps, Mecca here is reduced to the *Ka'bah* and its immediate surroundings. The portrayal is thoroughly contemporary: the *Ka'bah* is not shown in a nineteenth-century photograph or a medieval painting, but against a prominent backdrop of recently constructed buildings. Even so, the app describes its images as providing "the best pictures of Mecca," highlighting that for pious users "Mecca" is synonymous with the Mecca of pilgrimage, prayer, and ritual—signaled by the *Ka'bah*.

Even apps that reference the contemporary city tend to do so in the context of the *Ka'bah* and the *hajj*. For example, the description of *Hajj tv*

FIGURE 10.2 Mecca Live Wallpaper, *sample home page (Google Play).*

live, kabah tv live, mecca live: Mecca tv, a Google Play livestreaming app with over 1,000 downloads, begins by explaining why Mecca matters to Muslim, spotlighting the location of Muhammad's birth, the direction for prayer, and the location of the *hajj*. "In the 20th and 21st centuries, the city underwent vast improvements," the description adds—but then mentions only those changes related to pilgrimage, like the Great Mosque expansion and housing, sanitation, and transportation improvements designed to "accommodate the continually increasing number of pilgrims."[27] This statement frames all the various forms of Mecca's twentieth-century development as support for the *hajj*, rather than for the city's residents. In doing so, it reflects and reinforces a normalized assumption, developed over centuries and instantiated in a new form via religious apps, that "Mecca" signifies the part of the city central to Muslim pilgrimage, prayer, and ritual.

This reduced, synecdochic Mecca carries powerful meaning for digital users, who turn to these apps for worship and ritual support. Yet the large number of these apps and their descriptions also suggests that they play a role beyond worship and ritual: they help cultivate affective relationships between users and the ritual Mecca. This is an instance of what Catellani terms "digital affect culture": a culture constructed through the process of sharing emotional, affective responses via digital media forms, individually and communally.[28] As noted earlier, *Mecca Live Wallpaper* claims that its high-definition photos of Mecca "will strengthen your faith in [God]."[29] In a similar fashion, *Mecca in Saudi Arabia*, a Google Play wallpaper app with over 100,000 downloads, encourages users: "If you are not able to [get] to Makkah this year, download these free live wallpapers and be closer to your religion!" Going further, it suggests that by looking at the images it offers, which focus primarily on the *Ka'bah* and Great Mosque, the user is drawn closer both to God and to other Muslims: "you will never be alone as long as you have these background images on your phone or tablet!"[30] These statements indicate that developers expect their apps to play a meaningful role in users' spiritual lives, beyond the details of ritual acts of worship.

The various Mecca-themed photo frame apps seem to operate similarly, harnessing an affective response through user engagement. They enable viewers to superimpose one of their own photos, ideally a self-portrait, onto a photo of the *Ka'bah* and *matāf* (or the entire *Masjid al-Haram* or Great Mosque) during *hajj*.[31] The actions of these apps connect with the process of cultivating pious selves through bodily practices and the fostering of particular ethical dispositions—an idea that Saba Mahmood's Egyptian interlocutors considered foundational to their efforts.[32] In the process of creating images with these Mecca-focused photo frames—which this app and others constitute as a creative and aesthetic act—and in then viewing and sharing them, users cultivate an affective relationship with Mecca as a locus of individual and communal pious identity. While most scholarship on religious apps has focused on apps for ritual or educational purposes, these Mecca-focused apps illustrate the role that religious apps can play in supporting users who work to cultivate pious selves through affective and dispositional digital engagement.

Although pilgrimage guide, wallpaper, and livestream apps focus users' attention on Mecca in terms of prayer and pilgrimage, developers do not suggest that a virtual pilgrimage experience could ever replace the physical *hajj* or *'umrah*. As Bunt notes, apps—like earlier efforts at virtual *hajj*—"may offer a glimpse into the experience of pilgrimage" but do not fulfill Muslims' religious obligation to complete the *hajj*.[33] While virtual pilgrimages do not "count," however, they are still meaningful to users. As Sophia Arjana notes, they may be understood as alternatives to physical pilgrimage experiences for those who—for any reason—may be unable to participate physically.[34] Virtual pilgrimages may also be understood as supplemental pilgrimages: tours of the eye, mind, and heart that do not require travel or ritual purity, but bring devotees closer to Islam.

One salient absence from these Mecca-focused apps is any visible presence of Saudi Arabia as a state or of significant references to the Saudi government. To the extent that the Royal Mecca Clock Tower might be seen as representing modern Saudi Arabia, apps that include images of it may indirectly evoke the state. But few apps directly mention Saudi Arabia, and when they do, it seems to be simply a description of geographical location. For example, *Umrah Guide Hajj Guide & Makkah Map*, a Google Play app with over 10,000 downloads, offers guidance on performing the rituals of *hajj* and *'umrah*, as well as practical advice for finding everything from cash machines to parking lots. It promises to help provide Muslims on pilgrimage with "a convenient stay at Saudi Arabia" but focuses on the Mecca of pilgrimage, not on the Saudi state.[35] While numerous Mecca-focused apps emphasize that Mecca and the *hajj* connect Muslims to God and to one another as a global faith community—as Bulliet argues—they do not present the Saudi government as having a central role.

The only Mecca-focused apps that refer substantively to Saudi Arabia are those created by Saudi government ministries or other national entities. For example, *Smart Hajj* is a Saudi government app that describes itself as "a gift [to pilgrims] from the Kingdom of Saudi Arabia" that integrates "several government apps" together for easy access while on pilgrimage. Its home page includes the logo of the Ministry of Communications and Information Technology, but not the Ministry of *Hajj* and *'Umrah* or any other official state branding.[36] Similarly, *Manasikana*, the pilgrimage app produced by the Ministry of *Hajj* and *'Umrah*, displays the Ministry's logo and name on its home page and uses the Ministry's image—a stylized depiction of the *Ka'bah* and the Prophet's Mosque in Medina under a tent and atop an open Qur'ān on a *rehal* (Qur'ān stand)—in its own logo.[37] For the average user of these and similar apps, however, the Saudi state and government's presence would be minimal. In this respect, the Mecca-focused apps fit more with Sardar's description of Mecca as a central node for Muslim identity that is seen as both personal and universal, and distinct from any particular state or government.

Conclusion

Mecca-focused religious apps offer an important case study for scholars of digital Islam and digital religion. Both the large number of such apps and their many user downloads attest to their expanding role in supporting Muslim piety through affective relationships and religious observance centered around Mecca. Like other religious apps, they act as digital connective tissue that brings together users' online and offline experiences. Most Mecca-focused apps support users in carrying out ritual practices, but some also facilitate affective efforts at pious self-fashioning by drawing users into a closer relationship with the *Ka'bah* and Mecca's other key religious sites. The number of downloads, positive user reviews, and user comments suggests that users engage with these apps with the intent to cultivate their piety. Viewing a Mecca livestream or wallpaper, participating in a virtual *ṭawāf*, listening to the call to prayer as performed in the Great Mosque, and using location-based services to find the *qiblah* for prayer are active engagements that connect users to Islam's most sacred geography.

These apps also translate ways in which Muslims have historically engaged with Mecca into an alternative digital form. As Bulliet notes, Mecca has been politically and affectively central to Islam since the medieval period, with the *hajj* pilgrimage and the daily prayers toward the *Ka'bah* standing at the heart of Islam. Mecca-focused apps translate this emphasis on Mecca to the digital realm. They also continue the long-standing tradition of love and devotion toward Mecca, which Sardar describes as a relationship with both individual and community dimensions. Significantly, this relationship has little to do with Saudi Arabia or the Saudi government—in part because the Mecca of religious devotion is the Mecca of pilgrimage and prayer. As Mater indicates, Muslims outside Saudi Arabia tend to reduce the modern city of Mecca, with its more than two million inhabitants and over 400 square miles, to the much smaller space of its sacred geographies. This synecdochic view of Mecca, often further reduced to the *Ka'bah*, holds powerful meaning for users.

These apps also allow individual believers to seek out the religious support most meaningful or useful to them. Calculating the *qiblah* direction and providing guidance for pilgrims are certainly nothing new. However, moving those functions to mobile apps provides opportunities for contemporary Muslims across the global *ummah* to connect with Mecca— considered the spiritual heart of Islam—in real time and to do so with the digital technology that best fits their interests and needs. In doing so, these apps participate in the broader processes by which contemporary Islam supports individual interpretations of faith, piety, and ritual performance to cultivate a personal relationship between a believer and their religion. In this sense, mobile apps have helped reconfigure the contours of Muslim piety and ritual performance by acting as digital material objects that bridge the virtual and material worlds.

CHAPTER 11

Seeing a Global Islam?:

Eid al-Adha on Instagram

Rosemary Pennington

Introduction

Images of Islam in global popular media include everything from gauzily veiled women, to black-clad terrorists, to minarets jutting into a sky painted orange-red by a setting sun. Appearing in films, TV shows, and fashion magazines, these images are shaped by geopolitics as well as histories of cross-cultural interaction and European imperialism. These ubiquitous visual tropes have sometimes fueled reductive and distorting views of what Islam is and who Muslims are—stereotypes that, in turn, have exacerbated xenophobia, Islamophobia, and other types of anti-Muslim sentiment. Increasingly, Muslims are working to push back against this historic misrepresentation, countering images characterizing Islam or Muslims as threats with alternative depictions that portray Islam as a faith like any other and Muslims as the diverse individuals they are. The internet has helped facilitate this counter framing, with blogs and social media such as Instagram providing spaces where Muslims can share their own lived experiences and particular understandings of their faith. At times, these images foreground the ordinariness of everyday life, showing individuals grocery shopping or attending school. At other times, they focus on representations of piety: an individual praying alone in their room, the Qur'ān open to a particular passage, or Muslim communities coming together to worship during *Eid* or *Ramaḍān*. Such imagery displays moments of both individual and collective piety, reminding the viewer that while the faith is personal it is simultaneously situated within a broader community of believers. These visualizations of performances of piety can help make Islam, and its practitioners, seem less strange to viewers who have been conditioned to see them as enemy others. Instagram is full of such imagery.

Searching for the hashtag #Islam on Instagram returns tens of millions of posts, featuring everything from the Qur'ān and iconic *masjids* to inspirational quotes and *ḥijābi* fashion tips. Searching for the hashtag #Muslim also turns up millions of posts that frequently feature the photographs and perspectives of individual Muslims. What is clear from a cursory perusal of these hashtags in Instagram is that the individuals using them are working to make visible their lived experiences as Muslims. But what sense of Islam might a non-Muslim get from looking at these posts? What impression of Muslim identity or community might they glean from digging into the hashtags? These questions are at the heart of this research, which examines a series of Instagram posts visible during *Eid al-Adha* 2019 in order to understand the image of Islam that emerged there. *Eid al-Adha*, the Feast of the Sacrifice, is one of the major holidays of Islam, marking the end of the *hajj,* the annual pilgrimage to Mecca.[1] As a reflection of the interplay of religious piety and ritual performance, it seemed likely that Muslim Instagram users would post during the holiday to share *Eid* greetings and to connect to other Muslims celebrating the holiday in the space.

New Media and Community Connections

Media have long played a role in shaping the contours of religious community. As Feenberg and Barkadjieva note, "The great sacred communities of the past (Christendom, the Islamic Ummah, the Middle Kingdom) were imagined through the medium of a sacred language and script."[2] At the same time, there has often existed a tension between lived experience and the teachings of religious authorities—with individuals torn between their local realities and the expectations of a more global, and often distant, dogma. These dynamics have only become amplified by the hypermediated, hyperconnected environment in which believers now live. Woodhead suggests that the affordances of new media technologies provide religious individuals the opportunity to search out interactions of their faith which feel true to them, irrespective of physical distance.[3] For Stolow, "religion is everywhere now," thanks, in part, to digital communication technologies.[4] In similar fashion, Hoover argues that religion and media are so interconnected that they "are no longer separate 'spheres,'"[5] while Campbell asserts that "digital media and spaces are shaping and being shaped by religious practice."[6] In effect, social media can act as a kind of third space, where individuals work out issues related to religious identity and community away from those who might not approve of their explorations.[7]

Social media would seem an obvious place for religious individuals to flock online if, as Morgan suggests, "religions are ways of fabricating networks of relations among human beings."[8] In both theory and practice, social media are built upon "networks of relations" that connect individuals in digital spaces.

boyd and Ellison describe social networking sites as "web-based services that allow individuals to (1) construct a public or semi-public profile within a bounded system, (2) articulate a list of other users with whom they share a connection, and (3) view and traverse their list of connections and those made by others within the system."[9] An individual's list of connections, their network, is generally available for most others to see since these sites are built upon an expectation of interactivity among users.[10] Indeed, the interactivity of these sites (as well as other Web 2.0 spaces) led to the ecosystem it helped produce being labeled the "social web"—the idea being that you go online to be *with* others, not to avoid them. As Feenberg and Barkadjieva point out in their analysis of internet communities, however, "Online community arose from the margins of the medium, intruding on its original information-centered design."[11] Online community was, in effect, a happy accident of the increasingly interactive affordances of digital spaces. Even so, there is no guarantee that just because users are in a virtual space together that they will engage with one another. boyd reminds us that "Network publics' affordances do not dictate participants behavior, but they do configure the environment in a way that shapes participants' engagement."[12] This engagement can, in turn, influence an individual's self-performance and self-presentation.[13]

The architecture of social networking sites such as Facebook, Twitter, and Instagram is built upon displays of connection. Although they are visualized through friend or follower lists or the tagging of others in photographs and posts, connection in these sites is also established through the practice of hashtagging. Hashtags are an important way that social media users organize their posts as well as connect to others; they also help make social media posts more searchable and, therefore, visible. Bunt notes that they can be used to "flag specific themes and content across a variety of applications, which can then 'trend'."[14] This trending is what leads to broad visibility in social media. For instance, in 2017 Twitter users used the hashtag #MuslimWomensDay in order to draw attention to the diverse experiences of Muslim women.[15] As this example suggests, the desire for visibility—to be seen by others—seems to be driving young people to increasingly embrace more visually based social networking sites, such as Instagram and Snapchat, rather than Facebook or Twitter.[16]

Becoming highly visible on Instagram can catapult an individual into a kind of popular fame that leads to their being labeled an "influencer"—meaning they lead the way in shaping what is fashionable or trendy. A number of Muslims, particularly young women, have embraced Instagram's possibilities to shape a fashion agenda, to make visible what, for them, it means to live a virtuous, but stylish, life,[17] and to shape understandings and interpretations of their faith.[18] Other Muslim Instagram users work in digital spaces to trouble or "interrupt" particular interpretations of what it means to be Muslim. In her discussion of the American Black Muslim fashionista Leah Vernon, Peterson identifies how "social media interrupters" engage "with the visual style and discourse of Instagram fashion influencers while incorporating a subversive critique that points out the ways that this influencer industry perpetuates injustices and a neoliberal focus on individual solutions."[19] An interrupter, Peterson contends, is someone who uses their visibility to raise "concerns about those who have been marginalized" by mainstream, influencer culture.[20] In the case of Vernon, the interrupter works to foreground the experiences of Black and plus-sized Muslim women— women typically missing from influencer culture—while also discussing issues such as domestic violence or colorism that Muslim Instagram influencers often avoid altogether.[21]

In her broad critique, Yuan points out that issues of morality or culture are often not included in scholarly discussions of online community.[22] For many Muslims connecting online, however, those are very salient concerns which can influence with whom they connect, what communities they choose to participate in, and who they include in the groups they create in digital spaces.[23] For the "*hijabistas*" of Instagram, culture and morality are often central to their discussions of fashion and identity.[24] In fact, cultural identity was vitally important to the first Muslims who began building community on the internet. According to Anderson, among the earliest adopters of the internet were Muslim members of a Middle Eastern diaspora studying abroad who took advantage of the internet's ability to connect them to their homelands.[25] At the same time, cyberspace provided these individuals with the opportunity to experiment with new ways of being Muslim and practicing Islam—and they strategically deployed internet spaces to "re-create themselves." For Anderson, "identities are framed and formed through this communication. You are what you have to say on the net and, increasingly, what is 'said' is a variety of mixed discourses."[26] Given this diversity of experience, Bunt suggests that Muslims "can create online notions of Muslim identity and authority that echo similar notions in the 'real world'—but they can also nurture new networks of understandings in cyberspace."[27] Muslims online can connect with people, Muslim or non-Muslim, with whom they share other aspects of their identity as "there is no pure Islamic presence, separated from other relevant forms of identity, in cyberspace any more than there is in what still might nostalgically be called the real world."[28] Yet while there may be "no pure Islamic presence" online, there are certainly those who would like to create such a presence. In their work on Islamic message boards, for example, El-Nawawy and Khamis document spaces in which Muslims work to create a holistic sense of community while also marking clearly those who do not belong (such as the exclusion of Shi'a Muslims on sites run by a Sunni Muslim).[29] In short, as much as the social web can be used to create connection, it can also be weaponized to drive division.

For Bunt, "Use of the internet is significant in the way that it sometimes subverts traditional modes of religious authority and offers alternative approaches and information."[30] In his work on the media circulation of Islamic teachings, Echchaibi has shown how popular Muslim religious figures have utilized various media technologies to circumvent traditional religious leaders.[31] The "dislocalisation" of authority has allowed for the development of a more flexible experience of the religion for individuals seeking an alternative to forms of Islam approved by nation-states or established religious authorities.[32] This, Echchaibi suggests, has allowed some users to engage in a visible and open reexamination of some of the foundational tenets of Islam. In her work on the Muslim Indonesian and Iranian blogospheres, Lim documents evidence of such a reexamination, noting that a "mosaic" of meanings was constructed on the blogs, bringing together global concerns and local experiences.[33] Similarly, Bunt argues that the digital experience of Muslims is "influencing the representation of Islam to the wider world and the way Muslim societies perceive themselves and their peers" while also pointing out that many religious leaders are increasingly adopting the very technologies that once worked to disrupt their authority.[34] One digital space that manifests this disruptive potential is Instagram.

Analyzing Instagram

Instagram is a social media site and app in which visuals are paramount. Launched in 2010 as an app for the iPhone, users post visual images—either photographs or graphics—with minimal text captioning and abundant hashtags.[35] The app is designed to be used from a mobile phone; the advent of the camera phone has allowed users to easily capture images as they go about their daily lives.[36] Keep notes that "factors such as ease of use, connectivity, accessibility, and relative low-cost make the camera phone an ideal tool for capturing visual representations of personal and/or collective experiences."[37] Mobile phone photography has also allowed for a blurring of the boundaries between the public and private spheres which, in turn, can shape how users experience space as well as how they interact with strangers.[38] In Instagram, the visuals that appear in a user's feed are typically expected to be complete, with an underlying assumption that "a more detailed version" of the image does not exist.[39] Because cellphone photographs are generally meant to communicate something about lived experiences (whether real or imagined), they serve as a useful tool for determining how an individual sees their place in the world.[40] The dynamics of self-presentation are an important component in the creation of connections in social media spaces. In Instagram, this self-presentation can be used to frame both real experiences and idealized understandings of how one should move through the world.[41] Though the photo sharing in Instagram does not always lead to robust community-building in that specific site, connections individuals make there can facilitate the formation of communities in other social media or offline spaces.[42]

In order to understand how Islam and Muslim community are visualized on Instagram I chose to anchor my research on *Eid al-Adha*. As one of the major holidays in Islam, it seemed likely Muslims would post on Instagram to connect and celebrate this important event. Instagram has been an understudied new media space, but one which many young Muslims have embraced. For instance, in addition to the *ḥijāb* fashionistas who have taken to the space, there are also a number of Muslims posting #halal hashtags in multiple languages who seem to use Instagram to discuss *ḥalāl* (legally permissible) dietary restrictions while simultaneously pushing—or pushing back against—its commercialization as a concept.[43]

To begin building an archive for this project, I searched Instagram for the hashtags #Islam and #Muslim. There are tens of millions of posts on Instagram with these hashtags, exceeding those hashtagged #Christian and #Christianity combined. Since it would be virtually impossible to capture or qualitatively examine every published post, my analysis gathered posts hashtagged #Islam and #Muslim that were posted between 2 p.m. and 4 p.m. Eastern Standard Time on Sunday, August 11, 2019 (the first full day of *Eid al-Adha*). This window was chosen in an attempt to capture posts from both the Eastern and Western hemispheres given the global scope of both Instagram and Islam. Once duplicate posts, regrammed posts, and unrelated posts were excluded from the archive, 390 Instagram posts—189 hashtagged #Islam and another 201 hashtagged #Muslim—remained. I then conducted a qualitative textual analysis of these posts in order to understand the representation of Islam that emerged in the #Islam and #Muslim hashtags that day. What this research uncovered was a digital display of Islam which was contemplative and diverse in nature, often reflecting an image of a globally connected pious community.

Capturing Contemplation

Any day on Instagram you are bound to find images designed to make you consider your place in the world. Sometimes these are graphics featuring inspirational quotes and other times there are photographs captioned with inspiring text written by the user. During *Eid al-Adha*, a number of the posts hashtagged #Islam or #Muslim fit within this inspirational, or contemplative, framework. They often featured quotes from the *ḥadīth* (the sayings of the Prophet Muhammad), Qur'ān, or messages of support for those carrying burdens which felt hard to bear—texts and narratives seemingly designed to remind the viewer of the power of faith.[44]

One such contemplative image featured a man dressed in purple on his knees in a rosy colored desert, his back to the viewer. The play of color and light makes for a beautiful, serene atmosphere. The creator of this particular post anchored the text appearing above the man to this idea of beauty: "Every morning is beautiful when we talk to Allah first *fajr.*" The man on his knees appears to be in a pose of supplication, or prayer, seemingly engaged in *fajr*, the first of five daily prayers that Muslims around the world perform at sunrise. As the man gazes off toward the horizon, both his posture and the image itself encourage viewers to peer into the distance as well while considering their own relationship with God. Another post which appeared when searching for "Islam" in Instagram featured a black prayer rug with the *Ka'bah* printed on it. In the foreground of the image a grey striped cat lay stretched across the knees of an individual dressed in white. It was a cozy, comforting image, reminding the viewer of the importance of both prayer and caring for others. As with the purple prayer post, the image contained a bit of text set off in a box at the top. Rather than asking the viewer to consider their relationship to Allah, the post communicated a message of personal support. "I just want to see you happy always," the text read, "may Allah grant what you dearly desire."

Many of these contemplative posts featured images of individuals kneeling as though in prayer, prayer rugs or prayer beads, and occasionally *masjids* or the *Ka'bah* in Mecca. Though produced and shared by individual Instagram users, they appear designed to remind the viewer of particular embodied and performative articulations of piety that connect individual believers to one another. As Morgan notes, "By acting on themselves, they act on the group, and by submitting themselves to the ethos and behavior of the group, they act upon themselves."[45] By embodying the tenets and practices of a faith publicly, an individual can signal their connection to the body of believers while also working to shape the behavior of others. These contemplative posts in Instagram offer gentle reminders that there are particular ways that Muslims should move through the world, placing the love of Allah and care for others above personal needs, wants, and desires. They also help conjure up an Islamic social body, one sometimes framed by visualizations of piety. Morgan describes a social body as "an imagined, felt association to which the individual belongs and in which she experiences her connection in a variety of sensuous ways."[46] The feeling that one belongs to this social body, Morgan asserts, can strengthen an individual's perception of religious identity and sense of belonging. Visualizations of this community can, in turn, remind an individual of the other ways that the senses orient us to the world and to others, transforming religion from the realm of abstraction into that of lived experience.[47] Though the various Instagram users posting to the #Islam and #Muslim hashtags during *Eid al-Adha* were physically disconnected from one other, through their posts they seemed to be working to create the feeling of participating in a shared and collective experience. It is important to note that these affective displays were posted from accounts located across the globe, with images from Saudi Arabia mingling with those from the American Midwest or Indonesia. As a result, the Muslim social body created through the contemplative images posted during *Eid al-Adha* was marked as expansive and inclusive.

Though Instagram is a space in which images are the main currency, there are some posts which consist mostly of text or display some fanciful visual design while highlighting a particular portion of text. During *Eid al-Adha*, in addition to images meant to urge Muslims to pray or to at least deeply engage with the world around them, there were also posts consisting of text that aimed to remind the viewer of various lessons they should take into, and from, the holiday. Some of these consisted of quotes from the Qur'ān or the *ḥadīth*, emphasizing the importance of humility and piety amid the *Eid* celebrations. Other quotations came from *muftis* (jurists), *imams* (prayer leaders), or other teachers and seemed designed, as the posts that included verses from the Qur'ān, to remind the reader of the spiritual heart of the holiday. Among the most circulated quotes was this one from Yasmin Mogahed:

> Many years ago, our father Ibrahim (AS) made a choice. He loved his son. But He loved God more. The commandment came to sacrifice his son. But it wasn't his son that was slaughtered. It was his attachment. It was his attachment to anything that could compete with his love for God. And the beauty of such a sacrifice is this: Once you let go of your attachment, what you love is given back to you—now in a purer, better form. So let us ask ourselves in these beautiful days of sacrifice, which attachments do we need to slaughter?[48]

Originally posted to Mogahed's public figure Facebook page, a separate Instagram user created an image featuring the quote and then posted it to Instagram. This quotation was among those that appeared multiple times in searches of both the #Islam and #Muslim hashtags, affirming how the idea of sacrifice and of attachment to Allah resonated with a significant number of Muslim Instagram users during the Feast of the Sacrifice. Perhaps that should not be surprising: Mogahed is a popular writer and scholar and is also known for being the first woman instructor at the AlMaghrib Institute.[49] The writings of popular nonreligious writers, such as the poet Mary Oliver and author Terry Pratchett, are often posted in Instagram in a similar manner.

Though perhaps obvious and unsurprising for social media posts produced by religious individuals, the framing of Islam as a contemplative faith stands in stark contrast to pervasive Islamophobic caricatures of Islam as a faith of irrational and erratic believers, with Muslim piety often equated with violence. In news and popular media, Islam is often portrayed as being trapped in the past—with followers who never think about or question things, just swallowing whole whatever their religious leaders tell them.[50] The *Eid al-Adha* Instagram posts often displayed the opposite, spotlighting individuals reflecting deeply on their faith and their own relationship to it. They also demonstrated just how diverse those individual experiences of Islam can be.

Diverse, Not Monolithic

There are some 1.8 billion Muslims living around the world today, with Indonesia, Pakistan, and India the three countries with the largest Muslim populations.[51] Yet this is certainly not the reality most often reflected in media representations of Muslims. Instead, audiences are typically exposed to narratives that, over and over again, reinforce the idea that Islam is an Arab faith and that almost all Muslims are Arabs.[52] The image of Islam painted on Instagram during *Eid al-Adha* 2019, by contrast, offered a more accurate depiction of the racial and ethnic diversity of the faith.

A number of the photos posted in the #Muslim hashtag at this time featured Black or Asian Muslims, individuals who are often erased by the way that Islam is framed as a faith practiced by a homogenous group of believers in, or from, the Middle East.[53] The marginalization of these groups from the popular understanding of who Muslims are has ramifications both outside and inside Islam. For outsiders, the erasure of particular Muslim communities of color can make their experiences seem less authentic than Muslims who come from the Middle East or North Africa. Within some Muslim communities, the effacement of these same minority groups has helped fuel racism and colorism.[54] In her work on the social media interrupter Leah Vernon, Peterson showed how one Black Muslim woman was working to force difficult conversations about these issues in her community on Instagram.[55] In my own research on #MuslimWomensDay 2017 on Twitter, I found that a number of posts, particularly those of Black women, seemed to be aiming toward that same visibility.[56] While few of the Muslims who appear in this research on *Eid al-Adha* on Instagram were quite so overt in their attempts to push back against their own marginalization, their images did seem to be a challenge to that erasure. The women may not have been interrupters in the way that Leah Vernon is, but they certainly appeared to be working to make sure their experiences were not marginalized or hidden in the space.

When exploring a hashtag on Instagram, a user encounters either a linear stream of images in the app or a tiled organization of images on a computer. In order to access any captions or commentary associated with the images, a user has to click a photo. But if the user chooses not to do that, their experience of the space is something akin to viewing a photographic quilt as the images are all sewn together by the hashtag. By design, the images collectively aim to communicate some truth about whatever the subject of the hashtag happens to be. In the case of the hashtags #Islam and #Muslim, that message seemed to be that Muslim communities are more diverse than popular depictions of Muslims would suggest. Images of Black Muslim women were woven throughout the images shared during *Eid al-Adha*. Some of these were selfies of women dressed to celebrate the holiday, while others were staged to look like fashion photos. In one photograph, a Black Muslim woman dressed in a monochrome peachy-orange outfit stands in front of a glistening white mosque, her pose and the sunglasses she wears challenging the viewer to look past her or pretend she does not exist. When they appeared in the search results both images sat nestled among displays of traditional sweets, *Eid* greeting cards, mosques, and prayer rugs. They are each woven into the visual fabric of Islam on Instagram in a way that suggests they belong there and their experiences should not be ignored or overlooked.

Women from a variety of backgrounds shared similar images in Instagram and, significantly, they seemed to work to portray themselves as active participants in their own lives. These were women who were making choices about where they were, who they were with, and how they would celebrate *Eid al-Adha*. Even those women who appeared in photos wearing the *niqāb* or the *burqa*—two types of Islamic coverings which are often portrayed as oppressive in media and political framings of Muslims—posed in public spaces in ways that challenged the viewer to assert they were oppressed by their faith or their choice of covering. In the captions of their photographs they would often mention something about the struggles many Muslim women face, seemingly to situate their own experiences within a larger fabric and to connect their stories to those of others.

Muslim Instagram users also worked to emphasize the diversity of Muslim experience by sharing images of people from various racial or ethnic backgrounds sharing the same space, sometimes praying together. Often, however, such images would simply display the hands of individuals of different racial heritages in order to visualize the diversity within Islam. The images of Black Muslim women as well as those featuring people from different racial backgrounds coming together under Islam worked to counter the idea that Muslims exist as a racially and ethnically monolithic block of believers, working to connect Muslims from different backgrounds to one another.

Another way that individuals connect via social media is through the sharing of memes, which, as Baym notes, promote a feeling of community that allows for engagement between users.[57] Dawkins conceptualizes the "meme" as a cultural equivalent to the biological gene.[58] While genes are engines for the transmission of biological information in living beings, memes serve the same function in culture, providing a conduit for the transmission of jokes, insights, or ideas in tiny packages carried across vast distances. Dawkins imagines memes as having a kind of autonomous capacity for this transmission which does not fully account for the various ways that people shape what is shared. Dennett, writing of religious memes prior to the advent of the social web, notes that those who would dismiss

Dawkins's idea of the autonomy of memes often fail "to ask at every juncture just whose interests are being advanced: those of the individual, the elite, the social group as a whole, or those of some other selfish gene—or some other selfish meme."[59] A meme is meant to be shared and circulated— and the meanings associated with it are shaped by individuals, the cultures of digital spaces, and institutions. The sharing of memes in social media can also become ritualized. As Burroughs points out, digital rituals can "mediate the central authority of the church with the publication of personal worship."[60]

Memes appeared in some of the 2019 *Eid al-Adha* posts, constructed most often by appropriating images from popular TV shows or films and designed to poke fun at something from everyday experience. One popular meme featured an image of Pikachu from the *Detective Pikachu* movie holding up a large magnifying glass. The caption for the image said, "Me when I'm trying to figure out if there's something *haram* [legally impermissible] in the food I'm about to eat." Another meme showed a sheep, seemingly leaping into the air with joy, with a variety of captions all suggesting that *Eid al-Adha* is a time for Muslims to celebrate their devotion to Allah as well as love of their community. Other memes emphasized the idea of humility, gently poking fun of individuals for taking too much time with their appearance during *Eid* and not enough time for prayer. These memes were posted in a variety of languages, suggesting that though the expressions of Muslim faith are diverse, there are experiences people share no matter where they are.

Burroughs and Feller argue that religious memes are often used to communicate the "everydayness" of religion, the banal experience of just going about one's life as a person of faith.[61] At the same time, they can also be sites where issues of interpretation are worked out in a seemingly non-threatening manner. After all, it can be hard to become angry at the person sharing a meme featuring Pikachu, even if you disagree with the underlying idea the meme is being used to express. "In a transmediated religious ecology where multiple media platforms and texts are open to construct competing notions of faith," Burroughs and Feller note, "memes intervene in the struggle between institutions and individuals and mediate digital disjunctures."[62] In effect, memes help to make visible the diversity of thought and experience within a religious community.

When it comes to prevailing understandings of Islam, this diversity of thought is not acknowledged; instead, Muslims are often imagined as all thinking, voting, and acting as a monolithic block.[63] The memes in Instagram, as silly as some of them are, put the lie to that pervasive idea. They often show that Muslims are engaged with their religion not as some staid, unchanging thing but as a living faith—one that shapes their experiences in a relationship that changes over time. The Instagram memes, coupled with the images of Muslims in various settings, help communicate that Muslims are not a monolith. The way these images are used to connect Muslim

Instagram users to one another in the space also helps communicate the idea that these diverse individuals are members of a larger, global community.

The concept of *ummah* is important in Islam as it envisions a global body, a community of believers bound together by shared histories and understandings of Islam. Hassan demonstrates that *ummah* has come to be understood as a kind of "imagined community" and a "framework for maintaining religious unity and accommodating the cultural diversities of the believers."[64] At the same time, he notes that the globalizing reach of new media technologies has produced a struggle within the *ummah* over "hybridity" and "authenticity," leading to the question of whether there is space within the global body of believers for a diversity of thought, interpretation, and practice shaped by cultural difference.[65] In Instagram, a number of the posts reflected individual users' interpretations of faith, but often contextualized by the country in which the user lived. For instance, one user described the kinds of gifts his Pakistani family gives one another during *Eid*, while another discussed the Indonesian dishes her family prepares for an evening meal during *Eid* in Jakarta. While these discussions might not be as high stakes as those centered upon Islamic jurisprudence or the interpretation of *ḥadīth*, they still make visible to others the idea that the lived experience of Islam encompasses a multidimensional and hybrid dynamic, influenced by both Islamic teachings and local traditions.

Another way the global nature of Islam was visualized in Instagram was in the text posts published by select Muslim users. While a number of the messages were written in Arabic, posts in languages such as Malay, Indonesian, and English were just as visible—signaling to the viewer that Islam is not reducible to a single location but is, in fact, a faith lived by people all over the world. These text posts sat beside one another in Instagram when the hashtags #Islam and #Muslim were searched. There was no separation of Arabic posts from English ones or Urdu posts from Malay—they all mingled together in the digital space, emphasizing for the viewer that Islam is not a faith that belongs to one place, one people, or one culture. What is harder to ascertain from the exploration of these posts is precisely how much interaction there really is between users in Instagram. A viewer exploring the hashtag and coming across the colorful quilt of images might see a global faith with a diverse set of believers; what is much more difficult to assess from any cursory examination of images is exactly how the users see themselves fitting into this, or any other, image of Islam.

Conclusion: An Instagrammed Social Body

An individual who happens to stumble upon Instagram is met with a cavalcade of colors and a mix of photographs meant to be both "real" and inspiring. Since it is designed to engage the senses and imagination of the viewer, Instagram is a space where boundaries and borders can sometimes break down or blend. During *Eid al-Adha* 2019, an individual who casually browsed the #Islam or #Muslim hashtags would have found themselves immersed in a world of curved architecture, illuminated calligraphy, softly filtered quotes from the Qur'ān, and Muslim fashion designed to be both modest and chic. Unlike the historic representation of Islam as violent and Muslims as dangerous, the faith of the believers who posted during the Feast of the Sacrifice appeared accessible and non-threatening. The performances of piety often on display in these images seemed purposefully designed to invite the viewer in, to make them feel comfortable with the celebration, and the celebrants, captured in the photographs.

What viewers would also find in those hashtags during *Eid al-Adha* was a glimpse of an Islam that is both diverse and global. Featuring posts in a multitude of languages, including Arabic, French, Indonesian, Urdu, and English, the Islam that emerges in Instagram encapsulates a faith of anyone and everyone—regardless of race, ethnicity, or national identity. If an individual were to actually click on the image post, they might find in the short text a variety of discussions related to issues of gender, sect, and jurisprudence in Islam. But they would also discover jokes, memes, and other bits of silliness mixed in with the headier conversations. What emerges from all of this is the feeling that the Muslim community in Instagram is working to connect to other Muslims wherever they happen to be. At the same time, this constellation of texts and images helps bring into focus a community which is warm, welcoming, and full of humor—an *ummah* that takes its faith, but not itself, seriously. By design, it is a framing that runs counter to the historic and hegemonic framing of Muslims as threatening, humorless others.

Most importantly, an individual investigating the #Islam or #Muslim hashtags in Instagram during *Eid al-Adha* would have discovered ample evidence of a lived religion, not a faith trapped in the dusty pages of history or solidified into a static, unchanging thing. These displays of Muslim piety and ritual performance portrayed a vibrant, living, and lived faith embraced by diverse believers all across the globe, who seemed to want nothing more than to practice their religion in peace and to share their blessings with others. While it is hard to know how connected these Muslims were to one another, they all appeared eager to publicly share representations of their faith that reflected their own personal experiences of Islam. Above all, the images seen in the feed of an Instagram user, or collected together during a hashtag search, revealed the existence of a connected *ummah,* helping the viewing audience to visualize a global social body of Islam in Instagram.

Part IV

Visual and Cultural (Re)presentation

CHAPTER 12

Defining Islamic Art:

Practices and Digital Reconfigurations

Hussein Rashid

Introduction

Museums are sites for the curation and presentation of knowledge. In displaying material objects related to Muslim cultures, these institutions have historically fallen into Orientalist framings, which seek to tell Muslims who they are, rather than respecting how Muslims define themselves. The result is a limit on what artifacts can reveal about the cultures from which they emerge. Approaching objects as a means to classify and organize culture often results in a vision of Islam divorced from a religious grounding. Combining the principles of numerous academic fields—religious literacy, cultural studies, and digital humanities—with new organizing methods made available by digital technologies, I argue that it is possible to imagine museum spaces that communicate more nuanced narratives of Muslim cultures. These alternative paradigms are informed by recent experiments in physical museum spaces as well as alternative approaches to virtual spaces.[1]

This chapter explores the visual and cultural (re)presentation of Islam and Muslims both in physical museum spaces and on digital platforms. Drawing on multiple case studies, I spotlight certain relationships between these displays of Islamic art. By focusing on two encyclopedic museums, the Metropolitan Museum of Art in New York City and the British Museum in

London, I demonstrate some of the implications of museum organization with respect to religious communities. My analysis also explores an exhibit at the Children's Museum of Manhattan—where I served as a consultant—to illustrate the use of religious literacy principles in exhibit design. I then turn to the online spaces of Archnet and Artstor, websites where users can organize digital material as a way to engage different configurations of Islamic art. Using the knowledge gained from these various case studies, I speculate about what a truly encompassing project of Islamic art could look like. The interventions in this chapter are not an attempt to contribute to decolonization and its distinct set of methods and instigations.[2] Even so, my arguments do resonate with certain approaches to decolonization.[3]

Categorizing Islamic Art

It is important to understand how the limits of regional art displays contribute to the limitations of representing Islamic art. One of the critiques of museum displays of the Middle East is that the cultures of the region are presented as unchanging and unevolving.[4] One Orientalist trope insists that Middle Eastern cultures are immune to the effects of time, lacking in "civilization" and therefore unable to participate in Western notions of modernity.[5] The vehicles of describing the Other in this framework are numerous. They include ascriptions of violence, misogyny, a lack of culture and education, dirty and unhygienic practices, and superstition. It is this allegation of superstition which links the broad cultural critique to religion specifically.

Since religion and culture cannot be neatly separated, religion is also disciplined through comparison.[6] The study of religion emerges from comparative theology, which typically assumes forms of Protestant Christianity as the norm against which other religions are constructed, contrasted—and always found wanting.[7] Using this logic, Islam is academically "proven" to be a superstition, given its divergence from the "true religion" of Christianity. I argue that museological displays of Islam rely heavily on these early constructions of Islam in the study of religion, a linkage that has transformed both fields and continues to impact the visual and cultural (re)presentation of Muslims.

There is a broad chronological schema for understanding how Islamic art is presented in Western environments that increasingly employ contextual labeling of the objects on display.[8] Simply adding sociohistorical or anthropological context, however, does not remove an understanding of Islam from imperial interests—and, as a result, most museum exhibits in Western Europe and North America still discipline Muslims. The ways that we generally see Islamic art presented in Western museums in the contemporary period is based on a precedent established by the 1976 World of Islam Festival held in London.[9] Although funded by Muslim-majority countries, the primary drivers of this event were "Western seekers for an Eastern spiritual Path" who reinforced Orientalist views of a timelessness to Islamic art, immune for material contexts and inherently opposed to modernity.[10]

In practice, museums function as spaces where not only displayed cultures are disciplined but audiences are disciplined as well. In both form and function, they establish behaviors for the consumption of art, communicating what constitutes art, how to read and understand art.[11] If the curators, intentionally or not, cannot fully comprehend how to display Islamic art in a non-Orientalist fashion, audiences will continue to be disciplined to an Orientalist worldview.

The interpretation of Islamic art is inflected by present discourses around Islam which impact how curators and audiences understand the past.[12] When material objects are displayed as simply "things" that need to be explained, the results are too often dominated by current political concerns.[13] When artifacts are placed in isolation inside a glass case, they only have aesthetic value.[14] In effect, when the object is completely commodified and removed from its wider network of social meaning it loses its religious value and only has an exhibition value.[15] As a result, the function of modern galleries of Islamic art has more to do with art markets than a historically contextualized understanding of the religion and cultures of Muslims.[16] This emphasis on art value is inherent in museology, where the term "Islamic art" is used to describe "masterpiece" objects for art museums, as opposed to "material culture," which designates non-valuable items for ethnographic museums.[17] What this taxonomy ignores is the fact that this distinction may not exist in the cultures from where these materials are taken.

As objects are transformed from religious meaning to secular meaning, they are more easily adapted to civilizational narratives.[18] Civilizational discourses tend to be deeply inflected by colonialist notions of civilizational supremacy.[19] The removal of these objects from a religious framework also means that what is defined as "Islamic art" is an external label based on formal aesthetic qualities, rather than emic understandings of the material.[20] Wendy Shaw, an art historian, succinctly points out the Scylla and Charybdis of trying to classify Islamic art: either it is all about religion or it is not about religion at all. The problem, however, is that both approaches essentialize what Islam means to believers. Shaw suggests we navigate these perils by shifting attention from the object to the subject. Her approach collapses the artificial distinction between religion and culture, and embeds religion in lived realities which vary over time and space.[21]

Material objects have no agency of their own but are given meaning by people. Even if the formation of the object is informed by a religious worldview, the person engaging with the object does not have to be Muslim to give it meaning.[22] Shaw also insists that conceptions of art have to move beyond an exclusive focus on physical objects since art can and does exist in multisensory contexts.[23] Her multidisciplinary approach therefore destabilizes the standard narrative about how we should talk about Islamic art and the visual *and* cultural (re)presentation of Muslims.

Incorporating Religious Literacy, Cultural Studies, and Digital Humanities

In many ways, what Shaw proposes for thinking about Islamic art parallels the principles of religious literacy, which speaks to the situatedness of our knowledge and how it engenders inherently partial perspectives.[24] This means that our approach to religion—and, by extension, religious art—must engage with that partial knowledge, and we ought to structure our knowledge-seeking through that situatedness.

A search for alternative approaches to religious objects also invites consideration of the role of cultural studies which seeks to study "culture" as something that permeates all social practices.[25] Cultural studies highlights how people function and create within their material realities, and aims to "enhance and celebrate" social experiences by understanding their contexts. It understands culture as part of everyday life—not separate from it as the concept of "high art" would imply.[26] Moving the focus away from official, scholastic religion, it shifts attention to the lived realities of people, and how they engage and interact with texts and objects, among a multitude of other cultural creations.[27] Thus, by incorporating interventions from art history, religious studies, and cultural studies we discover alternative pathways to understand the Islamic art object. This reconceptualization takes emphasis away from the object and places it on people. By spotlighting lived experience, narrative frameworks, and participatory exercises museums can generate larger narratives of interpersonal connection.[28]

The role of digital humanities in all the fields discussed so far—art history, religious studies, cultural studies, and museology—is equally far-reaching. Rather than provide a survey of that material, I want to emphasize the impact of digital humanities on religious studies which, in my view, offers broad principles for rethinking method.[29] Since one of the crucial elements of digital spaces is that they are inherently participatory, simply transferring static versions of what happens offline into online spaces misses the norms, expectations, and possibilities of this environment.[30] Any new technology brings people together in new ways, opening up the possibility for new expressions and artistic creation to develop in this changed environment.[31]

Digital spaces are inherently collaborative. They can be leveraged by people doing specialized work to achieve a common goal, and facilitate communication and cooperation among those working on similar things in different contexts. Aided by digital media technologies, the scholar of Islam in anthropology can collaborate with another scholar in sociology while also engaging another scholar in philology—promoting a stronger sense of the commons and commitment to larger publics, particularly those with whom researchers are working.

Since museums are currently constrained by authorized sources and methods,[32] moving beyond those limitations requires multidisciplinarity in unarchiving emic notions of Islamic art.[33] In fact, what we now define as art history has never been Islamic.[34] Even so, it is possible that museums can move beyond Western models of curation and exclusively Western knowledge systems.[35] They can go beyond taxonomies that freeze people in time as a representation of their eternal essence[36] and, in doing so, can bring Islam out of the gaze of Medieval Europe.[37] Going further, we can even question the foundational ideas of Islamic art, enlivening entire disciplines in the process. As Shaw aptly notes, the key question to ask is not "what makes an image Islamic?" but "what is an image?"[38] This is an invitation to broaden our study of humanity, not from the vantage of power that seeks to narrowly define humanity, but rather from the perspective of individual agency and lived experience that aims to expand our understandings of others and of ourselves.

Museums have the potential to be multidisciplinary and collaborative spaces, breaking down geographic barriers, encouraging diachronic work, and recentering the subject.[39] The following case studies discuss how select presentation spaces, both physical and virtual, use these tools to reimagine how Islamic art is presented—and the new concerns that emerge from these efforts. As digital humanities emphasize, work is always iterative.

The Metropolitan Museum

The Metropolitan Museum of Art (The Met) is an encyclopedic museum that attempts to be a comprehensive "library of art" and claims to hold an array of artifacts that cover 5000 years of art.[40] Although still under the auspices of the Department of Islamic Art, in 2011 the Islamic art galleries were officially renamed the "Galleries for the Art of the Arab Lands, Turkey, Iran, Central Asia, and Later South Asia."[41] The most salient example this case study offers is in the conceptualization and articulation of how these disparate materials fit together.

The galleries' description moves from a sweeping geographic description (Arab lands) to the modern nation-states of Turkey and Iran, and then back to another broad geographic description of Central Asia. The term "Central Asia" is not culturally useful as an analytic category since, for example, there is an unresolved question as to what the connections are between Kazakhstan and Tajikistan—beyond the interests and constructions of "great power" conflict. Finally, the galleries' name ends with a temporal and regional reference. South Asia is a massive geographic region, and the holdings do not represent that breadth. In fact, there is a separate gallery of

South Asian art at the Met. The art of Muslims of South Asia is thus divorced from any connection or continuity with earlier South Asian artistic traditions. The overall result is that Muslims remain divorced from global history and continue to exist in a silo.

As a geographic system, the new name still privileges Orientalist conceptions of where "Islam" happens—namely, in places where "Brown people" are.[42] The nation with the largest number of Muslims, Indonesia, is entirely absent from this framing, as is the rest of Southeast Asia. Similarly, all of sub-Saharan Africa, which includes a large number of Muslims and a significant land area, is erased in this construction of the galleries. This is a glaring omission, since even if one thinks that the Arab world is the heartland of Islam, Zanzibar was the capital of the Sultanate of Oman in the mid-nineteenth century. Wendy Shaw also points out the erasure of different identities through this mixed ethnic/nation-state construction. Her critique rests on the fact that dominant ethnic identities, like Arab, are often based on the suppression of minoritized ethnic identities, like Amazigh.[43]

For uninformed visitors, the Met's new galleries provide no sense that producers of Islamic art still exist and that these are vibrant, diverse, living traditions. Since there are galleries of modern Western art elsewhere in the Met, this glaring absence cannot be based on the limit of the temporal holdings of the museum. As a result, Islamic art remains fossilized in its presentation, and the geographic shift does not ameliorate that shortcoming. In the galleries, there is a room called the "Kevorkian Gallery for Special Exhibitions," which hosts rotating short-term exhibits of materials, usually drawn from the Met's holdings. The space has been used to host displays of modern art, sometimes defined by region, sometimes by theme. Unfortunately, it is not consistently used for modern art exhibitions, so visitors do not always encounter Islamic art as part of dynamic traditions and living communities.

What is apparent from this collection of objects in the Met is that there is some type of continuity in this artwork, even if the descriptors fail to name and explain it. Intentional or not, these representations convey the idea that although we can recognize that Zanzibar, Java, and Baghdad are distinct, there is still something we can recognize as "Islamic art"—much as we understand that London, New York, and Sydney are distinct yet still part of a "Western art" tradition.[44]

The British Museum

The British Museum, another example of an encyclopedic museum, opened its renovated galleries of Islamic art in 2018 as "The Albukhary Foundation Gallery of the Islamic World." The galleries are framed around a conception of Islamic art that extends both geographically and diachronically to the present. Throughout, the distinction between material culture and art is collapsed, and the displays are invested in a breadth of human activity that is not limited to art objects.[45] The museum attempts to show that Islam is not bound to time or place, and that the Islamic world encompasses a "wider concept of contexts significantly impacted by the presence of Islam as a faith, political system or culture" that does not preclude highlighting other faith communities in those areas.[46] By taking an approach which recognizes the interrelationship between religion and culture, the galleries allow the voices of subjects to define what Islamic art is to them. In addition, Muslims are described as part of a broader history with other people, rather than being isolated and treated as exceptional, outside the flow of human history. Muslims are also portrayed as a living community, with contemporary Muslim art included in the displays.

Overall, the gallery is presented in a hybrid chronological-thematic format. It is structured to allow visitors to see as many objects as possible at the same time—both within display cases and across display cases—in order to highlight connections in stylistic relationships across time and space.[47] These relationships can be subtle, as evidenced in works that seem to be inspired by the same source. At other times, the material parallels are more obvious, sharing similar patterns. Outside of the chronological groupings, which are often linked to geography, there are also cases which focus on broader themes, such as "Music and Performance," "Bridal Headdresses," and "Arts of the Book."

Another distinct way in which the gallery integrates Muslims into world history is through "object histories." These labels explain how objects entered into the museum's collection. As a result, there are narratives of trade, colonization, commissioned works, and capitalist acquisition. Each of these types of stories helps place Muslims in relationship to others, rather than implying that these works simply exist as a collection, with no sense of the background of the objects and the people who may have engaged with them.

The curators use a "gateway object" in each display case which provides the "big picture" to make the assembled artifacts comprehensible to visitors. In their labeling, the curators also use local languages from the area each object originated to provide a palpable sense of the diverse worlds from which these materials emerged.[48] The use of languages other than English helps to make the unfamiliar familiar to viewers who may not have access to the various languages Muslims speak. This labeling also demonstrates that these objects had a life connected to people before they were publicly displayed in the museum. The gateway object seems to be connected to the concept of the "big idea": a museological approach to organizing material that gives an overarching coherence to discrete sections, with all displays designed in concert with the overall learning objectives of the exhibit or gallery.[49]

In this way, the Albukhary Gallery appears to integrate principles of religious literacy and cultural studies into the design of its new galleries. The end result replaces a unitary definition of Islamic art with a vision (both metaphorical and literal) that is organic, dynamic, and comprehensive. This approach positions Muslims inside history, and within diverse civilizational discourses, creating a more cohesive narrative of human interaction over time.

Children's Museum of Manhattan

Unlike an object museum, a children's museum focuses on a multisensory experiential approach that is often centered on reproductions of objects for people to interact with during their visits. In addition, children's museum exhibits are explicitly designed for multiple audiences: the children who are the primary users, as well as their caretakers who are their partners in learning. This strategy demonstrates that a children's museum is a space that is primed to rethink the presentation of Muslim cultures and objects, integrating art history, museology, religious literacy, and cultural studies into a coherent experience.

The Children's Museum of Manhattan (CMOM) engaged all these elements in the design of its 2016 exhibit, *America to Zanzibar: Muslim Cultures Near and Far* (AtoZ).[50] The goal of the exhibit was expressly framed "to showcase and celebrate the cultural diversity of those who self-identify as Muslim."[51] The aim was to represent how Muslims see themselves and to celebrate the diverse cultures of Muslims. Responding to other people's perceptions of Muslims was not the point, nor were the material objects the primary driving force of the exhibit.[52] Instead, the exhibit started with the premise that Muslims have agency with respect to the creation and reception of their own culture, and that culture is not limited to art objects.[53]

By accepting that different Muslim communities exist and evolve in relationship to one another, the exhibit also allowed for displays of Muslims living in varied geographic and temporal contexts. For example, the travel section of the exhibit included a camel from Afghanistan, a *dhow* (a sailing ship) from Oman, and a jingle truck (a highly decorated and personalized shipping truck) from Pakistan. Although the camel might be seen as stereotypical, in the exhibit it was removed from an Arab context, destabilizing that association. In conversation with the other conveyances, it became apparent that people choose the best tool for the job at hand, and that the camel was not just a premodern mode of transportation but an important part of the contemporary period as well. The jingle truck was a mock-up that visitors could get in and pretend to drive, and they were encouraged to decorate the outside through the use of magnetic tiles. There was also a jingle truck toy on display in two cases, one of which was loaned by a Bangladeshi American, highlighting the transnational nature of the art form. Among the New York City contemporary Muslim artists who were on display, one had done a modern miniature of the trucks, demonstrating that the art was alive and present in everyday, local contexts.

The materials on display comprised a mix of re-creations and loaned objects, including art objects. The difference between material culture and Islamic art was intentionally collapsed, and this diversity of material helped to attract diverse audiences who reacted to the exhibit with both awe and comfort.[54] We also engaged a variety of partners in conceiving and constructing the exhibit, including institutional and community groups, both Muslim and non-Muslim.[55] The exhibit did not address underlying questions of what "Islam" is or assert that there were religious impulses that tied these Muslim communities together. That decision was intentional. Although the focus throughout remained on Muslims, the exhibit did not privilege the lens of their religious lives. Admittedly, this approach risks effacing Muslim devotional life and theological difference. Nonetheless, the CMOM exhibit offered a glimpse of what an exhibit that centers people as creators of culture may look like. It embraced a more expansive view of culture, which collapses the space between material culture and Islamic art, and integrated Shaw's idea of the object being more than a thing. In short, the exhibit recognized Muslims in context and framed Muslims from their own perspectives rather than responding to other people's (mis)conceptions of Muslims.

Archnet and Artstor

CMOM launched an iOS app called "My Name Is" designed to teach children how to write and say their names in over twenty languages spoken by Muslims in New York City. The app engaged community contacts who taught the exhibit's organizers how to write in these languages, as well as providing recordings of the phrase "My Name Is." Like all museums that bring in people from outside the institution as partners rather than as advisors, this was a collaborative effort, highlighting one of the key principles of digital humanities. Languages in the app included Arabic, Persian, Urdu, and Turkish, as well as Wolof and Bahasa. It also included French, Spanish, and English in order to help users understand the breadth of Muslim diversity and to reinforce notions that Muslims are local neighbors. This type of juxtaposition was made possible through the digital environment.

In my view, digital technologies enable curation in novel ways. Unlike physical spaces, which are limited to their holdings, digital spaces can be more expansive, especially as more museums place their materials online under Creative Commons licenses.[56] This final case study examines two websites, Archnet and Artstor, as tools for organizing knowledge around Islamic art. Unfortunately, both sites focus solely on static images and do not yet highlight other digital objects, like sound recordings.[57]

Archnet places an emphasis on built environments rather than material objects.[58] This focus offers a unique resource for understanding Islamic art because the website provides the background context of where objects lived before they were museum pieces. The built environment also allows for the excavation of layered histories, as places are built over other places and, in that process, reference cultural idioms from multiple cultural systems. On the website, users can search for images, save them during the course of a session, and then share that collection with others. If this tool were persistent and public in nature it would offer a useful model for iterating ideas of how to present Muslim cultures. Archnet does include a limited selection of sound recordings as well—most notably Paul Bowles's recordings of Moroccan music—so there is a pathway to layer a multisensory experience. The site is also trying to create a multimedia archive for a book project: *Music, Sound, and Architecture in Islam.*[59]

By contrast, Artstor takes an entirely different approach that does not foreground Muslim cultures. According to their website, "Artstor provides faculty and students with a complete image resource in a wide array of subjects with the breadth and depth to add context beyond the confines of your discipline."[60] The opening statement delineates the website's audience as those formally involved in education. This approach suggests an emphasis on multidisciplinarity, if not interdisciplinarity. By design, Artstor functions as a collator and a portal to an array of image-based resources. Because of its focus on images and the sources nature of its materials, the website reifies the paradigm of the art object—although one presumes that as these sources diversify, the distance between material culture and art object will narrow.

To take one example, the website displays an image of a postcard that depicts an image of Imam ʿAli, the first Shīʿī *Imam*, believed to be the inheritor of Prophet Muhammad's authority.[61] The postcard, photographed in 1988, displays a bit of pop culture ephemera in an art object context. If the user so desired, this image could be displayed next to another image of Imam ʿAli from the Met, created a century earlier than the postcard.[62] In my view, Artstor's greatest potential is in facilitating these kinds of visual comparisons.

If we take seriously the concept that Muslims live in a shared environment with other people, then accessing different museum collections in order to trace ideas across time and through different milieus is vitally important. There is ample academic research that demonstrates how the leader of the Iranian Revolution, Ruhollah Khomeini, was depicted in ways akin to Western depictions of Jesus.[63] This use of Jesus imagery in Muslim contexts is not new; Muslim artists and writers have engaged the symbolism of Mary and Jesus for centuries. And, of course, this culture flow was never unidirectional; Muslim depictions of Jesus often circulated back into the West.[64] Literary scholars have documented innumerable examples of how poetic images have moved through time and place in a similar fashion.[65] This sort of diachronic and thematic work is useful in destabilizing unitary narratives of both Islam and Muslims.

The Possible of Digital Technologies

An interdisciplinary and comparative approach to cultural objects seems like an ideal place to leverage the power of digital technologies in service of the humanities. Digital tools offer us the ability to layer different types of knowledge with a particular thematic focus. For example, we could spotlight Touba, Senegal, and conduct an analysis of the biography and hagiography of the famous Sufi master, Cheikh Ahamadou Bamba (1853–1927), layered over a digital map of his travels. Doing so would allow us to connect the establishment of his tomb and the growth of the city around it. Going further, we could link this history to the rich musical traditions that emerge from the various Sufi orders that lay claim to Bamba's spiritual legacy. The annual pilgrimage to Touba, commemorating Bamba's passing, would add another sensory experience to our understanding of the city. There are also mystical readings of the location of the city that become important to understanding its central role in the life of believers and the ways in which Touba was designed.[66] For an additional layer of complexity, a digital construct of this world could trace the members of the various Sufi orders linked to Ahmadou Bamba as they move about the world, exploring the new social and aesthetic structures they create to achieve similar ethical ends. Street peddlers in New York, or the Bamba Parade in Harlem, offer salient examples of the continuing, evolving culture of these diasporic Sufi communities.[67]

This type of comprehensive narration—augmented through the use of digital tools—forces a discussion about the connection between visual and cultural (re)presentations of Muslims. It demonstrates the complexity of Islamic cultures and offers a way to think of the term "Islamic" in more comprehensive ways than simply through text or object.[68] Such a multidimensional and multisensorial mapping of a Muslim community would illustrate how culture permeates all aspects of life and reveal the role of ritual as a vital part of that culture.

New digital technologies can challenge the binaries that have emerged in modernity and have us rethink the ways in which Muslims lived—and actually still live—with adaptability and integration.[69] After all, religion and ritual are not divorced from other aspects of people's lives, and by challenging what we consider art we open up the possibility of breaking numerous other divisions. The sort of layering that I imagine achieves the end of a more complex, nuanced, and comprehensive strategy for thinking about religion in people's lives. It is something that Archnet and Artstor point us toward; while neither website fully achieves this sort of complexity on its own, each has elements that others can build upon. Here then is the promise of digital tools: to be simultaneously iterative and collaborative. No single scholar could do the grand project of Touba, but many researchers could contribute to it.

The mistake is to think that digital technologies are panaceas by themselves. There is a growing body of literature around the ways technologies inherit and reproduce the oppressive structures of current systems.[70] Of course, it seems obvious that if creators have internalized systems of oppression, they will reproduce them and not always consciously. Digital media may allow us to ask new questions, but those questions may not by themselves transform the fields in which they are being used—unless we are also conscious of the biases and limits that (mis)inform those fields. In my mind, it is the practical lessons of museums in real life that can inform how Islamic art is represented in the digital sphere. In addition to prompting new questions, digital spaces bring together multiple critiques and newer methods to craft more comprehensive iterations of the work that has come before it.

Conclusion

Digital technologies have the potential to enrich the visual and cultural representation of Muslims. The use of these tools, however, must be informed by the critiques of the fields in which they are being used. When theory informs practice, it is possible to recenter Muslims in the conversation, recognizing their agency and seeking to understand emic conceptions of Islam. This approach relies, in part, on applying the lessons of religious literacy and cultural studies.

The three museum case studies in this chapter expose differing ways in which responses to the critiques of Islamic art are implemented. Each draws on different approaches, but none is truly comprehensive in its response. Of course, that result is to be expected, as each museum is molded by the constraints of its collections, the space it occupies, and the limits of its curators' resources and time.[71] In contrast, the digital case studies point to the unrealized potential that new digital tools offer for presenting Islamic art, highlighting what is possible in not only the display of Islamic art but in representations of Muslim cultures in general.[72]

In considering visual and cultural (re)presentation of Muslims, we have to understand that museums are institutions of the present which narrate the past from that vantage point. Both in analog and digital spheres, the goal should be to construct histories that offer multiple ways of being in the present while, at the same time, offering us visions of the future.[73] What was is not what needs to be.[74] Although the physical museum is limited in what interventions it can make, it is still an important place for these discussions and transformations to happen. Being in conversation with digital spaces informs both locations with more inclusive ways of presenting Islamic art that operates within a larger cultural field.

CHAPTER 13

Dousing the Flame:

The Political Work of Religious Satire in Contemporary Indonesia

James B. Hoesterey

Introduction

This chapter examines the strategic use of humor in social media discourse in Indonesia, paying particular attention to the interpersonal ethics of Muslim visual and cultural representation. The study of religion and media has become a burgeoning field of increasing importance in a range of disciplines in the social sciences and humanities. Just as with the invention of the printing press centuries before, the rise of Islamic newspapers, magazines, cassette sermons, TV programs, and celebrity preachers online has led to a proliferation of novel claims on religious authority, what Eickelman and Piscatori refer to as the "fragmentation" of religious authority.[1] Without necessarily eclipsing the authority of formal Muslim clerics, a new generation of popular preachers and cyber Muslims have begun to make their own claims on religious authority, Islamic practice, and public piety.

This flourishing field researching Islam and media has provided incisive analyses of the (re)mediation of religion in contexts ranging from taxi cabs and hair salons in Egypt to pop preachers and naked bloggers in North

Africa.[2] The Arab Uprising began in Tunisia in late 2010 and quickly sparked popular protests across much of the Middle East and North Africa, eventually leading to the downfall of Egyptian dictator Hosni Mubarak. With both activists and repressive governments trying to take advantage of social media, scholars once again turned their attention to the relationship between social media and political change.[3] Misplaced dreams of the inherent democratic tendencies of social media gave way to the realities of national governments and military using these platforms for surveillance and crackdowns. Marwan Kraidy analyzes the politics of public spectacle in Egypt during the Arab Uprising, with special attention to the strategic deployment of online female nudity to shock and shame. By making her body visible, one blogger uses her nude female body—the object of social shame—to make a larger political point about transparency, corruption, and hypocritical ethics.[4] With an impressive range of case studies, Kraidy emphasizes the political importance of Muslim visual and cultural representation. In a similar fashion, Tarek El-Ariss explores mediated scandal during the Arab Uprising, especially the forms of online public exposure and scene-making that divulge self-righteous public figures for who they "really" are—a mediated form of social shaming that El-Ariss refers to as "affective hacking."[5]

Whereas some images publicly shame their subjects, other forms of visual culture summon their audience. Using the language of Althusser, images can "interpellate" viewers, hailing them from the vantage point of the state and summoning them to occupy a particular subject position.[6] As Christine Gruber has observed with respect to visual culture in the Middle East, "the image serves as a powerful carrier of meaning as well as a sign that hails viewers by 'speaking' to them through the symbolic language of form, a kind of interpellation that in turn requires of them a number of active, interactive, and interpretive acts."[7] Contrary to Althusser's concept, however, interpellation is not always about the state. There is also an intersubjective hailing going on between meme creators and their audience(s), civil society, and citizen subjects.

Much of the scholarship on Islam and media in Indonesia—the country with the world's largest Muslim population—examines how digital media reveal (and further entrench) religio-political fault lines between traditionalists, modernists, and a range of smaller-scale Islamic organizations among the aspirational middle classes. The digital divides between various online Muslim communities can run deep. Scholars have tried to make sense of how the privatization and proliferation of Islamic media have shifted discourses about public ethics and national morality (*moral bangsa*) in a post-authoritarian Indonesia, where major television networks are owned by various oligarchs with their own views on religion, power, and the state. To take one salient example, Merlyna Lim provides a trenchant analysis of the "tribal nationalism" that developed online in the lead-up to the 2019 Jakarta gubernatorial election.[8] There is indeed a competition of ideas among diverse religious groups, and social media provide important platforms on which these conflicts play out.

After scouring a broad range of online resources, articles, films, and memes (complemented by interviews with various producers of Islamic social media), I gradually began to wonder what sorts of religious and political online currents I was missing by focusing mostly on moving images that demand, provoke, and offend. How might I make sense of all of these other images that did not fit neatly into my analytic categories of how to see, and where to look for, the visual culture of political Islam? Beyond the more obvious figures and themes of political Islam, how might we make sense of this genre of clever memes that are not so easily recognizable as "political Islam," that mediate and make amends rather than antagonize and provoke, that discombobulate and defuse more than insist and oppose?

Amid the cacophony of social media shouting matches—whether about national politics, theological difference, or state power—many Indonesians of various religious attachments began to experience a certain level of exhaustion. One prominent trend in the online/offline worlds has been for some hard-liner groups to refuse theological argumentation, instead just labeling an opponent an unbeliever, or *kāfir*. Those Muslims who use conventional banking? *Kāfir.* Anyone who does not support the establishment of an Islamic state? *Kāfir.* Say "Merry Christmas" to Christians? *Kāfir.* This particular reimagining of *sharia* has become dogmatic and exclusivist. After all, to dismiss one's opponent as a *kāfir* is to end the conversation, to refuse even theological argumentation about religion, governance, and public ethics. Public argumentation was reaching its inevitable stalemate.

This chapter examines the strategic use of humor in social media discourse as a distinctly Indonesian mode of Muslim visual and cultural representation. The satirical voices and images I spotlight can be understood as a response to this climate of conflict and social media cocoons. Vibrant online spaces began to emerge where the focus was more about reparation than rupture, more play than politics. This trend of witty memes since 2015 reveals a different sensibility that deploys humor to preempt and defuse potential conflict. Over the last few years, diverse religious groups of young online activists—decidedly not the senior, national leaders—write in the name of what has become a group of various "Funny Brigades" (*Garis Lucu*). Though it is difficult to generalize about a diverse group of people—from amateur jokesters experimenting with Photoshop to humorists who spend long hours crafting visual jokes and theological (re)presentations—these online humorists post their work on every major social media platform: from Twitter and WhatsApp groups to Facebook and Instagram, the latter two being the most popular domain for visual satire. Many producers of online content often have an Islamic boarding school (*pesantren*) background, university education (including graduate training in some cases), and are able to play with semantics across Indonesian, Arabic, and English (as well as local languages such as Javanese).

Whereas some Islamic online content creators were once leading activists of the student movement that toppled authoritarian dictator Suharto in 1998, many others are much younger millennials who barely remember authoritarian rule but still have an invested stake in contemporary politics. As ethical commentary, these humorists value humility over proud proclamations of public piety, and they promote civic and religious pluralism over theological arrogance and sectarian division. As my analysis demonstrates, these netizens forge an inter-subjective space of ludic practice where humor is deployed to minimize difference and aspire toward intra-Muslim and interreligious harmony, a form of tolerance marked precisely through its jovial form.

The Funny Brigades of Indonesian Islam: Nahdlatul Ulama and Beyond

Indonesia is the world's most populous Muslim-majority country (roughly 270 million people, 87 percent Muslim), and its Muslim population rivals the number of Muslims in the entire Middle East. Over the last couple of decades, Indonesians have thoroughly embraced digital and social media technologies, and major religious and political leaders have adopted a prominent social media presence. In the academic study of Islam, at least in North America, Indonesia often looms on the periphery of inquiry and understanding—despite centuries of networks connecting the archipelago with great centers of learning in the Middle East and North Africa; its bumpy-yet-successful transition from authoritarian rule to democratic institutions; the 200,000 Indonesians each year that go on *hajj* pilgrimage; a strong civil society with Islamic organizations leading the way; and the modern establishment of a rigorous system of Islamic higher education that could well serve as a model for the world. Islam has a long history—or more precisely, several interlinking histories—in the archipelago now referred to as the nation-state of Indonesia. From the earliest centuries of Islam, various Muslim travelers criss-crossed the archipelago, first in major port cities and then later as Islamic teachings ventured from the Sultanates to much of the rural populace across the major islands of Sumatra, Java, Borneo, Sulawesi, as well as various kingdoms of eastern Indonesia, especially in Ternate.

In popular understanding, the "nine saints" (*wali songo*) spread Islam across the archipelago by fusing Islamic teachings with local arts and cultural traditions, such as *wayang* shadow puppet performances of the Hindu epics *Bhagavad Gita* and *Mahabharata*. Especially in the reckoning of contemporary members of the traditionalist Islamic organization, Nahdlatul Ulama (NU), Islam was able to peacefully convert people precisely because of this respect for local cultural traditions that do not conflict with

Islamic teachings. Founded in 1926, NU leaders defended these and other customs, such as grave visitation (*ziyārah*) and prayers to the deceased (*tahlilan*), that were scrutinized by modernist thinkers, who argued that they had no basis in the Qur'ān or traditions of the Prophet Muhammad (*ḥadīth*). Whereas NU members often came from upbringings in Islamic boarding schools (*pesantren*) and prioritized the learning of classical Islamic thinkers, reformist Muslims belonging to the organization Muhammadiyah (founded in 1912) were influenced by modernist movements in the Middle East that prioritized rationality and an individual's ability for independent reasoning (*ijtihād*). Despite their theological differences, both NU and Muhammadiyah were instrumental in the anticolonial struggle and have become important pillars of Indonesian civil society.

In 2015, NU evoked this history of an exceptional Indonesian Islam with the concept "Islam of the Archipelago," or *Islam Nusantara*. When NU's central leadership officially launched this theme for the National Congress, they did not present *Islam Nusantara* as an Islamic school of thought (*maḏhab*); instead, it was intended to conjure a particular spirit of inter- (and intra-) religious harmony and respect for difference during this current moment in Indonesia's history when a new generation of preachers openly challenge the civic virtues of religious pluralism and democratic governance. This concept of Islam of the Archipelago was not universally embraced, however. Reformists and other theologically conservative religious leaders decried it as an innovation that had no basis in the Qur'ān or *sunnah* (the example of the Prophet). Even within NU's loose organizational ranks, younger conservative preachers opposed the concept of *Islam Nusantara* and relished in social media controversy about its merits.

This group of young, media-savvy, and more conservative NU preachers took on the moniker "NU Straight Brigade" (*NU Garis Lurus*). As one of these Straight Brigade preachers allegedly put it, *Islam Nusantara* was akin to "pig meat disguised as goat."[9] Through print, digital, and social media the NU Straight Brigade took issue with what they felt was the wayward liberal direction of the current NU national leadership who take inspiration from prior NU champions of religious pluralism such as the late Abdurrahman Wahid. Popularly known as "Gus" Dur (an honorific granted to sons of esteemed religious leaders, *kyai*), Wahid was known for his humorous approach to piety and politics. Perhaps most famously, he liked to de-escalate political and theological differences with the quip, *Gitu aja, kok repot!* (Just that, why all the fuss!), a popular phrase that has been (re) presented on T-shirts and bumper stickers.

The figure of Gus Dur looms large in NU popular hagiography, especially when it comes to leveraging humor as a political asset. This rhetorical deployment of humor has deep histories within NU styles of preaching and social interaction. As an organization, NU is known for its loose structure and the independence of its regional leadership. As a result, spirited disagreement is nothing new within NU ranks.[10] At the same time, a generation of young NU activists inspired by the witty ethics of Gus Dur took exception to the political implications of the Straight Brigade's opposition. Rather than picking an online fight—what Indonesians refer to as a "Twitwar"—this group of young NU activists began circulating humorous memes in the name of the "NU Funny Brigade" (*NU Garis Lucu*), using an avatar meme of Gus Dur laughing hysterically as its official Twitter account picture in 2019 (Figure 13.1).[11] This visual imagery of a smiling Muslim stands in stark contrast to the stern faces and Arab garb depicted in standard images of Indonesia's hard-liners. In terms of Muslim visual culture, smiles and laughter thus serve an important (re)presentational dimension of a softer, funnier face of Islam.

By May 2015, NU Funny Brigade maintained a Twitter handle as well as Instagram and Facebook accounts, with the tagline "Speak the truth, even though it's funny." In accordance with their ludic practice, this phrase tweaks one of the sayings of the Prophet Muhammad, "Speak the truth, even if it's bitter." This witty way of transforming and refiguring discursive and visual meaning, I argue, has become an important dimension in the religio-political work of satirical memes that disorient, poke fun, or invite laughter and banter. In terms of audience, these images and jokes are primarily intended for NU audiences, even when they include visual

FIGURE 13.1 *The main text of this humorous Twitter meme is NU Funny Brigade's tagline: "Speak the truth, even though it's funny." The small print on the left is one of Gus Dur's famous phrases meant to cool tensions: "Just that, why all the fuss?" (Gitu aja kok repot!) (https://twitter.com/nugarislucu/status/1080013441010565121?lang =bg). Accessed February 28, 2021.*

satire about NU Straight Brigade or hard-liner groups. In this respect, visual satire serves to solidify the in-group sentiment among mainstream NU followers while simultaneously critiquing adversaries who espouse different theological and political views. They are not necessarily intended to convert opponents to one's way of thinking. Further, these memes are posted, reposted, shared, and reshared in ways that complicate any idea of target audiences.

In the years since NU Funny Brigade was founded, several other religious groups within and beyond Islam have formed their own variants of the Funny Brigade. Examples include Muhammadiyah Funny Brigade, Catholic Funny Brigade, Buddhist Funny Brigade, and Protestant Batak Church Funny Brigade (where religion and ethnicity are both summoned). Even more conservative Muslim groups such as Hizbut Tahrir-Indonesia have formed their own Funny Brigades. Whereas Muslims account for roughly 87 percent of Indonesia's population, the idea of religious freedom and interfaith relations plays an important part in the nation's story about itself. NU's paramilitary wing, Banser, prides itself on protecting Christian churches from possible bomb attacks during Christian Holy Days. Similarly, the public performance of interfaith respect is highly valued in Indonesia, even as government regulations make it more difficult for non-Muslims (and Muslim minorities) to get official permission to build new houses of worship.

Quite different from the idealized rational deliberation of the Habermasian public sphere, these various Funny Brigades are not interested in rational, public dialogue, nor are they consumed with disciplinary shaming or theological debates. Instead, their goal is to discombobulate, disorient, and then reorient the viewer away from various positions of anger, contempt, and righteous indignation, and toward a friendlier demeanor—or in Gus Dur's words, *Islam Ramah, Bukan Islam Marah* (Friendly Islam, not Angry Islam). Gus Dur's clever wordplay demonstrates how memes can operate as mediated rites of inversion that summon viewers to leave their current subjective, ethical, and affective frames. By design, memes in the spirit of the Funny Brigade are meant to disarm, to defuse, and even to confuse. Consider the following meme posted on the Facebook account of the self-proclaimed Islam Funny Brigade (Figure 13.2).

What are we to make of this? This is not of the "gotcha" genre of online satire that mocks self-proclaimed pietists who eventually find themselves embroiled in scandal. It makes no commentary on Indonesian party politics, nor does it spotlight any theological divides between Sufis and Salafists. If anything, the style of beard and head covering are meant to summon stereotypical Indonesian depictions of their co-religionists in the Middle East. Scrolling down to the "muah!" kiss, a certain unease sets in concerning the invasion of personal space and privacy—perhaps prompting the viewer to recoil in that moment. There is a certain absurdity about this scene, a flagrant violation of public ethics, that also feels like part of its ludic appeal.

FIGURE 13.2 *The creator of this meme borrowed from the broader playful ethos of NU Funny Brigade, but speaks in the name of the "Islam Funny Brigade" (https:// twitter.com/islamgarislucu). Accessed February 5, 2021.*

As one NU Funny Brigade admirer put it, "There are many examples where the semantic word play have us howling with laughter only a few seconds after we first tried to figure out, 'What does this mean?'"[12] These memes disorient, disarm, and defuse. In doing so, they shift the very affective frames of online debate and visual representation. These communities of humorists also inspire creative and entertaining ways of engaging religion and difference. Fed up with online vitriol, the aim is to tweak the angry tenor of online discourse.

In Figure 13.2, the cartoonish figure conjures pervasive stereotypes in the Indonesian imagination about course and ill-mannered Middle Easterners, often depicted in Indonesian visual media as typical "angry Muslims." But here the kiss and overdrawn smile serve as a visual reminder that even these Indonesian notions of angry, violent Middle Eastern Muslims could use some levity. These meme creators do not always intend to offer alternative interpretations, nor do they always have some didactic message. That would be too serious. Instead, the entire point is to play with juxtapositions of visual and religious representation that promote an ethics of emotional restraint that Indonesians refer to, using the English expression, as "cooling down."

Making Fun of Difference: Politics, Theology, Conversion

In 2016, Indonesia witnessed massive rallies to "defend Islam" (*Aksi Bela Islam*). Many of these public gatherings drew several hundred thousand people from a wide range of religious and political affiliations who, with diverse political agendas, temporarily joined together to demand the imprisonment of a Chinese Indonesian politician for supposed blasphemy. In the case of the hard-liner group "Islamic Defenders Front" (*Front Pembela Islam*, or *FPI*), however, it is often unclear exactly what they are trying to defend. In their organized protests against bars, discotheques, and brothels, for example, the FPI rationalized its actions as a call to carry out the Qur'ānic injunction to enjoin the good and forbid the evil. Despite any theological grievances these leaders may have genuinely felt, the political expediency of this movement was deeply connected to Jakarta's 2017 gubernatorial campaign, where public blasphemy charges were used to oust the Chinese Indonesian governor of Jakarta, Basuki Tjahaja Purnama, commonly known as "Ahok." Ahok was defeated and did ultimately serve two years in prison for blasphemy, despite the testimony from several religious scholars that he had not, in fact, blasphemed.

Adding to these tensions was the subsequent presidential campaign in 2019 that pitted one candidate largely backed by traditionalists in NU against another with substantial support from the modernists of Muhammadiyah. Against this charged political backdrop, online and social media worlds ignited into hot debate, name calling, liking, and defriending. WhatsApp groups regularly churned out dozens, sometimes hundreds of posts each day, and Twitter became the preferred place for heated contestation. Although social media worlds often become echo chambers of like-minded individuals, in Indonesia these political tensions frequently spill over into online arguments among members of diverse organizations. Even so, the online worlds of several Funny Brigades during this time were markedly different— avoiding the rhetoric of righteous indignation and mutual contempt.

Few topics are more sensitive in Indonesia's religious publics than electoral politics, theological divides, and religious conversion. Yet, these are the very topics engaged and reframed in online conversations between the respective Funny Brigade groups of diverse Muslim and non-Muslim online communities. These virtual exchanges, complete with viewer comments and conversations, provide an alternative narrative with lighter affect and interpersonal respect. To the extent that they do indeed represent a distinct online community, these myriad groups are only loosely affiliated and occasionally even nonmembers create and post memes in the name and spirit of a Funny Brigade, as has been the case with NU Funny Brigade.

In the context of electoral politics, the atmosphere on social media was especially cacophonous in the run-up to the 2019 presidential election. This combative campaign positioned President Joko Widodo and his running mate for vice president, Ma'aruf Amin (former head of both NU and the Indonesian Council of Ulama), against the former special forces commander and repeat presidential candidate, Prabowo Subianto, and his running mate business tycoon, Sandiaga Uno. Subianto and Uno had the backing of a motley bunch of hard-line Islamists and Muslim reformists, with notably strong support from members of the modernist group Muhammadiyah. In this heated online climate chock-full with accusations of deceit, many Indonesian voters once again mused online about not voting for any candidate at all. In response to this pervasive cynicism, a satirical third team for president and vice president, who went by the names Nurhadi and Aldo, mysteriously emerged on social media. This farcical presidential ticket, created by a group of anonymous millennials disaffected with the political system, quickly became an online sensation in late 2018 with a series of hilarious memes that reflected the broader absurdity of democracy run amok (what Indonesians refer to as *democrazy*). The fake presidential ticket referred to themselves by an abbreviated combination of both names, or DILDO. The proud vulgarity of the phrase DILDO reflects a particular political and moral valence, an exposure of the corruption and vulgarity of politics. By creating a scene through impious exposure, an "affective hacking" of typical campaign narratives, the absurdity of the satire makes transparent those darker corners of campaigning such as bribery, corruption, and broken promises to "the people" (*rakyat*).[13]

These memes resonate in Indonesia precisely because they draw from a different symbolic repertoire than typical campaign slogans that appeal to religious fervor, nationalist sentiment, or military symbolism.[14] Instead, the plight of the poor working class is emphasized, with some memes even showing Nurhadi-Aldo with the long beard of Karl Marx, speaking in terms of class consciousness—a dangerous affair in Indonesia where the ghost of communism still looms large following the anti-leftist purge in 1965–6.[15] Although the campaign itself was a total farce, Nurhadi is actually a real person: a massage specialist whose image was humorously (re)presented in dozens of funny memes.

Set against this surreal backdrop, numerous Funny Brigades engaged in speculation about this new satirical presidential campaign. An administrator for the website *Kumparan*, for example, asked the Funny Brigades of NU (NUGL) and Muhammadiyah (MGL) what they thought of this third presidential ballot. In this online interview, representatives of these groups responded:

> *Kumparan*: MGL and NUGL, do you support the campaign of Nurhadi-
>   Aldo?

MGL: The presence of Nurhadi-Aldo provides proof that the presidential campaign can still permit alternative candidates. Rather than support Nurhadi-Aldo, we are going to join forces with NU Funny Brigade. With 91.2 million NU members, in addition to Muhammadiyah members, we would surely win the presidency. A unified Muhammadiyah and NU could not be beat.

NUGL: We support every effort to calm the nerves of the nation. The Nurhadi-Aldo ticket is an alternative from the other contenders who are too tense due to a lack of being massaged.[16]

In this exchange, Muhammadiyah Funny Brigade sought to repair some of the increasing acrimonies between certain members of Muhammadiyah and NU whose respective followers largely supported different candidates. The NU Funny Brigade kept to the satire a bit more than Muhammadiyah, identifying the overall tensions of the campaign season as the real malady that needs to be addressed. And who, they suggested, could be more fitting (and absurd) than a satirical candidate who is a real massage specialist?

The exchange continued, with the interviewer from *Kumparan* trying to provoke some religio-political reflection:

Kumparan: This is a political year. What sorts of good deeds must be done to calm people's emotions?

NUGL: Concerning Twitter wars (*Twitwar*), it's enough to just drink coffee and always laugh, because the bitterness of the coffee will help us avoid the sweetness of the promises of politicians.

NU Funny Brigade used this latter joke across various social media, taking aim at both the empty promises of the campaign season and the vitriol that has accompanied it. *Kumparan's* final question asked each representative for their advice to the candidates:

Kumparan: What sorts of good deeds would you recommend the presidential and vice presidential candidates perform in order to win the election?

MGL: No way would we offer advice for rivals. No way, we want the presidency also!

NUGL: Pray that your opponent wins. Because good prayers will come back to the person who prays.[17]

Whereas Muhammdiyah Funny Brigade's humor falls a bit flat, NU Funny Brigade reworks a common saying about prayers coming back to a person in order to support the seemingly nonsensical approach to pray for your competitor's victory. In this sense, Funny Brigade administrators become ritual specialists of mediated rites of inversion.

Online dialogues between the Funny Brigades of NU and Muhammadiyah also play with the theological differences between NU traditionalists, who place great emphasis on learning from classical medieval Islamic scholars, and their modernist Muhammadiyah counterparts who privilege the individuals' capacity to interpret the Qur'ān and *sunnah* (and disapprove of many traditionalist practices as noted earlier). Historically, NU was founded in 1926 to counter the increasing prevalence of modernist thought marked by the founding of Muhammadiyah in 1912. In terms of cultural sensibilities, NU mostly drew its ranks from rural central and east Java, forming a loose network of Islamic schools and local leaders. Muhammadiyah, by contrast, is known for its expansive networks of modern schools and hospitals across the archipelago. Despite its founding in Central Java, Muhammadiyah members are associated more with the urban middle class.

Consider the following online exchange, when NU Funny Brigade joked with their Muhammadiyah counterparts:

> NUGL: When traveling to one's home village [at end of Ramadan], a favorite place for a rest is an NU mosque. In addition to a spacious bathroom, there is also a free religious tourism ride where you can swim in the pool where you wet your feet (after ablution, prior to entering the mosque). MuhammadiyahGL, where is your mosque?
>
> MGL: From the mosque, please proceed to one of our rest areas supported by Lazismu [Muhammadiyah's humanitarian organization] and Muhammadiyah hospital. There you can receive a health check. It's probably nothing, [we] just worry if the kids start to itch after swimming in a free pool, for example. Excuse me, just a reminder.[18]

These are the sorts of things most Indonesians would not typically say to each other face-to-face, yet somehow the online space of humor, play, and even entertainment inverts what is understood as normal, rational sociality. During a political moment when online accusations about infidels ring out on social media, Funny Brigade netizens try to reduce tensions precisely by joking about the most sensitive markers of theological, political, and class difference. In doing so, the goal is not to dismiss difference but to accept it while also easing the stakes of such controversial theological and political divides.

Religious conversion is another sensitive topic in Indonesia. Hard-liner Muslim magazines speak of the threat of "Christianization," a sentiment that has been stoked from the days of colonial rule when Protestant missionaries roamed the archipelago seeking converts, especially in eastern Indonesia. Whereas conversion away from Islam presents its own set of difficulties in a Muslim-majority nation, conversion from Christianity to Islam can also be a sensitive topic in Indonesia, where Christian minorities must tread lightly. When celebrity actor and eccentric entertainer Deddy Corbuzier (whose videos have over two billion views on YouTube) decided he would convert from Catholicisim to Islam in 2019, there was much fanfare in online and social media. Images of Corbuzier reciting the Islamic profession of faith (*shahādah*) circulated widely via digital media. Accompanying images of Corbuzier donning his new black *peci* hat, a symbolic marker of Muslim identity, provided the sartorial symbolism of the conversion of both person and persona.

Jumping into the online controversy, the Catholic Funny Brigade posted the image of Corbuzier's official conversion ceremony, tagging NU Funny Brigade, "Today we offer Corbuzier to NU Funny Brigade. From here on, please feel free to circumcise him and show him the way." In their subsequent Facebook status update on June 21, 2019, NU Funny Brigade proclaimed,

> Welcome Uncle Deddy Corbuzier. May this be a blessing for all worlds. To our Catholic Funny Brigade Friends, do not worry. God willing those good traditions of yours we will keep, in accordance with [NU principles of] *Al-muhafadzatu ala qadimis shalih* (maintain those traditions that are good and take what is even better from the new).[19] For the future, we all hope Uncle Deddy Corbuzier becomes even funnier. *Traktiiir*!!! (to treat someone for food and drink).[20]

In their reply, NU Funny Brigade administrators played with theological interreligious commentary from the Qur'ān that frames Islam as both a correction and extension of prior Abrahamic religions, invoking an ethos promulgated in NU Islamic schools that only prior errant theological beliefs would be changed by Islam (here implicitly referring to the difference between Christian and Muslim understandings of whether or not Jesus Christ was divine). This joke operates on two levels. First, it actually accentuates interreligious theological differences. Second, it minimizes the actual gravity of such differences that are often presented as insurmountable. The final exclamation about someone "treating" should not be interpreted literally; instead, its drawn-out and exaggerated form serves as a proclamation of hilarity, an allegiance to that which is funny (and those who are funny). In this context, these memes are rituals of the ridiculous, with humor exposing the absurdity of manufactured rancor online and in the streets.

Several religious minority groups in Indonesia, including Muslim minorities, are grateful for NU's legacy of interfaith harmony, especially Gus Dur's efforts to promote religious pluralism and understanding when he served as Indonesia's president from 1999 to 2001. Perhaps not surprisingly, a different Catholic Funny Brigade account (the Catholic Community Funny Brigade) emphasizes this relationship in their own online efforts at public diplomacy through humor. In one Facebook meme posted on September 5, 2020, the Catholic Community Funny Brigade shared an image of an avatar of a laughing Gus Dur, standing beside an avatar of the Catholic community (Figure 13.3). The Facebook status update read, "Come on, get

Romo Mangun menyebut Gus Dur sebagai orang Katolik
tapi tidak pernah ke gereja (misa),
Gus Dur membalas dengan mengatakan bahwa Romo
Mangun adalah orang Islam yang tak pernah Sholat.

Ayo Guyon Surga Milik Kita Bersama

NU Garis Lucu

Dikasih hadiah peci dan
sarung dari Gus NUGL

FIGURE 13.3 *A Facebook meme from the "Catholic Community Funny Brigade." The caption reads:"Father Mangun said that Gus Dur was a Catholic who just never went to church. Gus Dur replied by saying that Fr. Mangun was a Muslim that just didn't pray. Come on, joke. Paradise belongs to us all" (https://www .facebook.com/KatolikG/posts/ayo-sedulur-kita-guyon-surga-milik-kita-bersama /2682845881985516/). Accessed December 17, 2020.*

joking! Paradise belongs to all of us!" Beneath the image, the text narrates a story of interreligious friendship and mutual respect between Gus Dur and well-known Catholic priest writer, and architect, Father Mangun (Y. B. Mangunwijaya).

The image of the Catholic man shows him in sarong and *peci* hat, noting "Received a gift of *peci* and sarong from Gus NU Funny Brigade." In Indonesian Muslim culture, to gift a sarong and *peci* hat is a declaration of common humanity, and to wear those gifts is to honor the gifting relationships and sense of obligation and reciprocity that bind these interfaith friendships. In this way, the meme encapsulates the anthropological importance of online communities—the ways they encourage certain civic sensibilities and affective allegiances. The meme at once acknowledges Gus Dur's respect for other religions and religious leaders while also placing friendly interfaith relations in historical context. Without reducing these memes to political expediency alone, religious minorities in Indonesia are well aware of the benefit of maintaining solid interfaith relations. This ethic of interreligious cooperation is in fact a lodestone for NU, whose paramilitary wing, Banser, annually guards churches on Christmas Eve and, at least during the time of Gus Dur, defends various religious minorities.[21]

By spotlighting these cases of online interplay, I do not intend to imply that social media provides a liberating virtual space of interfaith *communitas*; nor should we understand the Funny Brigade phenomenon through a celebratory focus on transparency and accountability. On the contrary, as Karen Strassler has argued, such dreams of transparency in Indonesia are clouded by anxieties and ambivalences about truth and accountability.[22] From the perspective of Indonesia's religious minorities, there is ambivalence about whether these transactional gifting economies will actually have integrity when needed the most, whether outside a church where an angry mob has gathered or in the state bureaucratic chambers that give permits for places of worship. A purely instrumentalist understanding of online relations, in my view, misses the online genre of ludic play as one way to side step, if not disarm, the problem of online (and offline) rancor.

I would suggest that the administrators for diverse Funny Brigades have strategically embraced humor as part of their religious sensibilities, approaching the sublime through the ludicrous. To be sure, there is an archive of satirical memes designed specifically to mock, to shame, and to discipline people along various axes of difference. However, the troops of the Funny Brigades generally (though not always) lead with humor and seldom explicitly cast judgment. The style of visual interpellation here is not to hail citizen subjects from a particular position within the state apparatus. Instead, these images summon the audience by trying to jar viewers out of their comfort zones and media cocoons, to soothe their indignation, and to invite the viewer to crack a smile. It is in this sense that online humor aims to curtail resentment, disrespect, and violence in both online and offline worlds.

Funny Subjects: Some Concluding Reflections on Ludic Subjectivity

In a provocative essay, Christopher Pinney argues that "visual theory is in crisis, a crisis with revivifying potential, because we have rediscovered the potential of the visual to create crisis."[23] Certainly, we do not need to look too far to appreciate the capacity for the visual to create crisis. From insulting Danish cartoons about the Prophet Muhammad to unconventional cinematic portrayals of Jesus Christ, images can undoubtedly provoke, offend, and create religio-political chaos.[24] At the same time, the case studies considered in this chapter suggest that the political work of visual culture can also be leveraged to manage crisis, de-escalate conflict, and mend socioreligious bonds. The visual culture of political Islam, then, goes well beyond offensive cartoons, slick terrorist propaganda, and stereotypically angry Muslims. Whereas some images are intended to light the fuse, those considered here are meant to douse the flame.

This ludic impulse is not a secular shunning of religion but an ethical embrace of virtues such as tolerance, humility, and respect for humanity. These Funny Brigade memes suggest a distinct pleasure taken in the comical, an appreciation for a religious life taken in proportional seriousness. Such memes do not always have a didactic point, either. The ability to see humor in the everyday is itself valued as a personal virtue. Following the words of the Prophet Muhammad, even a smile can be an act of religious charity. One creative meme jokes about Islamic boarding school life (especially the sartorial struggle of keeping one's sarong at a perfect length) by tweaking the genre of movie posters for Islamic cinema in Indonesia. In this case, NU Funny Brigade meme creators played with the original film title, *Surga Yang Tak Dirindukan* (The Heaven None Missed), by replacing the word for heaven with the similarly spelled word for sarong, *sarung*: "NU Media Presents the Sarong that None Missed, a Film by NU Garis Lucu." A common situation among Islamic boarding school youth from NU backgrounds, properly folding and wearing the sarong can be serious business, especially when it might unravel at inopportune moments such as communal prayer, as pictured in the meme with one sarong clumsily hanging past the feet of a boy in the front line of prayer.[25]

Dozens of similar memes take pleasure in the juxtaposition of text and image, meaning and play. For example, rivalries among Indonesian soccer fans of both domestic and international leagues are often a source of humor and teasing. One meme shows the Liverpool soccer star Muhammad Salah (whose last name, in Indonesian, means "wrong") with the caption: "Salah brings blessings" (*Salah Membawa Barokah*).[26] As another example, in a NU Funny Brigade meme from July 2, 2018, an Indonesian soldier wearing the name badge "Yahudi" (which means "Jewish" in Indonesian) stares menacingly at the camera.[27] As the late historian Jeffrey Hadler has argued, anti-Semitism has a long history in Indonesia and is still prevalent in popular religious and political discourse.[28] Indonesia does not even have formal diplomatic relations with Israel. Given this backdrop of suspicion and prejudice, NU Funny Brigade added the caption: "Don't go on hating Jews because it might just be the case that they are defenders of the Indonesian nation's territorial integrity." This meme thus uses humor to de-escalate tensions. At the same time, the joke implicitly critiques anti-Semitism in contemporary Indonesia.

These mediated practices are also religious practices. Throughout the Qur'ān, in dozens of *ḥadīth*, as well as the writings of subsequent classical Islamic thinkers such as the renowned Persian medieval philosopher, theologian, and Sufi master al-Ghazālī (1058–1111 CE) there is a pervasive stress on the importance of reining in the emotions and cultivating one's sense of reason.[29] During a discussion of Nurhadi's satirical presidential campaign on a well-known TV Talk Show, NU politician Muhaimin Iskandar observed that many Indonesians embrace satirical figures like

"SESUNGGUHNYA SUMBU MANUSIA ITU SANGATLAH
FLEKSIBEL,BISA MEMANJANG DAN BISA MEMENDEK.
BISA MENJADI SANGAT PENDEK BILA BERHADAPAN
DENGAN LAWAN POLTIK,
DAN BISA MENJADI SANGAT PANJANG BILA BERHADAPAN
DENGAN KAWAN POLITIK."

-MBAH DUKI

fb.me/fihril

FIGURE 13.4 *Memes like this are circulated, refashioned, and remediated as part
of the intersubjective dimension of online sociality. Image by Fihril Kamal (https://
twitter.com/nugarislucu/status/1092710928708071424). Accessed February 28,
2021.*

Nurhadi precisely because they provide a "cooling down" of tensions, a
"safe zone" (*kanal aman*) in which people can connect without religious
or political vindictiveness.[30] Iskandar, who had lobbied hard for the vice
presidential candidacy, even cracked a joke on the TV program about his
own bitter disappointment at not being chosen for the position.

Consider one final example about this capacity for humor and Muslim
visual culture to cool down political hostilities. On February 5, 2019,
graphic artist Muhammad Fihril Kamal tweeted a meme that showed an
elder wise Muslim man, Mbah Duki, offering counsel to an angry young
Muslim boy with a furrowed brow and a flaming fuse coming up from his
peci hat. Mbah Duki was the wise moral protagonist of a series of cartoons
named "Sketches of Our Islam." Mbah Duki says, "Honestly, people's fuses
can be very flexible, getting longer or shorter. [People's fuses] can get very
short when face-to-face with their political opponents, and very long when
face-to-face with their political allies" (Figure 13.4). Along with the meme,
Kamal posed a question for NU Funny Brigade, "Are Mbah Duki's words
true?@ NUgarislucu?" NU Funny Brigade replied simply and sagaciously,
"Humor was created to douse the flame."[31]

CHAPTER 14

The Instagram Cleric:

History, Technicity, and Shīʿī Iranian Jurists in the Age of Social Media

Babak Rahimi

Introduction

"My name is Fāṭimah and I'm fourteen years old." So began a 2011 lecture by a Shīʿī Muslim cleric on the subject of digital media at the Computer Research Center of Islamic Science (*Markazi tahghighat-i computeri-ye ulum-i Islami [Noor]*) in Qum, Iran. Though at first stunned by the remark, the audience—comprised largely of male seminarians at the Research Center—later learned that "Fāṭimah" is actually the mid-ranking jurist's Facebook profile: an assumed virtual identity that allows him to pass as a female teenager on social media. The cleric, known for his views on the benefits of new technology for religious propagation, informed his amused audience that his Facebook profile does double duty as both a personal account (where he feels free to post commentaries, share videos, and maintain a friend list) and a fictional account (where he identifies as a female youngster).[1] Within this virtual realm, the cleric is therefore simultaneously both Fāṭimah and not Fāṭimah, both a middle-aged religious authority figure and a teenage girl. Realizing the ambiguity of these blurred offline and online identities, the audience laughed.

At the heart of this enigmatic story is a network space where the lecture took place. Founded in 1989 by the Islamic Republic, the Computer Research Center of Islamic Science is home to clerics, seminarians, and software engineers tasked with designing, producing, and disseminating Shīʿī Islamic literature through computer-mediated technologies—in particular software programs—for an Iranian and international Shīʿī public.[2] The Research Center is also known for hosting lectures and workshops on religious publications related to software computer technologies for educational and proselytizing purposes. The Center's educational and propagation mission has continued to operate since the end of Iran–Iraq War (1980–8), demonstrating the flexible ways that religious authority, with the support of the state, has worked closely with the Qum-based computer engineers. The result has been the network formation of collaborators: colleagues and friends engaged with computer technologies through multisensory interaction designs and internet outlets in the (re)production of religious authority and knowledge.

In this context, the cleric's social media profile may seem like an act of anonymity, or better yet pseudonymity: disguising himself as a teenage girl as a way to conceal an institutional identity while, at the same time, protecting his status (and preventing stigmatization) within a male-dominated conservative seminary community, where he officially self-identifies as an active member. In a similar fashion, the assumed profile of a teenage girl might also help the cleric to mask his "true" identity and thereby freely view other profiles, especially across gender lines, without the perils of judgment for his perceived male identity. However, there is something in this peculiar act of Facebook self-profiling that defies mere mischievous behavior; otherwise, why would the cleric begin his anticipated lecture with an apparent self-incriminating confession?

While the profile of "Fāṭimah" is hardly a deceptive act with the intention to harm, the cleric's feigned identity reveals a reflexive act of staging the self that playfully rearranges conventional notions of religious authority for an ambiguous effect. Even so, this representation of age and gender identity on social media did not undermine or discredit the authority of an established jurist. The seminary audience, in fact, recognized the humorous attempt to fake identity as something admirable. In my view, this performance of gender reversal on social media signals not fabrication but rather a freedom to play with identity. It provides an interlude in the everyday dynamics of official life that momentarily creates a new reality in virtual space and, in doing so, reworks the mediated possibility of self-expression beyond the rigid boundaries of officialdom. What this enigmatic story underscores is the dexterity of humor that helps refine the cleric's authorial image and enhance his agentive status. This agility offers a potential source of emulation for other clerics, whose awareness of traditional authority includes the interpersonal ability to negotiate self-presentation in shifting contexts. Both offline and online, legitimacy is achieved in the festive communicative frameworks that facilitate amenable authority.

With this story as a backdrop, this chapter explores Shī'ī Iranian clerical self-representation and participatory networks as mediums of authority. My analysis traces how such networks are enacted through social media technologies, focusing in particular on the photo-video sharing app, Instagram. In theoretical terms, this case study understands digital media technologies as a phenomenological performance that makes religious identity formation possible as a distinct social practice. I argue that since the 1990s, Shī'ī clerical authority has undergone a performative network transformation with digital technology playing a key role in the process. The term "performative network" refers to the complex repertoire of (self) representations that signal the confluence of repeatable and transferable frameworks, where the boundaries of "private" and "public" spheres blur into emerging social networks. Through ties that constitute diverse relations, Shī'ī clerics engage in diverse modes of authorial performances by carving out new spaces of public presence—an alternative landscape where self-representation becomes, despite physical absence, accessible, spreadable, and inherently more visible. Within the pathways of this network, the emergence of social media connectivity underlines what sociologist Scott Feld has described as a community marked by "foci" as the basis of distinct associations that interact in digitally mediated domains.[3] These online communities are personalized around certain performatives of self-presentation by male clerics of diverse age, most of them seminarians from mid-ranking status groups across Shī'ī dominated regions of Iran. The result, I suggest, is the creation of new bridges between social networks that go beyond conventional notions of state-society relations, many of which include mundane practices of clerical authority that are framed in everyday life.

The chapter is divided into two parts. The first section argues that Shī'ī authority should first be examined in its historical context, beginning from the juristic authority of early Shī'īsm to the clerical formation of an Islamist state in 1979. My analysis also draws attention to theory and examines the *hawza* (Shī'ī Islamic seminary) from the perspective of "technicity" in the production of jurisprudence and other forms of knowledge that have operated through technologies of dissemination and networks of connectivity. This production of authority, I argue, entails technicity *in* the performance of being a cleric in public life—a process which has always been integral to the *hawza*. The second section explores the changing practices of technicity in the performances of clerical authority on social media. Tracing the origins of clerical involvement in the Iranian internet during the 1990s, I chart how Shī'ī jurists continue to innovatively reconstruct authority in new social media practices. The chapter's case studies spotlight two clerical profiles on Instagram to analyze how chains of information, postings, commentaries, and followers flexibly reenact traditional authority in everyday and, at times, playful ways in situated contexts. The moniker "Instagram cleric" underlines the technologically mediated ways that Shīʿī religious authority and identity undergo dynamic change amid a visual and cultural repertoire of self-(re)presentations that preserves traditions through a process of constant reinvention.

The Technicity of Jurisprudence in the Era of Occultation

While the concept of authority has had complex historical meanings and practices in various Islamicate societies, we know little about either authority or communal identity in early Shīʿīsm.[4] This fact sharply contradicts the common perception that views Shīʿīsm as a sectarian movement born out of the political conflict over succession after the death of Prophet Muhammad (570–632 CE) who embodied legal-political and spiritual authority. The year 632, according to this view, precipitated a crisis of leadership for the *ummah* (Muslim community) as the Hashmite clan advanced the claim that the Prophet had designated ʿAli ibn ʾAbī Ṭālib (601–661 CE), his cousin and son-in-law, as successor—spawning competing claims over the legitimacy of the caliphate in the post-Prophetic period. Authority, in this view, was innate to the very foundation of Shīʿīsm in its allegiance to ʿAli as a protest religion.

As Najam Haider has shown, however, there is little historical evidence to support the view that a pro-ʿAlid "vociferous minority" community emerged in the years following the death of the Prophet.[5] It is most likely that following the battle of Karbala in 680, and the martyrdom of the grandson of the Prophet, Ḥussayn, an initial crystallization of Shīʿīsm took form, in particular in the city of Kufa. Such a speculative historical approach should help us identify early Shīʿī authority and communal identity not in canonical texts but rather in ritual and pilgrimage practices around sacred space devoted to the *Imams*, which emerged a century after the death of the Prophet. Shīʿī identity, by extension, remained firmly entrenched in its association with rituals, sacred sites, and associated pilgrimage rites, in particular at the shrine of Ḥussayn in Karbala, which played an integral role in the early community formation. In short: authority was inherently tied to particular ritual practices associated with *Imami* spaces of pilgrimage.

By the eighth century, under the leadership of Muhammad al-Baqir (Fifth *Imam*) and Jaʿfar ibn Muhammad al-Ṣādiq (Sixth *Imam*)—who embodied a direct bloodline of ʿAli via his son, Ḥussayn—a distinct Shīʿī identity developed around theological discourses. Although al-Ṣadiq rejected political ambition, under his leadership a discourse of authority was articulated that viewed male descents of the Prophet as the *Imam*, or guide, of the *ummah*. In Shīʿī eschatology, the appearance of the doctrine of Occultation (*ghaybah*) in the tenth century proclaimed that the twelfth descendant of the Prophet, Muhammad al-Mahdī, soon after the death of his father, Ḥasan al-ʿAskari, in 874, has remained hidden until God verdicts his return for a final apocalyptic fight against the forces of evil which will end in their defeat. In contrast to Sunni conceptions of authority that are primarily about worldly leadership of pious orientation, the early Shīʿī doctrine of *Imamate* emphasized the divinely led designation (*naṣṣ*) of the *Imams* based on a messianic worldview—an interpretation that continues to shape global Shīʿī communities on both devotional and doctrinal levels.

Since the Occultation of the Twelfth *Imam*, Shīʿī Muslims have continued to wrestle with the question of who should be given the reins of leadership in both temporal and spiritual terms. In the period of Occultation, Shīʿī authority held a relatively consistent position of the importance of keeping out of politics until the return of the promised Muhammad al-Mahdī (the Twelfth *Imam*). In a broad historical context, however, the resulting vacuum of leadership has in practice been filled with multiple sources of authority. In the case of Iran, the monarchy effectively served this role until the Revolution of 1979. Even so, on complex provincial and transnational levels—from Baghdad to Najaf and from Bahrain to Lebanon and Pakistan—Shīʿī jurists have claimed significant influence over communities, where their knowledge and (re)interpretation of textualist sources of Islamic law has legitimized authority in various spheres of life.

Two major historical changes brought about new institutional transformations in Shīʿī clerical authority. First, the Safavid dynasty (1501–1722 CE) gave rise to Shīʿī clerical authority as a sociopolitical institution tied to state power. The second, and more important, development was the 1979 Revolution and the establishment of the Islamic Republic.[6] In various stages of its development since the 1980s, the statization of the clerical authority reconfigured Shīʿī conceptions of authority in terms of governance. It also hardened the perception of Shīʿī clerical authority as a formal, disciplinary, and structural institution, inherently tied to local and (trans)national forms of governance. Of paramount concern to those who view Shīʿīsm as a political threat is the perception that Shīʿī authority has become a rigid form of "establishment" which by maintaining a strict hierarchy of state power projects legitimacy, with political claims extended over Iran and beyond. According to Mehdi Khalaji, in its postrevolutionary form, the independent institution of the *marjaʿ* has not only become a tool of state power but also lost its self-autonomy.[7] In this sense, the authority of the *marjaʿ* is now an empty claim in the era of Occultation.

In contrast to Khalaji's claim, Shīʿī clerical authority has never been singular, nor has it maintained a stable tradition in its apparent claim to traditional knowledge and its application to worldly life. Here, we could invoke Max Weber's tripartite classification of authority: traditional, legal-rational, and charismatic.[8] In its long history, especially since the nineteenth century when the *marjaʿ* was consolidated as a source of knowledge for the community, Shīʿī clerics in various contexts have effectively combined the practices of traditional and legal-rational authorities as representatives of the Hidden *Imam*. Since the Safavid period, in particular, legal-rational authority was enhanced, resulting in expanding clerical influence in the political sphere, along with close ties to the neighborhood, mosque, tribal, and also state networks. By contrast, the establishment of the Islamic Republic in the late twentieth century heightened the charismatic aspect of clerical authority, with Ayatollah Ruhollah Khomeini representing the office of the *Vilayat-i Faqih* (rule of the jurisconsult). The end result is the early twenty-first-century association of Shī'ī clerics with porous authorial identities and the ability to navigate through multiple networks in various spheres of life, including state power.

In theoretical terms, juristic expertise does not merely depend on textual knowledge of religious sources. Rather, it is grounded on the innovative ways jurists forge new interpretive relations with the changing world, a process that requires constant reexamination. In everyday practice, the key to Shī'ī clerics' success depends on the proficiency of scholars of high learning to transmit knowledge in the wavering space of rationality and revelation to younger seminarians in order to practice reason for the greater community. Such a conception of authority would also be legitimate if a cleric is able to apply legalistic tradition for practical and mundane purposes of *taqlid* (imitation). In this sense, the ability to enhance correct practice is the touchstone of authority.

The reference to practice, I argue, emphasizes the "technicity" of discursive and embodied action as acquired skills necessary to interpret law based on scriptural/legal sources. Such technicity of interpretative-embodied action also pertains to non-textual situations. It is marked by the application of correct conduct to changing settings that require vigorous and innovative reasoning according to *uṣūl al-fiqh* (the body of law gathered from textual sources). Along with consensus (*ijmā'*) and reason (*'aql*) as sources of knowledge, the technicity of Shī'ī jurisprudence lies in the rational and practical ability of a legal scholar (*faqīh*) to *produce* and *apply* his acquired knowledge in principled but flexible ways in response to changing circumstances. Rather than a strict institution of hierarchy, broadly speaking, the legitimacy of the *marja'* operates in the mundane orientation toward practical concerns across varied networks. The *marja'* also maintains legitimacy by demonstrating a prowess to rationally interpret and guide others to act beyond mere juridical or theological concerns—and accordingly attains public recognition for his abilities based on how he is perceived as a scholar and a public leader in the community.

Jurisprudence is an embodied practice. How effectively clerics of different ranks display their knowledge, and hence legitimize their authority, depends on the praxis to maintain disciplined enactments of piety in the world. Embodied knowledge is rooted in the visual and sensory attention to intricate appearances of piety, which often entails the enactment of ethical behaviors that, according to the principles of law, should resemble the conduct of the Prophet and the *Imams*. At the heart of the performative staging of clerical identity is the audio (verbal) and visual (nonverbal) ability to extract law for the purpose of encouraging emulation by others who, as non-*mujtahids* (jurisconsults), do not have the time or the intellectual potential to study and deeply understand the law. The normativity of jurisprudence, therefore, lies in the embodiment and display of authority that could be read as permanent and stable, but are in fact dynamic procedural activities that aim at affecting others to behave in meaningful and legally sanctioned ways.

The production, dissemination, and archivization of textual sources are equally important in the logic and practice of Shīʿī jurisprudence. Historically speaking, canonical texts have sustained a performativity of legal action amid the scriptural staging of clerical authority in the production of visual technological medium of manuscripts. From the middle (945–1500 CE) to the modern (1500 CE to the present) periods, canonical texts such as *al-Kāfī fī ʿIlm al-Dīn* (*The Sufficient, On the Knowledge of Faith*) by Muhammad ibn Yaʿqub al-Kulayni (d. 941) and *al-Nihāyah fī Mujarrad al-Fiqh wa al-Fatāwa* (*The Ultimate in Only Fiqh and Legal Rulings*) by Muhammad ibn al-Ḥasan al-Tūsī (d. 1067) have served as foundational sources on jurisprudence for the *hawza* in the Lebanon-Iraq-Iran-India nexus and beyond. As a distinct form of media, such texts have equally provided models of the continuity of knowledge, allowing the *hawza* to uphold authority while simultaneously undergoing change in the course of history. Robert Gleave has astutely described this paradoxical process as a sort of "trick" to "remain dynamic whilst appearing static," a challenge that has become exponentially more complex in the modern world.[9] Through multiple points of origin and circulation, the production of texts has functioned as the foremost feature of the performative networks, which materially and discursively inform the very performance of being a Shīʿī cleric in a changeable world whose meanings are both temporal and spiritual.

By the eighteenth century, the spread of print technology portended a new agency in the network reproduction of knowledge through colonial and imperial-state networks across the globe. Broadly speaking, the triumph of print publication introduced a revolutionary epoch that spurred the formation of new writing and reading publics, in which Shīʿī centers of learning actively participated in the late nineteenth and early twentieth centuries. As Nile Green observes, along with new modes of travel by train and steamship that allowed the movement of people across far-distant regions, a "global Muslim print sphere" emerged that was tied to the industrialization and consumerism of everyday life.[10] In late Qajar Iran, the publication and dissemination of newspapers and books via lithography developed alongside the growing use of the telegraph, spawning transformative changes in various spheres of life, including religion.

To take one prominent example, Grand Ayatollah Mirza Hasan Shirazi's famous 1891 *fatwā* (Islamic ruling by a recognized *mujtahid*), which sparked a nationwide boycott on the use of tobacco to protest a monopolistic concession to a British company, was not only delivered via telegraph but it was first prompted by ranking clerics in Isfahan and Tehran through telegraphic messages to Najaf.[11] Telegraphic discourse changed the styles and experiences of communication among clerics, as well as the ways they communicated with their followers (such as issuing a *fatwā* through a telegram). Equally important was the popular spread of radio as twentieth-century Iran underwent a sweeping political and social transformation in response to Pahlavi modernization. Beginning in 1939, radio served as an alternative medium for religious programs by a number of clerics who saw the new technology as a way to strengthen Islamic ethics and value in an increasingly modernizing society.[12]

In a similar fashion, the subsequent spread of typewriters, photocopiers, microphones, and especially cassette tapes provided new mediated technicities of jurisprudence, especially for activist clerics who appropriated these new technologies as an alternative way to develop new politicized conceptions of law for the growing educated middle-class population. In what Annabelle Sreberny-Mohammadi and Ali Mohammadi call "the electronic minbar," Ayatollah Khomeini's adroit use of cassette tapes during the 1960s and 1970s to propagate a radical new conception of clerical involvement in politics undeniably helped the establishment of the Islamic Republic in 1979.[13] With the establishment of the Shī'ī Islamist state, the expansion of radio and, even more importantly, television broadcasting introduced an official media sphere, wherein clerical authority was enacted through sermons, religious courses, and Qur'ānic interpretations—despite the occasional protests of quietist clerics based in Najaf. The introduction of the internet in the 1990s, however, represented a dramatic paradigm shift: transforming the Iranian media landscape and facilitating the rapid spread of personalized communications networks.

Iranian Social Media and Instagram Clerics

The internet was introduced to Iran in 1994 through the educational sector.[14] The Qum seminary soon followed suit, with Grand Ayatollah 'Ali Sistani emerging as the first *marja'* to approve the establishment of an Internet Center (Ahl al-Bayt Global Information Center) in 1996.[15] Sistani's personal website, www.sistani.com, offered information ranging from news articles about the Ayatollah to answers to practical questions of a religious nature. In the early 2000s, as the Najaf-based Grand Ayatollah's influence spread throughout Iran, Sistani and his religious representatives received more than a thousand questions a day in their small office—inquiries on a host of issues ranging from personal piety to politics.[16] The establishment of the Computer Research Center of Islamic Science in 2007—which undertook the digitization of Shīʿī texts of various literary, liturgical, and scripturalist genres—affirmed the expanding process of clerical involvement with digital technology. A key aim in the integration of digital media and Shīʿī discourse involved the modernist expression of multiple articulations of religious practices, ranging from prayers to rituals and jurisprudence. Digital technology also presented a new form of (trans)cultural capital for clerics, some of who combined the tasks of religious leaders and computer engineers to create a sense of distinction and affiliation with multiple communities (religious and technoscientific).

By the mid-2000s social media began to replace blogs, which had gained enormous popularity in the earlier phase of internet development. As a new medium of personalized but essentially networked expression, social media platforms increasingly became embedded in the everyday life of many Iranians, especially urban-based populations who had experienced major demographic shifts since the 1990s. With the Reformist push for open cultural policies aimed at the urban middle class, seminarians and mid-ranking clerics also became active participants in the emerging social media landscape. The most important development in this process was marked by the appearance of several *marjaʿ* Facebook profiles, most of which were set up by the seminarians or their lay followers. Mid-ranking jurists embraced a social media presence on Facebook as well. Their online usage was typically limited, however, to posting comments on religious or political matters, or displaying photos of religious rituals. At times, this included the use of fake profiles, as in the case of the cleric I introduced earlier. During the 2009 presidential election, the Green Movement adopted a limited but publicly visible presence on social media as well, focusing in particular on Facebook where certain preelection political campaigns were announced and organized.[17]

After 2009, Iran underwent a major economic transformation marked by the increasing neoliberalization of the economic sector. Social media—especially with the growing popularity of Telegram instant messaging beginning in 2015—gradually became identified as *fazaye majazi* (virtual space): a place where numerous companies advertised or promoted new brands and products in a simulated space of digital markets. In effect, E-commerce paved the path toward new spatial conceptions of social networks. Within these new digital spaces, self-presentation operated in close connection with communities of consumers that enabled leisure and consumption as a means for the reproduction of cultural capital. As a result, a new generation of internet users emerged to redefine the contours of public life.

The growing presence of Shīʿī clerics of various ranks on social media coincided with the economization of the internet. This dynamic was bolstered with the 2013 election of Hasan Rouhani and his subsequent push for liberalization. YouTube and, in particular, Instagram served as popular video-sharing platforms for secular self-representations, as young men and women danced to Pharrell Williams's song "Happy" and posted their own videos on social media platforms. Similar to moral urbanization, which seeks to tackle the spread of convivial spaces of transgression in the urban milieu, clerical participation on social media was partly a moral response to Iran's demographic and technological shifts. But it was also a philosophical reaction: an attempt to leverage online religious activities to reach a younger generation that increasingly relied on new technologies for self-expression. The coupling of faster internet service with the expanding opportunities for personalized involvement with multiple social networks through smart mobiles—which by 2016 had become a ubiquitous, everyday gadget for Iranians of both rural and urban backgrounds—enhanced the prestige and influence of social media for many clerics. In this context, Instagram, free from filter censorship, became the ideal social media site.

From "conservatives" to "reformists," from state actors to quietists, Shī'ī clerics have appeared on Instagram with a range of profiles. For them, the Instagram profile serves as the main staging prop for the visual and cultural (re)presentation of a public self via the medium of filtered photos and video clips. By 2016, Instagram's redesign for better user interface, colorful icons, and video postings (facilitating digital storytelling and live streams) introduced new performance features that changed the way profiles can be accessed and interacted with. The importance of these profile features cannot be underestimated. Instagram profiles allow jurists to narrate who they are through the display of various appearances. It is clear that these digital representations are strategically chosen for maximum visibility, with clerics posting photos of themselves in a variety of public and private settings in order to reach diverse audiences: from the religious devotee to Instagram *flânerie*. These Instagram profiles are also networked, in the sense that they are associated with the number of posts, followers, and the circulation of shared posts. The greater the number of followers, the higher the social capital; the more personalized and informative the profile, the better its performance of self-expressivity.

Shaykh Mostafa Shakori exemplifies a mid-ranking cleric—young and charismatic—whose Instagram profile as a "public figure" revolves around numerous posted photos and videos of his *rowzih khwani* (elegiac music) and *khuṭbahs* (sermons) (Figure 14.1). As public rituals, *rowzih khwani* performances—poetic narratives of the martyrs of Karbala and the Imams—reinforce a distinct form of traditional and charismatic authority that legitimizes the public standing of a cleric in a given local community. In a similar fashion, *khuṭbahs*, colloquial orations on various subjects of public concern that are often observed at the mosque congregations, serve as one of the most important traditional practices of communal authority, modeled after the Prophet and the *Imams*.

A closer look at Shakori's account shows that most of the *rowzih khwani* and *khuṭbah* sessions take place at the *Ḥussayniya*: congregational halls

FIGURE 14.1 *Shakori's* khuṭbah *in the weekly* Ḥussayniya *congregation, March 7, 2021 (https://www.instagram.com/mostafashakoriii/).*

where Shīʿī Muslims have traditionally gathered for mourning rituals in devotion to the Prophet and the *Imams*.[18] The spatial register of his Instagram account is critical since it specifies a distinct physical locality of communal importance to the visual posts. From photographic depictions of prayers to fasting rituals, from mourning ceremonies for the martyred soldiers in Iran–Iraq War to celebrations of the *Imams* at the *Ḥussayniya Ya Zahra* (a congregation hall for devotional mourning), Shakori's account is visually solemn. The visuals of elegies and sermons fuse the intensely fervent with the fraternal convivial, heightening an ambience of devotional zeal. Melodic music can often be heard in the background of lamentation elegies as well, instilling a sense of melancholy in ritualized visual gestures prescribed to male performers, such as *sinih zani* (chest beating). Distinct from most of Shakori's posts are his sporadic critiques of the celebrity culture that has become the most popular theme in the Iranian Instagram sphere. Shakori's moral stance is best articulated on a posted *khuṭbah*, titled "*shaytani majazi*" (diabolical virtuality). If in the past, he argues, the devil enticed humans to do evil to others in austere conditions, the same devil now deceives humanity through modern digital technologies such as Instagram, but in far easier and instantaneous ways. The irony, of course, is the fact that Shakori uses Instagram to warn his virtual audience against Instagram's potential for evil.

Shakori's Instagram profile also reveals a hub of network connections. Links on the account to Telegram indicate a social media convergence aimed across social media audiences, though mostly composed of Iranian men of religious leaning. Since its launch in 2018, commentary, messaging, and tagging practices show the network effects among a growing followership. Clips with over 6,000 views reveal an interactive spectator community that is led by key male members of the Ḥussayniya. Without a doubt, there is real social capital here. For follower-members, friends, and other acquaintances or visitors, the Ḥussayniya-led Instagram account extends a resilient network of associations based on mutual interest, shared trust, and value-laden emotions. Significantly, Shakori's account serves as one single node among many different networks that link younger male (and also some female) Instagramers who participate in the account through shares, likes, commentaries, and messages.

It is in the repertoire of images mostly centered around Shakori's authorial aura, however, that a mythical conception of spiritual life is re-presented and then networked through the sharing of accounts. If we are to accept the image, following Roland Barthes, as signification of persuasive messages, then Shakori's Instagram is a movable feast of explicit and implicit significations, a readable if at times opaque sequence of floating messages with affective implications.[19] In intricate forms, discourse and visibility are intertwined as Shakori performs clerical authority in his Ḥussayniya in polysemous ways. The key to these multiple-meaning performances is the technicity to project piety and devotion in a praxis of responses to the changing world, where celebrities, new technologies, and politics are all legitimate sites for moral reflection.

While Shakor's Instagram account typifies a ritual-centric profile, the account of another mid-ranking jurist, Mohammad Sedarat, is more personalized, spotlighting a collage of images and videos about his daily life as a "*talabi inghelabi ijtimai*" (seminarian social revolutionary). Sedarat's Instagram feed is more about visible presence in matters of public concern and, at times, domestic nature. This partly reflects the cleric's institutional association with the Islamist state. However, one can also identify here a jurisprudential precedence based on traditional authority grounded on a commitment to social welfare via a wide range of service-oriented activities. Providing help to people who are in need or to those who remain invisible to the broader public is a Prophetic tradition that was upheld by the *Imams* and now adopted by clerics who represent them on earth. In this sense, Instagram serves as the new minbar to propagate a modality of piety.

Sedarat's Instagram profile also insinuates the performance of the authority of guardianship, which traditionally has been associated with clerics in the era of *ghayba*, the period of Occultation when the Twelfth *Imam* remains in hiding. On his account, Sedarat plays the role of a rather minor guardian—relative to his clerical status—for orphans, the needy, and the destitute. In doing so, he combines the tradition of helping the socially marginalized and the dispossessed with the technicity of performing the truth of piety in conduct in accordance with Islamic jurisprudence. The bank account run by a "*jihād* group" named after Majid Gharabankhani, a volunteer soldier who died a martyr's death against ISIS in Syria in January 2016, appears on top of Sedarat's profile page. The account is devoted to the cause of *mahroman* (the deprived) and solicits support in the form of financial contributions. Thus, the moral economy of Sedarat's Instagram activity is the mediation of catastrophic events and the technicity to care for those who have suffered as a result.

Here again, social capital also plays an important role. In Sedarat's Instagram page, however, social capital is gained through the traditional authority of charity and welfare for the common good. It is not that ritual is secondary to charity; instead, charity entails its own distinct ritual performativity that is made visible on social media. To this end, victims of earthquakes in villages are a common feature of Sedarat's public activities (Figure 14.2). Charity has multiple registers. Sedarat's scope of engagement includes a range of public relations activities with impoverished and marginalized people. This includes publicizing the condition of flood victims and sharing the views of street sweepers (*pakban*), known for their economic destitution. Sedarat's travels also serve as a way of networking across Iran, a process that ultimately aims at building social capital as a source of trust and cooperation across local communities, including Sunni-populated regions where natural calamity has caused considerable public damage. In Sedarat's Instagram account, networking operates across vast localities and populations—and is therefore not limited to a religious space. In other words, the context into which the cleric is socialized encompasses a matrix of followers both known and unknown: a wide network that is constituted by (in)visible connections built around his public-facing clerical activities.

Sedarat's Instagram is also distinguished by its display of numerous family photos. In these images, his children appear at public events such as pilgrimage rites and in some instances within the private sphere of the home, as in the case of a modest birthday celebration (Figure 14.3). As with any family photographic images, Instagram depictions of children's lives prompt not only personal memory but also the public recognition of family as a vital social institution. When a cleric engages with networked connectivity, he therefore performs features of his "self": images of his home, family, and the quotidian moments of everyday life make his privacy a matter of public knowledge for moral growth. Such images that are displayed on Instagram

FIGURE **14.2** *Sedarat references the bank account to help earthquake victims (https://www.instagram.com/mohammadsedarat/).*

FIGURE **14.3** *Sedarat celebrates his son's fourth birthday (https://www.instagram .com/mohammadsedarat/).*

serve as calculated aspects of a personal life based on Islamic principles; this even includes a birthday, an annual rite of passage that is shared by all audiences.

In an important sense, it is the public re-presentation of the everyday private spaces that makes Sedarat's account a matter of jurisprudence of personalized significance. In doing so, it pronounces a distinct form of traditional authority that consciously emulates the private lives of the Prophet and the *Imams*. After all, the *aḥādīth* (recorded sayings and deeds) are replete with examples of the Prophets and the *Imams* spending time with their families, engaging in leisure, and pursuing educational and ethical activities with children, wives, and extended relatives. In this sense, the visualization of domesticity can be interpreted as a strategic display of family life that matches the ideals of Islamic ethics of parenthood and marriage.

Both of these Instagram profiles are representative of a diverse range of frameworks for clerical presence on social media: Shakori represents the sermon-elegy performative and Sedarat the charity performative. Both accounts include multiple images or videos in a single post or stories feature, but each emphasizes an aspect of traditional authority that is personalized around the figure of a unique cleric. This personalized stylization is communicated through innovative and strategic photographic and videographic practices. In a reflection of what Robert Rozehnal labels "cyber Islam," clerical engagement with social media underscores the effective leveraging of various internet practices couched in different understandings of Islamic identity and piety.[20] These visual performances illustrate a complex repertoire of (self) representations that signal the confluence of repeatable and transferable frameworks, where the boundaries of "private" and "public" spheres blur into emerging social networks.

Conclusion

This chapter has explored the multivalent and nuanced ways that Shīʿī clerics engage with social media, in particular Instagram, to reconstruct authority in complex visible technological spaces. Beginning the discussion with a jurist feigning as a teenage girl, I have underscored a prevalent adaptability in the presentation of religious authority in ways that ultimately help morally enrich the Shīʿī community in the era of Occultation. As the cases of these three clerics illustrate, the display of authority via digital media includes playful ways of self-representation that overlap with long-standing traditions of anecdotes (*muzah*), humorous and joyful tales, moral and poetical stories. Such changing self-representations serve to enhance the image of a Shīʿī cleric as someone who is pragmatically aware and publicly immersed in the affairs of the world for the benefit of Islam at large. This flexibility, I argue, has enabled Shīʿī jurists to reinvent authority while simultaneously presenting continuity.

The Shīʿī clerical presence on Instagram offers one example of this authorial flexibility in response to what Albert Borgmann has described as the technological character of contemporary life.[21] However, I argue that such flexibility is informed by a distinct historical formation of authority shaped by centuries of changing discursive traditions. Here an important aspect to bear in mind is the way clerical authority engages with technicity of jurisprudence to adapt to evolving circumstances. Seen this way, it is no wonder that some Shīʿī clerics have also been engineers, as both professional disciplines revolve around the technicity to build a range of specialized fields of applied knowledge to everyday situations. To that end, the strategic deployment of technology plays a key role.

Moreover, the agentive aspect of the jurists playing with identity on Instagram is not merely an individual expression. Underlying self-conscious rearrangement within an explicit authorial tradition is a complex web of stories that define social ties in networks or, to use Harrison C. White's description, "phenomenological realities" that shape the limits and boundaries of emerging relations in contention or cooperation.[22] How a person self-represents in measured (though spirited) ways is staged in significatory practices in which public performances—such as creating a Facebook or an Instagram profile—are to be understood in the process of reiterated citationality. In this sense, clerical self-representations in the form of either a teenage profile or an Instagram influencer can be understood as a strategic social fiction: a phenomenological move that enables a Shīʿī cleric to simultaneously *perform* (the theatrical self-presentation for an audience listening to a lecture) and conduct a performative action for a specific social *effect* (to speak with authority via the conventional procedure of the lecture).[23]

In the case of the cleric pretending to be a teenager girl, since the specific effect is less conventional than expected within the everyday dynamics of the Research Center, I would—echoing Austin's terminology—characterize his unceremonious use of humor in an unconventional way as an "unhappy performative." For the two jurists on Instagram, by contrast, the authorial playfulness on social media are examples of rather "happy performatives" with potential for "misapplication." In their Instagram profiles both Mostafa Shakori and Mohammad Sedarat seek to exert certain conducts with consequences—though with uncertain outcomes because of social media's participatory and therefore multidirectional orientation. In the end, all three cases illustrate the instability of identity in its official sense and the mundane, and at times ludic, attempt to express subjectivity. Echoing Austin, these three social media profiles—which in various ways evoke visuals of self-representation even without the addition of a photograph (in the case of the cleric's Facebook page)—are a reminder that the self is always constituted in relation to how it is perceived by audiences for "a certain conventional effect."[24]

"Space," de Certeau reminds us, "is a practiced place."[25] And since practice is about spatiality, religious authorial involvement on social media is fundamentally tied to complex spaces of visibilities—sometimes marked in a signified and discernible fashion, and at other times manifested in camouflaged, masqueraded, and (de)masked ways. In this sense, the visual and cultural (re)presentations in clerical Instagram practices are less about mere photographic or audiovisual expression of religious authority and more about the formation of new experiences. As Nathan Jurgenson has shown in his study of visual culture on social media, digital media technologies transform experience by facilitating "a broader development in self-expression, memory, and sociability."[26] By adapting to this new digital landscape, Shīʿī clerical authority is reclaiming space in virtual domains in ways that render everyday life visible and available for a participatory culture of network audiences—dissolving, at times, the fictive boundaries between public and private, mundane and sacred, tradition and modernity.

This chapter has approached authority and technology not as binaries but as an inseparable set of practices. In all its various historical and social forms, technology does not serve as a mere instrument or tool but instead constitutes an "irreducible prostheticity," an ontological extension of being human in the world.[27] In this sense, Shīʿī clerical authority on Instagram represents innovative technological practices of constituting authority in a world of changing circumstances. The technological becomes an extension of religious authority, a prosthesis of spiritual life amid the new technological space of digital media.

CHAPTER 15

Muslims between Transparency and Opacity

Nabil Echchaibi

I consider myself a Trojan poet, that poet whose text has been lost to us and literary history. What I wish to express, although not with any finality, but with a certain ambiguity, is that I belong to Troy, not because I am defeated, but because I am obsessed by the desire to write the lost text.

MAHMOUD DARWISH[1]

Introduction

In the 2014 documentary *UnMosqued,* New York–based director Ahmed Eid talks to millennial Muslims who share strong grievances against the mosque culture in the United States. Some lament cultural disharmony across generations, others oppose gender segregation, ethnocentrism, and social disconnection. The film raises critical questions about a growing social and religious alienation in the American mosque experience, but it also reveals a discounted but ordinary fact that Muslims are not all the same and require different things from their faith communities.[2] *UnMosqued* features alternative faith-based communities that target disconnected young Muslims with cultural and social activities similar to those in Evangelical churches and Jewish cultural centers.

I start with this film not because of its core argument about reclaiming the mosque as a culturally meaningful experience, but rather because it hints at a social dimension of Muslim life that is not necessarily tethered to faith and the mosque as exclusive anchors of reference for Muslims. I look at unmosquing differently to reflect on a vital need for an(other) Muslim expression, where the terms of speaking and being in the world are not conditioned by an inventory that interpellates Muslims as mere agents of their faith and suspect subjects legible only through the geopolitical lens of imperial politics. For a long time, Muslims have been invoked and addressed mainly from this compulsion to conform to a regime of snapshot visibility which has reduced them to a narrow order of conciliatory transparency. The transparent Muslim is a "good" or "bad" faith subject invented by a perpetual state of emergency and fear stabilized in the wake of the events of 9/11 and the interminable War on Terror.

The appearance of Muslims in a hypermediated economy of visibility is meant primarily to secure a shallow meaning, which translates as immediacy of security and management of threat. The hypervisible Muslim under the logic and calculations of this imperial gaze is compelled to unveil, expose, and resolve the incompatibilities of their faith in order to alleviate an obsessive anxiety of not "knowing" Islam. The visibility of Muslims, I argue, leads to a process of absenting, an epistemic erasure that denies them their right to abstraction and their singular density. An important argument in this chapter is how to speak *as Muslims* and *about Muslims* away from the spectacle of the bomb, the paranoia of terror, and the politics of premature and permanent suspicion imposed by the mandates of consented visibility. How Muslims suddenly appear—and around what events they are made to appear—determine and normalize a cultural script that silences the autonomy of their expression and instrumentalizes their presence based on a blackmail of (in)visibility fraught with control and manipulation.

An argument about unmosquing is designed not to undervalue the importance of faith or the mosque for Muslims but rather to underscore the limitations in this reductive form of address that minces the biographies of billions of people with complex cultures, long-standing civilizations, and creative energies into a uniform subject of religious sameness and irreconcilable otherness. Drawing on Édouard Glissant's concept of the right to opacity, I argue in favor of an ethics of Muslim narration that defies the totalizing frames of transparency and their insistence on strategic knowability and appropriation. The opaque Muslim is not a subject who willfully deceives by their mystery, but one who clamors for their right to retain the benefit of their mutable subjectivity and its core difference. It is the right to a singularity that resists being essentialized by the desire to be wholly figured out and brought in line for the sake of a universalizing ideology.

The Good Muslim Is a Transparent Muslim

My distinction of the transparent/opaque Muslim is an extension of Mahmood Mamdani's critique of the "Good Muslim, Bad Muslim" narrative and how a "culture talk" about Islam has transformed religious experience into a political question. Mamdani argues that this politicization, particularly of Muslim culture following 9/11, continues to generate a stark dichotomy between a culture that

> stands for creativity, for what being human is all about, in one part of the world, that called modern, but that in the other part, labeled "premodern," culture stands for habit, for some kind of instinctive activity whose rules are inscribed in early founding texts, usually religious, and mummified in early artifacts. . . . After that, it seems they—we Muslims—just conform to culture. Our culture seems to have no history, no politics, and no debates. It seems to have petrified into a lifeless custom.[3]

Under this logic, there is only one way to salvation and Muslims could only be good if they jettisoned their "premodern" ways and subscribed to a rather Manichean reading of their world in terms of good Muslims versus evil Muslims, not good versus evil persons, "nor . . . criminals and civic citizens."[4]

While Mamdani's excellent analysis attempts to historicize political Islam away from this narrow culture talk, my concern is about how a post-9/11 culture of racialized fear and crude geopolitical logistics has produced an even less conspicuous subject: the transparent Muslim, an iteration of Mamdani's good Muslim, a serviceable Muslim whose only appearance is restricted to denouncing violence without equivocation. Their visibility is enlisted as a tool to discipline Muslims publicly and contain their impending insubordination without having to deal with their nagging criticism. Muslims are then impelled to perform this command of transparency on a public stage to prove their basic humanity against an apolitical and ahistorical spectacle of terror invariably understood as a cosmic fight between good and evil. An injunction to break rank in order to affirm loyalty and restore faith in the moral exactitude of dominant ideology. Under this regime of transparency, there is in fact no escape from this economy of stereotypical reproduction whereby Muslim visibility is relentlessly tied to the hypervisibility of terrorism and its inescapable performance. The questions I grapple with, following this interpretation of transparency, are vexing but necessary: What kind of Muslim performativity is permissible in a culture grounded in these conditions of visibility? How can we truly know Muslims without the whip of transparency hanging over their head? And what is repressed in Muslims when their entire existence is perceived only through the prism of faith and geopolitics?

Faced with this kind of alienating encounters, Muslims themselves readily respond to the call of transparency by denouncing violence committed in the name of their religion and offering counter-narratives of peace and tolerance. American Muslim organizations such as the Council of American Islamic Relations (CAIR) and Muslim Public Relations Council (MPAC), among many others, have become quite adept at dispatching their advocates for this very purpose. A few Muslim pundits, who have become frequent guests on television and in the opinion columns of major publications, fulfill the same task with tact and erudition. But the problem is not whether Muslims should or should not condemn the use of violence against civilians but rather the tacit script lurking beneath these "invitations" to denounce which affirms the "stranger danger" status of the Muslim and forces them to perform again and again their assimilation. This kind of sanitized appearance of the Muslim becomes not only necessary to reduce the threat of terror but also vital, as Sara Ahmed writes, "as a reminder of the differences we must celebrate."[5] In other words, the ritual of Muslim transparency serves to name the outsider and the boundaries that constitute the nation and the terms of belonging to it. The stranger is placed on a loop to announce their reintegration into the fold of the nation despite never leaving it behind—and the nation needs the strangeness of the stranger to preserve its sameness and proclaim its difference. Muslims are quintessential strangers because they live inside that loop and such is, I argue, the fate of the transparent Muslim, stuck in a frustrating refrain of having to declare that they have nothing to hide.

Ahmed's analysis of the discursive and affective construction of the stranger and strangeness as constitutive elements of the nation is instructive for the purposes of my argument about transparency. Muslims are bound to always arrive as spectacular strangers whether they just disembarked as refugees and immigrants or when they appear on television news, reality shows, or Hollywood films. Consider, for example, the airport experience of an average Muslim today and how that encounter with metal detectors and Western customs control is fraught with dehumanizing tension. The metal detector has become the primary site of marginalization because its logic, as it searches for forbidden dangerous objects, is to reconstitute you into nothingness. Some will argue that everyone goes through this and therefore this experience cannot be singularly claimed by some bodies, but not everyone walks through that machine with the weight of suspicion and scorn as they raise their hands in the air as if to concede to an accusation. At the airport, it is hard to forget the gross caricature that the Muslim is a phobic object, a suspect, so you engage in a series of dehumanizing acts of erasure, suppression, and effacing of who you are. You become conscious of everything you do, who is listening to you, who is calling you on the phone, and which language to use at a close distance of the gate, in the security line, in a crowd situation, whether you have anything on you that will give away where you are from and who you pray to. As a Muslim, you feel like you must be neutralized as a subject: your identity, beliefs, and body all have to be contained and managed carefully by you and the surveilling system surrounding you so you can have an uneventful airport experience. At the airport, only one's Muslimness is invoked. Nothing else is significant anymore. Your presence is partial, excised because visibility in this space leads to an epistemic closure: once you are made visible as a "safe" Muslim, there is nothing else to know or be learned about you.

While the airport, as Lisa Parks writes, has become the place with "a charged and volatile domain punctuated by shifting regimes of biopower,"[6] for Muslims and other "suspect" populations, it is decidedly the Fanonian zone of nonbeing where these bodies are marked as perpetual strangers and reminded of the contingent nature of their mobility. Asad Malik, a British filmmaker of Pakistani origin, created *Terminal 3*, an augmented reality documentary to capture the volatility of airport screening for Muslim travelers.[7] Malik's AR experience prompts viewers to take on the role of a border officer to determine whether "Muslim-looking" travelers at the Abu Dhabi International Airport can be authorized to travel to the United States or be detained for further screening. Based on real-life situations, the film features six digitized subjects who appear in a hologram answering scripted questions about their reasons for travel. The subjects are complex and range from devout to secular Muslims, American citizens traveling back home from Pakistan, or tourists who sit nervously in a holding screening room to answer a barrage of prying questions about their faith and personal life. Malik insists that only AR can approximate the ostracizing feeling of the airport checkpoint by inviting viewers to empathize with the plight of the Muslim traveler who is subjected to interrogation as a test of transparency. "The whole idea with this piece for me has not been like, oh look, good Muslim, or not a good Muslim," Malik says. "The whole idea is more about showing a complex identity, it's about showing contradictions in people themselves."[8]

This basic fact about who Muslims are is further obscured in what Rachel Hall calls "a cultural performance of risk management" in airport security.[9] In her book *The Transparent Traveler*, Hall describes how a post-9/11 risk management culture, ingrained in fear and paranoid demands of security, has produced a climate where "the threat of terrorism remains hidden, enfolded, or tucked away."[10] The invisibility, and permanence, of the threat is what animates the obsession of the state, its apparatuses of surveillance and control, the media, as well as citizens to constantly ascertain the absence of terrorism. "Consequently," Hall writes, "passengers and their belongings appear to the eyes of security experts, petty officials, surveillance technologies, and alert citizens as an endless and overlapping series of mobile interiors-in-crisis."[11] It is this impending criminalization of the interior, the opacity of the traveler and the Muslim, that is of relevance to the argument of transparency. The all-is-suspect approach of the airport is the experience of Muslims in and outside of the airport because media representation of terrorism and the state reaction to the threat to security have turned this population into a mystery box of secrets in need of both tacit and discreet revelation. These opacity effects, as Hall calls them, "picture a desire to rid the warring world of pockets, caves, spider holes, and veils. They . . . communicate and invite a shared compulsion to ferret out all secrets . . . and nourish a political culture of compulsory transparency in the citizenry at large."[12]

That same energy of collective fear that prompts the TSA officer to search bags and pat down bodies to weed out bad and suspicious travelers is what Muslims often experience when their "interiors"—their bags, their bodies, their places of worship, their homes, their veils, and their beings— are permanently called into question. This paranoid quest for transparency to establish security and restore innocence may be suspended for many after the suspicion of the threat is cleared, but for others like Muslims, the threat simply mutates from one space to another, from one agent to another, and from one technique of surveillance to another.

Muslim Transparency: We Have Nothing to Hide

In his brilliant art project *Tracking Transience*, Hasan Elahi created a self-tracking device that permanently records details of his whereabouts and activities and posts them to a website.[13] Elahi, an artist whose work explores questions of surveillance, migration, and citizenship, wanted to expose the arbitrariness of surveilling Muslim civilians after a mistaken tip to the FBI landed him on the no-fly list in 2002. Apparently, the informant gave a physical description of an "Arab man" moving explosives in Florida that was similar to Elahi's. It took months of intense interrogation and traveling disruption for him to clear his name and resume his life as normal. In an Orwellian twist, Elahi began to track himself while in his apartment in New York, traveling in the United States, and around the world for his art exhibits—taking thousands of pictures of hotel rooms, food in restaurants, public bathrooms, his meeting schedule, and posting the exact time of these activities and other data. Elahi's project began as a collaborative attempt to voluntarily supply information to the FBI to ward off unnecessary suspicion. His website, *Tracking Transience*, has become a provocative artveillance project that seeks to neutralize the flow of secret data about Muslims and suspect citizens by making them available to a larger public. Elahi inundated the FBI with detailed information about his whereabouts without revealing anything of substance about his personality or his beliefs, a deliberate gesture to demonstrate how surveillance serves to annihilate the personhood of those surveilled by making them a node of data in an endless archive of security.

Transparency, understood along this dyad of concealment versus revelation, of hiding versus unmasking, and of veiling versus unveiling, produces the same effect of guarantee of information but only for the sake of homogeneity and containment within an ideology that treats human interiority as an undesirable and suspicious opacity. The Park 51 controversy in New York in 2010 was a good case in point. Critics of the proposal to build a Muslim cultural center near Ground Zero contested its insensitivity to the significance of the hallowed grounds of the site where the Twin Towers of the World Trade Center once stood. Some called it a "clubhouse for terrorists"; others thought the project would be a symbol of "triumphalist stealth *jihad*."[14] But besides the bombastic nature of these protests, one common feature was an acute concern about the secrecy of Muslim spaces of worship and what really goes on inside a mosque, despite the fact that the Park 51 proposal was not about a mosque but more of a community center like YMCA or JCC (Jewish cultural center). This assumption of a dangerous secrecy was equated with the deceit and betrayal of the 9/11 terrorists who feigned their way into attacking America. In order to avoid further escalation of this controversy, the architects and proponents of the Park 51 cultural center had to withdraw their proposal and agree to move their project to a different location.

There have been many other controversies involving mosque or Muslim cultural center construction in other American and European cities, and very often the conflict is framed around a rhetoric of cultural loyalty and religious identity.[15] Over the years, these incidents have prompted Muslim communities to open up their mosques to the public in an attempt to respond to this demand of transparency and alleviate concerns of secrecy or duplicity. Many mosques across the United States and in many other Western countries regularly hold "open houses" to show how these places of worship and social connection are embedded in local neighborhoods and harbor no ill will toward their communities. But the subtext of these initiatives is in fact to allow non-Muslims to penetrate the mysterious cloud cast over these spaces to ascertain for themselves the absence of harm and remove the obstacle to transparency. The point here is not to question the sincerity of these "unveiling rituals" or doubt the will of non-Muslim visitors to learn more about Islam, but it is impossible to read these events independently of larger tropes of transparency already ingrained and carefully deployed in the politics and aesthetics of the War on Terror. In fact, the frames of geopolitics, national security, and everyday life blur in complex fashion and work in tandem to harden a narrative of infinite mistrust and anxiety that can be satisfied only through the comforting certainty of transparency.

It is worth noting at this point that my argument is not to categorically reject any measure of transparency as a genuine desire of comprehension and elimination of uncertainty. Instead, I argue against transparency serving as a ploy for obfuscation, that is, when the demand for more information acts only to affirm a worldview that seeks coherence and security through a process of a homogenizing simplification and a radical disintegration of the undesired secret. An excess of transparency in dealing with complex relations of difference, I argue, is no guarantee of ethical discernment and honest care. In a society of publicity and self-exposure, the ideal of transparency, according to Samuel Weber, is understood as a facilitator of communication, whereas the secret is almost always castigated as an obstacle to communication. This duality is misleading because it assumes the secret can only be an intentional occlusion carefully designed to mislead and impede comprehension.

Weber opposes the facile presumption behind the equation of the secret as terror and transparency as counter-terror. A rethinking of this relationship between transparency and secrecy is indeed necessary in a modern society that fetishizes flow and circulation more than it values the content of information. Even so, in the context of Muslims and Islam, learning how to live with the secret appears as no option at all. In fact, this drive to render things perceptible is also internalized by Muslims themselves who, in the wake of their relentless scrutiny, respond to appease this desire for "perfect" revelation. Think of the "Hug a Muslim" phenomenon: a street performance in which a blindfolded Muslim offers free hugs to passersby to soften the anxiety of non-Muslims, particularly following terrorist attacks in Western cities. This is the ultimate display of transparency whereby a Muslim offers their body in order to make things secure again. After the 2017 attack in Manchester during an Ariana Grande concert, Baktash Noori, a video blogger, began to conduct what he called "an experiment of trust." Standing in a busy street of Manchester with a blindfold and his arms stretched, Noori invited hugs by holding a sign that read: "I'm a Muslim and I trust you. Do you trust me enough for a hug?"[16] It is certainly heartening to see dozens of people embracing Noori and showing their solidarity in the wake of anti-Muslim incidents across Europe, but the premise of the hug gesture rests on a dangerous presumption that the Muslim body must be literally touched to reveal its potential peacefulness and publicly tamed to discover its impassivity. This performance of public innocence is of course in contrast with the other sinister deployment of the Muslim body in suicide bombing, a scene made spectacularly familiar since 9/11. While the suicide bomber disintegrates his body to inflict as much damage to other bodies, the promise of the hug supposedly reverses the symbolism of the Muslim body to communicate peace and human warmth. The act, however, not only imposes a new condition to test the welcome docility of the Muslim body through the visceral touch but it also limits "knowing" that body only in terms of its possibility of peace and its occasional propensity for terror. It is as if the legible safety of that non-terrorist embrace were the only thing a Muslim could ever offer or should be inclined to offer. Ultimately, the hug accomplishes very little by way of comprehension of the Muslim since it perpetuates a dominant rhetoric that traps Muslims in a discursive archive of self-inflicted violence and their reaction to it.

This rhetoric of concealment is also prevalent in the epistemology of the War on Terror, which has normalized the permanence of the undefined threat and the "unconsummated surplus of danger," as Brian Massumi describes it.[17] That lurking of the threat in the future authorizes an eternal politics of preemption which prolongs fear of Islam and Muslims as an affective experience that can only be attenuated through the guarantee of transparency. Immediately after 9/11, an old Orientalist trope of a mysterious Islam was compounded by a fierce rhetoric of Muslims hiding in caves, concealing weapons of mass destruction, hiding bombs in their backpacks, and forcing their women behind veils and *burqas*. It did not matter whether these threats actually materialized or if these demeaning cultural assumptions about Muslims were true. The affective tangibility of fear had already blended with the mandates of national security and the realness of the threat dwells forever in the future. Preemption is now both a war logic and an affective aesthetic that "suffuses the atmosphere" and regulates the modulation of fear.[18]

The impending but unrealized threat necessitates then a mobilization of feeling permanently afraid that is tied to a performative politics of outing the Muslim. What do they hide? Are they with us or against us? Are they moderate Muslims or fanatic extremists? Is their religion compatible with modern democratic society? Would they tell us when the next strike is coming? Are they honest when they denounce violence? Why do they hate us? These are the nagging questions that fuel the affective discharge of uncertainty around the unspecified threat of Islam and authorize oppressive tactics to manage fear without ever seeking the definitive answer. Abu Ghraib, the extraterritorial jurisdiction of Guantanamo, the extraordinary rendition and outsourcing of torture, the surveillance programs of Muslims, drone killings, Trump's and Muslim travel ban, among others, are all examples of what this ontology of the hidden has legitimated over the years with a clear and simple message to Muslims everywhere: show yourselves and always reveal what is inside so we know where and with whom you stand.

Such is the operative logic of Massumi's "ontopower," an iteration of power that is born of a new ecology of fear and perception and that mixes the hard power of the War on Terror with the soft power of surveillance.[19] In fact, the logic of ontopower quickly metastasizes into the media and popular culture as they, for the most part, reinforce and normalize the frame of the need to pierce through the "real" interiority of Muslims to witness the enigma that is their faith and adjudicate their innocence. In the wake of 9/11, news accounts readily adopted the rhetorical lens of "lifting the veil" on Islam and Muslim countries.[20] Reality television shows such as *All-American Muslim*, sitcoms such as *Alien in America*, and television hit shows such as *Homeland* and *24* are all premised on a plotline of peeping into the "ordinary" life of Muslims to decipher their mystery and verify their loyalty.[21] This does not mean that Muslims have not created more culturally nuanced narratives of themselves, but that mainstream portrayals are still freighted with this burden of the transparent Muslim who services the needs of a non-Muslim audience. Shows such as *Ramy*, a Hulu series about a young American Muslim who lives his Muslimness with all its contradictions and complexities, the Apple TV series *Little America*, which features a gay Muslim refugee in its finale, or *Hala* about an American Muslim teenager struggling to balance her faith with social life are all recent efforts commendable for resisting the PR transparency function of television. Despite these welcome strides, it remains difficult to escape the unrelenting metascript of Islam, violence, and incompatible tradition which still calibrates and conditions how we know Muslims today.

But perhaps nothing captures more emphatically this doctrine of transparency than the unveiling spectacle Oprah hosted in Madison Square Garden with the cosmetic company L'Oréal in the lead-up to the US invasion of Afghanistan when she invited Zoya, an Afghan woman and member of the activist group RAWA (the Revolutionary Association of the Women of Afghanistan), on stage and removed her *burqa* in the presence of hundreds of cheering women. Later in her book *My Forbidden Face*, Zoya narrated the event in these terms:

When the time came for me to go on stage, after Oprah Winfrey had read [Eve Ensler's poem] "Under the *Burqa*," all the lights went off save for one that was aimed directly at me. I had been asked to wear my *burqa*, and the light streamed in through the mesh in front of my face and brought tears to my eyes. A group of singers was singing an American chant, a melody full of grief, and I was to walk as slowly as possible . . . I had to climb some steps, but because of the *burqa* and the tears in my eyes, which wet the fabric and made it cling to my skin, I had to be helped up the stairs. Slowly, very slowly, Oprah lifted the *burqa* off me and let it fall to the stage.[22]

Many scholars have written about the cultural and political significance of this facile amalgamation of unveiling with the rhetoric of liberation of the Muslim woman, but I use this iconic incident to underscore how the imperative of transparency has bluntly infiltrated our habitual perception of Islam and triggered in the general public an affective necessity of denuding Muslims to "figure them out." My point is not to deny Zoya her right to remove the *burqa* but to spotlight how her agency in unveiling was eroded by a performance and an audience that refused to see her in any other way but through the hypervisibility of her veil. In other words, the *burqa* acted as an insurmountable hindrance to the transparency of Zoya's face and only its removal could usher her in as a modern and free woman. Anything else about Afghan women is immaterial despite their valiant struggles against the Taliban and their articulate grievances for a free and democratic Afghanistan. As Jennifer Fluri argues, this is not Zoya's tale but that of Western women "who played the role of savior" and imposed their paternalistic vision of freedom which conveniently aligned with the geopolitical rationale for invading Afghanistan.[23] Zoya's tale in this spectacle is in fact less about her liberation and more about securing comfort in the familiar, to bring women like Zoya, as Gillian Whitlock says, "into 'our' civilization."[24] This performance of transparency, I argue, reduces Muslim subjectivity to a paradoxical state of absent presence, whereby appearance leads only to a superficial and truncated knowledge of the Muslim. This excision forces Muslims to perform exhausting autobiographical, intellectual, and emotional contortions only to belabor a banal fact: that their existence is not reducible to the "problem" of Islam in a Western imaginary.

"One enters a room and history follows": How Does It Feel to Be "the Muslim Problem"?

I begin this section borrowing a piercing statement from poet and essayist Dionne Brand, who reminds us how history haunts the lived experience of Black people in the diaspora: "One enters a room and history follows; one enters a room and history precedes. History is already seated in the chair in the empty room when one arrives."[25] Muslims inhabit an iteration of this historical haunting every time they appear or their appearance is foisted upon them through the fictive archive that conditions their presence. What does it mean to appear as a fragment, as an ellipsis because your story is obstinately preceded and followed by the antipathy of this archive? How does it feel to be made into the "Muslim problem," I ask, since that is the perceptual and lived reality of Muslims?

Moustafa Bayoumi asked this question about young Arab and Muslim Americans in the aftermath of 9/11 whom he described as the new illustration of the DuBoisian "problem" of the American imaginary, an alienating ascription of pathological difference to a minority that codes its existence in society as malignant and dangerous.[26] The color line that W. E. B. DuBois argued regulated the racial antagonism of American society has developed another layer that designates Muslims as the new sociological problem. This assignment of the label "problem" is not something Muslims can simply ignore or turn down. It is rather the culmination of all the excesses of description and the silences of the archive that haunt Muslims and persist in hailing them as menacing subjects and provisional citizens. Once the label of the "Muslim Problem" sticks, Muslim presence can mean only one thing: a menacing appearance. My argument is not that Muslims are incapable of constituting themselves despite the oppression of this archive, but that the demands of the archive exert tremendous power and strain a great deal of energy. These demands are a direct consequence of this commanding power—and my attempt in developing this argument is to analyze the complexity of this mode of address and the terms of recognition that are embedded in this transactional relationship with a Muslim.

Conclusion: Muslim Opacities, Fugitive Muslims

I began this chapter with an argument about "unmosquing" Muslims not as a suggestion to rebuke one's faith but as a way to retrieve the movement and fullness of Muslimness away from its essentialist frames of analysis of religious singularity and cultural unity. To write against the transparent Muslim is to resist a framing that insists on locating a fixed and legible Muslim ontology and to refuse to consent to an imaginary that sees in difference only a threatening pathology and in relationality strictly a redemptive impulse for conversion. What of the fugitivity of Muslimness when it seeks a path in the wake of and beyond a historical record that restrains its visibility? What about the right of Muslims to their own opacity as subjects in their own history, an unresolved opacity that defies the calculus of security politics and the aphasias of the archives? And what of the multiple ways in which we can learn to know Muslims without the expedient relief of an ontological foundation that is also a blueprint to resolve the "incomprehension" of Islam and its "threat" to modern society?

My argument is about a refusal to be subjugated by the blackmail of conditional recognition. It is not simply a critique of a stifling cultural and political paternalism, nor is it a call to return to the comfort of some form of Muslim essence. It is rather a vindication of the voices, subjectivities, histories, knowledges, and aspirations long disqualified and amputated by a cruel imaginary of self-serving transparency and possessive relationality. Speaking about the "partial truths of the archives" for the Black experience, Christina Sharpe writes, "Despite knowing otherwise, we are often disciplined into thinking through and along lines that reinscribe our own annihilation, reinforcing and reproducing what Sylvia Wynter . . . has called our 'narratively condemned status'."[27] The locus of enunciation of Muslims, I argue, is never singular or determined, but it is condemned by a meta-narrative that traps it in a politics of defensive riposte and transparent reconciliation. It is this condemnation that requires Muslims to live in the gaze of others, overdetermined by the authority of its interpretation and the tenacity of its projection, which is the target of my reflection. My point then is not to negate the role of religion in the progression of Muslim identity but to interrogate the experience of recognition that suffocates that progression. My question is rather an iteration of Frantz Fanon's "what does the black want?"[28]—"What does the Muslim want?" Such a looming question cannot be answered with definitive certainty, but like Fanon's Black subject, and without assuming an equivalence of suffering, the Muslim too wants to be recognized as a full human and to be free from the epistemic closure that absorbs them into a homogenizing same. Fanon refuses to live in a white world where his blackness is stifled and scripted for the perfection of others. He writes:

A cripple of the Pacific War told my brother: "Adjust to your color as I did my stump; we're both victims of misfortune." Yet with all my being, I refuse the amputation. I feel my soul as vast as the world, truly a soul as deep as the deepest rivers, my chest has power of infinite expansion. I offered myself and I was advised to take the humility of the cripple. . . . Yesterday, opening my eyes to the world, I saw the sky from one side while abhorred by the other. I tried to get up, but the silence eviscerated and flowed over me, leaving my wings paralyzed.[29]

It is precisely this sentiment of paralysis that I invoke in vindicating the desire of Muslims to escape the terms of recognition which presume a need for rehabilitation and an order of reconciliation. Paralysis in this sense is about subordinating Muslims into subject positions predetermined by a dominant structure in which even the terms of resistance are dictated by the demands of that structure. Muslims must first denounce the violence of their "brethren," answer to the radicalism in their midst, and reveal their inner innocence as a condition of their speech. This permission to speak, I argue, is predicated on a crude belief that Muslims must graduate to the status of modern subjects without rewards and constantly suffer the fate of the dangerous stranger who, as Sara Ahmed reminds us, must be vigilantly managed and governed.[30] "The permitted Muslim" is the one who has passed the test of transparency by containing their "Muslimness" within the parameters tolerated by the dominant society.

In contrast, Muslim opacity is negatively perceived as a risk to be eliminated because in this imaginary of absolute transparency, the opaque can only be translated into an ominous secret, a threat that cannot be reconciled with the immediate certainty of security. By opacity, I do not mean the Muslim who refuses to condemn terrorist violence or those who insist on providing the contextual analysis to explain the reasons behind such violence. Rather, it is the Muslim who struggles to break free from the interpellative blackmail of this regime of recognition. The opaque Muslim is neither only religious nor only secular, neither deceptive nor assimilative; neither threatening nor amicable, and neither compromising nor combative. By opacity, I simply mean a capacity to reclaim an unpoliced presence for Muslims so their existence is not rigidly tied to a structuring schema of fragmented transparency. It is a demand to preserve the potentiality of Muslimness despite and in excess of the coercive forces of a provisional system of recognition.

But for such a hospitable vision of opacity to emerge, we must adopt a decolonial approach to what we mean by "really knowing" a Muslim. Here I turn to the work of Caribbean poet and philosopher Édouard Glissant, whose reflections on the ethics, poetics, and politics of relation insist on safeguarding the power of genuine diversity. This is not the multiculturalism of liberal democracy which has been heavily faulted for its emphasis on toleration and management of cultural difference and its amplification of an essentialized conception of culture.[31] Opacity, for Glissant, is equated with departure and the errantry of identification. It is, he writes, "the moment when one consents not to be a single being and attempts to be many beings at the same time."[32] This refusal to be pinned down and figured out only as an inevitable extension of one's culture, one's faith, and one's nation is at the heart of Glissant's epistemology of opacity.

The opaque is not a foreclosure of meaning, according to Glissant. It is a value that enables everyone to maintain their "thick shadow," a pyscho-cultural thickness which cannot be diverted from its natural course of evolution. Glissant's keywords throughout his work underline a fundamental poetics of movement and an ideal of ethical relationality: nomadity, errantry, travel, multiplicity, entanglement, rhizome, archipelago, Tout-Monde (All-World), creolization, ripening, uprising, and, of course, opacity. It is important to note that Glissant's dissent takes at its target a Western colonial and universalizing view of the world that impoverishes the organic potentiality of relation, thanks in most part to its obsession with a pathological conception of difference and a redemptive impulse to remake the world in its image.

Glissant's intervention constitutes a kind of epistemic insurrection against the demands of this imaginary to free up relationality from the burdens of this transaction. Why should the "other" be seen as a contrary, as holding no truth, as possessing no viable alternative, and as destined only for conversion? Under this imaginary of subjective negation, there is indeed no salvation for this "other," no possibility for cognitive autonomy because their instrumentalized repression is deemed necessary for the preservation of trust and order. Transparency then can only serve to uphold this order at the expense of one's opacity. In Glissant's words:

> There's a basic injustice in the worldwide spread of the transparency and projection of Western thought. Why must we evaluate people on the scale of transparency of the ideas proposed by the West? I understand this, I understand that and the other—rationality. I said that as far as I'm concerned, a person has the right to be opaque. That doesn't stop me from liking that person, it doesn't stop me from working with him, hanging out with him, etc. A racist is someone who refuses what he doesn't understand. I can accept what I don't understand. Opacity is a right we must have.[33]

Glissant contends that one of the basic principles of relationality is not knowability but a respect for multiplicity and divergence as a true measure of the richness of the world. This is a philosophical injunction of how to inhabit a complex planet where only this attunement to our differences can preserve our true diversity. Opacity then is a call to liberate relation from the chains of the "Same" and resist strategies of visibility and subjectivity, which serve someone else's desire to tame, manage, and understand. "In order to understand and thus accept you," Glissant comments on an anemic version of relationality, "I have to measure your solidity with the ideal scale providing me with grounds to make comparisons and perhaps, judgments. I have to reduce. . . . The opaque is not the obscure, though it is possible for it to be so and be accepted as such."[34]

I do not use opacity as a way to further mystify Muslims and Islam, but rather as a necessary corrective to the ways in which Muslim differences are manipulated to fit the calculus of transparency. It is about Muslims who clamor for the right to their opacity because they do not exist in a pendulum only to appease the fear of others or arouse fantasies. Nor do they live as spectators of history trapped in a closed script of fixed assumptions and predictable behaviors. Like everyone else, Muslims are fractal beings who live in entanglement, movement, and circulation. They are not locked in a closed archive of neatly contained truths and meanings. Thus, opacity upholds the fecundity of Muslim subjectivity and recognizes the sufficiency of Muslim presence without the violence of subsumption and the demand of transmutation.

The epigraph at the opening of this chapter is from Mahmoud Darwish, the Palestinian poet who spent his entire existence fighting a vicious system of physical and symbolic erasure. His poetry was notable for insisting on reconstituting Palestinian presence to bear witness to the violent effects of its excision. Darwish's command of the word and its cadences were not only a beautiful exercise in poetics but also an exalted demonstration of the insufficiency of the language of carcerality, security, and legibility to capture the absented fullness of Palestinian reality, memory, and opacity. That excision is the haunting noise Muslims continue to battle against in order to fulfill a simple "desire to write the lost text."[35]

NOTES

Introduction

1 Gibson (1984).

2 Freedom House (2016: 1).

3 Bhabha (1994: 37).

4 Habermas (1991). For a discussion of Habermas's notion of the public sphere and its relevance to Islamic online discourse, see El-Nawawy and Khamis (2009: 23–79).

5 For an overview of the scholarship on digital religion, see Rozehnal (2019: 21–8). Sections of this Introduction are drawn from *Cyber Sufis*, particularly the following brief survey of research on Islamic digital media (2019: 28–37).

6 On the use of digital media by Islamist militant groups, see Aggarwal (2016); Aly et al. (2016); Brandon (2008); German and Pennington (2019); Krona and Pennington (2019); Lim (2005); Ramsay (2013).

7 In his groundbreaking 1983 work *Imagined Communities*, Benedict Anderson argued that the convergence of print technology and capitalism spurred the rise of the modern nation-state—an "imagined political community" bound together by a common "print language." On the history of print media in the Muslim world, see Robinson (1996).

8 cooke and Lawrence (2005: 27).

9 Eickelman and Anderson (1999: 2).

10 Anderson (1995).

11 Anderson (1999b: 49).

12 Anderson (2002: 301).

13 Anderson (1999b: 49–50). See also Anderson (2001, 2003, 2005).

14 Anderson (1997).

15 Anderson (1999a: 10).

16 For a full listing of Bunt's publications, see his professional web page: www.virtuallyislamic.com.

17 In *iMuslims*, Bunt provides a visual diagram outlining the interdependent spaces of "Cyber Islamic Environments" (2009: 44–5).

18 Bunt (2009: 276).

19 Bunt (2018: 39–44); (2009: 81–7); (2000: 18–30).

20 Bunt (2000: 33–6).

21 Bunt (2018: 63–98); (2003: 114–18; 124–83); (2000: 108–31).

22 Bunt (2018: 45–7); (2009: 87–129); (2000: 104–8).

23 Bunt (2000: 30–3).

24 Bunt (2018: 48–53); (2009: 45–53).

25 Bunt (2018: 33–4); (2010); (2009: 64–8).

26 Bunt (2009: 131–76).

27 Bunt (2009: 117–20).

28 Bunt (2000: 37–47).

29 Bunt (2018: 55–60); (2003: 184–98); (2000: 47–57).

30 Bunt (2018: 54–5); (2014: 187–91); (2003: 198–200); (2000: 58–65).

31 Bunt (2000: 66–103).

32 Bunt (2018: 24–32); (2014: 196–200); (2009: 69–75); (2003: 37–66); (2000: 135–8).

33 Bunt (2018: 99–140); (2014: 191–6); (2009: 177–274); (2005); (2003: 25–36; 67–111).

34 Bunt (2009: 247).

35 El-Nawawy and Khamis (2009).

36 Echchaibi (2012); Larsson (2007); Lawrence (2002); Zaman (2008).

37 Baldanzi and Rashid (2020); Echchaibi (2013); Elfenbein (2021); Khamis (2018); Morales (2018); Peterson and Echchaibi (2017); Rozehnal (2019).

38 Faris and Rahimi (2015); Rahimi (2011, 2013, 2015a, 2015b, 2016, 2018).

39 Adi (2014); El-Nawawy and Khamis (2012a, 2012b, 2013, 2014); Hofheinz (2005); Howard and Hussain (2013); Jamali (2015); Khamis (2010, 2019, 2020); Khamis, Gold, and Vaughn (2020); Khamis and Mili (2018); Nunns and Idle (2011); Pennington (2019); Stanton (2020); Wheeler (2005).

40 Alatas (2017, 2021); Hoesterey (2015, 2019); Lim (2005).

41 Baulch and Pramiyanti (2018); Echchaibi (2014); Goehring (2019); Kavakci and Kraeplin (2017); Khamis (2010, 2017, 2020); Khamis and Mili (2018); Marcotte (2010); Oshan (2009); Pennington (2018a); Peterson (2020a, 2020b); Piela (2012, 2015, 2021); Radsch and Khamis (2013); Sreberny (2015).

42 Khabeer and Al Hassen (2013: 309).

43 Echchaibi (2011a); Maguire (2006); Pennington (2018b, 2018c); Stanton (2017).

44 Rippin (2014).

45 Echchaibi (2011b); Hermansen (2014); Hirshkind (2012); Larsson (2016); Sisler (2011).

46 Echchaibi (2008); Howard (2010); Mandaville (1999, 2002, 2003).

47 El-Nawawy and Khamis (2013, 2014); Larsson (2005); Pennington (2019); Sands (2010); Varisco (2010).

48 Lo and Aziz (2009).

49 Sisler (2013).

50 Alatas (2017); Rozehnal (2019); Sijapati (2019).

51 Cantwell and Rashid (2015); https://mappingislamophobia.org/ (edited and directed by Caleb Elfenbein); www.cyberorient.net (editor-in-chief, Daniel Martin Varisco).

52 Echchaibi, "Taming the West," p. 145.

53 In 1965, Intel cofounder Gordon Moore noted that the number of transistors per square inch on integrated circuits had doubled every year since their invention. "Moore's law" predicts this trend will continue in the future, an observation that also serves as shorthand for the exponential growth of digital technologies in general.

Chapter 1

1 In this context, *imam* refers to a religious leader or functionary with responsibilities for leading the prayers; *mullah* refers to a religious leader or scholar; *shaykh* refers to a religious leader. The terms can have other meanings, depending on the religious orientation and tradition of the individual. The focus in this chapter is primarily on Sunni perspectives and interpretations. I have written extensively elsewhere on other approaches.

2 Bunt (2018).

3 Bunt (2000).

4 Bunt (2009).

5 Bunt (1996). This was a common feature of my discussions with Muslim scholars during fieldwork on religious authority issues in the mid-1990s, when the use of the internet as a form of communication of religious ideas was in its early stages (often through mailing lists and chatrooms).

6 Cox (2020). Islamically oriented apps were not without issues or problems. In 2020, for example, there were allegations that some Muslim apps had been compromised and their data shared with a variety of partners, including security-oriented organizations.

7 Bunt (2003); El-Nawawy and Khamis (2009).

8 Abusharif (2019).

9 Mandaville (2014).

10 Darul Ifta (2020).

11 *Associated Press* (2019); *Virtual Ifta* (2019).

12 *IQRA Cartoon* (2018). *Sīra* refers to the biographical genre associated with the life of the Prophet Muhammad.

13 *The Islamic Information* (2019).

14 *OnePath Network* (2020).

15 *TikTok* (2020); Stanton (2020); Bunt (2015); Arjana (2017). *Hajj* refers to the "major" annual pilgrimage; *'umrah* is the "minor" pilgrimage. Both take place in Mecca and focus on the *Ka'bah*, the central cube-like structure in the Great Mosque. The 2020 *hajj* took place in the year 1441 in the Islamic calendar.

16 *TVQuran* (2020).

17 *Mudasir_100* (2020).

18 *Reminder4Believer* (2020).

19 Bunt (2020: 39–44); Smith Galer (2020). *Suwar* (singular: *sūrah*) are chapters in the Qur'ān.

20 The term *ifṭār* relates to breaking the *Ramaḍān* fast. Practices vary in diverse religious and cultural contexts. *Laylat al-Qadr*, the "Night of Power," is associated with marking the day of the initial Revelation received by Muhammad. It is celebrated with additional prayers and readings of the Qur'ān, often over several nights as there is no precise contemporaneous date.

21 Versi (2020).

22 The term *ṭawāf* refers to the ritual circumambulation of the *Ka'bah* at the commencement and conclusion of the *hajj*.

23 Khan (2020).

24 Kutty (2018–); *About Islam* (2021). Kutty is Director of the Islamic Center of Toronto and resident scholar at the Islamic Institute of Toronto. His religious opinions have been widely circulated online on prominent Islamic websites. His opinions are also featured on his personal *Ask the Scholar* website, which links to *About Islam*.

25 Kutty (2020).

26 *State Information Services* (2020).

27 *Akhbar el-Yom* (2020); *ShoroukNews* (2020).

28 Brown (2020).

29 Al-Qaradaghi (2020).

30 Fakude (2014); Lauzière (2015); Wiktorowicz (2005); Thomas Hegghammer (2009). The term "Salafi" is complex, relating here to a spectrum of political-religious movements associated with "reform" and "renewal" of Islam. The term can have negative connotations from observers (Muslim and other) in relation to its perceived association with so-called fundamentalism(s) and *jihād*-oriented militancy.

31 *Middle East Monitor* (2020).

32 *Jumu'ah* refers to the Friday prayer, which is conventionally seen as most beneficial when undertaken communally in a mosque. The term *aḥādīth* (singular: *ḥādīth*) is associated with the reports, traditions, and sayings and actions attributed to the Prophet Muhammad.

33 *IslamQA* (2020c).

34 *IslamQA* (2020b).

35 *IslamQA* (2020a).

36 *Islamic Portal* (2020b).

37 *Islamic Portal* (2020a).

38 *Islamic Portal* (2020c).

39 *Deenspiration* (2020b).

40 *Deenspiration* (2020a).

41 Durmaz (2020); *Arab News* (2020).

42 *Al-Azhar* (2020b).

43 *Al-Azhar* (2020c).

44 *Al-Azhar* (2020a).

45 *TalabeToday* (2020). Shīʿī and other diverse perspectives would require a wider study than this present overview.

46 Webb (2020).

Chapter 2

1 El-Nawawy and Khamis (2009); Marcotte (2016); Bunt (2018); Rozehnal (2019).

2 Permission from the participants and REB approval have been obtained for publication purposes.

3 For more info, see www.risconvention.com

4 Campbell (2013).

5 Helland (2007).

6 Hoover (2016).

7 Bunt (2018).

8 Peterson and Echchaibi (2017).

9 Rozehnal (2019: 14).

10 Orsi (2006).

11 Ammerman (2007).

12 McGuire (2008).

13 Jeldtoft (2011).

14 Orsi (2006: 188).

15 Ammerman (2007).

16 McGuire (2008: 8–13, 120).

17 Jeldtoft (2011).

18 At the time of research, I assigned this age group for millennials.

19 The participants were required to be repeat attendees so they could discuss their reasoning for returning to this conference.

20 Qadhi resigned from this institution in 2019 to join the Islamic Seminary of America.

21 Personal interview, P26, January 2020. In this study, the names of all interviewees are anonymous. The participants have been labeled by numbers.

22 Personal interview, P20, September 2019.

23 Personal interview, P45, April 2020.

24 Personal interview, P37, April 2020.

25 Personal interview, P24, January 2020.

26 For more information, see Furlanetto (2013); Lewis (2000).

27 Personal interview, P25, January 2020.

28 Personal interview, P10, May 2019.

29 Personal interview, P9, February 2019.

30 Personal interview, P3, July 2019.

31 Personal interview, P45, April 2020.

32 Personal interview, P12, May 2019.

33 Personal interview, P50, May 2020. For more on *IslamQ&A*, see Bunt (2018).

Chapter 3

1 Coleman (2010); de la Cruz (2015); de Vries (2001); Engelke (2010); Stolow (2005).

2 Eisenlohr (2009); Hirschkind (2006); Meyer (2009).

3 Hirschkind (2006); Eisenlohr (2018); Larkin (2004); Rasmussen (2010); Rozehnal (2019).

4 Campbell (2010); Engelke (2007); Husein and Slama (2018).

5 Arendt (2006 [1954]: 122).

6 Arendt (2006 [1954]: 93).

7 Hirschkind and Larkin (2008).

8 Latour (2005: 39).

9 Chih (2007); Halman (2013).

10 Meri (2010); Renard (2008).

11 Brenner (1996); Hefner (2000); Liddle (1996).

12 Latif (2005).

13 Howell (2001); Hoesterey (2015).

14 *alKisah* (1, 2004: 36–41; 25, 2004: 30–3).

15 *alKisah* (7, 2005: 14–21, 32–4).

16 *alKisah* (5, 2003: 82–3).

17 *alKisah* (8, 2007: 132–3).

18 *alKisah* (24, 2004: 82–4); *alKisah* (1, 2005: 86–8).

19 Slama (2017).

20 Messick (1993: 25–6).

21 Pandolfo (1997: 91).

22 Eickelman and Anderson (1999).

23 Zito (2008: 81).

24 Rozehnal (2019: 177).

25 Keane (2018: 65).

Chapter 4

1 See original data on www.mappingislamophobia.org.

2 Dr. Qamar's full remarks are available at https://www.argusleader.com/story/news/2017/02/27/speech-what-s-like-muslim-sioux-falls/98479368/ (accessed October 4, 2021).

3 Mohamed et al. (2017).

4 #GoodMuslimBadMuslim recently completed a successful five-year run of new episodes. See https://www.goodmuslimbadmuslim.com for more information.

5 Annear (2015).

6 Balmeseda (2015).

7 Moriki (2018).

8 Fraser (1990).

9 Warner (2002).

10 In a speech at Portland State University, Morrison told the audience, "The very serious function of racism . . . is distraction. It keeps you from doing your work. It keeps you explaining, over and over again, your reason for being" (Morrison 1975).

11 See, for example, Nagel and Staeheli (2005).

12 Smith (2018).

13 Elfenbein (2021).

14 Mohamed and Diament (2019).

15 See, for example, GhaneaBassiri (2010), Abdul Khabeer (2016), and Curtis (2002).

16 Ratliff (2019).

17 In the interest of transparency: I am a modest financial supporter of *See Something, Say Something*. My decision to support the podcast predates the start of research for this project.

18 Akbar (2019).

19 Akbar (2020).

20 Akbar (2016).

21 Mohamed et al. (2017).

22 Alice (2020).

23 Alice submitted her response to my questionnaire on February 20, 2020.

24 Megan (2020).

25 Maureen (2020).

26 The work of the Muslim Anti-Racism Collaborative (Muslim ARC), a human rights educational group, provides an example of how organizations and groups might enact a "stream if you want approach" IRL. Its workshops and trainings are primarily meant for Muslim publics, addressing racism and its effects within Muslim communities. Yet through its work the organization also provides opportunities for non-Muslim publics to learn from, with, and about Muslims in practical, meaningful ways. Margari Aziza, the group's cofounder, also features in a *See Something, Say Something* podcast episode about the importance of cultural production through antiracist lens. Aziza prepared trainings and served as a consultant and collaborator on a web series called *East of LaBrea*, addressing questions of race and representation for Muslim and non-Muslim writers alike. See https://seesomethingsaysomething.libsyn .com/east-of-la-brea-with-sameer-gardezi-and-margari-aziza.

Chapter 5

1 Reza (2005).

2 Mohamed (2018).

3 Morales (2018: 108).

4 Bowen (2010: 410) and Leonard (1992: 130). The Ahmadiyya are a group of Muslims who first emerged in India in the late nineteenth century as followers of Ghulam Ahmad. A faction of this community proclaimed that their leader had been a divine reformer, a prophet, and the returned messiah awaited by Christians and the Mahdi awaited by Muslims at the end of times. Ahmadi Muslims practice the five pillars of Islam and recite from the same Qur'ān as Sunni and Shīʿah Muslims. Ahmadis began arriving in North America in 1913. These *daʿwah* workers concluded that African Americans had not only been largely ignored by other Muslim proselytizers, but that they were in many ways more receptive to Islam than white Americans. Morales (2018: 29).

5 Padilla-Alvarez (2017). In one of the few texts describing the Bani Saqr, Padilla-Alverez describes the group as a small community of Puerto Rican Muslims in Newark during the 1970s.

6 Jameel and Johnson (2016).

7 Webb (2012).

8 See Brasher (2001).

9 Brasher (2001).

10 Galvan (2017).

11 Galvan (2012).

12 Galvan (2012).

13 Hernandez (2011).

14 Espinoza (2004).

15 Espinoza (2004).

16 Green and Giammona (2016).

17 Haleem (2008: 173).

18 Robinson (2014: 276).

19 Maffei (2016: XI).

20 Maffei (2016).

21 Anzaldúa (1987).

22 Martínez-Vazquez (2010: 37).

23 Maffei (2008, 2016).

24 Abeytia (2016).

25 Abeytia (2016).

26 Abeytia (2016).

27 Lofgren (2013).

28 Gallegos (2005: 99).

29 Abarca (2006: 118).

30 Abarca (2006).

31 Cognard-Black and Goldthwaite (2014: 2).

32 Latimer and Gamboa (2016).

33 Reddy and El-Ghobashy (2010).

34 United States and Donald J. Trump, Presidential Document (2017).

35 Tuathail (1996) and Brady (2002).

36 Sandoval (2000: 112).

37 Duran (2017).

38 Do (2017).

39 See Anderson (2003: 53).

40 Chan-Malik (2018: 186).

41 Tareen (2019).

Chapter 6

1 Bunt (2018).

2 Howard (2011).

3 El-Nawawy and Khamis (2009).

4 Khamis (2017).

5 A "self-reflexivity" note is worth highlighting in this context. As a bilingual, Muslim American, Arab American woman, who is a mother, an academic, a media commentator and analyst, and an interfaith activist, I was able to secure easy, and natural, access to many of these gender-based, faith-based, online communities, including women-only closed Facebook groups.

6 See McDonald (2008), Khamis (2010), Badran (2013).

7 Hoover and Echchaibi (2014).

8 Pennington (2018b).

9 Radsch and Khamis (2013).

10 Gallup (2018).

11 Tyrer (2013: 3).

12 Khamis (2018).

13 Khamis (2018).

14 Khamis (2018).

15 These tweets were posted at: https://twitter.com/i/events /760197573839876097?lang=en.

16 *Karamah* means "dignity" in Arabic.

17 https://shortyawards.com/2nd-socialgood/canyouhearusnow.

18 Ibid.

19 https://wagingnonviolence.org/2016/08/muslim-women-broadcast-their -strength-with-canyouhearusnow/.

20 Khamis (2018).

21 El-Nawawy and Khamis (2009); Khamis (2010).

22 https://muslimskeptic.com/2021/04/01/france-bans-ḥijāb-for-anyone-under-18- secular-tyranny-rises/.

23 Croucher (2008).

24 https://www.dw.com/en/french-burqa-ban-violates-human-rights-rules-un -committee/a-46007469.

25 These tweets were all posted at: https://mobile.twitter.com/lsarsour/status /1378173660058550272.

26 Throughout this chapter, I quote from a number of "closed" women's Facebook groups. Out of ethical considerations, and to respect the privacy of the participants in these gated online communities, no links are shared from these groups' postings, and the names of individual participants who post in these groups are kept anonymous.

27 Karim (2006).

28 Hoover and Echchaibi (2014); Pennington (2018b).

29 Waninger (2015: 2).

30 Peterson (2020).

31 Kavakci and Kraeplin (2017).

32 Al-Heeti (2019).

33 Kavakci and Kraeplin (2017: 856).

34 Kavakci and Kraeplin (2017).

35 Kavakci and Kraeplin (2017: 866).

36 Pennington (2018a).

37 Al-Khatahtbeh (2016).

38 Pennington (2018a: 207).

39 Pennington (2018a: 206).

40 https://metro.co.uk/2019/03/27/muslim-women-should-look-to-the-past-to
    -find-the-empowerment-we-need-today-9034825/.

41 Ibid.

42 The video and the tweets were all posted at: https://muslimgirl.com/20-tweet
    -highlights-from-our-fifth-annual-muslimwomensday/.

43 https://muslimgirl.com/get-ready-for-the-first-muslimwomensday-digital
    -summit/.

44 Ibid.

45 Bunt (2009, 2018).

46 El-Nawawy and Khamis (2009).

47 McDonald (2008), Khamis (2010), Badran (2013).

48 El-Nawawy and Khamis (2009).

49 El-Nawawy and Khamis (2009).

50 El-Nawawy and Khamis (2009).

51 Habermas (1992).

52 El-Nawawy and Khamis (2009).

53 Habermas (1992).

54 Radsch and Khamis (2013).

55 Hammer (2012).

56 Campbell and Evolvi (2019).

57 Harris (2008).

58 Goehring (2019: 34).

59 Goehring (2019).

60 Goehring (2019: 23).

61 McDonald (2008); Khamis (2010); Badran (2013).

62 Tzoreff (2014).

Chapter 7

1 Al-Khatahtbeh has expanded her work beyond *Muslim Girl* with other activism
   projects like partnering with *Teen Vogue* in 2016 to provide content on Muslim
   women's experiences, starting Muslim Women's Day in 2017 on social media,

hosting a podcast called *Antidote*, and even running (unsuccessfully) for political office in New Jersey's Sixth Congressional District in 2020.

2 Al-Khatahtbeh (2020).

3 Al-Khatahtbeh (2016: 79).

4 Al-Khatahtbeh (2016: 81).

5 Al-Khatahtbeh (2016: 1).

6 Al-Khatahtbeh (2016: 3).

7 Al-Khatahtbeh (2016: 46).

8 McRobbie (1991: 84).

9 McRobbie (1991: 145).

10 Kaiser (2012: 4).

11 Moors and Tarlo (2013: 3).

12 Kearney (2006: 13).

13 Kearney (2006: 139).

14 Harris (2008: 482).

15 Harris (2008: 485).

16 Harris (2008: 486).

17 Al-Khatahtbeh (2016: 85).

18 Keller (2012: 430).

19 Keller (2012: 432).

20 Keller (2012: 440).

21 Al-Khatahtbeh (2016: 45).

22 Magearu (2018: 138).

23 Magearu (2018: 149).

24 Glaser and Strauss (1967).

25 Avishai, Gerber, and Randles (2013: 418–19).

26 Biographical information is not provided for most of the writers on *Muslim Girl*. Some of the contributors use screen names or are anonymous. For those authors who share relevant background, I include this information.

27 Ali (2018).

28 Saleh (2018b).

29 Elshamy (2018).

30 Diaf (2018).

31 Ahmed (2018).

32 Ahmed (2018).

33 Vernon (2018).

34 Matan (2018).

35 Matan (2018).

36 For more background on Latino Muslims in the United States, see Nuñez (2019), Allaudeen (2020), and Espinosa, Morales, and Galvan (2017).

37 Khatib (2017).

38 Guest Blogger (2017b).

39 Colon (2018b).

40 Colon (2018a).

41 Yousaf (2018).

42 Asim (2019).

43 Iman (2017).

44 Guest Blogger (2017a).

45 Guest Blogger (2017a).

46 Saleh (2018a).

Chapter 8

1 *Niqāb* is a face covering worn by some Muslim women as part of their religious garments.

2 Nisa (2013: 251).

3 Piela (2015, 2017).

4 Piela (2021).

5 Piela (2021).

6 Tarnovskaya (2017).

7 Evolvi (2018).

8 Campbell and Evolvi (2019).

9 Sreberny (2015: 359).

10 Hoover and Echchaibi (2014).

11 Bhabha (2012: 312).

12 Campbell and Evolvi (2019: 7).

13 Helland (2016: 183).

14 Campbell and Evolvi (2019).

15 Bhabha (2012); Brah (2001); Hall (2003).

16 Brah (2001: 183).

17 Hall (2003).

18 Bhabha (1990: 211).

19 Bhabha (2012).

20 Hoover and Echchaibi (2014: 13).

21 Campbell (2012: 71).

22   Hall (2003: 234).

23   Campbell (2012: 71).

24   Campbell (2012: 74).

25   https://www.youtube.com/watch?v=Q84ypQdBsPc (accessed February 24, 2021).

26   https://www.youtube.com/watch?v=gfePNIAr_I0&list=PL-XSVKFDxcV6-17C
     r0kfNwKBEbMnDrlQX (accessed February 24, 2021).

27   Rivka Sajida's Twitter account is set to "private," therefore I do not share her
     Twitter handle.

28   https://www.etsy.com/shop/AWishForWinsomeWorks. Site no longer active.

29   https://www.youtube.com/watch?v=NJ9xnQP4mho (accessed February 24,
     2021).

30   http://hijabininjette.blogspot.com/2016/09/ (accessed February 24, 2021).

31   *Pew Research Center* (2018).

32   http://hijabininjette.blogspot.com/2016/09/ (accessed February 24, 2021).

33   https://www.youtube.com/watch?v=UxV6E3mg4wo (accessed February 24,
     2021).

34   https://www.youtube.com/watch?v=UxV6E3mg4wo (accessed February 24,
     2021).

35   http://hijabininjette.blogspot.com/2018/09/grwm-yemeni-style.html (accessed
     February 24, 2021).

36   Khamis, Ang, and Welling (2017: 197).

37   Thompson (2020) analyzes in her work worship practices of American
     LGBTQ+ Muslims.

38   Peterson (2020) discusses another woman whose online identity challenges
     preconceptions regarding Islam, feminism, and the *niqāb*.

39   http://hijabininjette.blogspot.com/2016/09/ (accessed February 24, 2021).

40   Zebiri (2008).

41   Zebiri (2008: 252).

42   Piela (2012).

43   Zebiri (2008: 39).

44   Evolvi (2018).

45   https://www.youtube.com/watch?v=hTeMHoocYHs (accessed February 24,
     2021).

46   It is those biases, mainly the antireligious trope, that cause many Muslim
     women to only accept a qualified label "Muslim" or "Islamic" feminist, or
     to shun the "feminist" identity altogether. See Badran (2013) for an in-depth
     discussion of feminism and Islam.

47   Clark Mane (2012).

48   For a useful glossary of the terms *niqāb*, *jilbab*, and *burka* with illustrations,
     see https://www.open.edu/openlearn/history-the-arts/veiling/content-section-1.3
     (accessed February 24, 2021).

49 Piela (2013).

50 Johnson (2017: 278–9).

51 For photographs of these styles, see http://hijabininjette.blogspot.com/2019/ (accessed February 24, 2021).

52 https://www.youtube.com/watch?v=LqQzyXzJpaA (accessed February 24, 2021).

53 Piela (2021).

54 Bolognani and Mellor (2012).

55 https://www.youtube.com/watch?v=j4QIDfRNp6Q (accessed February 24, 2021).

56 https://www.youtube.com/watch?v=JnjdQFhCB6A (accessed February 24, 2021).

57 https://www.youtube.com/watch?v=sY5eajF78h4 (accessed February 24, 2021). "Deen" (*dīn*) means "religion."

58 *Ṣalāh* is a daily prayer ritual and one of the five pillars of Islam; *khuṭba* is a sermon given by the *imam* to the congregation; *iftar* is a meal which breaks the *Ramaḍān* fast.

59 https://www.youtube.com/watch?v=Y2J0lb_pjuo (accessed February 24, 2021).

60 Personal communication, May 22, 2020.

61 Personal communication, May 22, 2020.

62 Bano and Kalmbach (2011); Hammer (2012); Sharify-Funk and Haddad (2012).

63 Hammer (2012).

64 Thompson (2020).

65 https://www.youtube.com/watch?v=Lsy2oioTQOw&t=857s (accessed February 24, 2021).

66 Ali (2019).

67 Thompson (2020).

68 Personal communication, May 22, 2020.

69 Hoover and Echchaibi (2014).

70 Hooks (1990: 149).

71 Khamis, Ang, and Welling (2017: 6).

72 Schielke (2009, 2010).

73 Habermas (1992).

74 Johnson (2005).

75 Habermas (1998: 121).

76 Downey and Fenton (2002: 194).

77 Khamis, Ang, and Welling (2017: 198).

78 Evolvi (2018).

Chapter 9

1 "Meditation marketplace" is a term I use to refer to the digital landscape of apps for meditation and mindfulness (the terms are used interchangeably in this genre), including their marketing, consumption, and content (Sijapati 2019). I situate this as a subcategory within what Wade Clark Roof (2001) in the late 1990s first called the "spiritual marketplace" and as a dimension of what Sofia Rose Arjana (2020) has recently identified as the "mystical marketplace."

2 Sijapati (2019).

3 Sijapati (2019). *Dhikr* means remembrance, or recollection, and refers to the ritual practice of recollecting the divine through repetition of a word, phrase, or breathing technique either silently or aloud.

4 *Duʿāʾ* is a personal prayer to God in the form of an appeal or invocation. It is distinct from ritual or liturgical prayer (*ṣalāh*) and may be done for oneself or on behalf of others. *Duʿāʾ* can be composed freely by the person making it or employ a preformulated statement containing excerpts from *ḥadīth* (the recorded sayings of the Prophet Muhammad) or the Qurʾān.

5 Chappel (2020).

6 Sijapati (2019).

7 Sijapati (2019).

8 https://www.sakeenah.io.

9 https://www.sakeenah.io.

10 "Sakeenah, Improve your mental wellbeing," Apple App Store, https://apps .apple.com/us/app/sakeenah/id1488712495.

11 https://www.sakeenah.io.

12 A *madhab* is a school of Islamic law, of which there are four in the Sunni tradition.

13 "Sakeenah, Improve your mental wellbeing," Apple App Store, https://apps .apple.com/us/app/sakeenah/id1488712495.

14 "The All-Hearing and the All-Seeing"—two names of God in the Qurʾān.

15 Another two of God's names, "The Most Gracious and the Most Merciful."

16 "Sakeenah, Improve your mental wellbeing," Apple App Store, https://apps .apple.com/us/app/sakeenah/id1488712495.

17 Sufi psychology elaborates various forms of the individual's *nafs* (ego, human self, or lower soul) and the ways its base forms are transcended on the path toward experiential awareness of God. Various forms of the *nafs* are mentioned in the Qurʾān. It is contrasted with *rūḥ*, or spirit.

18 Sabr: Meditation and Sleep," Apple App Store, https://apps.apple.com/us/app/ sabr-meditation-sleep/id1529988831.

19 "Sabr: Meditation and Sleep," Apple App Store, https://apps.apple.com/us/app/ sabr-meditation-sleep/id1529988831.

20 https://sabrapp.com.

21 "Sabr: Meditation and Sleep," Apple App Store, https://apps.apple.com/us/app/sabr-meditation-sleep/id1529988831. https://sabrapp.com. Also see the *Sabr* promotional video: https://www.youtube.com/watch?v=9gTN_ASTOGw&t=31s.

22 Ashrafi is an Illinois-based professional YouTuber, whose channel, SGT, is dedicated to sports entertainment. https://www.youtube.com/c/SubTheGamer/about.

23 Altaleb (2021).

24 LaunchGood is a crowdfunding platform founded in 2013 for Muslim organizations.

25 "Sabr: Meditation and Sleep," Apple App Store, https://apps.apple.com/us/app/sabr-meditation-sleep/id1529988831.

Nasheed (nashīd), an Arabic term meaning "chant," is a genre of vocal music popular in Islamic cultures as a form of devotional or religious expression, usually containing Islamic religious motifs. AMSR is the acronym for "autonomous sensory meridian response," generally referring to feelings of calmness created in a person when listening to sounds, from nature or otherwise, that are laid in a repetitive loop on an audio track.

26 https://sabrapp.com/our-team/.

27 "Sabr: Meditation and Sleep," Apple App Store, https://apps.apple.com/us/app/sabr-meditation-sleep/id1529988831.

28 "Sabr: Meditation and Sleep," Apple App Store, https://apps.apple.com/us/app/sabr-meditation-sleep/id1529988831.

29 The Arabic phrase here is from the Qur'ān, *Surah al Baqara* (2:201) ("Our Lord! Give us good in this world and good in the Hereafter, and defend us from the torment of the Fire!").

30 "Sabr: Meditation and Sleep," Apple App Store, https://apps.apple.com/us/app/sabr-meditation-sleep/id1529988831.

31 This is part of a *du'ā'* derived from the end of the last verse of *Surah al Imran* (3:173): "*ḥasbunā Allahu wa ni'ma al-wakilu*" ("Allah is enough for us, He is the best protector").

32 "Sabr: Meditation and Sleep," Apple App Store, https://apps.apple.com/us/app/sabr-meditation-sleep/id1529988831.

33 Suleiman is an American Muslim scholar and founder of Yaqeen Institute for Islamic Research in Dallas, Texas. See https://yaqeeninstitute.org/.

34 https://www.myhalaqah.com/home/about/.

35 https://www.myhalaqah.com/home/about/.

36 "Halaqah—Muslim Meditation," Apple App Store, https://apps.apple.com/us/app/halaqah-muslim-meditation/id1522290777.

37 https://www.myhalaqah.com/home/our-story/.

38 https://www.youtube.com/watch?v=0P3xEsoFRZo.

39 It is not uncommon for these terms to be used interchangeably in English to describe Muslim contemplative practices. These apps do not delineate which of their practices are *dhikr*, *fikr*, or *murāqabah*.

40 Jubair (2020).

41 Other digital content platforms such as Hulu use similar approaches to content curation, naming the user's choices as their personal "My Stuff," for example.

42 "Halaqah—Muslim Meditation," Apple App Store, https://apps.apple.com/us/app/halaqah-muslim-meditation/id1522290777.

43 *Bismillāh* is the shorthand term for the Arabic phrase and opening words of the Qur'ān: *Bismillāh ar-Raḥmān ar-Raḥīm* (In the Name of God the Compassionate, the Merciful). The phrase is recited daily in Muslim liturgical prayers and can be also recited at the commencement of nonreligious endeavors.

44 "Halaqah—Muslim Meditation," Apple App Store,

https://apps.apple.com/us/app/halaqah-muslim-meditation/id1522290777.

45 *Dīn*, the Arabic term for "religion," is most commonly used in the sense of the obligations a Muslim has to God, codified in the tradition and customs of ritual practice (*'ibādah*). *Dīn* is contrasted with *dunyā*, which refers to the realm of worldly, material matters.

46 For example, Qur'ān 13:28, 2:235.

47 An example of this is *The Mindful Muslimah* who runs podcasts, webinars, support groups, and maintains a YouTube channel: https://www.youtube.com/watch?v=wVyCPDTQpi0.

Despite the title, she promotes a Muslim women's lifestyle, not just mindfulness. Her identity is not public; her name is undisclosed and she wears *niqāb* in her online appearances.

48 Goyal (2014).

49 http://www.shifaacounseling.com/about.html. Rothman is the executive director of the International Association of Islamic Psychology and Principal of the Cambridge Muslim College.

50 Rothman (2018, 2019). On Muhāsibī, see Schimmel (1975: 54 and note 31) and Sells (1996: 171–95).

51 Yaqeen Institute (2018).

52 Yaqeen Institute (2018).

53 Yaqeen Institute (2018).

54 Isgandarova (2019: 1157).

55 Isgandarova (2019: 1158).

Chapter 10

1 See *Saudi Gazette* (2020) and Oxford Business Group (2018).

2 Bunt (2010).

3 Stanton (2020).

4 See Fewkes (2019) and Fakhruroji (2019).

5 See Bazaar Android Market, https://cafebazaar.ir, and Myket Android Store, https://myket.ir.

6 Bulliet (2013: 6–7) and (2020).

7 For *hajj* paintings, see Parker and Neal (2009). For *hajj* certificates, see, for example, Marzolph (2014).

8 Bulliet (2013: 10).

9 Sardar (2014: xiii–xiv).

10 Sardar (2014: 104).

11 Mater (2016: 55–6).

12 Mater (2016).

13 See, for example, Sardar (2014: 314–17 and 345–7).

14 Mater (2016: 207).

15 Campbell et al. (2014: 159).

16 Apps with robust institutional support also appear more likely to have had regular updates, as indicated in this study by the app's version number.

17 See Google Play's Developers page: https://developer.android.com/distribute.

18 Iqbal (2020).

19 "Number of apps" (2021). The report notes that Windows Store has not released updated app data in several years, but the other three are current as of the first quarter of 2021.

20 "vMakkah," Google Play, https://play.google.com/store/apps/details?id=com.semaphorelab.vmakkah&hl=en_US&gl=US (last accessed November 12, 2020).

21 "Athan," Google Play, https://play.google.com/store/apps/details?id=com.athan&hl=en_US&gl=US (last accessed December 11, 2020). The Islamic *Hijri* calendar is a lunar calendar that begins with the year 622 CE, when Muhammad and the early Muslim community (*ummah*) migrated from Mecca to Medina.

22 Campbell et al. (2014: 163–4).

23 "Qibla Compass – Find Direction," Google Play, https://play.google.com/store/apps/details?id=com.sstsmartapps.qiblahcompass.finddirection (last accessed November 5, 2020).

24 Campbell et al. (2014: 154–72).

25 "Mecca Live Wallpaper," Google Play, https://play.google.com/store/apps/details?id=com.MeccaWallpaperWorld&hl=en_US&gl=US (last accessed December 11, 2020).

26 "Mecca Live Screen Lock," Google Play, https://play.google.com/store/apps/details?id=com.mrsniper.mecca.live.lock (last accessed November 4, 2020).

27 "Hajj tv live, kabah tv live, mecca live: Mecca tv," Google Play, https://play.google.com/store/apps/details?id=com.icaali.makkah (last accessed May 11, 2020).

28 Catellani (2020). The app's long and somewhat awkward name reflects the differing degrees of professionalization and efforts to brand apps for users.

29   "Mecca Live Wallpaper," Google Play, https://play.google.com/store/apps/details?id=com.MeccaWallpaperWorld (last accessed May 11, 2020).

30   "Mecca in Saudi Arabia," Google Play, https://play.google.com/store/apps/details?id=com.meccainsaudiarabia.

31   See, for example, "Mecca Photo Frame," Myket, https://myket.ir/app/com.beauty.mecca.photo.frame.wallpapers?lang=en. Interestingly, the Mecca photo frame apps available on Myket all show women in elaborate *ḥijābs* in their sample photographs.

32   See Mahmood (2005).

33   See Bunt (2016: 233).

34   See Arjana (2017).

35   "Umrah Guide Hajj Guide & Makkah Map," Google Play, https://play.google.com/store/apps/details?id=com.makkah.map.offline.

36   "Smart Hajj," Google Play, https://play.google.com/store/apps/details?id=com.vegas.smarthajj.

37   "Manasikana," Google Play, https://play.google.com/store/apps/details?id=com.hajj.manasikana.

Chapter 11

1   In this chapter, I use the Standard English rendering of this term rather than the formal Arabic transliteration with diacritics (*ʿīd al-ʾaḍḥā*).

2   Feenberg and Barkadjieva (2004: 37).

3   Woodhead (2009).

4   Stolow (2005: 119).

5   Hoover (2011: 613).

6   Campbell (2013: 2).

7   Hoover and Echchaibi (n.d.); Pennington (2018a).

8   Morgan (2009: 15).

9   boyd and Ellison (2007: 211).

10   Burgess and Green (2009); Choi and Toma (2014); Papacharissi (2009).

11   Feenberg and Barkadjieva (2004: 38).

12   boyd (2007: 39).

13   Papacharissi (2011).

14   Bunt (2018: 2).

15   Pennington (2018b).

16   Alhabash and Ma (2017).

17   Nisa (2018).

18   Baulch and Pramiyanti (2018).

19 Peterson (2020: 1195).

20 Peterson (2020).

21 Peterson (2020).

22 Yuan (2012).

23 Bunt (2018); El-Nawawy and Khamis (2009); Pennington (2018b, 2020).

24 Baulch and Pramiyanti (2018); Nisa (2018).

25 Anderson (1995).

26 Anderson (1995): 14.

27 Bunt (2005: 68).

28 Varisco (2010: 176).

29 El-Nawawy and Khamis (2009).

30 Bunt (2018: 3).

31 Echchaibi (2011).

32 Echchaibi (2011).

33 Lim (2008).

34 Bunt (2018: 9).

35 Zappavigna (2016).

36 Hjorth and Pink (2014).

37 Keep (2014: 15).

38 Lasén and Gómez-Cruz (2009).

39 MacDowall and Souza (2017: 9).

40 Zappavigna (2016).

41 Smith and Sanderson (2015).

42 Serafinelli (2017).

43 Mejova, Benkhedda, and Khairani (2017).

44 Images similar to those posted during *Eid al-Adha* 2019 can be found by exploring the #Islam hashtag in Instagram: https://www.instagram.com/explore/tags/islam/

45 Morgan (2009: 15).

46 Morgan (2009: 17).

47 Morgan (2009).

48 Mogahed (2011).

49 The AlMaghrib Institute is based in Houston, Texas, and seeks to give English-speaking students access to an "authentic" Islamic education. https://www.almaghrib.org/about/

50 Arjana (2015); Iftikhar (2018).

51 Lipka (2015).

52 Gottschalk (2013); Iftikhar (2018).

53 Searching the #Muslim hashtag outside of holidays also turns up a diverse array of images, suggesting that the space regularly offers up a representation of Muslim experience that may serve to challenge the stereotype that all Muslims are Arab and/or from Arab countries. https://www.instagram.com/explore/tags/muslim/.

54 Abdelaziz (2020); Dinee (n.d.); Karim (2006).

55 Peterson (2020).

56 Pennington (2018).

57 Baym (2010).

58 Dawkins (1976).

59 Dennett (1998: 119).

60 Burroughs (2013: 79).

61 Burroughs and Feller (2015).

62 Burroughs and Feller (2015: 373).

63 Gottschalk (2013); Iftikhar (2018).

64 Hassan (2006: 312).

65 Hassan (2006).

Chapter 12

1 Thanks to Raha Rafii, Courtney Bender, Abigail Balbale, and Kathleen Foody, who provided resources and sounding boards for this chapter.

2 For a discussion of decolonization and the museum, see Hicks (2020).

3 Wajid and Minott (2019: 30–1). For discussion on the politics of inclusion, see Ahmed (2012).

4 Rafii (2019).

5 See Said (1979). For further connections between Orientalism to religion, see Said (1981) and Ernst (2003: 55).

6 On engaging the connection between religion and culture in museum contexts, see Shatanawi (2012: 188).

7 Masuzawa (2005).

8 Rey (2019: 250).

9 Grinell (2018: 74).

10 Grinell (2018: 75, 77, 86). For discussions of other ways museums dehumanize Muslims, see Shatanawi (2012: 179) and Rey (2019: 250).

11 For a general discussion of the disciplinary nature of museums, see Levine (1988: 171–242). See also Bennett (1995: 163) and Paine (2013: 33).

12 Coones (2017: 126); Bennett (1995: 130).

13 Bennett (1995: 129).

14 Berns (2016: 163).

15 Paine (2013: 16, 33). See also Coones (2017: 139).

16 Reeve (2019: 55).

17 Gonnella (2012: 144).

18 Shaw (2019: 7).

19 See Mamdani (2004: 16–72).

20 Shaw (2019: 25).

21 Shaw (2019: 8, 2). See also Paine (2013: 15).

22 Shaw (2019: 2). This last point is reminiscent of Marshall Hodgson's idea of "Islamicate," which recognizes that non-Muslims are impacted by, consume, and can produce things that are informed by Islam, without believing themselves. Hodgson (1974: 59).

23 Shaw (2019: 6).

24 Moore (2007: 79–80).

25 Hall and Morley (2019: 44, 51).

26 During (2005: 1).

27 King (1999: 53); Rashid (2018: 92); Paine (2013: 22); Hall and Morley (2019: 38); Shaw (2019: 2).

28 Gökçiğdem (2016: xx). See also Demerdash-Fatemi (2020: 19–21). For a critique of the role of empathy in art, see Winner (2019: 189–210). For additional discussion on how cultural production embedded in narrative can change perceptions of Muslims, see Rashid (2021).

29 Cantwell and Rashid (2015).

30 Cantwell and Rashid (2015: 7).

31 Hall and Whannel (2018: 43).

32 Cantwell and Rashid (2015: 39).

33 Shaw (2012: 27).

34 Shaw (2019: 11).

35 Kreps (2003: 1, 7).

36 Demerdash-Fatemi (2020: 17).

37 Grinell (2020: 32).

38 Shaw (2019: 26).

39 Gökçiğdem (2016: xxvi); McCarthy (2019: 42); Kluszczyski (2017: 70).

40 "About the Met" (2021).

41 Bier (2017: 5).

42 See also Shaw (2019: 10).

43 Shaw (2019: 14).

44 Shaw (2019: 17–18).

45 "The British Museum: Islamic Gallery" (2021).

46 Porter and Greenwood (2020: 109–10).

47 Porter and Greenwood (2020: 112).

48 Porter and Greenwood (2020: 111).

49 Masteller (2020: 149). See also Grinell (2020).

50 Since opening in New York City in 2016, the exhibit traveled across the country to various cities. The "AtoZ" abbreviation that was used for the exhibit had a nice resonance with the librarian Mr. Atoz from *Star Trek: The Original Series* ["All Our Yesterdays," Season 3, Episode 23, 1969], as a reference to seeking as much knowledge as possible. For a brief discussion of how speculative fiction and Islamic studies intertwined in this exhibit, see Rashid (2016).

51 Martin (2019).

52 See Gökçiğdem (2016: xx–xxi). The author argues that museum exhibits mirror "our collective behavior, knowledge, conscience, complex histories, and values." However, that mirror does not have to reflect what we have done with collective knowledge but what we could do with that collective knowledge.

53 See Shaw (2019: 26).

54 Norton-Wright (2020: 3).

55 See Wajid and Minott (2019: 30); Kreps (2003: 10); Reeve (2019: 61).

56 For an introduction to Creative Commons, see https://creativecommons.org.

57 An example of an archive of religious sounds is the American Religious Sounds Project. See https://religioussounds.osu.edu.

58 "About: Archnet" (2020).

59 Frishkopf and Spinetti (2018).

60 "About Artstor" (2020).

61 https://library-artstor org.ezproxy.cul.columbia.edu/asset/ISLAMIC_DB_1031 0753078.

62 Jalayir (1860).

63 For example, see Chelkowski and Dabashi (1999).

64 See Leirvik (2010); Qa'im (2005).

65 For example, see Lewis (1994).

66 See Cantwell and Rashid (2015: 39); Ross (2006); Hill (2018).

67 See Abdullah (2009); Abdullah (2010).

68 Shaw (2019: 19).

69 Shaw (2019). See also Sila-Khan (2003).

70 For example, see Noble (2018).

71 See Junod et al. (2012: 12).

72 See Shaw (2019: 29).

73 See McCarthy (2019: 41).

74 See Coones (2017: 140).

Chapter 13

1 Eickelman and Piscatori (1996: 58).

2 For examples of this burgeoning field, see Eickelman and Anderson (1999); Hirschkind (2006), Mandaville (2007), Flood (2013), Gruber (2013), Schulz (2012), Hoesterey (2016), Izharuddin (2017), Kraidy (2017), Slama and Jones (2017), Wijaya (2017), Moll (2018), Slama and Barendregt (2018), El-Ariss (2019).

3 See essays by Shirky (2011) and Pollock (2011).

4 Kraidy (2017).

5 El-Ariss (2019: 2).

6 Althusser (1972).

7 Gruber (2013: xxiii).

8 Lim (2017).

9 I learned this while staying at a *sharī'a* hotel next to NU Garis Lurus preacher Buya Yahya (who allegedly made the remarks) in Cirebon, West Java, where I was attending *Islam Nusantara* training sessions at the local NU headquarters.

10 For expansive analyses of NU, see Robin Bush (2009), Fealy (1998).

11 NU Funny Brigade administrators granted permission to use all images from their public Instagram account: https://www.instagram.com/nugarislucu/ (accessed December 17, 2020).

12 Latu (2019).

13 El-Ariss (2019).

14 Duile (2020).

15 Roosa (2006).

16 https://kumparan.com/kumparannews/cerdas-cermat-muhammadiyah-vs-nu
-garis-lucu-1547173324641163599/full.

17 https://kumparan.com/kumparannews/cerdas-cermat-muhammadiyah-vs-nu
-garis-lucu-1547173324641163599/full.

18 https://alif.id/read/muhammad-asad/akun-garis-lucu-dan-dialog-antaragama
-b220462p/.

19 For a discussion on NU's embrace of this concept, see Fairozi (2019).

20 https://seword.com/umum/ketika-kelompok-beragama-garis-lucu-menanggapi
-muallafnya-corbuzier-fmpNIYEYwb. NU Funny Brigade also posted on their Facebook: https://www.facebook.com/NUgarisLUCU/photos /2453572134921645/ (accessed December 17, 2020).

21 This reputation aside, more recently some NU figures have fueled sectarian divides within the Muslim community. For example, Robin Bush (2015) argues persuasively that former NU leader (and current Indonesian vice president) Ma'aruf Amin stoked anti-Shi'a sentiment while serving as advisor for former president Susilo Bambang Yudhoyono.

22 Strassler (2020); see also Spyer and Steedly (2013).

23   Pinney (2016: 73).

24   Kruse, Meyer, and Korte (2018).

25   The image can be viewed on Facebook: https://www.facebook.com/
NUgarisLUCU/photos/a.1583831908562343/2496748860603972/.

26   This image can be viewed on Facebook: https://www.facebook.com/
NUgarisLUCU/photos/2438288523116673/.

27   This image can be viewed on Facebook: https://www.facebook.com/
NUgarisLUCU/photos/a.1583831908562343/2183969168548611/.

28   Hadler (2004).

29   For an analysis of Islamic concepts of passion and reason in Malaysia, see
Peletz (1996).

30   https://www.youtube.com/watch?v=QJQ2uq9Bhio.

31   https://twitter.com/nugarislucu/status/1092710928708071424.

Chapter 14

1   This narrative is based on observations made during a conversation with two
seminarians at the Computer Research Center of Islamic Science in Qum on
December 20, 2011. At the time of the interview, I was unable to learn if the
cleric had a photo associated with his Facebook profile, in which he pretended
to be a teenage girl. In the social media context of 2011, however, it is highly
unlikely that the profile would have included a photo—and even if it did, it
would probably have not displayed the person's face.

2   https://hawzah.net/fa/Occation/View/70267/-ویژه-نامه-سی-سال-حضور -(به-مناسبت-سی-
نور-—-اسلامی-علوم-کامپیوتری-تحقیقات-مرکز-تأسیس-سال-امین) (accessed March 1, 2021).

3   Feld (1981).

4   The primary focus of this study is Twelver Shīʿīsm, the largest branch of the
Shīʿī tradition that maintains a foundational belief in the leadership of the
Prophet's cousin and son-in-law, ʿAli, and his male descendants until the return
of the Twelfth *Imam*.

5   Haider (2011: 24–53).

6   The 1979 Revolution was partly a response to political and social changes in
Iran and the Global South, social disruptions that sought to create alternative
political options to the American and Soviet models.

7   *Marjaʿ* (*marājiʿ*, plural) refers to a high-ranking *mujtahid*, or jurisconsult. For
Khalaji's alarmist position, see Khalaji (2006).

8   Weber (1978: 215–16).

9   Gleave (2017: 113).

10   Green (2013: 402).

11   Amanat (2017: 309).

12 Kamaly (2018: 104).

13 See Annabelle Sreberny-Mohammadi and Ali Mohammadi (1994: 119–35).

14 Rahimi (2008: 38–9).

15 Sistani's son-in-law, Shahrestani, who first introduced the idea to the Grand Ayatollah, established the Center. Since 1996, the Center has become the host domain to a number of religious organizations and clerical websites based in Iran. According to one of his aides in Qum, Sistani and his son-in-law viewed the internet as a way to reach out to Sistani's millions of followers in an age of globalization. They saw no vice in the new technology, only the ability to spread the cause of Shīʿism. Islam, he claims, is the heart of science and the internet its capillary.

16 Most of the questions are forwarded to Najaf, where Sistani replies and his representatives forward the answer back to Qum; the rest are answered by clerics who are personally approved by Sistani as his representatives at the Center in Qum.

17 Rahimi (2011).

18 In fact, it is the Ḥussayniya's members who appear to be responsible for maintaining and updating Shakori's account.

19 Barthes (1999).

20 Rozehnal (2019: especially 28–35).

21 Borgmann (1984).

22 White (1992: 65).

23 The term "performative" is borrowed from Austin (1962).

24 Austin (1962: 14).

25 De Certeau (1984: 117).

26 Nathan Jurgenson (2020: 10).

27 Wills (2021: xiii).

Chapter 15

1 Bitton (1998).

2 Eid (2013).

3 Mamdani (2004: 18).

4 Mamdani (2004).

5 Ahmed (2000: 4).

6 Parks (2009: 163).

7 Malik (2018).

8 Cited in Caffier (2018).

9 Hall (2015: 2).

10 Hall (2015: 5).

11 Hall (2015).

12 Hall (2015: 7).

13 Hasan Elahi's "Tracking Transience" was an art installation in the Sundance
    Film Festival in 2008.

14 Moore (2010).

15 Bowe and Makki (2016).

16 Revesz (2017).

17 Massumi (2010: 53).

18 Massumi (2010: 62).

19 Massumi (2010).

20 Stabile and Kumar (2005).

21 Echchaibi (2013).

22 Cited in Whitlock (2006: 60).

23 Fluri (2009: 245).

24 Whitlock (2007: 31).

25 Brand (2002: 7).

26 Bayoumi (2009).

27 Sharpe (2016: 13).

28 Fanon (1967: 10).

29 Quoted in Gordon (2015: 58).

30 Ahmed (2014).

31 For a critique of multiculturalism and liberal theory, see Benhabib (2002) and
    Appiah (2005).

32 Glissant (1997: 5).

33 Cited in Diawara (2011: 14).

34 Glissant (1997: 190–1).

35 Bitton (1998).

BIBLIOGRAPHY

Introduction

Adi, Mohammed Munir (2014), *The Usage of Social Media in the Arab Spring: The Potential of Media to Change Political Landscapes throughout the Middle East and Africa*, Berlin: LIT Verlag.

Aggarwal, Neil Krishnan (2016), *The Taliban's Virtual Emirate: The Culture and Psychology of an Online Militant Community*, New York: Columbia University Press.

Alatas, Ismail Fajrie (2017), "Sufi Sociality in Social Media," in Carla Jones and Martin Slama (eds.), *Piety, Celebrity, Sociality: A Forum on Islam and Social Media in Southeast Asia*, American Ethnologist, November 8. Available online: http://americanethnologist.org/features/collections/piety-celebrity-sociality/sufi -sociality-in-social-media.

Alatas, Ismail Fajrie (2021), *What Is Religious Authority?: Cultivating Islamic Communities in Indonesia*, Princeton: Princeton University Press.

Aly, Anne, Stuart Macdonald, Lee Jarvis and Thomas Chen, eds. (2016), *Violent Extremism Online: New Perspectives on Terrorism and the Internet*, New York: Routledge.

Anderson, Benedict (1983), *Imagined Communities: Reflections on the Origin and Spread of Nationalism*, London: Verso.

Anderson, Jon W. (1995), "'Cyberites': Knowledge Workers and New Creoles on the Superhighway," *Anthropology Today*, 11 (4): 13–15.

Anderson, Jon W. (1997), "Globalizing Politics and Religion in the Muslim World," *The Journal of Electronic Publishing*, 3 (1). Available online: http://quod.lib .umich.edu/j/jep/T3336451.0003.116?view=text;rgn=main.

Anderson, Jon W. (1999a), "Technology, Media and the Next Generation in the Middle East," a paper delivered at the Middle East Institute, Columbia University, September 28. Available online: http://www.mafhoum.com/press3 /104T45.htm.

Anderson, Jon W. (1999b), "The Internet and Islam's New Interpreters," in Dale F. Eickelman and Jon W. Anderson (eds.), *New Media in the Muslim World: The Emerging Public Sphere*, 41–56, Bloomington: Indiana University Press.

Anderson, Jon W. (2001), "Muslim Networks, Muslim Selves in Cyberspace: Islam in the Post-Modern Public Sphere," NMIT Working Papers. www.mafhoum .com/press3/102S22.htm.

Anderson, Jon W. (2002), "Internet Islam: New Media of the Islamic Reformation," in Donna Lee Brown and Evelyn A. Early (eds.), *Every Life in the Muslim Middle East*, 300–5, Bloomington: Indiana University Press.

Anderson, Jon W. (2003), "New Media, New Publics: Reconfiguring the Public Sphere of Islam," *Social Research*, 70 (3): 887–906.

Anderson, Jon W. (2005), "Wiring Up: The Internet Difference for Muslim Networks," in miriam cooke and Bruce B. Lawrence (eds.), *Muslim Networks: From Hajj to Hip Hop*, 252–63, Chapel Hill: University of North Carolina Press.

Baldanzi, Jessica, and Hussein Rashid, eds. (2020), *Ms. Marvel's America: No Normal*, Jackson: University Press of Mississippi.

Baulch, Emma, and Alila Pramiyanti (2018), "Hijabers on Instagram: Using Visual Social Media to Construct the Ideal Muslim Woman," *Social Media+ Society*, October–December: 1–15.

Bhabha, Homi (1994), *The Location of Culture*, New York: Routledge.

Brandon, James (2008), *Virtual Caliphate: Islamic Extremists and Their Websites*, London: Centre for Social Cohesion.

Bunt, Gary R. (2000), *Virtually Islamic: Computer-Mediated Communication and Cyber Islamic Environments*, Cardiff: University of Wales Press.

Bunt, Gary R. (2003), *Islam in the Digital Age: E-Jihad, Online Fatwas and Cyber Islamic Environments*, London: Pluto Press.

Bunt, Gary R. (2005), "Defining Islamic Interconnectivity," in miriam cooke and Bruce B. Lawrence (eds.), *Muslim Networks: From Hajj to Hip Hop*, 235–51, Chapel Hill: University of North Carolina Press.

Bunt, Gary R. (2009), *iMuslims: Rewiring the House of Islam*, Chapel Hill: University of North Carolina Press.

Bunt, Gary R. (2010), "Surfing the App Souq: Islamic Applications for Mobile Devices," *CyberOrient*, 4 (1): 3–18.

Bunt, Gary R. (2014), "#islam, Social Networking and the Cloud," in Jeffrey Kenney and Ebrahim Moosa (eds.), *Islam in the Modern World*, 177–208, New York: Routledge.

Bunt, Gary R. (2018), *Hashtag Islam: How Cyber-Islamic Environments Are Transforming Religious Authority*, Chapel Hill: University of North Carolina Press.

Cantwell, Christopher D., and Hussein Rashid (2015), *Religion, Media, and the Digital Turn*, Brooklyn: Social Science Research Council.

cooke, miriam, and Bruce B. Lawrence (2005), "Introduction," in miriam cooke and Bruce B. Lawrence (eds.), *Muslim Networks: From Hajj to Hip Hop*, 1–30, Chapel Hill: University of North Carolina Press.

Echchaibi, Nabil (2008), "Hyper-Islamism?: Mediating Islam from the Halal Website to the Islamic Talk Show," *Journal of Arab and Muslim Media Research*, 1 (3): 199–214.

Echchaibi, Nabil (2011a), "From Audio Tapes to Video Blogs: The Delocation of Authority in Islam," *Nations and Nationalism*, 17 (1): 25–44.

Echchaibi, Nabil (2011b), "Gendered Blueprints: Transnational Masculinities in Muslim Televangelist Cultures," in Radha Hegde (ed.), *Circuits of Visibility: Gender and Transnational Media Cultures*, 80–102, New York: New York University Press.

Echchaibi, Nabil (2012), "Alt-Muslim: Muslims and Modernity's Discontents," in Heidi Campbell (ed.), *Digital Religion: Understanding Religious Practice in New Media Worlds*, 119–38, New York: Routledge.

Echchaibi, Nabil (2013), "American Muslims and the Media," in Juliane Hammer and Omid Safi (eds.), *The Cambridge Companion to American Islam*, 119–38, Cambridge: Cambridge University Press.

Echchaibi, Nabil (2014) "Muslimah Media Watch: Muslim Media Activism and Social Change," *Journalism: Theory, Practice and Criticism*, 14 (7): 852–67.

Eickelman, Dale F., and Jon W. Anderson (1999), "Redefining Muslim Publics," in Dale F. Eickelman and Jon W. Anderson (eds.), *New Media in the Muslim World: The Emerging Public Sphere*, 1–18, Bloomington: Indiana University Press.

Elfenbein, Caleb et al. (website), "Mapping Islamophobia: Visualizing Islamophobia and Its Effects in the United States." Available online: http://mappingislamophobia.org.

Elfenbein, Caleb (2021), *Fear in Our Hearts: What Islamophobia Tells Us about America*, New York: New York University Press.

El-Nawawy, Mohammed, and Sahar Khamis (2009), *Islam Dot Com: Contemporary Islamic Discourses in Cyberspace*, New York: Palgrave Macmillan.

El-Nawawy, Mohammed, and Sahar Khamis (2012a), "Cyberactivists Paving the Way for the Arab Spring: Voices from Egypt, Tunisia and Libya," *CyberOrient*, 6 (2): 4–27. Available online: https://cyberorient.net/2012/11/10/cyberactivists -paving-the-way-for-the-arab-spring-voices-from-egypt-tunisia-and-libya/.

El-Nawawy, Mohammed, and Sahar Khamis (2012b), "Political Activism 2.0: Comparing the Role of Social Media in Egypt's 'Facebook Revolution' and Iran's 'Twitter Uprising'," *CyberOrient*, 6 (1): 8–33. Available online: https:// cyberorient.net/2012/05/10/political-activism-2-0-comparing-the-role-of-social -media-in-egypts-facebook-revolution-and-irans-twitter-uprising/.

El-Nawawy, Mohammed, and Sahar Khamis (2013), *Egyptian Revolution 2.0: Political Blogging, Civic Engagement, and Citizen Journalism*, New York: Palgrave Macmillan.

El-Nawawy, Mohammed, and Sahar Khamis (2014), "Blogging against Violations of Human Rights in Egypt: An Analysis of Five Political Blogs," *International Journal of Communication*, 8: 962–82.

Faris, David M., and Babak Rahimi, eds. (2015), *Social Media in Iran: Politics and Society after 2009*, Albany: Statue University of New York Press.

Freedom House (2016), "Silencing the Messenger: Communication Apps under Pressure," *Freedom on the Net*. Available online: https://freedomhouse.org/ report/freedom-net/freedom-net-2016.

German, Kathleen, and Rosemary Pennington (2019), "Sisters of the Caliphate: Media and the Women of ISIS," *Journal of Vincentian Social Action*, 4 (2): Available online: https://scholar.stjohns.edu/jovsa/vol4/iss2/7.

Gibson, William (1984), *Neuromancer*, New York: Penguin Random House.

Goehring, Dorothy Lee (2019), "Muslim Women on the Internet: Social Media as Sites of Identity Formation," *Journal of South Asian and Middle Eastern Studies*, 42 (3): 20–34.

Habermas, Jurgen (1991), *The Structural Transformation of the Public Sphere: An Inquiry into a Category of Bourgeois Society*, Boston, MA: MIT Press.

Hermansen, Marcia (2014), "The Emergence of Media Preachers: Yusuf al-Qaradawi," in Jeffrey Kenney and Ebrahim Moosa (eds.), *Islam in the Modern World*, 301–18, New York: Routledge.

Hirshkind, Charles (2012), "Experiments in Devotion Online: The YouTube Khutba," *IJMES*, 44 (1): 5–21.

Hoesterey, James Bourk (2015), *Rebranding Islam: Piety, Prosperity, and a Self-Help Guru*, Palo Alto: Stanford University Press.

Hoesterey, James Bourk (2019), "Politicians, Pop Preachers, and Public Scandal: A Personal Politics of *Adab*," in Robert Rozehnal (ed.), *Piety, Politics, and Everyday Ethics in Southeast Asian Islam: Beautiful Behavior*, London: Bloomsbury Academic.

Hofheinz, Albrecht (2005), "The Internet in the Arab World: Playground for Political Liberalization." Available online: http://library.fes.de/pdf-files/id/ipg/02941.pdf.

Howard, Philip (2010), *The Digital Origins of Dictatorship and Democracy: Information Technology and Political Islam*, Oxford: Oxford University Press.

Howard, Philip, and Muzammil M. Hussain (2013), *Democracy's Fourth Wave?: Digital Media and the Arab Spring*, Oxford: Oxford University Press.

Jamali, Reza (2015), *Online Arab Spring: Social Media and Fundamental Change*, Waltham: Chandos Publishing.

Kavakci, Elif, and Camille R. Kraeplin (2017), "Religious Beings in Fashionable Bodies: The Online Identity Construction of *Hijabi* Social Media Personalities," *Media, Culture & Society*, 39 (6): 850–68.

Khabeer, Su'ad Abudul, and Maytha Al Hassen (2013), "Muslim Youth Cultures," in Juliane Hammer and Omid Safi (eds.), *The Cambridge Companion to American Islam*, 299–311, Cambridge: Cambridge University Press.

Khamis, Sahar (2010), "Islamic Feminism in New Arab Media: Platforms for Self-Expression and Sites for Multiple Resistances," *Journal of Arab and Muslim Media Research*, 3 (3): 237–55.

Khamis, Sahar (2017), "The Internet and New Communication Dynamics among Diasporic Muslims: Opportunities, Challenges and Paradoxes," in Merve R. Kayikci and Leen D'Haenens (eds.), *European Muslims and New Media*, 35–52, Leuven: Leuven University Press.

Khamis, Sahar (2018), "American Muslims' E-Jihad: Trumping Islamophobia in the Trump Era," *CyberOrient*, 12 (1): 87–94. Available online: https://cyberorient .net/2018/05/10/american-muslims-e-jihad-trumping-islamophobia-in-the-trump -era/.

Khamis, Sahar (2019), "The Arab Media Landscape One Year after Khashoggi: Louder Opposition, More Repressions, and Zero Accountability," Inside Arabia: Voice of the Arab People, October 29. Available online: https://insidearabia.com /the-arab-media-landscape-one-year-after-khashoggi-louder-opposition-more -repression-and-zero-accountability/.

Khamis, Sahar, and Eliza Campbell (2020), "Info-Deficiency in an Infodemic: The Gender Digital Gap, Arab Women, and the COVID-19 Pandemic," *Arab Media & Society*, September 27. Available online: https://www.arabmediasociety.com /info-deficiency-in-an-infodemic-the-gender-digital-gap-arab-women-and-the -covid-19-pandemic/.

Khamis, Sahar, and Amel Mili, eds. (2018), *Arab Women's Activism and Socio-Political Transformation: Unfinished Gender Revolutions*, Cham: Palgrave Macmillan.

Khamis, Sahar, Paul B. Gold, and Katherine Vaughn (2020), "Beyond Egypt's 'Facebook Revolution' and Syria's 'YouTube Uprising': Comparing Political Contexts, Actors, and Communication Strategies," *Arab Media & Society*,

March 28. Available online: https://www.arabmediasociety.com/beyond-egypts
-facebook-revolution-and-syrias-youtube-uprising-comparing-political-contexts
-actors-and-communication-strategies/.

Krona, Michael, and Rosemary Pennington, eds. (2019), *The Media World of ISIS*,
Bloomington: Indiana University Press.

Larsson, Goran (2005), "The Death of a Virtual Muslim Discussion Group: Issues
and Methods in Analyzing Religion on the Net," *Online Heidelberg Journal of
Religions on the Internet*, 1 (1): 1–18.

Larsson, Goran (2007), "Cyber-Islamophobia?: The Case of Wikiislam,"
Contemporary Islam, 1: 53–67.

Larsson, Goran (2016), *Muslims and the New Media: Historical and
Contemporary Debates*, New York: Routledge.

Lawrence, Bruce B. (2002), "Allah On-Line: The Practice of Global Islam in the
Information Age," in Stewart M. Hoover and Lynn Schofield Clark (eds.),
*Practicing Religion in the Age of the Media: Explorations of Media, Religion
and Culture*, 237–53, New York: Columbia University Press.

Lim, Merlyna (2005), *Islamic Radicalism and Anti-Americanism in Indonesia: The
Role of the Internet*, Washington, D.C.: East West Center.

Lo, Mbaye, and Taimoor Aziz (2009), "Muslim Marriage Goes Online: The Use of
Internet Matchmaking by American Muslims," *Journal of Religion and Popular
Culture*, 21 (3): 1–22.

Maguire, Musa (2006), "The Islamic Internet: Authority, Authenticity and
Reform," in Daya Thussu (ed.), *Media on the Move: Global Flow and Contra-
Flow*, 237–50, London: Routledge.

Mandaville, Peter (1999), "Digital Islam: Changing the Boundaries of Religious
Knowledge?" *ISIM Newsletter* 2.

Mandaville, Peter (2002), "Reimagining the *Ummah*?: Information Technology and
the Changing Boundaries of Political Islam," in Ali Mohammadi (ed.), *Islam
Encountering Globalization*, 61–90, London: Routledge.

Mandaville, Peter (2003), "Communication and Diasporic Islam: A Virtual
Ummah?" in Karim H. Karim (ed.), *The Media of Diaspora*, 135–47, London:
Routledge.

Marcotte, Roxanne (2010), "Gender and Sexuality Online on Australian Muslim
Forums," *Contemporary Islam*, 4 (1): 117–38.

Morales, Harold (2018), *Latino and Muslim in America: Race, Religion, and the
Making of a New Minority*, New York: Oxford University Press.

Nunns, Alex, and Nadia Idle, eds. (2011), *Tweets from Tahrir: Egypt's Revolution
as It Unfolded, In the Words of the People Who Made It*, New York: OR Books.

Oshan, Maryam (2009), *Saudi Women and the Internet: Culture and Gender
Issues*, Saarbrucken: VDM.

Pennington, Rosemary (2018a), "Making Space in Social Media:
#MuslimWomensDay in Twitter," *Journal of Communication Inquiry*, 42 (3):
199–217.

Pennington, Rosemary (2018b), "New Media and Muslim Voices," in Rosemary
Pennington and Hilary E. Khan (eds.), *On Islam: Muslims and the Media*,
110–20, Bloomington: Indiana University Press.

Pennington, Rosemary (2018c), "Social Media as Third Spaces?: Exploring Muslim
Identity and Connection Tumblr," *The International Communication Gazette*,
80 (7): 620–36

Pennington, Rosemary (2019), "Witnessing the 2014 Gaza War in Tumblr," *The International Communication Gazette*, 0 (0): 1–19.

Peterson, Kristin M. (2020a), "Hybrid Styles, Interstitial Spaces, and the Digital Advocacy of the Salafi Feminist," *Critical Studies in Media Communication*, 37 (3): 254–66.

Peterson, Kristin M. (2020b), "The Unruly, Loud, and Intersectional Muslim Woman: Interrupting the Aesthetic Styles of Islamic Fashion Images on Instagram," *International Journal of Communication*, 14: 1194–213.

Peterson, Kristin M., and Nabil Echchaibi (2017), "Mipsterz: Hip, American and Muslim," in Bryce David Forbes and Jeffrey H. Mahan (eds.), *Religion and Popular Culture in America*, 144–58, Oakland: University of California Press.

Piela, Anna (2012), *Muslim Women Online: Faith and Identity in Virtual Space*, New York: Routledge.

Piela, Anna (2015), "Online Islamic Spaces as Communities of Practice for Female Muslim Converts Who Wear the Niqab," *Hawwa: Journal of Women of the Middle East and the Islamic World*, 13 (3): 363–82.

Piela, Anna (2021), *Wearing the Niqab: Muslim Women in the UK and US*, London: Bloomsbury Academic.

Radsch, Courtney, and Sahar Khamis (2013), "In Their Own Voice: Technologically Mediated Empowerment and Transformation among Young Arab Women," *Feminist Media Studies*, 13 (5): 881–90.

Rahimi, Babak (2011), "The Agonistic Social Media: Cyberspace in the Formation of Dissent and Consolidation of State Power in Post-Election Iran," *The Communication Review*, 14: 158–78.

Rahimi, Babak (2013), "The State of Digital Exception: Censorship and Dissent in Post-Revolutionary Iran," in Muzammil Hussain and Philip Howard (eds.), *State Power 2.0: Authoritarian Entrenchment and Political Engagement Worldwide*, 33–44, New York: Routledge.

Rahimi, Babak (2015a), "Censorship and the Islam Republic: Two Modes of Regulatory Measures for Media in Iran," *The Middle East Journal*, 69 (3): 358–78.

Rahimi, Babak (2015b), "Rethinking Digital Technologies in the Middle East," *International Journal of the Middle East Studies*, 47 (2): 362–5.

Rahimi, Babak (2016), "*Vahid* Online: Post-2009 Iran and Politics of Citizen Media Convergence," *Social Sciences*, 5 (4): 77. Available online: http://www.mdpi.com/2076-0760/5/4/77.

Rahimi, Babak (2018), "Digital *Javanmardi*: Chivalric Ethics and Imagined Iran on the Internet," in Lloyd Ridgeon (ed.), *Javanmardi: The Ethics and Practice of Persianate Perfection*, 281–96, London: Gingko Library.

Ramsay, Gilbert (2013), *Jihadi Culture on the World Wide Web*, New York: Bloomsbury.

Rippin, Andrew (2014), "The Quran on the Internet: Implications and Future Possibilities," in Thomas Hoffman and Goran Larsson (eds.), *Muslims and the New Information and Communication Technologies: Notes From an Emerging and Infinite Field*, 113–28, New York: Springer.

Robinson, Francis (1996), "Islam and the Impact of Print in South Asia," in Nigel Crook (ed.), *The Transmission of Knowledge in South Asia: Essays on Education, Religion, History and Politics*, Delhi: Oxford University Press.

Rozehnal, Robert (2019), *Cyber Sufis: Virtual Expressions of the American Muslim Experience*, London: Oneworld Academic.

Sands, Kristin Zahra (2010), "Muslims, Identity and Multimodal Communication on the Internet," *Contemporary Islam*, 4 (1): 139–55.

Sijapati, Megan Adamson (2019), "Sufi Remembrance Practices in the Meditation Marketplace of a Mobile App," in Jacqueline H. Fewkes (ed.), *Anthropological Perspectives on the Religious Uses of Mobile Apps*, 19–41, Cham: Palgrave Macmillan.

Sisler, Vit (2011), "Cyber Counsellors: Online *Fatwas*, Arbitration Tribunals and the Construction of Muslim Identity in the UK," *Information, Communication and Society*, 14 (8): 1136–59.

Sisler, Vit (2013), "Play Muslim Hero: Construction of Identity in Video Games," in Heidi Campbell (ed.), *Digital Religion: Understanding Religious Practice in New Media Worlds*, 136–46, New York: Routledge.

Sreberny, Annabelle (2015), "Women's Digital Activism in a Changing Middle East," *International Journal of Middle East Studies*, 47 (2): 357–61.

Stanton, Andrea (2017), "Islamic Emoticons and Religious Authority: Emerging Practices, Shifting Paradigms," *Journal of Contemporary Islam*, 12: 153–71.

Stanton, Andrea (2020), "Saudi Arabia's Ministry of *Hajj* Apps: Managing the Operations and Piety of the *Hajj*," *Journal of Religion, Media, and Digital Culture*, 9 (2): 228–46.

Varisco, Daniel Martin (2010), "Muslims and the Media in the Blogosphere," *Contemporary Islam*, 4 (1): 157–77.

Wheeler, Deborah (2005), *The Internet in the Middle East: Global Expectations and Local Imaginations in Kuwait*, New York: State University of New York Press.

Zaman, Saminaz (2008), "From *Imam* to Cyber *Mufti*: Consuming Identity in Muslim America," *The Muslim World*, 98 (October): 465–74.

Chapter 1

About Islam (2021). Available online: https://aboutislam.net (accessed January 7, 2021).

Abusharif, Ibrahim N. (2019), "Cyber-Islamic Environments and Salafī-Ṣūfī Contestations Appropriating Digital Media and Challenges to Religious Authority," PhD diss., University of Wales Trinity Saint David.

Akhbar el-Yom (2020), "Statement from Minister of Endowments Muhammad Mukhtar Jumaa." Available online: https://akhbarelyom.com (accessed March 18, 2020).

Al-Azhar (2020a), Twitter, November 11. Available online: https://twitter.com/AlAzhar/status/1326484004032360454.

Al-Azhar (2020b), "*Eid ul-Fitr*," *Twitter*, May 24. Available online: https://twitter.com/AlAzhar/status/1264409252505911297.

Al-Azhar (2020c), "Tweet Emphasizing Precautionary Measures," *Twitter*, September 4. Available online: https://twitter.com/AlAzhar/status/1264409252505911297.

Al-Qaradaghi, Ali Mohieddin (2020), *International Union of Muslim Scholars*, March 3. Available online: http://iumsonline.org/ar/ContentDetails.aspx?ID=11019.

Arab News (2020), "Hagia Sophia Prayers Sparked Turkey's New COVID-19 Cases," August 12. Available online: https://arab.news/crbkh.

Arjana, Sophia Rose (2017), *Pilgrimage in Islam: Traditional and Modern Practices*, London: Oneworld Academic.

Associated Press (2019), "AI-powered Chatbot Gives Muslims Religious Guidance." Available online: https://youtu.be/-V4yRuEgaAA (accessed November 6, 2019).

Brown, Nathan J. (2020), "Death on the Nile," Malcolm H. Kerr Carnegie Middle East Centre, March 27. Available online: https://carnegie-mec.org/diwan/81379 (accessed September 7, 2020).

Bunt, Gary R. (1996), "Decision Making and Idjtihad in Islamic Environments: A Comparative Study of Pakistan, Malaysia, Singapore and the United Kingdom," PhD diss., University of Wales, Lampeter.

Bunt, Gary R. (2000), *Virtually Islamic: Computer-Mediated Communication and Cyber Islamic Environments*, Cardiff: University of Wales Press.

Bunt, Gary R. (2003), *Islam in the Digital Age: E-jihad, Online Fatwas and Cyber Islamic Environments*, London & Michigan: Pluto Press.

Bunt, Gary R. (2009), *iMuslims: Rewiring the House of Islam*, Chapel Hill: University of North Carolina Press.

Bunt, Gary R. (2015), "Decoding the *Hajj* in Cyberspace," in Eric Tagliacozzo and Shawkat M. Toorawa (eds.), *The Hajj: Pilgrimage in Islam*, 231–40, Cambridge: Cambridge University Press.

Bunt, Gary R. (2018), *Hashtag Islam: How Cyber Islamic Environments Are Transforming Religious Authority*, Chapel Hill: University of North Carolina Press.

Bunt, Gary R. (2020), "#FemaleReciters," Virtually Islamic Blog. Available online: https://virtuallyislamic.com/virtuallyislamicblog/?id=femalereciters.

Cox, Joseph (2020), "How the U.S. Military Buys Location Data from Ordinary Apps," Motherboard/Vice, November 16. Available online: https://www.vice .com/amp/en/article/jgqm5x/us-military-location-data-xmode-locate-x.

Darul Ifta, Darul Uloom Deoband India (2020). Available online: http://www .darulifta-deoband.com (accessed December 10, 2020).

Deenspiration (2020a), "Episode 44: Covid-19 through the Lens of Spirituality— Shaykh Ruzwan Mohammed," October 22. Available online: https:// deenspiration.com/covid-19-through-the-lens-of-spirituality-shaykh-ruzwan -mohammed/.

Deenspiration (2020b), "Ramadan Q&A with Shaykh Amer Jamil: The *Fiqh* of Fasting in Light of COVID-19," April 21. Available online: https://deenspiration .com/fiqh-of-Ramadan-shaykh-amer-jamil/.

Durmaz, Mucahid (2020), "Friday Prayer with Social Distancing at Istanbul's Fatih Mosque," *Twitter*, April 29. Available online: https://twitter.com/ mucahiddurmaz/status/1266347899908231169?lang=en.

El-Nawawy, Mohamed A., and Sahar Khamis (2009), *Islam Dot Com*, New York: Palgrave Macmillan.

Fakude, Thembisa (2014), "Al Jazeera Studies, Arab World Journalist in a Post-Beheading Era." Available online: http://studies.aljazeera.net/en/reports/2014/12 /2014121095622836950.html (accessed December 10, 2014).

Hegghammer, Thomas (2009), "Jihadi-Salafis or Revolutionaries: On Religion and Politics in the Study of Militant Islamism," in Roel Meijer (ed.), *Global Salafism: Islam's New Religious Movement*, 244–66, London: C. Hurst & Company.

IQRA Cartoon (2018), "Childhood-Muhammad Story Ep 2." Available online: https://youtu.be/lNP_QsSQkoA (accessed January 6, 2021).

Islamic Portal (2020a), "Covid-19: Status of Performing Salah in the Masjids and Restrictions," July 9. Available online: https://islamicportal.co.uk/covid-19 -status-of-performing-salah-in-the-masjids-and-restrictions/.

Islamic Portal (2020b), "Hadith Transmission via Internet and Phone," June 14. Available online: https://islamicportal.co.uk/hadith-transmission-via-internet -and-phone/ (accessed August 9, 2020).

Islamic Portal (2020c), "Wearing a Mask in Ihram," June 14. Available online: https://islamicportal.co.uk/wearing-a-mask-in-ihram/.

IslamQA (2020a), "Because of Lockdown and the Coronavirus, Is It Permissible to Offer the Eid Prayer at Home?" number18351, May 20. Available online: https://islamqa.info.

IslamQA (2020b), "How Can Someone Who Is Wearing PPE (Personal Protective Equipment) to Guard against Viruses Do Wudoo' and Pray?" Available online: https://islamqa.info.

IslamQA (2020c), "What Is the Ruling on Not Attending Friday (*Jumu'ah*) Prayer in Congregation in the Event of an Epidemic or Fear of an Epidemic?," #333514, March 12. Available online: https://islamqa.info.

Khan, Aina J. (2020), *Twitter*. Available online: https://twitter.com/ainajkhan (accessed July 31, 2020).

Kutty, Sheikh Ahmad (2018), "Ask the Scholar." Available online: https:// askthescholar.com/ (accessed January 7, 2021).

Kutty, Sheikh Ahmad (2020), "On Holding Virtual/Online *Jumu'ahs* and *Taraweeh Salats* During COVID-19 Precautions," *Islamic Institute of Toronto*, April 2. Available online: https://islam.ca/virtual-jumuah-and-taraweeh-during-covid/ (accessed April 2, 2020).

Lauzière, Henri (2015), *The Making of Salafism: Islamic Reform in the Twentieth Century*, New York: Columbia University Press.

Mandaville, Peter (2014), "Globalisation and Muslim Societies," in Kate Fleet, Gudrun Krämer, Denis Matringe, John Nawas and Everett Rowson (eds.), *Encyclopaedia of Islam, THREE*, Leiden: Brill. Available online: http://dx.doi .org/10.1163/1573-3912_ei3_COM_27486 (accessed March 3, 2021).

Menk, Mufti Ismail (2020), Available online: https://muftimenk.com/ (accessed November 1, 2020).

Mudasir_100 (2020), "Corona Virus," TikTok. Available online: https://www.tiktok .com/@mudasir_100/video/6805950696962264325 (accessed September 9, 2020).

OnePath Network (2020), "The Reason Why Mufti Menk Is NOT on TikTok," March 29. Available online: https://youtu.be/O8yJmcQj6Iw (accessed January 7, 2021).

Reminder4Believer (2020), "Dr Muhammad Salah, Islamic Ruling for Or@l $ex," TikTok. Available online: https://www.tiktok.com/@reminder4believer/video /6887244140367727873 (accessed November 1, 2020).

ShoroukNews (2020), Available online: https://www.shorouknews.com/news/ view.aspx?cdate=21032020&id=865da3c7-e0c2-46d2-860d-078cbace63ac (accessed March 21, 2020).

Smith Galer, Sophia (2020), "Heart and Soul, The Lives of Female Qur'an Reciters," BBC World Service, September 18. Available online: https://www.bbc .co.uk/programmes/w3ct0x63.

Stanton, Andrea L. (2020), "Saudi Arabia's Ministry of Hajj Apps: Managing the Operations and Piety of the Hajj," *Journal of Religion, Media and Digital Culture*, 9: 228–46.

State Information Services (2020), "Council of Senior Scholars Urges Egyptians to Abide by Anti-COVID-19 Measures." Available online: https://sis.gov.eg/Story /145378/Council-of-Senior-Scholars-urges-Egyptians-to-abide-by-anti-COVID -19-measures?lang=en-us (accessed April 4, 2020).

TalabeToday (2020), September 9. Available online: https://www.instagram.com/ talabetoday/?hl=en.

The Islamic Information (2019), "Is Making TikTok Haram in Islam or for Muslims?" Available online: https://theislamicinformation.com/tiktok-haram-in -islam/ (accessed October 9, 2019).

TikTok (2020), "Search: #haramain." Available online: https://www.tiktok.com/tag/ haramain?lang=en (accessed June 9, 2020).

TVQuran (2020), "Islamic Guidance." Available online: https://www.tiktok.com/ tag/tvquran (accessed November 13, 2020).

Versi, Miqdaad (2020), "Video: Shaykh Yunus Dudhwala, National Burial Council, Senior Hospital Chaplain, London," Twitter, April 3. Available online: https:// twitter.com/miqdaad/status/1245774544104828929.

Virtual Ifta (2019), Available online: www.iacad.gov.ae (accessed October 30, 2019).

Webb, Suhail (2020), *Instagram*, May 7. Available online: https://www.instagram .com/suhaib.webb/?hl=en.

Wiktorowicz, Quintan (2005), "The Salafi Movement," in miriam cooke and Bruce B. Lawrence (eds.), *Muslim Networks from Hajj to Hip Hop*, 208–34, Chapel Hill: University of North Carolina Press.

Chapter 2

Ammerman, Nancy (2007), *Everyday Religion: Observing Modern Religious Lives*, New York: Oxford University Press.

Ammerman, Nancy T. (2016), "Lived Religion as an Emerging Field: An Assessment of Its Edges and Frontiers," *Nordic Journal of Religion and Society*, 2: 83–99.

Bunt, Gary R. (2018), *Hashtag Islam: How Cyber-Islamic Environments Are Transforming Religious Authority*, Chapel Hill: University of North Carolina Press.

Campbell, Heidi (2013), *Digital Religion: Understanding Religious Practice in New Media Worlds*, London: Routledge.

El-Nawawy, Mohammed, and Sahar Khamis (2009), *Islam Dot Com: Contemporary Islamic Discourses in Cyberspace*, New York: Palgrave Macmillan.

Furlanetto, Elena (2013), "The 'Rumi Phenomenon' between Orientalism and Cosmopolitanism: The Case of Elif Shafak's *The Forty Rules of Love*," *European Journal of English Studies*, 17 (2): 201–13.

Helland, Christopher (2007), "Diaspora on the Electronic Frontier: Developing Virtual Connections with Sacred Homelands," *Journal of Computer-Mediated Communication*, 12 (2): 956–76.

Hoover, Stewart M. (2016), *The Media and Religious Authority*, University Park: Penn State University Press.

Jeldtoft, Nadia (2011), "Lived Islam: Religious Identity with 'Non-Organised' Muslim Minorities," *Ethnic and Racial Studies*, 34 (7): 1134–51.

Lewis, Franklin (2000), *Rumi: Past and Present, East and West: The Life, Teaching and Poetry of Jalâl Al-Din Rumi*, Oxford: Oneworld Publications.

Marcotte, Roxanne D. (2016), "*Fatwa* Online: Novel Patterns of Production and Consumption," in Noha Mellor and Khalil Rinnawi (eds.), *Political Islam and Global Media: The Boundaries of Religious Identity*, 231–45, Abington: Routledge.

McGuire, Meredith (2008), *Lived Religion: Faith and Practice in Everyday Life*, New York: Oxford University Press.

Orsi, Robert (2006), *Between Heaven and Earth: The Religious Worlds People Make and the Scholars Who Study Them*, Princeton: Princeton University Press.

Peterson, M. Kristin and Nabil Echchaibi (2017), "Mipsterz: Hip, American and Muslim," in Bruce D. Forbes (ed.), *Religion and Popular Culture in America*, 3rd ed., 145–57, Oakland: University of California Press.

Rozehnal, Robert (2019), *Cyber Sufis: Virtual Expressions of the American Muslim Experience*, Oneworld Publications.

Chapter 3

AlKisah (2003), "Konsultasi Spiritual: Misteri Mengamalkan Doa Nurbuwat," no. 5, September 15–28: 82–3.

AlKisah (2004), "Habib Lutfi bin Yahya: Meneduhkan Hati Umat dengan Doa," no. 1, January 5–18: 36–41.

AlKisah (2004), "Habib Luthfi bin Yahya: Tokoh dengan 30 Juta Umat," no. 25, December 6–19 December: 30–3.

AlKisah (2004), "Konsultasi Spiritual: Bertarekat tanpa Guru," no. 24, November 22–December 5: 83–4.

AlKisah (2005), "Habib M. Luthfi bin Yahya: Menanamkan Kalimat Tauhid di Kalbu," no. 7, March 28–April 10: 32–4.

AlKisah (2005), "Konsultasi Spiritual: Ingin Masuk Tarekat Sadzaliyah," no. 1, January 3–16: 87–8.

AlKisah (2005), "Muktamar Tarekat: Banyak jalan menuju Allah," no. 7, March 28–April 10: 14–21.

AlKisah (2007), "Konsultasi Spiritual: Makna Mimpi dan Minta Jodoh," *alKisah*, no. 8, April 9–22: 132–3.

Arendt, Hannah ([1954] 2006), *Between Past and Future: Eight Exercises in Political Thought*, New York: Penguin.

Brenner, Suzanne (1996), "Reconstructing Self and Society: Javanese Muslim Women and 'The Veil'," *American Ethnologist*, 23 (4): 673–97.

Campbell, Heidi A. (2010), *When Religion Meets New Media*, New York: Routledge.

Chih, Rachida (2007), "What Is a Sufi Order? Revisiting the Concept through a Case Study of the Khalwatiyya in Contemporary Egypt," in Martin van

Bruinessen and Julia Day Howell (eds.), *Sufism and the "Modern" in Islam*, 21–38, London: I.B. Tauris.

Coleman, E. Gabriella (2010), "Ethnographic Approaches to Digital Media," *Annual Review of Anthropology* 39: 487–505.

De La Cruz, Deridre (2015), *Mother Figured: Marian Apparitions and the Making of a Filipino Universal*, Chicago: University of Chicago Press.

de Vries, Hent (2001), "In Media Res: Global Religion, Public Spheres, and the Task of Contemporary Religious Studies," in Hent de Vries and Samuel Weber (eds.), *Religion and Media*, 3–42, Stanford: Stanford University Press.

Engelke, Matthew (2010), "Religion and the Media Turn," *American Ethnologist*, 37 (2): 371–9.

Engelke, Matthew (2007), *A Problem of Presence: Beyond Scripture in an African Church*, Berkeley: University of California Press.

Eickelman, Dale F., and Jon W. Anderson, eds. (1999), *New Media in the Muslim World: The Emerging Public Sphere*, Bloomington: Indiana University Press.

Eisenlohr, Patrick (2018), *Sounding Islam: Voice, Media, and Sonic Atmosphere in an Indian Ocean World*, Berkeley: University of California Press.

Eisenlohr, Patrick (2009), "Technologies of the Spirit: Devotional Islam, Sound Reproduction, and the Dialectics of Mediation and Immediacy in Mauritius," *Anthropological Theory*, 9 (3): 273–96.

Halman, Hugh T. (2013), *Where the Two Seas Meet: The* Qur'ānic *Story of Al-Khiḍr and Moses in Sufi Commentaries as a Model of Spiritual Guidance*, Knoxville: Fons Vitae.

Hefner, Robert W. (2000), *Civil Islam: Muslims and Democratization in Indonesia*, Princeton: Princeton University Press.

Hirschkind, Charles (2006), *The Ethical Soundscape: Cassette Sermons and Islamic Counterpublics*, New York: Columbia University Press.

Hirschkind, Charles, and Brian Larkin (2008), "Introduction: Media and the Political Forms of Religion," *Social Text* 26 (3): 1–9.

Hoesterey, James B. (2016), *Rebranding Islam: Piety, Prosperity, and a Self-Help Guru*, Stanford: Stanford University Press.

Howell, Julia D. (2001), "Sufism and the Indonesian Islamic Revival," *Journal of Asian Studies*, 60 (3): 701–29.

Husein, Fatimah, and Martin Slama (2018), "Online Piety and Its Discontent: Revisiting Islamic Anxieties on Indonesian Social Media," *Indonesia and the Malay World*, 46 (134): 80–93.

Keane, Webb (2018), "On Semiotic Ideology," *Signs and Society*, 6 (1): 64–87.

Larkin, Brian (2004), "Bandiri Music, Globalization, and Urban Experience in Nigeria," *Social Text*, 22 (4): 91–112.

Latif, Yudi (2005), *Inteligensia Muslim dan Kuasa: Genealogi Inteligensia Muslim Indonesia abad ke-20*, Bandung: Mizan.

Latour, Bruno (2005), *Reassembling the Social: An Introduction to Actor-Network-Theory*, Oxford: Oxford University Press.

Liddle, William R. (1996), "The Islamic Turn in Indonesia: A Political Explanation," *Journal of Asian Studies*, 55 (3): 613–34.

Meri, Josef. W. (2010), "Relics of Piety and Power in Medieval Islam," *Past and Present*, 206, (s. 5): 97–120.

Messick, Brinkley (1993), *The Calligraphic State: Textual Domination and History in a Muslim Society*, Berkeley: University of California Press.

Meyer, Birgit, ed. (2009), *Aesthetic Formations: Media, Religion, and the Senses*, New York: Palgrave Macmillan.

Pandolfo, Stefania (1997), *Impasse of the Angels: Scenes from a Moroccan Space of Memory*, Chicago: University of Chicago Press.

Rasmussen, Anne (2010), *Women, the Recited Qur'an, and Islamic Music in Indonesia*, Berkeley: University of California Press.

Renard, John (2008), *Friends of God: Islamic Images of Piety, Commitment, and Servanthood*, Berkeley: University of California Press.

Rozehnal, Robert (2019), *Cyber Sufis: Virtual Expressions of the American Muslim Experience*, London: Oneworld Academic.

Slama, Martin (2017), "Social Media and Islamic Practice: Indonesian Ways of Being Digitally Pious," in Edwin Jurriens and Ross Tapsell (eds.), *Digital Indonesia: Connectivity and Divergence*, 146–62, Singapore: ISEAS.

Stolow, Jeremy (2005), "Religion and/as Media," *Theory Culture & Society*, 22 (4): 119–45.

Zito, Angela (2008), "Culture," in David Morgan (ed.), *Key Words in Religion, Media and Culture*, 69–82, New York: Routledge.

Chapter 4

Abdul Khabeer, Su'ad (2016), *Muslim Cool: Race, Religion, and Hip Hop in the United States*, New York: New York University Press.

Akbar, Ahmed Ali (2016), "Preview," *See Something, Say Something* [Podcast], October 16. Available online: https://seesomethingsaysomething.libsyn.com/preview (accessed March 29, 2021).

Akbar, Ahmed Ali (2017a), "Lost in the Sauce," *See Something, Say Something* [Podcast], April 20–23. Available online: https://seesomethingsaysomething.libsyn.com/episode-21-lost-in-the-sauce (accessed March 20, 2021).

Akbar, Ahmed Ali (2017b), "A 91-Year-Old Imam Still Finds Joy in the Podcast Studio," *See Something, Say Something* [Podcast], September 14. Available online: https://seesomethingsaysomething.libsyn.com/episode-33-a-91-year-old-imam-still-finds-joy-in-the-podcast-studio (accessed March 18, 2021).

Akbar, Ahmed Ali (2019), phone interview, October 23.

Akbar, Ahmed Ali (2020), phone interview, October 29.

Alice (2020), phone interview, March 4.

Annear, Steve (2015), "Coffee, Doughnuts, and a Muslim to Answer Your Questions," *Boston Globe*, December 21. Available online: https://www.bostonglobe.com/metro/2015/12/21/couple-sets-ask-muslim-booth-cambridge/aOiTfhSp8wtM5zYhqaWdnO/story.html (accessed April 10, 2021).

Balmeseda, Liz (2015), "In Vandal's Wake, Islamic Center Opens Doors, Makes Friends," *Palm Beach Post*, December 19. Available online: https://www.palmbeachpost.com/news/local/vandal-wake-islamic-center-opens-doors-makes-friends/GOowoT5PkU7cwx2DktegEM/ (accessed April 10, 2021).

Curtis, Edward (2002), *Islam in Black America*, Albany: SUNY Press.

Elfenbein, Caleb. (2021), *Fear in Our Hearts: What Islamophobia Tells Us about America*, New York: New York University Press.

Fraser, Nancy (1990), "Rethinking the Public Sphere: A Contribution to the Critique of Actual Democracy," *Social Text* 25/26: 56–80.

GhaneaBassiri, Kambiz (2010), *A History of Islam in America*, New York: Cambridge University Press.

Maureen (2020), phone interview, March 10.

Megan (2020), phone interview, March 25.

Mohamed, Bashir, and Jeff Diament (2019), "Black Muslims Account for a Fifth of All US Muslims, and about Half Are Converts to Islam," Pew Research Center. Available online: https://www.pewresearch.org/fact-tank/2019/01/17/black -muslims-account-for-a-fifth-of-all-u-s-muslims-and-about-half-are-converts-to -islam/ (accessed March 27, 2021).

Mohamed, Bashir, Gregory Smith, Alan Cooperman, and Anna Schiller (2017), "US Muslims Concerned about Their Place in Society, but Continue to Believe in the American Dream," Pew Research Center. Available online: https://www .pewforum.org/2017/07/26/how-the-u-s-general-public-views-muslims-and -islam/ (accessed March 14, 2021).

Moriki, Darin (2018), "Hayward Man Bridges Gap between Muslims and the Community," *East Bay Times*, January 26. Available online: https://www .eastbaytimes.com/2018/01/26/hayward-man-bridges-gap-between-muslims-and -the-community/ (accessed April 10, 2021).

Morrison, Toni (1975), "A Humanists View," Portland State University, May 30, 1975. Available online: https://mackenzian.com/wp-content/uploads/2014/07/ Transcript_PortlandState_TMorrison.pdf (accessed March 21, 2021).

Nagel, Caroline, and Lynn A. Staeheli (2005), "We're Just Like the Irish: Narratives of Assimilation, Belonging and Citizenship Amongst Arab-American Activists," *Citizenship Studies* 9 (5): 485–98.

Ratliff, Evan (2019), "Kiese Laymon," *Longform* [Podcast], March 20. Available online: https://longform.org/posts/longform-podcast-335-kiese-laymon (accessed March 27, 2021).

Smith, Mychal Denzel (2018), "The Gatekeepers: On the Burden of the Black Public Intellectual," *Harper's Magazine*, December: 41–6.

Warner, Michael (2002), "Publics and Counterpublics," *Public Culture* 14 (1): 49–90.

Chapter 5

Abarca, Meredith E. (2006), *Voices in the Kitchen*, Vol. 9, College Station: Texas A&M University Press.

Abeytia, Anisa (2016), "Curries, Tajeens, and Moles," *Edible East Bay*, October 9. Available online: edibleeastbay.com/2016/10/08/curries-tajeens-and-moles/.

Alvarado, Juan (unknown publication date), "The Lado Genesis: Evolution of the Latino American Dawah Organization," *Latino American Dawah Organization*. Available online: http://www.latinodawah.org/about/ladogenesis.html (accessed July 24, 2017).

Anderson, Jon W. (2003), "The Internet and Islam's New Interpreters," in Dale F. Eickelman and Jon W. Anderson, *New Media in the Muslim World: The Emerging Public Sphere*, 2nd ed., 45–60, Bloomington: Indiana University Press.

Anzaldúa, Gloria (1987), *Borderlands/La Frontera: The New Mestiza*, San Francisco: Aunt Lute Press.

Besheer, Mohamed (2020), "A New Estimate of U.S. Muslim Population," Pew Research Center, May 30. Available online: www.pewresearch.org/fact-tank /2018/01/03/new-estimates-show-u-s-muslim-population-continues-to-grow/.

Bowen, Patrick D. (2010), "Early U.S. Latina/o African-American Muslim Connections: Paths to Conversion," *The Muslim World*, 100 (4): 390–413.

Brady, Mary Pat. (2002), *Extinct Lands, Temporal Geographies: Chicana Literature and the Urgency of Space*, Durham: Duke University Press.

Brasher, Brenda E. (2001), *Give Me That Online Religion*, San Francisco: Jossey-Bass.

Cognard-Black, Jennifer, and Melissa A. Goldthwaite, eds. (2014), *Books That Cook: The Making of a Literary Meal*, New York: New York University Press.

Chan-Malik, Sylvia (2018), *Being Muslim: A Cultural History of Women of Color in American Islam*, New York: New York University Press.

Do, Anh (2017), "Muslim and Latino Groups Unite during Ramadan, Breaking Fast with Tacos at Mosques," *Los Angeles Times*, June 6. Available online: www .latimes.com/local/lanow/la-me-ln-tacos-ramadan-20170604-story.html.

Duran, Jeanette (2017), "'Taco Trucks at Every Mosque' Goes to Rosarito for Cross-Border Latino-Muslim Unity . . . and Tacos!," *OC Weekly*, September 26. https://web.archive.org/web/20180216005136/www.ocweekly.com/taco-trucks -at-every-mosque-goes-to-rosarito-8406717/.

Espinoza, Kathryn (2004), "Latino Muslim Cultural Night," *The Latino Muslim Voice*, October–December 2004.

Espinosa, Gaston, Harold D. Morales, and Juan Galvan (2017), "Latino Muslims in the United States Reversion, Politics, and Islamidad," *Journal of Race, Ethnicity, and Religion*, 8 (1): 1–48.

Fletcher, Mujahid, and Isa Parada (2010), "Journey to Islam: Latino Muslims Share Their Story," Islamic Institute of Orange County, January 30. Available online: https://www.youtube.com/watch?v=QAjfUWmenBI.

Gallegos, Danielle (2005), "Cookbooks as Manuals of Taste," in David Bell and Joanne Hollows (eds.), *Ordinary Lifestyles: Popular Media, Consumption and Taste*, 99–110, Maidenhead: Open University Press.

Galvan, Juan (2012), "Faqs about the LADO Group," United States of Islam: Latino American Dawah Organization. Available online: http://www.usislam.org/latinos /English/faqs_about_the_lado_group.htm (accessed February 10, 2012).

Galvan, Juan (2017), Latino Muslims: Our Journeys to Islam, Scotts Valley: CreateSpace Independent Publishing Platform.

Garcia, Matt, E., Melanie Dupuis and Don Mitchell, eds. (2017), *Food across Borders*, New Brunswick: Rutgers University Press.

Green, Jeff, and Craig Giammona (2016), "How Halal Food Became a $20 Billion Hit in America," *Bloomberg.com*, September 14. Available online: www .bloomberg.com/news/articles/2016-09-14/america-loves-muslim-food-so-much -for-a-clash-of-civilizations.

Haleem, Abdel M. A. S., trans. (2008), *The Qur'an*, Oxford: Oxford University Press.

Hernandez, Abdul Daniel (2011), "Raices Islamicas en la Cultura Latina," *IslamInSpanish Show*. Available online: https://www.youtube.com/watch?v =6DxfudTEVew&t=9s.

Jameel, Maryam, and Michael Johnson (2016), "Muslim & Latino," *National Public Radio*, December 2. Available online: https://www.latinousa.org/episode/muslim-latino/.

Latimer, Brian, and Suzanne Gamboa (2016), "Latinos for Trump Founder: 'Defend Your Country' from Hispanics," *NBCNews.com*, September 2. Available online: www.nbcnews.com/news/latino/latinos-trump-founder-warned-others-defend-your-country-hispanics-n641976.

Leonard, Karen Isaksen (1992), *Making Ethnic Choices: California's Punjabi Mexican Americans*, Philadelphia: Temple University Press.

Lofgren, Jennifer (2013), "Food Blogging and Food-Related Media Convergence," *Media Convergence Journal*, 16 (3 June): 1.

Maffei, Yvonne M. (2008), "My Halal Kitchen." Available online: www.myḥalālkitchen.com.

Maffei, Yvonne M. (2016), *My Halal Kitchen: Global Recipes, Cooking Tips, and Lifestyle Inspiration*, Evanston: Agate Publishing.

Martínez-Vazquez, Hjamil A. (2009), *Latina/o y Musulmán: The Construction of Latina/o Identity among Latina/o Muslims in the United States*, Eugene: Pickwick Publications.

Mohamad, Basheer, and Elizabeth Podrebarac Sciupac, "The Share of Americans Who Leave Islam is Offset by Those Who Become Muslim." *Pew Research Center*, January 26, 2018. https://www.pewresearch.org/fact-tank/2018/01/26/the-share-of-americans-who-leave-islam-is-offset-by-those-who-become-muslim/ (accessed March 11, 2021).

Morales, Harold (2018), *Latino and Muslim in America: Race, Religion, and the Making of a New Minority*, New York: Oxford University Press.

Padilla-Alvarez, Al-Hajj Yusuf Abdul Rahman "A Historical Review of the Bani Saqr." *The Alianza Islamica Blog*, July 21, 2017. https://alianzaislamica.org/a-historical-review-of-bani-saqr (accessed July 24, 2017).

Reddy, Sumathi, and Tamer El-Ghobashy (2010), "Trump Offers to Buy Out Islamic Center Investor," *The Wall Street Journal*, September 9. www.wsj.com/articles/SB10001424052748704644404575482093330879912.

Reza, H. G. (2005), "Embracing Islam, Praying for Acceptance," *Los Angeles Times*, October 29.

Rivera, Khadijah (2007), "Dr. T B Irving. —Frontier for Latino Dawah in USA," *Piedad-LatinoDawah.Blogspot.com*. Available online: http://piedad-latinodawah.blogspot.com/2007/02/dr-t-b-irving-frontier-for-latino-dawah.html (accessed August 12, 2012).

Robinson, Sarah E. (2014), "Refreshing the Concept of Halal Meat: Resistance and Religiosity in Chicago's Taqwa Eco-Food Cooperative," in Benjamin E. Zeller, Marie W. Dallam, Reid L. Neilson, and Nora L. Rubel (eds.), *Religion, Food, and Eating in North America*, 274–93, New York: Columbia University Press.

Sandoval, Chela (2000), *Methodology of the Oppressed*, Minneapolis: University of Minnesota Press.

Tareen, Sher Afgan (2019), "Raising Children on the Ice Skating Rink: Corporate Stewardship, Race, and the Muslim Practices of Motherhood in Reston, Virginia," unpublished presentation, American Academy of Religion Conference, San Diego, California.

Tuathail, Gerard (1996), *Critical Geopolitics: The Politics of Writing Global Space*, Minneapolis: University of Minnesota Press.

United States, and Donald J. Trump, Presidential Document (2017), *Protecting the Nation from Foreign Terrorist Entry into the United States*, The Executive Office of the President, document number 2017-02281. Available online: https://www.federalregister.gov/documents/2017/02/01/2017-02281/protecting-the-nation-from-foreign-terrorist-entry-into-the-united-states (accessed April 6, 2021).

Webb, Suhaib (2012), "In Honor of Khadijah Rivera." Available online: http://www.suhaibwebb.com/miscellaneous/announcements/in-honor-of-khadijah-rivera/ (accessed February 21, 2012).

Chapter 6

Al-Heeti, Abrar (2019), "At Home in My Hijab: How the Internet Helped Me Embrace Modest Clothing." Available online: https://www.cnet.com/news/at-home-in-my-ḥijāb-how-the-internet-helped-me-embrace-modest-clothing/ (accessed December 30, 2019).

Al-Khatahtbeh, Amani (2016), *Muslim Girl: A Coming of Age*, New York: Simon and Schuster.

Badran, Margot (2013), *Feminism in Islam: Secular and Religious Convergences*, New York: Simon and Schuster.

Bunt, Gary (2018), *Hashtag Islam: How Cyber-Islamic Environments Are Transforming Religious Authority*, Chapel Hill: University of North Carolina Press.

Bunt, Gary (2009), *iMuslims: Rewiring the House of Islam*, Chapel Hill: University of North Carolina Press.

Campbell, Heidi A., and Giulia Evolvi (2019), "Contextualizing Current Digital Religion Research on Emerging Technologies," *Human Behavior and Emerging Technologies*, 2 (1): 5–17.

Croucher, Stephen M. (2008), "French-Muslims and the Hijab: An Analysis of Identity and the Islamic Veil in France," *Journal of Intercultural Communication Research*, 37 (3): 199–213.

El-Nawawy, Mohammed, and Sahar Khamis (2009), *Islam Dot Com: Contemporary Islamic Discourses in Cyberspace*, New York: Palgrave Macmillan.

Gallup (2018), "Islamophobia: Understanding Anti-Muslim Sentiment in the West," World, Gallup Online. Available online: http://news.gallup.com/poll/157082/islamophobia-understanding-an-ti-muslim-sentiment-west.aspx (accessed December 15, 2018).

Goehring, Dorothy Lee (2019), "Muslim Women on the Internet: Social Media as Sites of Identity Formation," *Journal of South Asian and Middle Eastern Studies*, 42 (3): 20–34.

Habermas, Jürgen (1992), "Further Reflections on the Public Sphere," in Craig Calhoun (ed.), *Habermas and the Public Sphere*, 421–61, Cambridge, MA: MIT Press.

Hammer, Juliane (2012), *American Muslim Women, Religious Authority, and Activism: More Than a Prayer*, Austin: University of Texas Press.

Harris, Anita (2008), "Young Women, Late Modern Politics, and the Participatory Possibilities of Online Cultures," *Journal of Youth Studies*, 11 (5): 481–95.

Hoover, Stewart M., and Nabil Echchaibi (2014), "Media Theory and the 'Third Spaces of Digital Religion,'" Center for Media, Religion, and Culture, University of Colorado Boulder. Available online: https://www.researchgate.net/profile /Stewart_Hoover/publication/287644204_The_Third_Spaces_of_Digital _Religion/links/567825d108aebcdda0ebcb9f/The-Third-Spaces-of-Digital -Religion (accessed November 30, 2014).

Howard, Philip N. (2011), *The Digital Origins of Dictatorship and Democracy: Information Technology and Political Islam*, London: Oxford University Press.

Karim, Jamillah A. (2006), "To Be Black, Female, and Muslim: A Candid Conversation about Race in the American Ummah," *Journal of Muslim Minority Affairs*, 26 (2): 225–33.

Kavakci, Elif, and Camille R. Kraeplin (2017), "Religious Beings in Fashionable Bodies: The Online Identity Construction of *Hijabi* Social Media Personalities," *Media, Culture & Society*, 39 (6): 850–68.

Khamis, Sahar (2010), "Islamic Feminism in New Arab Media: Platforms for Self-Expression and Sites for Multiple Resistances," *Journal of Arab and Muslim Media Research*, 3 (3): 237–55.

Khamis, Sahar (2017), "The Internet and New Communication Dynamics among Diasporic Muslims: Opportunities, Challenges and Paradoxes," in Merve R. Kayikci and Leen D'Haenens (eds.), *European Muslims and New Media*, 35–52, Leuven: Leuven University Press.

Khamis, Sahar (2018), "American-Muslims' E-Jihad: Trumping Islamophobia in the Trump Era," *CyberOrient*, 12 (1): 87–94. Available online: http://www .cyberorient.net/article.do?articleId=9923 (accessed December 10, 2018).

Mcdonald, Laura Zahra (2008), "Review: Islamic Feminism," *Feminist Theory*, 9 (3): 347–54.

Pennington, Rosemary (2018a), "Making Space in Social Media: #MuslimWomensDay in Twitter," *Journal of Communication Inquiry*, 42 (3): 199–217.

Pennington, Rosemary (2018b), "Social Media as Third Spaces? Exploring Muslim Identity and Connection in Tumblr," *International Communication Gazette*, 80 (7): 620–36.

Peterson, Kristin M. (2020), "The Unruly, Loud, and Intersectional Muslim Woman: Interrupting the Aesthetic Styles of Islamic Fashion Images on Instagram," *International Journal of Communication*, 14: 1194–213.

Piela, Anna (2010), "Muslim Women's Online Discussions of Gender Relations in Islam," *Journal of Muslim Minority Affairs*, 30 (3): 425–35.

Piela, Anna (2012), *Muslim Women Online: Faith and Identity in Virtual Space*, Abingdon: Routledge.

Radsch, Courtney, and Sahar Khamis (2013), "In Their Own Voice: Technologically Mediated Empowerment and Transformation among Young Arab Women," *Feminist Media Studies*, 13 (5): 881–90.

Sreberny, Annabelle (2015), "Women's Digital Activism in a Changing Middle East," *International Journal of Middle East Studies*, 47 (2): 357–61.

Tyrer, David (2013), *The Politics of Islamophobia: Race, Power and Fantasy*, London: Pluto Press.

Tzoreff, Mira (2014), "The Hybrid Women of the Arab Spring Revolutions: Islamization of Feminism, Feminization of Islam," *Journal of Levantine Studies*, 4 (2): 69–111.

Waninger, Kelsey (2015), "The Veiled Identity: Hijabistas, Instagram and Branding in the Online Islamic Fashion Industry," Master's Thesis, Georgia State University, Atlanta, Georgia.

Chapter 7

Ahmed, Sarah (2018), "Hey Muslims, Black History Month Doesn't End Here," *Muslim Girl*, February 28. Available online: http://muslimgirl.com/47440/hey-muslims-black-history-month-doesnt-end-here/ (accessed October 27, 2021).

Al-Khatahtbeh, Amani (2020), "The #MuslimGirlArmy Enters the Roaring Twenties," *Muslim Girl*, January 16. Available online: https://muslimgirl.com/muslimgirlarmy-roaring-twenties/ (accessed October 27, 2021).

Al-Khatahtbeh, Amani (2016), *Muslim Girl: A Coming of Age*, New York: Simon and Schuster.

Ali, Rabia (2018), "This Is Why Pink Feminist Hats Don't Represent Me," *Muslim Girl*, February 15. Available online: http://muslimgirl.com/47458/this-is-why-pink-feminist-hats-dont-represent-me/ (accessed October 27, 2021).

Allaudeen, Aqilah (2020), "U.S. Latino Muslims Speak the Language of Shared Cultures," U.S. News & World Report, July 2. Available online: https://www.usnews.com/news/best-countries/articles/2020-07-02/numbers-of-us-latino-muslims-growing-rapidly (accessed October 27, 2021).

Asim, Imaan (2019), "Is Colonization Responsible for Global Warming?," *Muslim Girl*, September 17. Available online: http://muslimgirl.com/56402/is-colonization-responsible-for-global-warming/ (accessed October 27, 2021).

Avishai, Orit, Lynne Gerber, and Jennifer Randles (2013), "The Feminist Ethnographer's Dilemma: Reconciling Progressive Research Agendas with Fieldwork Realities," *Journal of Contemporary Ethnography*, 42 (4 August): 394–426.

Colon, Breonnah (2018a), "See How This Latina Found Empowerment in Wearing Ḥijāb," *Muslim Girl*, March 1. Available online: http://muslimgirl.com/47617/see-how-this-latina-found-empowerment-in-wearing-hijab/

Colon, Breonnah (2018b), "5 Questions I Get Asked Frequently as a Latina Revert," *Muslim Girl*, February 14. Available online: http://muslimgirl.com/47378/5-questions-i-get-asked-frequently-as-a-latina-revert/

Diaf, Marwa (2018), "Are Women of Color Ever Treated Equal in Sports?," *Muslim Girl*, October 18. Available online: http://muslimgirl.com/49675/are-women-of-color-ever-treated-as-equals-in-sports/ (accessed October 27, 2021).

Elshamy, Vanessa (2018), "The March for Black Women and Why We Need It," *Muslim Girl*, October 17. Available online: http://muslimgirl.com/49620/the-march-for-black-women-and-why-we-need-it/

Espinosa, Gaston, Harold Morales, and Juan Galvan (2017), "Latino Muslims in the United States: Reversion, Politics, and Islamidad," *Journal of Race, Ethnicity, and Religion*, 8 (1 June): 1–48.

Glaser, Barney G., and Anselm L. Strauss (1967), *The Discovery of Grounded Theory: Strategies for Qualitative Research*, Chicago: Aldine.

Guest Blogger (2017a), "This Ramadan, I Didn't Shame Myself for Being Queer," *Muslim Girl*, July 12. Available online: http://muslimgirl.com/43720/ramadan -didnt-shame-queer/ (accessed October 27, 2021).

Guest Blogger (2017b), "Watch These Muslim Latinas Speak Out against Stereotypes," *Muslim Girl*, March 10. Available online: http://muslimgirl.com /39355/watch-muslim-latinas-speak-stereotypes/ (accessed October 27, 2021).

Harris, Anita (2008), "Young Women, Late Modern Politics, and the Participatory Possibilities of Online Cultures," *Journal of Youth Studies*, 11 (5): 481–95.

Iman, Zarina (2017), "Gay Muslim Man Faces Threats after Wedding," *Muslim Girl*, July 21. Available online: http://muslimgirl.com/43850/gay-muslim-man -faces-threats-wedding/ (accessed October 27, 2021).

Kaiser, Susan B. (2012), *Fashion and Cultural Studies*, London: Berg.

Kazmi, Humeira (2019), "America, Stop Dragging Sharia into Your Abortion Ban Mess," *Muslim Girl*, May 18. Available online: http://muslimgirl.com/54989/ america-stop-dragging-sharia-into-your-abortion-ban-mess/ (accessed October 27, 2021).

Kearney, Mary Celeste (2006), *Girls Make Media*, New York: Routledge.

Keller, Jessalynn Marie (2012), "VIRTUAL FEMINISMS: Girls' Blogging Communities, Feminist Activism, and Participatory Politics," *Information, Communication & Society*, 15 (3): 429–47.

Khatib, Maysoon (2017), "Find Out Why Latino Muslims Are Growing in Numbers," *Muslim Girl*, July 15. Available online: http://muslimgirl.com/43803/ find-latino-muslims-growing-numbers/ (accessed October 27, 2021).

Magearu, Alexandra (2018), "A Phenomenological Reading of Gendered Racialization in Arab Muslim American Women's Cultural Productions," *The Comparatist*, 42: 135–57.

Matan, Amal (2018), "Black Spirituality Is the Muslim Revolution," *Muslim Girl*, February 24. Available online: http://muslimgirl.com/47402/black-spirituality-is -the-muslim-revolution/ (accessed October 27, 2021).

McRobbie, Angela (1991), Feminism and Youth Culture: From "*Jackie*" to "Just Seventeen," Boston: Unwin Hyman.

Moors, Annelies, and Emma Tarlo (2013), *Islamic Fashion and Anti-Fashion: New Perspectives from Europe and North America*, London: Bloomsbury.

Nuñez, Madelina (2019), "Latino Muslims in the United States," *Why Islam*, July 23. Available online: https://www.whyislam.org/islam/latino/ (accessed October 27, 2021).

Saleh, Aisha (2018a), "Trump Wants to Ban Abortions for Immigrant Teens," *Muslim Girl*, October 9. Available online: http://muslimgirl.com/49615/trump -wants-to-ban-abortions-for-immigrant-teens/ (accessed October 27, 2021).

Saleh, Aisha (2018b), "What Feminism Means to Me," *Muslim Girl*, October 3. Available online: http://muslimgirl.com/49530/what-feminism-means-to-me/ (accessed October 27, 2021).

Vernon, Leah (2018), "Muslim Women Are Trending But Some of Us Are Still Invisible," *Muslim Girl*, February 20. Available online: http://muslimgirl.com /47449/muslim-women-are-trending-but-some-of-us-are-still-invisible/ (accessed October 27, 2021).

Yousaf, Uyala (2018), "Why We Shouldn't Celebrate Christopher Columbus," *Muslim Girl*, October 8. Available online: http://muslimgirl.com/49654/why-we -shouldnt-celebrate-christopher-columbus/ (accessed October 27, 2021).

Chapter 8

Ali, Tazeen Mir (2019), "Rethinking Interpretative Authority: Gender, Race, and Scripture at the Women's Mosque of America," unpublished PhD diss., Boston University.

Badran, Margot (2013), *Feminism in Islam: Secular and Religious Convergences*, New York: Simon and Schuster.

Bano, Masooda, and Hilary E. Kalmbach, eds. (2011), *Women, Leadership, and Mosques: Changes in Contemporary Islamic Authority*, Leiden: Brill.

Bhabha, Homi K. (1990), "The Third Space: An Interview with Homi Bhabha," in Jonathan Rutherford (ed.), *Identity: Community, Culture, Difference*, 207–21, London: Lawrence and Wishart.

Bhabha, Homi K. (2012), *The Location of Culture*, 3rd ed., London: Routledge.

Bolognani, Marta, and Jody Mellor (2012), "British Pakistani Women's Use of the 'Religion versus Culture' Contrast: A Critical Analysis," *Culture and Religion*, 13 (2): 211–26.

Brah, Avtar (2001), *Cartographies of Diaspora: Contesting Identities*, New York: Routledge.

Campbell Heidi, A. (2012), "Understanding the Relationship between Religion Online and Offline in a Networked Society," *Journal of the American Academy of Religion*, 80 (1): 64–93.

Campbell, Heidi A., and Giulia Evolvi (2019), "Contextualizing Current Digital Religion Research on Emerging Technologies," *Human Behavior and Emerging Technologies*, 2 (1): 5–17.

Clark Mane, Rebecca L. (2012), "Transmuting Grammars of Whiteness in Third-Wave Feminism: Interrogating Postrace Histories, Postmodern Abstraction, and the Proliferation of Difference in Third-Wave Texts," *Signs: Journal of Women in Culture and Society*, 38 (1): 71–98.

Downey, John, and Natalie Fenton (2002), "New Media, Counter Publicity and the Public Sphere," *New Media & Society*, 5 (2): 185–202.

Etsy (no date). Available online: https://www.etsy.com/shop/AWishForWin someWorks. Site no longer active.

Evolvi, Giulia (2018), Blogging My Religion: Secular, *Muslim, and Catholic Media Spaces in Europe*, Abingdon: Routledge.

Habermas, Jürgen (1992), "Further Reflections on the Public Sphere," in Craig Calhoun (ed.), *Habermas and the Public Sphere*, 421–61, Cambridge, MA: The MIT Press.

Habermas, Jürgen (1998), "The European Nation-State: On the Past and Future of Sovereignty and Citizenship," in Ciaran Cronin and Pablo De Greiff (eds.), *The Inclusion of the Other: Studies in Political Theory*, 105–27, Cambridge, MA: MIT Press.

Hall, Stuart (2003), "Cultural Identity and Diaspora," in Jana Evans Braziel and Anita Mannur (eds.), *Theorizing Diaspora: A Reader*, 233–46, Malden: Blackwell Publishing.

Hammer, Juliane (2012), *American Muslim Women, Religious Authority, and Activism: More Than a Prayer*, Austin: University of Texas Press. Available online: https://books.google.com/books?id=HiGNhMPMnFcC

Helland, Christopher (2016), "Digital Religion," in David Yamane (ed.), *Handbook of Religion and Society*, 177–96, Springer: Cham.

Hoover, Stewart M., and Nabil Echchaibi (2014), "Media Theory and the 'Third Spaces of Digital Religion,'" Center for Media, Religion, and Culture, University of Colorado Boulder. Available online: https://www.researchgate.net/profile /Stewart_Hoover/publication/287644204_The_Third_Spaces_of_Digital _Religion/links/567825d108aebcdda0ebcb9f/The-Third-Spaces-of-Digital -Religion (accessed February 24, 2021).

hooks, bell (1990), *Yearning: Race, Gender, and Cultural Politics*, Boston: South End Press.

Johnson, Azeezat (2017), "Getting Comfortable to Feel at Home: Clothing Practices of Black Muslim Women in Britain," *Gender, Place & Culture*, 24 (2): 274–87.

Johnson, David (2005), *The Popular and the Canonical: Debating Twentieth-Century Literature 1940–2000*, London: Psychology Press.

Khamis, Susie, Lawrence Ang, and Raymond Welling (2017), "Self-branding, 'Micro-celebrity' and the Rise of Social Media Influencers," *Celebrity Studies*, 8 (2): 191–208.

Nisa, Eva F. (2013), "The Internet Subculture of Indonesian Face-Veiled Women," *International Journal of Cultural Studies*, 16 (3): 241–55.

Peterson, Kristin M. (2020), "Hybrid Styles, Interstitial Spaces, and the Digital Advocacy of the Salafi Feminist," *Critical Studies in Media Communication*, 37 (3): 254–66.

Pew Research Center (2018), "The Share of Americans Who Leave Islam Is Offset by Those Who Become Muslim," Pew Research Center, January 26. Available online: https://www.pewresearch.org/fact-tank/2018/01/26/the-share-of -americans-who-leave-islam-is-offset-by-those-who-become-muslim/ (accessed February 24, 2021).

Piela, Anna (2012), *Muslim Women Online: Faith and Identity in Virtual Space*, Abingdon: Routledge.

Piela, Anna (2013), "I Am Just Doing My Bit to Promote Modesty": *Niqabis' Self-portraits on Photo-sharing Websites," *Feminist Media Studies*, 13 (5): 781–90.

Piela, Anna (2015), "Online Islamic Spaces as Communities of Practice for Female Muslim Converts Who Wear the Niqab," *Hawwa: Journal of Women of the Middle East and the Islamic World*, 13 (3): 363–82.

Piela, Anna (2017), "How do Muslim Women Who Wear the *niqab* Interact with Others Online? A Case Study of a Profile on a Photo-Sharing Website," *New Media & Society*, 19 (1): 67–80.

Piela, Anna (2021), *Wearing the Niqab: Muslim Women in the UK and the US*, London: Bloomsbury.

Schielke, Samuli (2009), "Being Good in Ramadan: Ambivalence, Fragmentation, and the Moral Self in the Lives of Young Egyptians," *The Journal of the Royal Anthropological Institute*, 15: 24–40.

Schielke, Samuli (2010), "Second Thoughts about the Anthropology of Islam, or How to Make Sense of Grand Schemes in Everyday Life," ZMO Working Papers 2. Available online: https://nbn-resolving.org/urn:nbn:de:0168-ssoar -322336 (accessed February 24, 2021).

Sajida, Rivka (2016), "Chai and Chocolate," September 26. Available online: http:// hijabininjette.blogspot.com/2016/09/ (accessed February 24, 2021).

Sajida, Rivka. (2017a), "Deen Talk!: Introduction," February 12. Available online: https://www.youtube.com/watch?v=gfePNIAr_I0&list=PL-XSVKFDxcV6-17C r0kfNwKBEbMnDrlQX (accessed February 24, 2021).

Sajida, Rivka (2017b), "Deen Talk!: Mental/Physical Illness, Disability, and Ramadan," May 26. Available online: https://www.youtube.com/watch?v =j4QIDfRNp6Q (accessed February 24, 2021).

Sajida, Rivka (2017c), "Deen Talk!: Women and Islam, Part 3: Feminism," October 25. Available online: https://www.youtube.com/watch?v=hTeMHoocYHs (accessed February 24, 2021).

Sajida, Rivka (2017d), "Product Review: Tasnim Collections Jilbab and XXL Niqab!" September 27. Available online: https://www.youtube.com/watch?v =NJ9xnQP4mho (accessed February 24, 2021).

Sajida, Rivka (2018a), "A Day in the Life of a Disabled Niqabi," May 17. Available online: https://www.youtube.com/watch?v=Q84ypQdBsPc (accessed February 24, 2021).

Sajida, Rivka (2018b), "Deen Talk!: Helping Our D/deaf Brothers and Sisters This Ramadan," May 4. Available online: https://www.youtube.com/watch?v =sY5eajF78h4 (accessed February 24, 2021).

Sajida, Rivka (2018c), "#GRWM: Yemeni Style," September 6. Available online: http://hijabininjette.blogspot.com/2018/09/grwm-yemeni-style.html (accessed February 24, 2021).

Sajida, Rivka (2018d), "My Revert Story," May 29. Available online: https://www .youtube.com/watch?v=UxV6E3mg4wo (accessed February 24, 2021).

Sajida, Rivka (2019a), "A Day in the Life of a Disabled Niqabi," February 2. Available online: https://www.youtube.com/watch?v=Y2J0lb_pjuo (accessed February 24, 2021).

Sajida, Rivka (2019b), "Product Review: @Asiyah_Umm_Ammar Haul with Qibtiyyah Niqāb!" February 18. Available online: https://www.youtube.com/ watch?v=JnjdQFhCB6A (accessed February 24, 2021).

Sajida, Rivka (2019c), "Review: Mantilla Transformer Jilbab by ScarfTurbanHijab!" April 7. Available online: https://www.youtube.com/watch ?v=LqQzyXzJpaA (accessed February 24, 2021).

Sajida, Rivka (2020d), "Daar ul-Gharib, Ramadan Khutbah, 15 Ramadan 2020/1441." May 8. Available online: https://www.youtube.com/watch?v =Lsy2oioTQOw&t=857s (accessed February 24, 2021).

Sharify-Funk, Mona, and Munira Kassam Haddad (2012), "Where Do Women 'Stand' in Islam? Negotiating Contemporary Muslim Prayer Leadership in North America," *Feminist Review*, 102 (1): 41–61.

Sreberny, Annabelle (2015), "Women's Digital Activism in a Changing Middle East," *International Journal of Middle East Studies*, 47 (2): 357–61.

Tarnovskaya, Veronika (2017), "Reinventing Personal Branding: Building a Personal Brand through Content on YouTube," *Journal of International Business Research and Marketing*, 3 (1): 29–35.

Thompson, Katrina Daly (2020), "Making Space for Embodied Voices, Diverse Bodies, and Multiple Genders in Nonconformist Friday Prayers: A Queer Feminist Ethnography of Progressive Muslims' Performative Intercorporeality in North American Congregations," *American Anthropologist*, 122 (4): 876–90.

Zebiri, Kate (2008), *British Muslim Converts: Choosing Alternative Lives*, London: Oneworld Publications.

Chapter 9

Altaleb, Omama (2021), "There's a New Meditation App and This One Is Designed Specifically with Muslims in Mind," Layali Blog. Available online: https://layaliblog.com/theres-a-new-meditation-app-and-this-one-is-designed -specifically-with-muslims-in-mind/

Arjana, Sophia Rose (2020), *Buying Buddha, Selling Rumi: Orientalism and the Mystical Marketplace*, London: Oneworld Academic.

Chappel, Craig (2020), "Downloads of Top English-Language Mental Wellness Apps Surged by 2 Million in April Amid COVID-19 Pandemic," Sensor Tower Blog: Authoritative Insights into the Global App Economy, May 28. Available online: https://sensortower.com/blog/top-mental-wellness-apps-april-2020 -downloads (accessed April 1, 2021).

Ernst, Carl (1997), *Sufism: An Introduction to the Mystical Tradition of Islam*, Boston: Shambala Publications.

Gardet, L. (2012), "Fikr," in P. Bearman, Th Bianquis, C. E. Bosworth, E. van Donzel, and W. P. Heinrichs (eds.), *Encyclopedia of Islam*, 2nd ed. Available online: http://dx.doi.org.ezpro.cc.gettysburg.edu:2048/10.1163/1573-3912 _islam_SIM_2366 (accessed April 27, 2021).

Goyal, Madhav et al. (2014), "Meditation Programs for Psychological Stress and Well-being: A Systematic Review and Meta-analysis," *JAMA Internal Medicine*, 174 (3): 357–68.

Isgandarova, Nazila (2019), "*Muraqaba* as a Mindfulness-Based Therapy in Islamic Psychotherapy," *Journal of Religion and Health*, 58 (4 August): 1146–60.

Khan, Jubair (2020), "Bismillah," Halaqah, December 11. Available online: https://www.myhalaqah.com/home/halaqah/bismillah/ (accessed December 20, 2020).

Perez, Sarah (2020), "Meditation and Mindfulness Apps Continue Their Surge amid Pandemic," Tech Crunch, May 28. Available online: https://techcrunch .com/2020/05/28/meditation-and-mindfulness-apps-continue-their-surge-amid -pandemic/ (accessed July 23, 2020).

Roof, Wade Clark (2001), *Spiritual Marketplace: Baby Boomers and the Remaking of American Religion*, Princeton: Princeton University Press.

Rothman, Abdullah, and Adrian Coyle (2018), "Toward a Framework for Islamic Psychology and Psychotherapy: An Islamic Model of the Soul," *Journal of Religion and Health*, 57 (5): 1731–44.

Rothman, Abdullah (2019), "What Islam Offers to Modern Self-Help: An Islamic Paradigm of Psychology," The Productive Muslim Company, December 31. Available online: https://productivemuslim.com/what-islam-offers-to-modern -self-help/ (accessed April 1, 2021).

Rozehnal, Robert (2019), *Cyber Sufis: Virtual Expressions of the American Muslim Experience*, London: Oneworld Academic (accessed April 1, 2021).

Schimmel, Anne Marie (1975), *Mystical Dimensions of Islam*, Chapel Hill: University of North Carolina Press.

Sells, Michael Anthony (1996), *Early Islamic Mysticism: Sufi, Qur'an, Mi'raj, Poetic, and Theological Writings*, New York: Paulist Press.

Sijapati, Megan Adamson (2019), "Sufi Remembrance Practices in the Meditation Marketplace of a Mobile App," in Jacqueline H. Fewkes (ed.), *Anthropological Perspectives on the Religious Uses of Mobile Apps*, 19–41, Cham: Palgrave Macmillan.

Yaqeen Institute (2018), "How to Be a Mindful Muslim," Yaqeen Institute, September 13. Available online: https://yaqeeninstitute.org/justin-parrott/how-to -be-a-mindful-muslim-infographic (accessed July 23, 2020).

Chapter 10

Arjana, Sophia (2017), "Modern Muslim Pilgrims: Tourism, Space, and Technology," in *Pilgrimage in Islam: Traditional and Modern Practices*, 148–89, London: Oneworld Academic.

Bulliet, Richard W. (2020), *The End of Middle East History and Other Conjectures*, Cambridge: Harvard University Press.

Bulliet, Richard W. (2013), "Religion and the State in Islam: From Medieval Caliphate to Muslim Brotherhood," Denver: University of Denver Center for Middle East Studies Occasional Paper #2.

Bunt, Gary (2016), "Decoding the Hajj in Cyberspace," in Eric Tagliacozzo and Shawkat Toorawa (eds.), *The Hajj: Pilgrimage in Islam*, 231–49, New York: Cambridge University Press.

Bunt, Gary (2010), "Surfing the App Souq: Islamic Applications for Mobile Devices," *CyberOrient*, 4 (1): 3–18.

Catellani, Andrea (2020), "Religions and Communication: Digital Transformations," in David Kergel, Birte Heidkamp-Kergel, Ronald C. Arnett, and Susan Mancino (eds.), *Communication and Learning in an Age of Digital Transformation*, 117–35, London: Routledge.

Campbell, Heidi A., Brian Altenhofen, Wendi Bellar, and Kyong James Cho (2014), "There's a Religious App for That!: A Framework for Studying Religious Mobile Applications," *Mobile Media and Communication*, 2 (2): 154–72.

Fakhruroji, Moch (2019), "Digitalizing Islamic Lectures: Islamic Apps and Religious Engagement in Contemporary Indonesia," *Contemporary Islam*, 13: 201–15.

Fewkes, Jacqueline (2019), "'Siri Is Alligator Halal?': Mobile Apps, Food Practices, and Religious Authority among American Muslims," in Jacqueline Fewkes (ed.), *Anthropological Perspectives on the Religious Uses of Mobile Apps*, 107–29, Cham: Palgrave Macmillan.

Iqbal, Mansoor (2020), "App Download and Usage Statistics (2020)," The Business of Apps, October 30, updated September 22, 2021. Available online: https:// www.businessofapps.com/data/app-statistics/ (accessed October 23, 2021).

Mahmood, Saba (2005), *The Politics of Piety: The Islamic Revival and the Feminist Subject*, Princeton: Princeton University Press.

Mater, Ahmed (2016), "Beyond Concept and Construction: Divergent City", 54–82; and "Accommodating Rupture", 207–41, in *Desert of Pharan: Unofficial Histories behind the Mass Expansion of Mecca*, Catherine David (ed.), Zurich: Lars Muller Publishers.

Marzolph, Ulrich (2014), "From Mecca to Mashhad: The Narrative of an Illustrated Shi'i Pilgrimage Scroll from the Qajar Period," *Muqarnas Online*, 31 (1 Fall): 207–42.

Oxford Business Group (2018), "Saudi Arabia Aims to Increase Pilgrim Numbers and Non-religious Tourism." Available online: https://oxfordbusinessgroup.com /overview/grand-plans-sustained-focus-raising-pilgrim-numbers-and-expanding -beyond-religion-oriented-tourism (accessed October 24, 2021).

Parker, Ann, and Avon Neal (2009), *Hajj Paintings: Folk Art of the Great Pilgrimage*, Cairo/New York: American University in Cairo Press.

Sardar, Ziauddin (2014), *Mecca: The Sacred City*, New York/London: Bloomsbury.

Saudi Gazette (2020), "19 Million Pilgrims Performed *Umrah* in 2019," April 30. Available online: https://saudigazette.com.sa/article/592545 (accessed December 4, 2020).

Stanton, Andrea (2020), "Saudi Arabia's Ministry of *Hajj* Apps: Managing the Operations and Piety of the *Hajj*," *Journal of Religion, Media, and Digital Culture*, 9 (2): 228–46.

Statista (2021), "Number of Apps Available in Leading App Stores as of First Quarter 2021," September. Available online: https://www.statista.com/ statistics/276623/number-of-apps-available-in-leading-app-stores/ (accessed October 24, 2021).

Chapter 11

Abdelaziz, Rowaida (2020), "Arab and Muslim Communities Need to Talk about Anti-Blackness," *Huffington Post*, July 3. Available online: https://www .huffpost.com/entry/the-need-for-arab-and-muslim-communities-to-reckon-and -reconcile-anti-blackness_n_5efdfc24c5b6acab284cce95 (accessed August 15, 2020).

Alhabash, Saleem, and Mengyan Ma (2017), "A Tale of Four Platforms: Motivations and Uses of Facebook, Twitter, Instagram, and Snapchat among College Students?," *Social Media + Society*, 3 (1): DOI: 2056305117691544.

Arjana, Sophia Rose (2015), *Muslims in the Western Imagination*, New York: Oxford University Press.

Baulch, Emma, and Alila Pramiyanti (2018), "Hijabers on Instagram: Using Visual Social Media to Construct the Ideal Muslim Woman," *Social Media + Society*, 4 (4): DOI: 2056305118800308.

Baym, Nancy (2010), *Personal Connections in the Digital Age*, Malden: Polity Press.

boyd, d., and Nicole Ellison (2007), "Social Network Sites: Definitions, History, and Scholarship," *Journal of Computer Mediated Communication*, 13 (1): 210–30.

Bunt, Gary (2005), "Negotiating Islam and Muslims in Cyberspace," in Erik Borgman, Stephan van Erp, and Hille Haker (eds.), *Cyberspace – Cyberethics – Cybertheology*, London: SCM Press.

Bunt, Gary (2018), *Hashtag Islam: How Cyber-Islamic Environments Are Transforming Religious Authority*, Chapel Hill: University of North Carolina Press.

Burgess, Jean, and Joshua Green (2009), *YouTube*. Malden: Polity Press.

Burroughs, Benjamin (2013), "And I'm a (Social Media) Mormon: Digital Ritual, Techno-Faith, and Religious Transmedia," *Qwerty-Open and Interdisciplinary Journal of Technology, Culture and Education*, 8 (2): 71–81.

Burroughs, Benjamin, and Gavin Feller (2015), "Religious Memetics: Institutional Authority in Digital/Lived Religion," *Journal of Communication Inquiry*, 39 (4): 357–77.

Campbell, Heidi (2013), "Introduction: The Rise in the Study of Digital Religion," in Heidi Campbell (ed.), *Digital Religion: Understanding Religious Practice in New Media Worlds*, 1–22, New York: Routledge.

Choi, Mina, and Catalina L. Toma (2014), "Social Sharing through Interpersonal Media: Patterns and Effects on Emotional Well-Being," *Computers in Human Behavior*, 36: 530–41.

Dawkins, Richard (1976), *The Selfish Gene*, Oxford: Oxford University Press.

Dennett, Daniel C. (1998), "Review: The Evolution of Religious Memes: Who—or What—Benefits?," *Method & Theory in the Study of Religion*, 10 (1): 115–28.

Dinee, Fatima (n.d.), "Anti-Blackness in the Ummah," Between Borders. Available online: https://www.between-borders.com/blog/anti-blackness-in-the-ummah (accessed August 15, 2020).

Echchaibi, Nabil (2011), "From Audio Tapes to Video Blogs: The Delocalisation of Authority in Islam," *Nations and Nationalisms*, 17 (1): 25–44.

El-Nawawy, Mohammed, and Sahar Khamis (2009), *Islam Dot Com: Contemporary Islamic Discourses in Cyberspace*, New York: Palgrave Macmillan.

Feenberg, Andrew, and Maria Bakardjieva (2004), "Virtual Community: No 'Killer Implication'," *New Media & Society*, 6 (1): 37–43.

Gottschalk, P. (2013). *American Heretics: Catholics, Jews, Muslims, and the History of Religious Intolerance*, New York: St. Martin's Press.

Hassan, Riaz (2006), "Globalisation's Challenge to the Islamic 'Ummah'," *Asian Journal of Social Science*, 34 (2): 311–23.

Hjorth, Larissa, and Sarah Pink (2014), "New Visualities and the Digital Wayfarer: Reconceptualizing Camera Phone Photography and Locative Media," *Mobile Media & Communication*, 2 (1): 40–57.

Hoover, Stewart (2011), "Media and the Imagination of Religion in Contemporary Global Culture," *European Journal of Cultural Studies*, 14 (6): 610–25.

Hoover, Stewart, and Nabil Echchaibi (2014), "Media Theory and the 'Third Spaces of Digital Religion.'" Working Paper.

Iftikhar, Arsalan (2018), "Shattering the Muslim Monolith," in Rosemary Pennington and Hilary Kahn (eds.), *On Islam: Muslims and the Media*, 18–26, Bloomington: Indiana University Press.

Karim, Jamillah A. (2006), "To Be Black, Female, and Muslim: A Candid Conversation about Race in the American Ummah," *Journal of Muslim Minority Affairs*, 26 (2): 225–33.

Keep, Dean (2014), "Artist with a Camera-Phone: A Decade of Mobile Photography," in Marsha Berry and Max Schleser (eds.), *Mobile Media Making in an Age of Smartphones*, 14–24, New York: Palgrave Pivot.

Lasén, Amparo, and Edgar Gómez-Cruz (2009), "Digital Photography and Picture Sharing: Redefining the Public/Private Divide," *Knowledge, Technology & Policy*, 22 (3): 205–15.

Lim, Merlyna (2008), "Muslim Voices in the Blogosphere: Mosaics of Local-Global Discourses," in Gerard Goggin and Mark McLelland (eds.), *Internationalizing Internet Studies: Beyond Anglophone Paradigms*, New York: Routledge.

Lipka, Michael (2015), "Muslims and Islam: Key Findings in the U.S. and around the World," Pew Research Center: Fact Tank, August 9. Available online: https://www.pewresearch.org/fact-tank/2017/08/09/muslims-and-islam-key-findings-in-the-u-s-and-around-the-world/ (accessed July 18, 2020).

MacDowall, Lachlan John, and Poppy de Souza (2017), "'I'd Double Tap That!': Street Art, Graffiti, and Instagram Research," *Media, Culture & Society*, 40 (1): 3–22.

Mejova, Yelena, and Youcef Benkhedda (2017), "#Halal Culture on Instagram," *Frontiers in Digital Humanities*, 4. DOI: 10.3389/fdigh.2017.00021. https://www.frontiersin.org/articles/10.3389/fdigh.2017.00021/full (accessed July 15, 2020).

Mogahed, Yasmin (2011), *Facebook*. [Public figure.] Posted November 5. Available online: https://www.facebook.com/YMogahed/posts/many-years-ago-our-father-ibrahim-as-made-a-choice-he-loved-his-son-but-he-loved/302868309740498/ (accessed June 1, 2020).

Morgan, David (2009), "The Material Culture of Lived Religion: Visuality and Embodiment," *Mind and Matter: Selected Papers of Nordic Conference*, 14–31.

Nisa, Eva F. (2018), "Creative and Lucrative Da'wa: The Visual Culture of Instagram amongst Female Muslim Youth in Indonesia," *Asiascape: Digital Asia*, 5: 68–99.

Papacharissi, Zizi (2009), "The Virtual Sphere 2.0. The Internet, the Public Sphere, and Beyond," in Andrew Chadwick and Philip N. Howard (eds.), *Routledge Handbook of Internet Politics*, 230–45, New York: Routledge.

Papacharissi, Zizi (2011), "Conclusion: A Networked Self," in Zizi Papacharissi (ed.), *A Networked Self: Identity, Community and Culture on Social Network Sites*, 304–18, New York: Routledge.

Pennington, Rosemary (2020), "Witnessing the 2014 Gaza War in Tumblr," *International Communication Gazette*, 82 (4): 365–83.

Pennington, Rosemary (2018a), "Making Space in Social Media: #MuslimWomensDay in Twitter," *Journal of Communication Inquiry*, 42 (3): 199–217.

Pennington, Rosemary (2018b), "Social Media as Third Spaces?: Exploring Muslim Identity and Connection in Tumblr," *International Communication Gazette*, 80 (7): 620–36.

Peterson, Kristin M. (2020), "The Unruly, Loud, and Intersectional Muslim Woman: Interrupting the Aesthetic Styles of Islamic Fashion Images on Instagram," *International Journal of Communication*, 14: 1194–213.

Serafinelli, Elisa (2017), "Analysis of Photo Sharing and Visual Social Relationships: Instagram as Case Study," *Photographies*, 10 (1): 91–111.

Smith, Lauren Reichart, and Jimmy Sanderson (2015), "I'm Going to Instagram It!: An Analysis of Athlete Self-Presentation on Instagram," *Journal of Broadcasting & Electronic Media*, 59 (2): 342–58.

Stolow, Jeremy (2005), "Religion and/as Media," *Theory, Culture & Society*, 22 (4): 119–45.

Varisco, Daniel Martin (2010), "Muslims and the Media in the Blogosphere," *Contemporary Islam*, 4: 157–77.

Woodhead, Linda (2009). "Old, New, and Emerging Paradigms in the Sociology of the Study of Religion," *Nordic Journal of Religion and Society*, 22 (2): 103–21.

Yuan, Elaine J. (2012), "A Culturalist Critique of 'Online Community' in New Media Studies," *New Media & Society*, 15 (5): 665–70.

Zappavigna, Michele (2016), "Social Media Photography: Construing Subjectivity in Instagram Images," *Visual Communication*, 15 (3): 271–92.

Chapter 12

Abdullah, Zain (2009), "Sufis on Parade: The Performance of Black, African, and Muslim Identities," *Journal of the American Academy of Religion*, 77 (2): 199–237

Abdullah, Zain (2010), *Black Mecca: The African Muslims of Harlem*, New York: Oxford University Press.

"About: Archnet" (2020). Available online: https://archnet.org/pages/about (accessed March 6, 2021).

"About: Artstor" (2020). Available online: https://www.artstor.org/about/ (accessed March 6, 2021).

"About the Met" (2021). Available online: https://www.metmuseum.org/about-the -met (accessed March 6, 2021).

Ahmed, Sara (2012), *On Being Included: Racism and Diversity in Institutional Life*, Durham: Duke University Press.

Bennett, Tony (1995), *The Birth of the Museum: History, Theory, Politics*, New York: Routledge.

Berns, Steph (2016), "Considering the Glass Case: Material Encounters between Museums, Visitors and Religious Objects," *Journal of Material Culture*, 21 (2): 153–68.

Bier, Carol (2017), "Reframing Islamic Art for the 21st Century," *Horizons in Humanities and Social Sciences: An International Refereed Journal*, 2 (2): 1–25.

Cantwell, Chris, and Hussein Rashid (2015), *Religion, Media, and the Digital Turn*, New York: Social Science Research Council.

Chelkowski, Peter J., and Hamid Dabashi (1999), *Staging a Revolution: The Art of Persuasion in the Islamic Republic of Iran*, New York: New York University Press.

Coones, Wendy (2017), "Museum on Mars: Re-Define, Re-Auratize, Re-Territorialize," in Oliver Grau, Wendy Coones, and Viola Rühse (eds.), *Museum and Archive on the Move: Changing Cultural Institutions in the Digital Era*, 124–42, Boston: De Gruyter.

Demerdash-Fatemi, Nancy (2020), "Objects, Storytelling, Memory and Living Histories: Curating Islamic Art Empathically in an Era of Trauma and Displacement," in Jenny Norton-Wright (ed.), *Curating Islamic Art Worldwide*, 15–30, Cham, Switzerland: Springer.

During, Simon (2005), *Cultural Studies: A Critical Introduction*, New York: Routledge.

Ernst, Carl W. (2003), *Following Muhammad: Rethinking Islam in the Contemporary World*, Chapel Hill: University of North Carolina Press.

Frishkopf, Michael Aaron, and Federico Spinetti, eds. (2018), *Music, Sound, and Architecture in Islam*, Austin: University of Texas Press.

Gökçiğdem, Elif M. (2016), "Introduction," in Elif M. Gökçiğdem (ed.), *Fostering Empathy through Museums*, xix–xxxii, Lanham: Rowman and Littlefield.

Gonnella, Julia (2012), "Islamic Art versus Material Culture: Museum of Islamic Art or Museum of Islamic Culture?," in Benoît Junod, Georges Khalil, Stefan Weber, and Gerhard Wolf (eds.), *Islamic Art and the Museum*, 144–50, London: Saqi.

Grinell, Klas (2018), "Framing Islam at the World of Islam Festival, London, 1976," *Journal of Muslims in Europe*, 7 (1): 73–93.

Grinell, Klas (2020), "Labelling Islam: Structuring Ideas in Islamic Galleries in Europe," in Jenny Norton-Wright (ed.), *Curating Islamic Art Worldwide*, 31–44, Cham, Switzerland: Springer.

Hall, Stuart, and David Morley (2019), *Essential Essays*, Durham: Duke University Press.

Hall, Stuart, and Paddy Whannel (2018), *The Popular Arts*, Durham: Duke University Press.

Hicks, Dan (2020), *The Brutish Museums: The Benin Bronzes, Colonial Violence and Cultural Restitution*, London: Pluto Press.

Hill, Joseph (2018), *Wrapping Authority: Women Islamic Leaders in a Sufi Movement in Dakar, Senegal*, Toronto: University of Toronto Press.

Hodgson, Marshall G. S. (1974), *The Classical Age of Islam*, Chicago: University of Chicago Press.

Jalayir, Isma'il (1860), "Imam 'Ali and Sons with a Lion." Available online: https://www.metmuseum.org/art/collection/search/773289 (accessed March 6, 2021)

Junod, Benoît, Georges Khalil, Stefan Weber, and Gerhard Wolf (2012), "Islamic Art and the Museum," in Benoît Junod, Georges Khalil, Stefan Weber, and Gerhard Wolf (eds.), *Islamic Art and the Museum*, 11–16, London: Saqi.

King, Richard (1999), *Orientalism and Religion: Post-colonial Theory, India and the Mystic East*, New York: Routledge.

Kluszczyski, Ryszard W. (2017), "The Museum, Public Space and the Internet: Environments for Presenting Interactive Film," in Oliver Grau, Wendy Coones, and Viola Rühse (eds.), *Museum and Archive on the Move: Changing Cultural Institutions in the Digital Era*, 70–83, Boston: De Gruyter.

Kreps, Christina F. (2003), *Liberating Culture: Cross-Cultural Perspectives on Museums, Curation, and Heritage Preservation*, New York: Routledge.

Leirvik, Oddbjørn (2010), *Images of Jesus Christ in Islam*, New York: Continuum.

Levine, Lawrence W. (1988), *Highbrow/Lowbrow: The Emergence of Cultural Hierarchy in America*, Cambridge: Harvard University Press.

Lewis, Franklin D. (1994), "The Rise and Fall of a Persian Refrain: The *Radif* '*Ātash u Āb*'," in Suzanne Pinckney Stetkevych (ed.), *Reorientations: Arabic and Persian Poetry*, 199–226, Bloomington: Indiana University Press.

Mamdani, Mahmood (2004), *Good Muslim, Bad Muslim: America, the Cold War, and the Roots of Terror*, New York: Pantheon Books.

Martin, Lizzy (2019), "A Global Education for All." Available online: https://www.aam-us.org/2019/03/01/a-global-education-for-all/ (accessed March 6, 2021).

Masteller, Kimberly (2020), "Curating Islamic Art in the Central United States: New Approaches to Collections, Installations and Audience Engagement," in Jenny Norton-Wright (ed.), *Curating Islamic Art Worldwide*, 145–56, Cham, Switzerland: Springer.

Masuzawa, Tomoko (2005), *The Invention of World Religions: Or, How European Universalism Was Preserved in the Language of Pluralism*, Chicago: University of Chicago Press.

McCarthy, Conal (2019), "Indigenisation: Reconceptualising Museology," in Simon J. Knell (ed.), *The Contemporary Museum: Shaping Museums for the Global Now*, 40–54, New York: Routledge.

Moore, Diane L. (2007), *Overcoming Religious Illiteracy: A Cultural Studies Approach to the Study of Religion in Secondary Education*, New York: Palgrave Macmillan.

Noble, Safiya Umoja (2018), *Algorithms of Oppression: How Search Engines Reinforce Racism*, New York: New York University Press.

Norton-Wright, Jenny (2020), "Introduction," in Jenny Norton-Wright (ed.), *Curating Islamic Art Worldwide*, 1–12, Cham, Switzerland: Springer.

Paine, Crispin (2013), *Religious Objects in Museums: Private Lives and Public Duties*, New York: Berg Publishers.

Porter, Venetia, and William Greenwood (2020), "Displaying the Cultures of Islam at the British Museum: The Albukhary Foundation Gallery of the Islamic World," in Jenny Norton-Wright (ed.), *Curating Islamic Art Worldwide*, 107–16, Cham, Switzerland: Springer.

Qa'im, Mahdi Muntazir (2005), *Jesus through Shi'ite Narrations*, Elmhurst: Tahrike Tarsile Quran, Inc.

Rafii, Raha (2019), "Destruction on Display: The Politics of Preservation." Available online: https://therevealer.org/destruction-on-display-the-politics-of -preservation/ (accessed January 29, 2021).

Rashid, Hussein (2016), "My Secret Thoughts of America to Zanzibar at the Children's Museum of Manhattan." Available online: https://ummahwide .com/my-secret-thoughts-of-america-to-zanzibar-at-the-children-s-museum-of -manhattan-22bda56b799e (accessed March 6, 2021).

Rashid, Hussein (2018), "Plural Voices in the Teaching of Islam," *Thresholds in Education*, 41 (2): 87–100.

Rashid, Hussein (2021), "The Incidental Muslim: The Characters We Overlook," in Kristian Petersen (ed.), *Muslims in the Movies: A Global Anthology*, 45–57, Boston: Ilex Foundation.

Reeve, John (2019), "Islam: Islamic Art, the Islamic World—and Museums," in Simon J. Knell (ed.), *The Contemporary Museum: Shaping Museums for the Global Now*, 55–70, New York: Routledge.

Rey, Virginie (2019), "Islam, Museums, and the Politics of Representation in the West," *Material Religion*, 15 (2): 250–52.

Ross, Eric (2006), *Sufi City: Urban Design and Archetypes in Touba*, Rochester: University of Rochester Press.

Said, Edward W. (1979), *Orientalism*, New York: Vintage.

Said, Edward (1981), *Covering Islam: How the Media and the Experts Determine How We See the Rest of the World*, New York: Pantheon Books.

Shatanawi, Mirjam (2012), "Curating against Dissent: Museums and the Public Debate on Islam," in Christopher Flood, Stephen Hutchings, Galina Miazhevich, and Henri Nickels, (eds.), *Political and Cultural Representations of Muslims: Islam in the Plural*, 177–92, Boston: Brill.

Shaw, Wendy M. K. (2012), "The Islam in Islamic Art History: Secularism and Public Discourse," *Journal of Art Historiography*, 6: 1–34.

Shaw, Wendy M. K. (2019), *What Is "Islamic" Art?: Between Religion and Perception*, Cambridge: Cambridge University Press.

Sila-Khan, Dominique (2003), *Crossing the Threshold: Understanding Religious Identities in South Asia*, London: I.B. Tauris.

"The British Museum: Islamic Gallery" (2021). Available online: https://islamicworld.britishmuseum.org (accessed March 6, 2021).

Wajid, Sara, and Rachael Minott (2019), "Detoxing and Decolonising Museums," in Robert R. Janes and Richard Sandell (eds.), *Museum Activism*, 25–35, New York: Routledge.

Winner, Ellen (2019), *How Art Works: A Psychological Exploration*, New York: Oxford University Press.

Chapter 13

Althusser, Louis (1972), *Lenin and Philosophy, and Other Essays*, New York: Monthly Review Press.

Bush, Robin (2009), *Nahdlatul Ulama and the Struggle for Power within Islam and Politics in Indonesia*, Singapore: ISEAS.

Bush, Robin (2015), "Religious Politics and Minority Rights during the Yudhoyono Presidency," in Edward Aspinall, Marcus Mietzner, and Dirk Tomsa (eds.), *The Yudhoyono Presidency: Indonesia's Decade of Stability and Stagnation*, 239–57, Singapore: ISEAS.

Duile, Timo (2020), "Challenging Hegemony: Nurhadi-Aldo and the 2019 Election in Indonesia," *Journal of Contemporary Asia*, 50: 1–27.

Eickelman, Dale F., and Jon W. Anderson, eds. (1999), *New Media in the Muslim World: The Emerging Public Sphere*, Bloomington: Indiana University Press.

Eickelman, Dale F., and James Piscatori, eds. (1996), *Muslim Politics*, Princeton: Princeton University Press.

El-Ariss, Tarek (2019), *Leaks, Hacks, and Scandals: Arab Culture in the Digital Age*, Princeton: Princeton University Press.

Fairozi, Ahmad (2019). "Paradigma Manhaji al-Muhafadzah dan al-Akdu," *Pesantri*, February 21. Available online: https://penasantri.id/paradigma-manhaji-al-muhafadzah-dan-al-akhdu/ (accessed March 12, 2021).

Fealy, Greg (1998), "Ulama and Politics in Indonesia: A History of Nahdlatul Ulama, 1952–1967," PhD diss., Monash University.

Flood, Finbarr Barry (2013), "Inciting Modernity?: Images, Alterities, and the Contexts of 'Cartoon Wars'," in Patricia Spyer and Mary Margaret Steedly (eds.), *Images that Move*, 257–93, Santa Fe: School for Advanced Research Press.

Gruber, Christine, ed. (2013), *Visual Culture in the Modern Middle East: The Rhetoric of Image*, Indianapolis: Indiana University Press.

Hadler, Jeffrey (2004), "Translations of Antisemitism: Jews, the Chinese, and Violence in Colonial and Postcolonial Indonesia," *Indonesia and the Malay World*, 32 (94): 291–313.

Hirschkind, Charles (2001), "Civic Virtue and Religious Reason: An Islamic Counter-Public," *Cultural Anthropology*, 16: 3–34.

Hoesterey, James B. (2018), "Politicians, Pop Preachers, and Public Scandal: A Personal Politics of *Adab*," in Robert Rozehnal (ed.) *Piety, Politics, and Everyday Ethics in Southeast Asia: Beautiful Behavior*, 123–46, London: Bloomsbury.

Iqbal, Asep M. (2020), "Challenging Moderate Islam in Indonesia: NU Garis Lurus and Its Construction of the "Authentic" NU Online," in Leonard C. Sebastian, Syafiq Hasyim, and Alexander R. Arifianto (eds.), *Rising Islamic Conservatism in Indonesia*, 95–115, New York: Routledge.

Izharuddin, Alicia (2017), *Gender and Islam in Indonesian Cinema*, Singapore: Palgrave Macmillan.

Kraidy, Marwan M. (2017), *The Naked Blogger of Cairo: Creative Insurgency in the Arab World*, Cambridge: Harvard University Press.

Kruse, Christiane, Birgit Meyer, and Anne-Marie Korte, eds. (2018), *Taking Offense: Religion, Art, and Visual Culture in Plural Configurations*, Leiden: Brill.

Kumparan News (2019), "The Propagation of NU-Muhammadiyah Funny Brigades," January 11. Available online: https://kumparan.com/kumparannews /dakwah-garis-lucu-nu-muhammadiyah-1547175616360531881/full (accessed July 4, 2020).

Latu, Jonathan (2019), "*Fenomena @NUgarislucu dan Jamaah GL lainnya*" [The Phenomenon of NU Funny Brigade and Other Funny Brigades], Kompasiana, May 17. Available online: https://www.kompasiana.com/qitmr/5cde68ec957 60e63d90d5112/fenomena-atnugarislucu-dan-jamaah-gl-lainnya?page=all (accessed May 13, 2020).

Lim, Merlyna (2017), "Freedom to Hate: Social Media, Algorithmic Enclaves, and the Rise of Tribal Nationalism in Indonesia," *Critical Asian Studies* 49 (3): 411–27.

Mandaville, Peter (2007), "Globalization and the Politics of Religious Knowledge: Pluralizing Authority in the Muslim World," *Theory, Culture & Society*, 24 (2): 101–15.

Moll, Yasmin (2018), "Television Is Not Radio: Theologies of Mediation in the Egyptian Islamic Revival," *Cultural Anthropology*, 33 (2): 233–65.

Peletz, Michael G. (1996), *Reason and Passion: Representations of Gender in a Malay Society*, Berkeley: University of California Press.

Pinney, Christopher (2016), "Crisis and Visual Critique," *Visual Anthropology Review*, 32 (1): 73–8.

Pollock, John (2011), "Streetbook: How Egyptian and Tunisian Youth Hacked the Arab Spring," *Technology Review*, September/October. Available online: http://www.technologyreview.com/featured-story/425137/streetbook/ (accessed February 28, 2012).

Roosa, John (2006), *Pretext for Mass Murder: The September 30th Movement and Suharto's Coup d'état in Indonesia*, Madison: University of Wisconsin Press.

Schulz, Dorothea (2012), *Muslims and New Media in West Africa: Pathways to God*, Bloomington: Indiana University Press.

Shirky, Clay (2011), "The Political Power of Social Media: Technology, the Public Sphere, and Political Change," *Foreign Affairs*, 90 (1): 28–41.

Slama, Martin, and Bart Barendregt (2018), "Online Publics in Muslim Southeast Asia: In Between Religious Politics and Popular Pious Practices," *Asiascape: Digital Asia* 5 (1–2): 3–31.

Slama, Martin, and Carla Jones (2017), "Piety, Celebrity, Sociality: A Forum on Islam and Social Media in Southeast Asia," *American Ethnologist* online. Available online: https://americanethnologist.org/features/collections/piety -celebrity-sociality/heart-to-heart-on-social-media (accessed November 8, 2017).

Strassler, Karen (2020), *Demanding Images: Democracy, Mediation, and the Image-Event in Indonesia*, Durham: Duke University Press.

Spyer, Patricia, and Mary Margaret Steedly (2013), "Introduction," in Patricia Spyer and Mary Margaret Steedly (eds.), *Images that Move*, 3–40, Santa Fe: School for Advanced Research Press.

Wahid, Abdurrahman (2000), *Melawan Melalui Lelucon [To Counter Through Jokes]*, Jakarta: Tempo.

Wijaya, Pungkit (2017), "Merawat 'Dakwah' Garis Lucu" [Taking Care of the Funny Brigade Propagation], *Detik News*, Available online: https://news.detik .com/kolom/d-3568538/merawat-dakwah-garis-lucu (accessed July 28, 2019).

Chapter 14

Amanat, Abbas (2017), *Iran: A Modern History*, New Haven: Yale University Press.

Austin, J. L. (1962), *How to Do Things with Words*, Cambridge: Harvard University Press.

Barthes, Roland (1999), "Rhetoric of Image," in Jessica Evans and Stuart Hall (eds.), *Visual Culture: The Reader*, 33–50, London: Sage Publications.

Borgmann, Albert (1984), *Technology and the Character of Contemporary Life: A Philosophical Inquiry*, Chicago: University of Chicago Press.

De Certeau (1984), *Michel, Practice of Everyday Life*, Berkeley: University of California Press.

Feld, Scott (1981), "The Focused Organization of Social Ties," *American Journal of Sociology*, 86: 1015–35.

Gleave, Robert (2017), "Najaf: Learned Authority and Scholarly Pre-eminence," in Sabrina Mervin, Robert Gleave, and Géraldine Chatelard (eds.), *Najaf: Portrait of a Holy City*, 111–31, Reading: Ithaca Press.

Green, Nile (2013), "Spacetime and the Muslim Journey West: Industrial Communications in the Making of the 'Muslim World'," *The American Historical Review*, 118 (2): 401–29.

Haider, Najam (2011), *The Origins of the Shīʿa: Identity, Ritual and Sacred Space in Eight-Century Kūfa*, Cambridge: Cambridge University Press.

Jurgenson, Nathan (2020), *The Social Photo: On Photography and Social Media*, London: Verso.

Kamaly, Hossein (2018), *God and Man in Tehran: Contending Visions of the Divine from the Qajars to the Islamic Republic*, New York: Columbia University Press.

Khalaji, Mehdi (2006), "The Last *Marja*: Sistani and the End of Traditional Religious Authority in Shiism." Available online: https://www .washingtoninstitute.org/policy-analysis/last-marja-sistani-and-end-traditional -religious-authority-shiism (accessed October 29, 2021).

Rahimi, Babak (2008), "The Politics of the Internet in Iran," in Mehdi Semati (ed.), *Media, Culture and Society in Iran: Living with Globalization and the Islamic State*, 36–56, New York: Routledge.

Rahimi, Babak (2011), "The Agonistic Social Media: Cyberspace in the Formation of Dissent and Consolidation of State Power in Postelection Iran," *The Communication Review*, 14 (3): 158–78.

Rozehnal, Robert (2019), *Cyber Sufis: Virtual Expressions of the American Muslim Experience*, London: Oneworld Academic.

Sreberny-Mohammadi, Annabelle, and Ali Mohammadi (1994), *Small Media, Big Revolution: Communication, Culture, and the Iranian Revolution*, London; Minneapolis: University of Minnesota Press.

Weber, Max (1978), "The Types of Legitimate Domination," in Guenther Roth and Claus Wittich (eds.), *Economy and Society*, Berkeley: University of California Press.

White, Harrison C. (1992), *Identity and Control: A Structural Theory of Social Action*, Princeton: Princeton University Press.

Wills, David (2021), *Prothesis*, Minneapolis: University of Minnesota Press.

Chapter 15

Ahmed, Sara (2000), *Strange Encounters: Embodied Others in Post-Coloniality*, London: Routledge.

Ahmed, Sara (2014), "Making Strangers," *feministkilljoys*, August 4. Available online: https://feministkilljoys.com/2014/08/04/making-strangers/ (accessed September 8, 2020).

Appiah, A. Kwame (2005), *The Ethics of Identity*, Princeton: Princeton University Press.

Bayoumi, Moustafa (2009), *How Does It Feel to Be a Problem?: Being Young and Arab in America*, London and New York: Penguin Books.

Benhabib, Seyla (2002), *The Claims of Culture: Equality and Diversity in the Global Era*, Princeton: Princeton University Press.

Bitton, Simone (1998), *Mahmoud Darwish: As the Land Is the Language*, Documentary Film, France 3/ PDJ Productions.

Bowe, J. Brian, and W. Makki Taj (2016), "Muslim Neighbors or an Islamic Threat? A Constructionist Framing Analysis of Newspaper Coverage of Mosque Controversies," *Media, Culture & Society*, 38 (4): 540–58.

Brand, Dionne (2002), *A Map to the Door of No Return: Notes to Belonging*, Toronto: Vintage Canada.

Caffier, Justin (2018), "Screen Muslims Like a Real Customs Officer in This New AR Experience," *Vice*, April 30. Available online: https://www.vice.com /en/article/3kjgaw/screen-muslims-like-a-real-customs-officer-in-this-new-ar -experience (accessed September 9, 2020).

Diawara, Manthia (2011), "Édouard Glissant in Conversation with Manthia Diawara," *Journal of Contemporary African Art*, 28 (1): 4–19.

Echchaibi, Nabil (2013), "American Muslims and the Media," in Juliane Hammer and Omid Safi (eds.), *The Cambridge Companion to American Islam*, 119–38, Cambridge: Cambridge University Press.

Eid, Ahmed, Marwa Aly, and Atif Mahmud (prod.) (2013), Unmosqued: A Film
   about the Mosque in America. DVD. Written by Ahmed Eid, Atif Mahmud.
   Mountain View, CA: Eidfilms.
Fanon, Frantz, and Charles L. Markmann (1967), *Black Skin, White Masks*,
   New York: Grove Press.
Fluri, Jennifer (2009), "The Beautiful 'other': A Critical Examination of 'western'
   Representations of Afghan Feminine Corporeal Modernity," *Gender, Place &
   Culture*, 16 (3): 241–57.
Glissant, Édouard (1997), *Poetics of Relation*, Ann Arbor: University of Michigan
   Press.
Gordon, R. Lewis (2015), *What Fanon Said: A Philosophical Introduction to His
   Life and Thought*, New York: Fordham University Press.
Hall, Rachel (2015), *The Transparent Traveler: The Performance and Culture of
   Airport Security*, Durham: Duke University Press.
Malik, Asad (2018), *Terminal 3*, Los Angeles: 1Ric.
Mamdani, Mahmood (2004), *Good Muslim, Bad Muslim: America, the Cold War,
   and the Roots of Terror*, New York: Three Leaves Press.
Massumi, Brian (2010), "The Future Birth of the Affective Fact: The Political
   Ontology of Threat," in Melissa Gregg and Gregory Seigworth (eds.), *The Affect
   Theory Reader*, 52–70, Durham: Duke University Press.
Massumi, Brian (2015), *Ontopower: War, Powers, and the State of Perception*,
   Durham: Duke University Press.
Moore, Rowan (2010), "Why Park51 Is Much More than the 'Mosque at Ground
   Zero'," *The Guardian*, November 6. Available online: https://www.theguardian
   .com/world/2010/nov/07/ground-zero-park51-new-york (accessed September
   10, 2020).
Parks, Lisa (2009), "Points of Departure: The Culture of US Airport Screening,"
   in Rosi Braidotti, Claire Colebrook, Patrick Hanafin (eds.), *Deleuze and Law:
   Forensic Futures*, 163–78, London: Palgrave Macmillan.
Phillips, W. P. John (2011), "Secrecy and Transparency: An Interview with Samuel
   Weber," *Theory, Culture & Society*, 28 (7–8): 158–72.
Revescz, Rachael (2017), "Blindfolded Muslim Gives Free Hugs in Manchester
   in Trust Experiment after Terror Attack," *Independent*, May 30. Available
   online: https://www.independent.co.uk/news/uk/home-news/blindfolded-muslim
   -manchester-free-hugs-terrorist-attack-kindness-strangers-baktash-noori
   -a7761696.html (accessed September 9, 2020).
Sharpe, Christina (2016), *In the Wake: On Blackness and Being*, Durham: Duke
   University Press.
Stabile, A. Carol, and Deepa Kumar (2005), "Unveiling Imperialism: Media, Gender
   and the War on Afghanistan," *Media, Culture & Society*, 27 (5): 765–82.
Whitlock, Gillian. (2006), *Soft Weapons: Autobiography in Transit*, Chicago:
   University of Chicago Press.

INDEX